Applied Mathematics for Database Professionals

Lex de Haan and Toon Koppelaars

Applied Mathematics for Database Professionals

Copyright © 2007 by Lex de Haan and Toon Koppelaars

ISBN-13: 978-1-4302-1184-6

ISBN-10: 1-4302-11184-9

Lead Editor: Jonathan Gennick

Technical Reviewers: Chris Date, Cary Millsap

Editorial Board: Steve Anglin, Ewan Buckingham, Gary Cornell, Jonathan Gennick, Jason Gilmore, Jonathan Hassell, Chris Mills, Matthew Moodie, Jeffrey Pepper, Ben Renow-Clarke, Dominic Shakeshaft, Matt Wade, Tom Welsh

Project Manager: Tracy Brown Collins

Copy Edit Manager: Nicole Flores

Copy Editor: Susannah Davidson Pfalzer

Assistant Production Director: Kari Brooks-Copony

Production Editor: Kelly Winquist

Compositor: Dina Quan

Proofreader: April Eddy

Indexer: Brenda Miller

Artist: April Milne

Cover Designer: Kurt Krames

Manufacturing Director: Tom Debolski

For information on translations, please contact Apress directly at 2855 Telegraph Avenue, Suite 600, Berkeley, CA 94705. Phone 510-549-5930, fax 510-549-5939, e-mail info@apress.com, or visit http://www.apress.com.

The source code for this book is available to readers at http://www.apress.com in the Source Code/ Download section. You will need to answer questions pertaining to this book in order to successfully download the code.

Lex de Haan
1954–2006

"Tall and narrow, with a lot of good stuff on the upper floor"
"A missing value"

Contents at a Glance

PART 1 ■■■ The Mathematics

PART 2 ■■■ The Application

PART 3 ■ ■ ■ The Implementation

PART 4 ■ ■ ■ Appendixes

Contents

PART 1 ▪▪▪ The Mathematics

PART 2 ▪▪▪ The Application

PART 3 ■ ■ ■ The Implementation

PART 4 ■■■ Appendixes

Foreword

We welcome this contribution to the database literature. It is another book on the theory and practice of relational databases, but this one is interestingly different. The bulk of the book is devoted to a treatment of the theory. The treatment is not only rigorous and mathematical, but also rather more approachable than some other texts of this kind. The authors clearly recognize, as we do, the importance of logic and mathematics if database study is to be taken seriously. They have done a good job of describing a certain formalism developed by their former teachers, Bert de Brock and Frans Remmen. This formalism includes some ideas that will be novel to many readers, even those who already have a degree of familiarity with the subject. A particularly interesting novel idea, to us, is the formalization of updating and transactions in Chapter 10.

The formalism is interestingly different from the approach we and several others have adopted. The differences do not appear to be earth-shattering, but the full consequences are not immediately obvious to us, and we hope they will provoke discussion. One major difference is the omission of any in-depth treatment of types. This omission can be justified because relations are orthogonal to the types available for their attributes, so the two issues are somewhat separable even though any relational database language must of course deal with both of them. Closely related to the issue of types, and possibly a consequence of the omission we have noted, is the fact that there is only one empty relation under the De Brock/Remmen approach; by contrast, we subscribe to the notion that empty relations of distinct types are themselves distinct. Distinguishing empty relations of different types is in any case needed for static type checking, regarded as a *sine qua non* for database languages intended for use by robust applications. However, our approach is explicitly intended to provide, among other things, a foundation for database language design. The De Brock/Remmen approach appears to be more focused on getting the specifications of the database and its transactions right.

The authors turn from theory to practice in Chapter 11. Here they deal exclusively with *current* practice, showing how to translate the theoretical solutions described in Part 2 into concrete syntax using a particular well-known implementation of SQL. In doing this they have to face up not only to SQL's well-known deviations from the theory (especially its deviations from the classical logic used in that theory) but also to some alarming further deficiencies in many of the implementations of that language. This chapter can therefore be read as a thinly veiled wake-up call to DBMS vendors. We would like to take this opportunity to lift that veil a little.

The two deficiencies brought out by the authors' example solutions are (a) severe limitations on the extent to which declarative database constraints can be expressed, and (b) lack of proper support for serializability. If a DBMS does not suffer from (a), then (b) comes into play only when declarative constraints would lead to unacceptable performance. In that case, custom-written procedures, preferably triggered procedures, might be needed as a workaround. Such procedures require very careful design, as the authors eloquently demonstrate, so they are prone to some of those very errors that the relational approach from its very beginning was expressly designed to avoid. Deficiency (b) compounds this exposure by requiring the developers of these procedures to devise and implement some form of concurrency control within them. The authors describe a method requiring them first to devise a locking scheme, appropriate to the particular requirements of the database, then inside the procedures, in accordance with that scheme, to acquire locks at appropriate points. If the DBMS suffers from deficiency (a), then procedural workarounds will be needed for many more constraints, regardless of performance considerations. The worst-case scenario is clearly when the DBMS suffers from both (a) and (b). That is the scenario the authors feel compelled to assume, given the current state of the technology. To our minds, a relational DBMS that suffers from (a) is not a relational DBMS. (Of course, we have other reasons for claiming that no SQL DBMS is a relational DBMS anyway.) A DBMS that suffers from (b) is not a DBMS.

Standard SQL is relationally complete in its support for declarative constraints by permitting the inclusion of query expressions in the CHECK clause of a constraint declaration. However, it appears that few SQL products actually support that particular standard feature. The authors offer a polite excuse for this state of affairs. The excuse is well understood. It goes like this: a constraint that includes a possibly complex query against a possibly very large database might take ages to evaluate and might require frequent evaluation in the presence of a high transaction rate. We do not yet know—and it is an important and interesting research topic—how to do the kind of optimization that would be needed for the DBMS to work out efficient evaluation strategies along the lines of the authors' custom-written solutions. Performance considerations would currently militate against big businesses with very large databases and high transaction rates expressing the problematical constraints declaratively. Such businesses would employ—and could afford to employ—software experts to develop the required custom-written procedures. But what about small businesses with small databases and low transaction rates? And what about constraints that are evaluated quickly enough in spite of the inclusion of a query expression (which might be nothing more than a simple existence test, for example)? In any case, our history is littered with good ideas (for example, FORTRAN in the 1960s, the relational model in the 1970s) that have initially been shunned on advice from the performance sages that has eventually turned out to be ill-founded. As the years go by machines get faster, memory gets bigger, research comes up with new solutions. So much, then, for that excuse.

Sadly, Lex de Haan did not live to see the completion of this joint project. We would like to express our appreciation to Toon Koppelaars for the work that he has undertaken single-handedly since the untimely death in early 2006 of his friend and ours.

Hugh Darwen and Chris Date

About the Authors

LEX DE HAAN studied applied mathematics at the University of Technology in Delft, the Netherlands. His experience with Oracle goes back to the mid 1980s, version 4. He worked for Oracle Corp. from 1990 until 2004 in various education-related roles, ending up in Server Technologies (Oracle product development) as senior curriculum manager for the advanced DBA curriculum group. In that role, he was involved in the development of Oracle9*i* and Oracle Database 10*g*. In March 2004, he decided to go independent and founded his own company, Natural Join B.V. (http://www.naturaljoin.nl). From 1999 until his passing in 2006, he was involved in the ISO SQL language standardization process as a member of the Dutch national body. He was also one of the founding members of the OakTable network (http://www.oaktable.net). He wrote the well-received *Mastering Oracle SQL and SQL*Plus* (Apress, 2005).

TOON KOPPELAARS studied computer science at the University of Technology in Eindhoven, the Netherlands. He is a longtime Oracle technology user, having used the Oracle database and tool software since 1987. During his career he has been involved in application development (terminal/host in the early days, GUI client/server later on, and J2EE/web development nowadays), as well as database administration. His interest areas include performance tuning (ensuring scalability and SQL tuning), architecting applications in a database-centric way, and database design. Within the database design area, the mathematical specification and robust implementation of database designs—that is, including the data integrity constraints (often referred to as business rules)—is one of his special interest areas. He is employed as a senior IT architect at Centraal Boekhuis B.V., a well-known Oracle shop in the Netherlands. Toon is also a frequent presenter at Oracle-related conferences.

About the Technical Reviewers

 **CHRIS DATE** is an independent author, lecturer, researcher, and consultant specializing in relational database systems. He was one of the first people anywhere to recognize the fundamental importance of Ted Codd's pioneering work on the relational model. He was also involved in technical planning for the IBM products SQL/DS and DB2 at the IBM Santa Teresa Laboratory in San Jose, California. He is best known for his books—in particular *An Introduction to Database Systems*, Eighth Edition (Addison-Wesley, 2003), the standard text in the field, which has sold nearly three quarters of a million copies worldwide—and (with Hugh Darwen and Nikos A. Lorentzos) *Temporal Data and the Relational Model* (Morgan Kaufmann, 2002).

 **CARY MILLSAP** is the principal author of *Optimizing Oracle Performance* (O'Reilly, 2003) and the lead designer and developer of the Hotsos PD101 course. Prior to cofounding Hotsos in 1999, he served for ten years at Oracle Corp. as one of the company's leading system performance experts. At Oracle, he also founded and served as vice president of the 80-person System Performance Group. He has educated thousands of Oracle consultants, support analysts, developers, and customers in the optimal use of Oracle technology through his commitment to writing, teaching, and speaking at public events.

Acknowledgments

This project started at the end of the summer in 2005, and due to unfortunate circumstances took much longer than originally planned. My coauthor was already diagnosed when he contacted me to jointly write a book "about the mathematics in our profession." We started writing in October 2005 and first spent a lot of time together developing the example database design—especially the involved data integrity constraints—that would be used throughout the book. "I'll start at the beginning, you start at the end, then we will meet somewhere in the middle," is what he said once the database design was finished. In the months that followed Lex put in a big effort to create the Introduction through Chapter 3. Unfortunately, around Christmas 2005 his situation deteriorated rapidly and he never saw the rest of this book.

Thankfully, I received the support of many other people to complete this project.

The contribution of my main reviewers to the quality of this book has been immense. I'd like to thank Chris Date, Cary Millsap, Hugh Darwen, and Frans Remmen for their efforts in reviewing the manuscript and offering me many comments and suggestions to improve the book.

I also greatly appreciate the time some of my colleagues at Centraal Boekhuis put into this book: Jaap de Klerk, Lotte van den Hoek, and Emiel van Bockel for reviewing several chapters; Petra van der Craats for helping me out when I was struggling with the English language; and Ronald Janssen for his overall support for this project.

I must mention the support I received from the people at Apress, especially my editor Jonathan Gennick for remaining committed to this book even when the original plan had to be completely revised, and the other people at Apress involved in the production of this book—the only ones I've never met in person: Tracy Brown Collins, Tina Nielsen, Susannah Davidson Pfalzer, Kelly Winquist, and April Eddy.

I would like to mention a few other people: Mogens Nørgaard, for his support early in 2006 in the time right after Lex's passing; Juliette Nuijten, for her continued support of this project; and Bert de Brock, for the influential curriculum on database systems he provided together with Frans Remmen more than 20 years ago. Without those courses this book would not exist.

I must of course also thank my wife for giving me the opportunity to embark upon this project and to finish it, and our kids for their patience, especially these last three months; I had to promise them not even to think about writing another book.

And finally, I thank Lex, who initiated this book and decided to contact me as his coauthor. Well Lex, we finally did it, your last project is done.

Toon Koppelaars
Zaltbommel, the Netherlands, March 2007

Preface

This book is not an easy read, but you will have a great understanding of mathematics as it relates to database design by the end.

We'll introduce you to a mathematical methodology that enables you to deal with database designs in a clear way. Those of you who have had a formal education in mathematics will most likely enjoy reading this book. It demonstrates how you can apply two mathematical disciplines—logic and set theory—to your current profession.

For those of you who lack a formal education in mathematics, you'll have to put in an effort when reading this book. We do our best to explain all material in a clear way and provide sufficient examples along the way. Nevertheless, there is a lot of new material for you to digest.

We assume that you are familiar with designing a database. This book will not teach you how to design databases; more specifically, this book will not explain what makes a database design a good one or a bad one. This book's primary goal is to teach you a formal methodology for specifying a database design; in particular, for specifying all involved data integrity constraints in a clear and unambiguous manner.

This book is a *must* for every IT professional who is involved in any way with designing databases:

- Database designers, data architects, and data administrators

- Application developers with database design responsibilities

- Database administrators with database design responsibilities

- IT architects

- People managing teams that include any of the preceding roles

We wrote this book because we are convinced that the mode of thought required by this formal methodology will—as an important side effect—contribute to your database design capabilities. Understanding this formal methodology will benefit you, the database professional, and will in the end make you a better database designer.

Introduction

This book will not try to change your attitude towards mathematics, which can be anywhere between hate and love. The sole objective of this book is to show you how you can use mathematics in your life as a database professional, and how mathematics can help you solve certain problems. We, the authors, are convinced that familiarity with the areas of mathematics that will be presented in this book, and on which *the relational model of data* is based, is a strong prerequisite for anybody who aims to be professionally involved with databases.

This book tries to fill a space that is not yet covered by the many books on databases that are already available. In Part 1, we cover just the part of mathematics that is useful for the practice of the database professional; the mathematical theory covered in this part is linked to the practice in Parts 2 (specifying database designs) and 3 (implementing database designs).

One thing is for sure: mathematics forces you to think clearly and precisely, and then to write things down as formally and precisely as possible. This is because the language of mathematics is both formal and rich in expressive power. Natural languages are rich in expressive power but are highly informal; on the other hand, programming languages are formal but typically have much less expressive power than mathematics.

Mathematicians

Mathematicians are strange people. Most of them have all sorts of weird hobbies, and they all share a passionate love for puzzles and games. To be more precise, they love to create their own games and then play those games. Well, how do you create a game? You simply establish a set of rules, and start playing. If you are the creator of the game, you have a rather luxurious position: if you don't like the game that much, you simply revisit the rules, implement some changes, and start playing again—until you like the game.

Mathematicians always strive for elegance and *orthogonality*—they dislike exceptions. A game is said to be designed in an orthogonal way if its set of components that together make up the whole game capability are non-overlapping and mutually independent. Each capability should be implemented by only one component, and one component should only implement one capability of the game. Well-separated and independent components ensure that there are no side effects: using or even changing one component does not cause side effects in another area of the game.

Note For more information, see for example "A Note on Orthogonality" by C. J. Date, originally published in *Database Programming & Design* (July 1995), or visit http://en.wikipedia.org/wiki/ Orthogonality.

Why do things in a complicated way if you can accomplish the same thing in a more simple way? Why allow tricks in certain places, but at the same time forbid them in other places where the same trick would make a lot of sense? Exceptions are the worst of all. Therefore, mathematicians always explore the boundaries of their games. If the established rules don't behave nicely at the boundaries, there is room for improvement.

High-Level Book Overview

Over time, mathematicians have spawned several formal disciplines. This book pays special attention to the following two formal disciplines, because they are the most relevant ones in the application of mathematics to the field of databases:

- Logic

- Set theory

The first part of this book consists of four chapters; they introduce the mathematics as such. While reading these chapters, you should try to exercise some patience in case you don't immediately see their relevance for you; they lay down the mathematical concepts, techniques, and notations needed for the second and third parts of the book.

■**Note** Even if you think at first glance that your mathematical skills are strong enough, we advise you to read and study the first four chapters in detail and to go through all exercises, without looking at the corresponding solutions first. This will help you get used to the mathematical notations used throughout this book; moreover, some exercises are designed to make you aware of certain common errors.

The second part consists of Chapters 5 through 10, showing the application of the mathematics to database issues. Chapter 5 introduces a formal way to specify table designs and introduces the concept of a database state. Chapter 6 establishes the notion of data integrity predicates; we use these to specify data integrity constraints. Chapter 7 specifies a full-fledged example database design in a clear mathematical form. You'll discover through this example that specifying a database design involves specifying data integrity constraints for the most part. Chapter 8 adds the notion of state transition constraints, and formally specifies these for the given example database design. Chapter 9 shows how you can precisely formulate queries in mathematics, and Chapter 10 shows how you can formally specify transactions.

The third part consists of Chapter 11 and Chapter 12. Chapter 11 goes into the details of realizing a database design, especially its data integrity constraints, in a database management system (DBMS)—a crucial and challenging task for any database professional. In Chapter 11, we establish a further link from the theory to the SQL DBMS practice of today.

■**Note** Chapter 11 is an optional chapter. However, if you're involved in implementing database designs in Oracle's SQL DBMS, you'll appreciate it.

Chapter 12 summarizes the book, lists some conclusions, and provides some general guidelines.

The book contains several appendixes:

- Appendix A gives the full formal definition of the database design used in the book.

- Appendix B contains a quick reference of all mathematical symbols used in the book.

- Appendix C provides a reference for further background reading.

- Appendix D provides a brief exploration of the use of NULLs.

- Appendix E provides solutions for selected exercises.

We assume that you're aware of the existence of the relational model, and perhaps you also have some in-depth knowledge of what this model is about (that's not required, though). We also assume that you have experience in designing databases, and you're therefore familiar with concepts such as keys, foreign keys, (functional) dependencies, and the third normal form (the latter two aren't required).

This book's main focus is on specifying a relational database design in general and specifying the data integrity constraints involved in such a design, specifically. We demonstrate how elementary set theory (in combination with logic) aids us in producing solid database design specifications that give us a good and clear insight into the relevant constraints.

Other authors, most notably C. J. Date in his recent book *Database In Depth* (O'Reilly, 2005), lay out the fundamentals of the relational model but sometimes assume you are knowledgeable in certain mathematical disciplines. In this book no mathematical knowledge is preassumed; we'll deliver the theoretical—set-theory—concepts that are necessary to define a relational database design from the ground upwards.

We must mention up front that the approach taken in this book is a different approach (for some, maybe radically different) to the one taken by other authors. The methodology that is developed in this book uses merely elementary set theory in conjunction with logic. Elementary set theory suffices to specify relational database designs, including all relevant data integrity constraints. We'll also use set theory as the vehicle to specify queries and transactions on such designs.

▪**Note** We (the authors) are not the inventors of the methodology presented in this book. Frans Remmen and Bert de Brock originally developed this methodology in the 1980s, while they were both engaged at the Eindhoven University of Technology. Appendix C lists two references of books authored by Bert de Brock in which he introduces this methodology to specify database designs.

Database Design Implementation Issues

The majority of all DBMSes these days are based on the ISO standard of the SQL (pronounced as "ess-cue-ell") language. This is where you'll get into some trouble. First of all, the SQL language is far from an elegant and orthogonal database language; furthermore, it is not too difficult to see that it is a product of years of political debates and attempts to achieve consensus.

In hindsight, some battles were won by the wrong guys. Indeed, this is one of the reasons why C. J. Date and Hugh Darwen wrote their book on what they call "the third manifesto." A fully revised third edition was published in 2006: *Databases, Types, and the Relational Model: The Third Manifesto* (Addison-Wesley).

On top of this, several database software vendors have made mistakes—sometimes small ones, sometimes big ones—in their attempts to implement the ISO standard in their products. They also left certain features out and added nonstandard features to enrich their products, thus deviating from the ISO standard. As soon as you try to step away from mathematics (and thus from the relational model) and start using an SQL DBMS, you'll inevitably open up several cans of worms.

This book tries to stay away as much as possible from SQL, thus keeping the book as generic as possible. Chapters 9 (data retrieval) and 10 (data manipulation) display SQL expressions; they serve only to demonstrate (in)abilities of this language in comparison to the mathematical formalism introduced in this book. Both authors happen to have extensive experience with the SQL DBMS from Oracle; the SQL code given in these chapters is compliant with the 10g release of Oracle's SQL DBMS. Chapter 11 (implementing database designs) displays SQL expressions even more. We'll also maintain the Oracle-specific content of Chapter 11; you can download the code from the Source Code/Download area of the Apress Web site (http://www.apress.com).

PART 1

■ ■ ■

The Mathematics

Everything should be made as simple as possible, but not simpler.

Albert Einstein (1879–1955)

CHAPTER 1

Logic: Introduction

The word "logic" has many meanings, and is heavily overloaded. It's derived from the Greek word *logicos*, meaning "concerning language and speech" or "human reasoning."

The section "The History of Logic" gives a concise overview of the history of logic, just to show that many brilliant people have been involved over several centuries to develop what's now known as mathematical logic. The section is by no means meant to be complete.

In the section "Values, Variables, and Types," we'll discuss the difference between *values* (constants) and *variables*. We'll also introduce the notion of the *type of a variable*. We'll use these notions in the section "Propositions and Predicates" to introduce the concept of a *predicate*, and its special case, a *proposition*—the main concepts in logic.

The section "Logical Connectives" explains how you can build new predicates by combining existing predicates using *logical connectives*. Then, in the section "Truth Tables" you'll see how you can use *truth tables* to define logical connectives and to investigate the truth value of logical expressions. Truth tables are an important and useful tool to start developing various concepts in logic.

Functional completeness is covered in the section "Functional Completeness"; it's about which logical connectives you need (as a minimum) to formulate all possible logical expressions.

The following two sections introduce the concepts of *tautologies* and *contradictions*, *logical equivalence*, and *rewrite rules*. You can use a rewrite rule to transform one logical expression into another (equivalent) logical expression.

This chapter is an introductory chapter on logic. Chapter 3 will continue where this one stops—the two chapters make up one single topic (logic). The split is necessary because some concepts concerning logic require the introduction of a few set-theory notions first. Chapter 2 will serve that purpose.

The introduction of the crucial concept of *rewrite rules* at the end of this chapter opens up the first possibility to do some useful exercises. They serve two important purposes:

- Learning how to use truth tables and rewrite rules to investigate logical expressions

- Getting used to the mathematical symbols introduced in this chapter

Therefore, we strongly advise you to spend sufficient time on these exercises before moving on to other chapters.

The History of Logic

The science of logic and the investigation of human reasoning goes back to the ancient Greeks, more than 2,000 years ago. Aristotle (384–322 BC), a student of Plato, is commonly considered the first logician.

Gottfried Wilhelm Leibnitz (1646–1716) established the foundations for the development of mathematical logic. He thought that symbols were extremely important to understand things, so he tried to design a universal symbolic language to describe human reasoning. The logic of Leibnitz was based on the following two principles:

- There are only a few simple ideas that form the "alphabet of human thought."

- You can generate complex ideas from those simple ideas by a process analogous to arithmetical multiplication.

George Boole (1815–1864) invented the general concept of a Boolean algebra, the foundation of modern computer arithmetic. In 1854 he published *An Investigation of the Laws of Thought on Which Are Founded the Mathematical Theories of Logic and Probabilities*, in which he shows that you can perform arithmetic on logical symbols just like algebraic symbols and numbers.

In 1922, Ludwig Wittgenstein (1889–1951) introduced truth tables as we know them today, based on the earlier work of Gottlob Frege (1848–1925) and others during the 1880s.

After a formal notation was introduced, several attempts were made to use mathematical logic to describe the foundation of mathematics itself. The attempt by Gottlob Frege (that failed) is famous; Bertrand Russell (1872–1970) showed in 1901 that Frege's system could produce a contradiction: the famous Russell's paradox (see sidebar). Later attempts to achieve the same goal were performed by Bertrand Russell and Alfred North Whitehead (1861–1947), David Hilbert (1862–1943), John von Neumann (1903–1957), Kurt Gödel (1906–1978), and Alfred Tarski (1902–1983), just to name a few of the most famous ones.

RUSSELL'S PARADOX

Russell's paradox can be difficult to understand for readers who are unfamiliar with mathematical logic in general and with setting up a mathematical proof in particular. The paradox goes as follows:

1. Consider the set of all sets that are not members of themselves; let's call this set X.

2. Suppose X is an element of X—but then it must *not* be a member of itself, according to the preceding definition of set X. So the supposition is FALSE.

3. Similarly, suppose X is *not* an element of X—but then it must be a member of itself, again according to the preceding definition of set X. So this supposition is FALSE too.

4. But surely one of these two suppositions must be TRUE; hence the paradox.

Don't worry if this puzzles you; it isn't important for the application of the mathematics that this book deals with.

It's safe to say that the science of logic is sound; it has existed for many centuries and has been investigated by many brilliant scientists over those centuries.

■Note If you want to know more about the history of logic, or the history of mathematics in general, `http://en.wikipedia.org` is an excellent source of information.

These days, formal methods derived from logic are not only used in mathematics, informatics (computer science), and artificial intelligence; they are also used in biology, linguistics, and even in jurisprudence.

The importance of data management being based on logic was envisioned by E. F. (Ted) Codd (1923–2003) in 1969, when he first proposed his famous relational model in the IBM research report "Derivability, Redundancy and Consistency of Relations Stored in Large Data Banks." The relational model for database management introduced in this research report has proven to be an influential general theory of data management and remains his most memorable achievement.

Every science is (should be) based on logic: every theory is a system of sentences (or statements) that are accepted as true and can be used to *derive* new statements following some well-defined rules. It's one of the main goals of this book to explain the mathematical concepts on which the science of relational data management is based.

Values, Variables, and Types

You probably have some idea of the two terms *values* and *variables*. However, it's important to define these two terms precisely, because they are often misunderstood and mixed up.

A *value* is an individual constant with a well-determined meaning. For example, the integer 42 is a value. You cannot update a value; if you could, it would no longer be the same value. Values can be represented in many ways, using some encoding. Values can have any arbitrary complexity.

A *variable* is a holder for a value. Variables in the course of time and space get a different value. We call the changing of values the *updating* of a variable. Variables have a *name*, allowing you to talk about them without knowing which value they currently represent.

In this book, we'll always use variables that are of a given *type*. The *set of values* from which the variable is allowed to hold a value is referred to as the *type of that variable*.

A database—containing table values—is an example of a variable; at any point in time, it has a certain (complex) value. *We will specify the type of a database variable in a precise way in Part 2 of this book.*

Propositions and Predicates

In logic, the main components we deal with are propositions and predicates. A proposition is a *declarative sentence* that's either TRUE or FALSE.

■**Note** A sentence S is a declarative sentence, if the following is a proper English question: "Is it true that S?"

If a proposition is true we say it has a "truth value" of TRUE; if a proposition is false, its truth value is FALSE. Here are some examples of propositions:

- This book has two authors.

- The square root of 16 equals 3.

- All mathematicians are liars.

- If Toon is familiar with SQL, then Lex has three daughters.

All four examples are declarative sentences; if you prefix them with "Is it true that," then a proper English question is formed and you can decide if the declarative sentences are TRUE or not. The truth value of the first proposition is TRUE; it is a TRUE proposition. The second proposition is obviously FALSE; the square root of 16 equals 4. The third example is a proposition too, although you might find it difficult to decide what its truth value is. But in theory you *can* decide its truth value. Assuming you have a clear definition of who is and who isn't a mathematician, you can determine the set of persons that need to be checked. You would then have to check every mathematician, in this rather large but finite set, to find the truth value of the proposition. If you find a non-lying mathematician, then the proposition is FALSE; on the other hand, if no such mathematician can be found, then the proposition is clearly TRUE. In the last example, "Toon" and "Lex" are the authors of this book. Therefore, you should be able to decide whether this predicate is TRUE or FALSE if you know enough about the authors of this book. The proposition is FALSE, by the way; Toon is indeed familiar with SQL, but Lex does not have three daughters.

■**Note** It's a common misconception to consider only TRUE statements to be propositions; propositions can be FALSE as well.

The following examples are not propositions:

- x + y > 10

- The square root of x equals z.

- What did you pay for this book?

- Stop designing databases.

The first two examples hold embedded variables; the truth value of these sentences depends on the values that are currently held by these variables. The last two examples aren't declarative sentences and therefore aren't propositions.

A *predicate* is something having the form of a declarative sentence. A predicate holds embedded variables whose values are unknown at this time; you cannot decide if what is declared is either TRUE or FALSE without knowing the value(s) for the variable(s). We'll refer to the embedded variables in a predicate as the *parameters* of the predicate.

The first two examples in the preceding list are predicates; they hold embedded variables x, y, and z. Following are some other examples of predicates:

- i has the value 4.

- x lives in y.

- If Toon is familiar with SQL, then Lex has k daughters.

You cannot tell if the first example is TRUE or FALSE, because it depends on the actual value of parameter i. The same holds for the second example; as long as you don't know which human being is represented by parameter x and which city is represented by parameter y, you cannot say whether this predicate is TRUE or FALSE. Finally, the truth value of the last example depends on its parameter k. You already saw that if value 3 is substituted for parameter k, then the truth value of this predicate becomes FALSE.

A predicate with n parameters is called an n-place predicate. If you substitute one of the parameters in an n-place predicate with a value, then the predicate becomes an (n-1)-place predicate. For instance, the preceding second example is a 2-place predicate; it has two parameters, x and y. If you substitute the value Lex for parameter x, then this predicate turns into the following expression:

```
Lex lives in y
```

This expression represents a 1-place predicate; it has one parameter. The truth value still depends upon (the value of) the remaining parameter. If you now substitute value "Utrecht"—the name of a city in the Netherlands—for parameter y, the predicate turns into a 0-place predicate.

```
Lex lives in Utrecht
```

Do you see that this is now a proposition? You can decide the truth value of this expression. As this example shows, propositions can be regarded as a special case of predicates; they are predicates with no parameters. You can convert a predicate into a proposition by providing values that are substituted for the parameters. This is called *instantiating* the predicate with the given values.

Note A way to look at a predicate is as follows—here we quote from Chris Date's book *Database in Depth* (O'Reilly Media, 2005): "You can think of a predicate as a truth-valued function. Like all functions, it has a set of parameters, it returns a result when it is invoked (instantiated) by supplying values for the parameters, and, because it's truth valued, that result is either TRUE or FALSE."

The parameters of a predicate are also referred to as the *free variables* of a predicate. There's another way to convert predicates into propositions: by *binding* the involved free variable(s) with a *quantifier*. Free variables then turn into what are called *bound variables*. Quantification (over a set) is an important concept in logic and even more so in data management; we'll cover it in Chapter 3 (the section "Quantifiers") in great detail.

Table 1-1 summarizes the properties of a predicate and a proposition.

Table 1-1. *Predicates and Propositions*

Predicate	Proposition
Form of declarative sentence	Declarative sentence
With parameters	Without parameters
Truth-valued function	Either TRUE or FALSE
Input is required to evaluate truth/falsehood	Special case predicate (no input required)

Before we go on, let's briefly look at sentences such as the following:

```
This statement is false
I am lying
```

These are *self-referential* sentences; they say something about themselves. Sentences of this type can cause trouble in the sense that they might lead to a contradiction. The second example is known as the liar's paradox. If you assume these sentences to be TRUE then you can draw the conclusion that they are FALSE (and vice versa); you cannot decide whether they are TRUE or FALSE, which is a mandatory property for them to be valid propositions. The solution is simply to disqualify them as valid propositions.

You must also discard "ill-formed" expressions as valid predicates; that is, expressions that don't adhere to our syntax rules, such as the following:

```
3 is an element of 4
n = 4 ∨ ∧ m = 5
```

The first one is ill-formed because 4 is not a set; it is a numeric value. To say 3 is an element of it doesn't make any sense. Here we assume you have some idea of the concept of a set and for something to be an element of a set; we'll cover elementary set theory in Chapter 2. The second expression contains two consecutive connectives ∨ and ∧ (explained in the next section), which is illegal.

Logical Connectives

You can build new predicates by applying *logical connectives* to existing ones. The most well-known connectives are *conjunction* (logical AND), *disjunction* (logical OR), and *negation* (logical NOT); two other connectives we'll use frequently are *implication* and *equivalence*. Throughout this book, we use mathematical symbols to denote these logical connectives, as shown in Table 1-2.

Table 1-2. *Logical Connectives*

Symbol	Meaning	Also Referred to As	Example
¬	NOT	Negation	not (Toon lives in Utrecht)
∧	AND	Conjunction	(n = 4) and (m = 2)
∨	OR	Disjunction	(job = 'CLERK') or (salary > 5000)
⇒	IMPLIES	Implication (if . . . then . . .)	(x < 6) implies (x ≠ 7)
⇔	IS EQUIVALENT TO	Equivalence (if and only if)	(x = 10) is equivalent to (x/2 = 5)

Caution Although you probably have some idea about the meaning of most connectives listed in the preceding text, we must be prudent, because they're also used in natural languages. Natural languages are informal and imprecise; as a consequence, the meaning of words sometimes depends on the context in which they're used.

We'll precisely define the meaning of these five logical connectives in the section "Truth Tables" when the concept of a *truth table* is introduced.

Simple and Compound Predicates

Logical connectives can be regarded as *logical operators*; they take one or more predicates as their operands, and return another predicate. For instance, the logical AND in Table 1-2 has $n = 4$ and $m = 2$ as its operands (inputs) and returns the predicate listed under the Example column as its output predicate. We say that the AND operator is invoked with operands $n = 4$ and $m = 2$.

It's quite common to refer to predicates without logical connectives as *simple* predicates, and to refer to predicates with one or more logical connectives as *compound* predicates. The input predicates (operands) of a connective in a compound predicate are also referred to as the *components* of that predicate.

Another common term is the *complexity* of a compound predicate, which is the number of connectives occurring in that predicate. Here are some more examples of compound predicates, this time using the mathematical symbols.

Note You might have some difficulty reading the last example. This is because the *operator precedence* (explained in the following section) is unclear in that example.

- n = 4 ∧ m = 5

- x = 42 ∨ x ≠ 42

- Toon lives in Utrecht ⇒ 1 + 1 = 2

- P ∧ Q ⇒ P ⇒ Q

In the last example, P and Q are *propositional variables*. They denote an arbitrary proposition with an unspecified truth value. We'll use letters P, Q, R, and so on for propositional variables. You can use propositions, as well as propositional variables, to form new assertions using the logical connectives introduced in the preceding text. An assertion that contains at least one propositional variable is called a *propositional form*. If you substitute propositions for the variables of a propositional form, a proposition results.

In a similar way, we'll use the letters P, Q, R, and so on in expressions such as P(x), Q(s,t), R(y), and so on to denote arbitrary predicates with at least one parameter. The parameter(s) of such predicates are denoted by the letters—in these cases x, y, s, and t—separated by commas inside the parentheses of these expressions. For instance, the first compound predicate listed in the preceding text can be denoted as P(n,m). If we substitute the value 3 for the parameter n and the value 5 for the parameter m, the predicate changes to a proposition P(3,5) whose truth value is FALSE.

In mathematics, the precise meaning (semantics) of all logical connectives can be defined using truth tables, as introduced in the next section. With those definitions, you can "calculate" the truth values of compound predicates from the truth values of their components.

Using Parentheses and Operator Precedence Rules

You can use parentheses in logical expressions to denote operator precedence, just like in regular arithmetic, where you can overrule the customary operator precedence as defined by the mnemonic "Please Excuse My Dear Aunt Sally."

Note The first characters of these words signify operator precedence in arithmetic: Parentheses, Exponents, Multiplication, Division, Addition, Subtraction.

Even when a language defines formal operator precedence rules—allowing you to omit parentheses in certain expressions—it still is a good idea to use them for enhanced readability. It isn't wrong to include parentheses that could be omitted without changing the meaning. You can include parentheses into the previous four compound predicate examples as follows:

- (n = 4) ∧ (m = 5)

- (x = 42) ∨ (x ≠ 42)

- (Toon lives in Utrecht) ⇒ (1 + 1 = 2)

- (P ∧ Q) ⇒ (P ⇒ Q)

The readability of the last example is definitely enhanced by including the parentheses. It's customary to adopt the precedence rules as shown in Table 1-3 for the five logical connectives we introduced so far (note that some have the same rank).

Table 1-3. *Logical Connective Precedence Rules*

Rank	Connective
1	$\neg$
2	$\wedge, \vee$
3	$\Rightarrow, \Leftrightarrow$

These precedence rules prescribe that, for example, the following compound predicate P $\wedge$ Q $\Rightarrow$ R—which has no included parentheses—should in fact be interpreted as (P $\wedge$ Q) $\Rightarrow$ R—not as P $\wedge$ (Q $\Rightarrow$ R), which is a different predicate (that is, it has a different meaning). When same-rank connectives are involved, it's customary to have them associate their operands from right to left; this is sometimes referred to as the *associativity rule*. This means that the predicate P $\Rightarrow$ Q $\Rightarrow$ R should in fact be interpreted as P $\Rightarrow$ (Q $\Rightarrow$ R).

Consider the following two example predicates, and check out the usage of parentheses:

1. $\neg$ (P $\Rightarrow$ Q) $\Leftrightarrow$ (P $\wedge$ $\neg$Q)

2. ((P $\Rightarrow$ Q) $\wedge$ (Q $\Rightarrow$ R)) $\Rightarrow$ (P $\Rightarrow$ R)

In the first example, the first set of parentheses is needed—otherwise the negation would affect P only. The second set can be omitted, because $\wedge$ takes precedence over $\Leftrightarrow$. In the second example, the outermost parentheses at the left-hand side are optional, as are the parentheses at the right-hand side (due to the associativity rule), but the other two sets of parentheses are needed.

In the remainder of this book when more than one connective is involved in a predicate, we'll always include parentheses and not depend on the precedence and associativity rules.

Truth Tables

Truth tables are primarily used in logic to establish the basic logical concepts. You can use them for two (quite different) basic purposes:

- To define the meaning of logical connectives

- To investigate the truth value of compound logical expressions

By investigating compound logical expressions using truth values, you can establish (develop) new logical concepts; the development of rewrite rules at the end of this chapter is a fine example of this. Once basic logical concepts have been established, you'll rarely use truth tables anymore.

Every truth table consists of a header and a body. When defining the meaning of logical connectives, the leftmost column headers list the variables involved with the connective you want to define, and the rightmost column header lists the connective itself.

When you investigate the truth value of a compound logical expression, the leftmost column headers list the variables involved in the compound expression, and the rightmost column header lists the compound expression. Optionally, you can have additional columns in the middle to help you gradually work towards the logical expression in the last column; this is especially useful if the logical expression under investigation is a complicated one.

Take a look at Figure 1-1. It shows the truth table that defines the meaning of the logical AND connective.

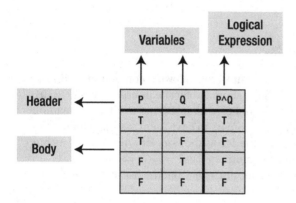

Figure 1-1. *Structure of the truth table for logical AND*

The body of a truth table always contains one row for every possible truth combination of the variables involved. That is, if you have only one variable you need two rows (one for TRUE and one for FALSE), if you have two variables you need four rows (TRUE/TRUE, TRUE/FALSE, FALSE/TRUE, FALSE/FALSE), and so on.

■**Note** The variables involved in a truth table are propositional variables.

Tables 1-4 through 1-8 show the truth tables for the five logical connectives introduced in the previous section, and as such formally define the semantics of these connectives. We'll use T and F as abbreviations for TRUE and FALSE, respectively.

Table 1-4. *Truth Table for NOT (Negation)*

P	¬P
T	F
F	T

¬P is FALSE if and only if P is TRUE. In the other case, ¬P is TRUE.

Table 1-5. *Truth Table for AND (Conjunction)*

P	Q	P ∧ Q
T	T	T
T	F	F
F	T	F
F	F	F

P ∧ Q is TRUE if and only if both P and Q are TRUE. In all other cases, P ∧ Q is FALSE. In a conjunction P ∧ Q, P and Q are referred to as the *conjuncts*.

Table 1-6. *Truth Table for OR (Disjunction)*

P	Q	P ∨ Q
T	T	T
T	F	T
F	T	T
F	F	F

P ∨ Q is FALSE if and only if both P and Q are FALSE. In a disjunction P ∨ Q, P and Q are referred to as the *disjuncts*.

Note The OR operator that is defined here is called the *inclusive* or. In natural language, we normally refer to the inclusive or when using the word "or." However, we sometimes use "or" to denote what is called the *exclusive* or (eor for short). Compared to the truth table for the inclusive or (Table 1-6), the truth table for the exclusive or differs only on the first row; the propositional form P eor Q is FALSE if both P and Q are TRUE. An example use of the exclusive or is in the statement, "You must clean up your room or you go to bed early." Clearly you aren't required to both clean up your room *and* go to bed early. In this book we will always use the inclusive or.

Table 1-7. *Truth Table for IF . . . THEN (Implication)*

P	Q	P ⇒ Q
T	T	T
T	F	F
F	T	T
F	F	T

P ⇒ Q is FALSE if and only if P is TRUE and Q is FALSE. In all other cases P ⇒ Q is TRUE. In an implication P ⇒ Q, P is often referred to as the *antecedent, hypothesis,* or *premise,* and Q as the *consequent* or *conclusion.*

Table 1-8. *Truth Table for IF AND ONLY IF (Equivalence)*

P	Q	P ⇔ Q
T	T	T
T	F	F
F	T	F
F	F	T

Logical equivalence is nothing more than the conventional = operator as it applies to Boolean values; P ⇔ Q is TRUE if and only if P and Q have the same truth value. Another common way to express equivalence is to use the words "necessary and sufficient."

Note that the negation (see Table 1-4) is a *monadic* operator; it accepts only one operand. The other connectives in Tables 1-5 through 1-8 are *dyadic;* they accept two operands.

■**Note** Other books sometimes use the terms unary, binary, and ternary instead of monadic, dyadic, and triadic when classifying operators.

Implication

In real life, implication plays a predominant role, because life is full of if-then situations. Database designs are meant to represent parts of real life. You'll see in Part 2 of this book that the implication is often used within formal specifications of data integrity constraints that play a role in these database designs. Therefore, it's important to understand fully the formal definition of the implication connective as given by Table 1-7.

Probably the most "controversial" truth table entry is this one: if P is FALSE and Q is TRUE, the implication P ⇒ Q is TRUE. You remember in the introduction of this book, when we described how mathematicians create their own games, changing the rules until they like the game? Well, the preceding definition of implication turns out to work better in practice than any other definition. One way to think about the implication P ⇒ Q is as follows:

- This implication says something about the truth of Q in case P is TRUE.

- If P is *not* true, the implication does not "say" anything; therefore, the truth of Q does not matter and the implication is considered TRUE.

Take a look at the following proposition:

```
Toon lives in Utrecht implies Lex has two daughters.
```

You can regard this as an instantiation of the propositional form P ⇒ Q where the proposition "Toon lives in Utrecht" is substituted as the value for propositional variable P, and the proposition "Lex has two daughters" is substituted as the value for variable Q. Because Toon doesn't live in Utrecht, the value for Q might as well have stated that Lex has three daughters (in reality there are two); the implication P $\Rightarrow$ Q would still be TRUE.

Another way of looking at this is as follows: if you believe a falsehood, you'll believe anything.

Predicate Strength

Implication can be considered to *order* the two predicates it has as its operands; it declares an order between the two operands, the hypothesis and the conclusion. This order is referred to as the *strength* of a predicate. If two predicates—say P and Q—are involved in an implication P $\Rightarrow$ Q, then predicate P is said to be *stronger* than predicate Q—or Q is *weaker* than P.

Assuming x is a variable of type integer, take a look at the following implication:

x > 42 $\Rightarrow$ x > 0

To declare that x is greater than 42 clearly implies that x is greater than 0. This implication is TRUE irrespective of the value that you supply for x, and the statement "x > 42" is said to be stronger than the statement "x > 0".

Two predicates, say P and Q, are of equal strength if and only if both P $\Rightarrow$ Q and Q $\Rightarrow$ P are TRUE. In this case P and Q are equivalent: P $\Leftrightarrow$ Q.

Note You aren't always able to state for two given predicates, say P and Q, which one is the stronger one. If neither P $\Rightarrow$ Q holds, nor Q $\Rightarrow$ P holds, then there is no order between P and Q. In mathematics this kind of ordering is referred to as a *partial ordering*.

Given this ordering of predicates, you can ask yourself whether there exists a predicate that is the strongest of all predicates, and likewise, is there one that is weakest of all? The strongest predicate would be the one *implying every other predicate*. Indeed there is such a predicate: FALSE is the strongest predicate because FALSE $\Rightarrow$ Q is TRUE for any conclusion Q. This follows from the third and fourth entry in the truth table listed in Table 1-7 that defines the implication.

The weakest predicate would be the one *implied by every other predicate*; TRUE is the *weakest* predicate because P $\Rightarrow$ TRUE is true for any hypothesis P. This follows from the first and third entry in the truth table listed in Table 1-7.

Going a Little Further

Let's explore the area of logical connectives a little further, just for fun. The preceding truth tables show five logical connectives. Why *five*? How many logical connectives, each with a distinct different meaning, can we come up with in total? How many of them do we need? What would be the theoretical minimum set of logical connectives to express all other ones?

For example, it's relatively easy to see that you can define four different monadic and sixteen different dyadic logical connectives. A truth table for a monadic connective has two rows, and a truth table for a dyadic connective has four rows; because you have two choices for each truth table cell (TRUE and FALSE), the total number of possibilities is 2 * 2 = 4 and 2 * 2 * 2 * 2 = 16, respectively. So, we could give all those 20 connectives a name, also choose a symbol to represent them, and start using them in our logical expressions. Obviously, we don't do that; it would be too difficult to remember all those operators, our expressions would become difficult to read, and apparently we don't need all those connectives. This leads to the important concept of functional completeness.

Functional Completeness

A given set of logical connectives is *truth functionally complete* if and only if all possible connectives can be expressed through suitable combinations of the ones in the given set.

It turns out the set of five logical connectives introduced in this chapter is truth functionally complete. In fact, the subset containing only the three connectives AND, OR, and NOT is also truth functionally complete (we'll come back on this in Chapter 3 when we discuss the disjunctive normal form). This means that you don't need the other two connectives—implication and equivalence—because you can express them in terms of NOT, AND, and OR:

$(P \Rightarrow Q)$ can be expressed as $(\neg P) \lor Q$

$(P \Leftrightarrow Q)$ can be expressed as $(P \land Q) \lor (\neg P \land \neg Q)$

We'll investigate (and prove) *equivalences* like the preceding ones in the section "Logical Equivalences and Rewrite Rules." Although the set of connectives {AND, OR, NOT} is indeed both sufficient and convenient to express all possible compound predicates, you can achieve the same goal with even a *single* logical connective: the NAND operator (not and), also known as the Sheffer stroke, and commonly represented by a vertical bar, as defined in Table 1-9. As you can see, the NAND connective returns FALSE if and only if both operands are TRUE, and returns TRUE in all other cases.

Table 1-9. *Truth Table for the NAND Connective (|)*

P	Q	P	Q
T	T	F
T	F	T
F	T	T
F	F	T

Note that this is purely a theoretical exercise, exploring the extreme edges of our game; although you can indeed rewrite all possible logical expressions using this single NAND connective, your expressions will become longer and much more difficult to read.

Table 1-10 shows how you can express NOT using NAND by using the same propositional variable (P) for the left and right operands of the NAND connective.

Table 1-10. *Expressing NOT with the NAND Connective*

P	¬P	P|P	(¬P)⇔(P|P)
T	F	F	T
F	T	T	T

The last column of Table 1-10 shows that regardless of the truth value of P, ¬P is always logically equivalent with P|P. The proof that you can also express AND and OR in terms of NAND is left as an exercise at the end of this chapter.

The main reason why every textbook on the science of logic ends up with the five operators introduced earlier lies in the origin of this particular science: "concerning language and speech" or "human reasoning." If you study natural languages, you'll discover that the five operators introduced here are the ones we (human beings) use when reasoning.

Caution Don't even try to imagine what it would be like to communicate with an alien species whose language (the reasoning part of it) would be based on just the NAND operator. :-)

Special Predicate Categories

Two predicate categories deserve a special name: tautologies and contradictions.

Tautologies and Contradictions

A *tautology* is a propositional form that's TRUE for every possible combination of truth values of the propositional variables. A *contradiction* is a propositional form that's false regardless of the truth values the propositional variables happen to take. Examples of tautologies are as follows:

```
x = 42 ∨ x ≠ 42
10 = 10
P ∨ TRUE
P ⇒ ( P ∨ Q )
```

The first example illustrates what is known in logic as "*Tertium non datur,*" or the law of the excluded middle. The second example is rather obvious. The third one is TRUE regardless of the truth value of P. You can prove the last tautology using a truth table, as shown in Table 1-11.

Table 1-11. *Proving a Tautology Using a Truth Table*

P	Q	P∨Q	P⇒(P∨Q)
T	T	T	T
T	F	T	T
F	T	T	T
F	F	F	T

As you can see, the last column of Table 1-11 contains only TRUE; this means that the predicate $P \Rightarrow (P \vee Q)$ in the corresponding column header is always TRUE regardless of the individual truth values of the variables P and Q, and therefore a *tautology*. Table 1-10 (expressing the NOT connective with NAND) also shows an example of a tautology.

Along the same lines, a propositional form is a *contradiction* if it always evaluates to FALSE, regardless of the individual truth values of its components. The following expression is a contradiction:

$$(P \vee Q) \wedge ((\neg P) \wedge (\neg Q))$$

If you set up a truth table for this predicate, you'll end up with only FALSE in the corresponding column. Do you think it's obvious that the expression is a contradiction? Perhaps this example will give you some feel for the importance of being able to perform purely formal analysis on logic expressions, without regard for what the variables P and Q involved stand for.

Modus Ponens and Modus Tollens

The *Modus Ponens* (Latin: *mode that affirms*) and *Modus Tollens* (Latin: *mode that denies*) are probably the most famous examples of tautologies in logic. In regular text, they respectively read as follows:

- If P implies Q and P is TRUE, then Q must be TRUE.

- If P implies Q and Q is FALSE, then P must be FALSE.

You can also express these two tautologies using the logic operator symbols:

$$((P \Rightarrow Q) \wedge P)) \Rightarrow Q$$
$$((P \Rightarrow Q) \wedge (\neg Q)) \Rightarrow \neg P$$

The Modus Ponens represents the most direct form of everyday reasoning; therefore it is also referred to as *direct reasoning*. The Modus Tollens is also known as *indirect reasoning*, a form of reasoning that's much less familiar. Take a look at the following example.

Let P represent the predicate "Employee e is a manager" and let Q represent "Employee e earns a monthly salary of more than 10K." Further assume that the company you work at has the following business rule: "Managers always earn more then 10K," or, using symbols, $P \Rightarrow Q$. Indirect reasoning allows you to deduce that if you aren't earning more than 10K monthly then you are not a manager.

Logical Equivalences and Rewrite Rules

Table 1-8 showed the truth table of the logical equivalence connective. Logical equivalences deserve our special attention because they're extremely important, for many reasons. The most important application of logical equivalences is that you can use them to derive new equivalent predicates from existing ones; as such, they provide an alternative for using truth tables, as you'll see in this section. They're especially important for specifying data integrity constraints in different ways; you'll see a lot of this in Part 2 of this book.

Setting up truth tables for complicated predicates can become quite labor intensive. For example, if the predicate you want to examine contains four proposition variables (say P, Q, R, and S), you need to set up a truth table with sixteen rows, reflecting all possible truth value combinations. You might want to use a spreadsheet to fill such a truth table efficiently once you have entered the first row, but you'll see that using (a particular kind of) logical equivalence can be much more efficient.

Rewrite Rules

A *rewrite rule* is a rule that allows us to replace a given propositional form X by another propositional form Y, in such a way that X and Y are guaranteed to have the same truth value regardless of the value of the propositional variables. Such a replacement is permissible if and only if the equivalence X ⇔ Y is a tautology. This equivalence is referred to as the rewrite rule.

You already encountered an equivalence that is a tautology in the section "Functional Completeness." It showed how implication can be expressed using a combination of disjunction and negation:

$$(P \Rightarrow Q) \Leftrightarrow (\neg P) \vee Q$$

The truth table shown in Table 1-12 proves that this equivalence is indeed a tautology.

Table 1-12. *Proving That an Equivalence Is a Tautology*

P	Q	P ⇒ Q	¬P	¬P ∨ Q	(P ⇒ Q) ⇔ (¬P ∨ Q)
T	T	T	F	T	T
T	F	F	F	F	T
F	T	T	T	T	T
F	F	T	T	T	T

As you can see, the last column of Table 1-12 contains only TRUE. *This tautology is an important rewrite rule allowing you to convert an implication into a disjunction (and vice versa).* If you encounter a propositional form—or component within a propositional form—that is of the form P ⇒ Q, then you're allowed to replace that with ¬P ∨ Q.

Table 1-12 lists the most important and well-known rewrite rules, divided in named categories. Using these rewrite rules you can replace a component (one that matches either side of a rewrite rule) in a compound predicate with some other expression (the other side of the rule) without changing the meaning of the compound predicate.

Table 1-13. *Some Important Rewrite Rules*

Category	Rewrite Rule
Idempotence	(P ∧ P) ⇔ P (P ∨ P) ⇔ P
Double negation	P ⇔ ¬¬P
Commutativity	(P ∧ Q) ⇔ (Q ∧ P) (P ∨ Q) ⇔ (Q ∨ P) (P ⇔ Q) ⇔ (Q ⇔ P)
Associativity	((P ∧ Q) ∧ R) ⇔ (P ∧ (Q ∧ R)) ((P ∨ Q) ∨ R) ⇔ (P ∨ (Q ∨ R))

Continued

Table 1-13. *Continued*

Category	Rewrite Rule
Distribution	((P ∨ Q) ∧ R) ⇔ ((P ∧ R) ∨ (Q ∧ R)) ((P ∧ Q) ∨ R) ⇔ ((P ∨ R) ∧ (Q ∨ R))
De Morgan Laws	¬ (P ∨ Q) ⇔ (¬P ∧ ¬Q) ¬ (P ∧ Q) ⇔ (¬P ∨ ¬Q)
Special cases	(P ∧ TRUE) ⇔ P (P ∨ FALSE) ⇔ P (P ∨ TRUE) ⇔ TRUE (P ∧ FALSE) ⇔ FALSE (P ∧ ¬P) ⇔ FALSE (P ∨ ¬P) ⇔ TRUE
Implication rewrite	(P ⇒ Q) ⇔ (¬P ∨ Q)

The preceding 19 rewrite rules constitute key knowledge for a database professional. Most of these are intuitively obvious. The Distribution and De Morgan Laws might need a little more thought to see that they are in fact reasonably intuitive too. We'll spend some more time on these rewrite rules in the first section of Chapter 3.

Rewrite rules will help you in your task of formulating queries and data integrity constraints. They are crucial for database management systems too; they allow optimizers to rewrite predicates in such a way that alternative execution plans (with possibly better performance) become available while guaranteeing the same results under all circumstances.

Using Existing Rewrite Rules to Prove New Ones

Suppose you want to investigate the following logical equivalence, to see whether it is a rewrite rule:

$$(P \Rightarrow Q) \Leftrightarrow ((P \land \neg Q) \Rightarrow FALSE)$$

■**Note** This rule has the effect of moving propositional variable Q to the left side of the implication, negating it on the way; the right-hand side is reduced to a constant, FALSE. This technique is similar to the way you solve quadratic equations (ax2 + bx + c = 0) in arithmetic, and it turns out to be a useful technique when implementing nontrivial constraints too, as you will see in Chapter 11 of this book.

You could use a truth table, as shown before, but you can also use existing rewrite rules such as the ones listed in Table 1-13 to prove that this logical equivalence is in fact a tautology. Table 1-14 shows what such a proof might look like. Here we make use of the aforementioned rewrite rule that enables you to convert an implication into a disjunction and vice versa:

$$(P \Rightarrow Q) \Leftrightarrow (\neg P \lor Q)$$

Table 1-14. *Proving Rewrite Rules with Rewrite Rules*

Input Expression	Equivalent Expression	Comment
(P ⇒ Q)	⇔ ((P ⇒ Q) ∨ FALSE)	Trivial; second special case in Table 1-13
	⇔ ((¬P ∨ Q) ∨ FALSE)	Convert implication into disjunction
	⇔ ((¬P ∨ ¬¬Q) ∨ FALSE)	Double negation
	⇔ (¬ (P ∧ ¬Q) ∨ FALSE)	De Morgan
	⇔ ((P ∧ ¬Q) ⇒ FALSE)	Convert disjunction to implication

This completes the proof; we have derived a new rewrite rule from the ones we already knew, without using a truth table. If you look back at Table 1-7 with the definition of the implication connective, our new rewrite rule in the preceding text makes sense; it precisely corresponds with the only situation where the implication returns FALSE, also known as the *broken promise*.

Chapter Summary

Before continuing with the exercises in the next section, you might want to revisit certain sections of this chapter if you don't feel comfortable about one of the following concepts, introduced in this first chapter about logic:

- A *value* is an individual constant with a well-determined meaning.

- A *variable* is a holder for a (representation of a) value.

- A *proposition* is a declarative sentence that is unequivocally either TRUE or FALSE.

- A *predicate* is a truth-valued function with parameters.

- You can convert a predicate into a proposition by providing values for the parameters or by binding parameters with a quantifier.

- You can build compound predicates by applying *logical connectives* to existing ones; this chapter introduced *negation, conjunction, disjunction, implication*, and *equivalence*.

- Logical connectives can be regarded as *logical operators*; they take one or more (input) predicates as their operands, and return another predicate as their output.

- The input predicates of a compound predicate are also referred to as the *components* of the compound predicate.

- The precise meaning of all logical connectives can be defined using *truth tables*, and you can use truth tables to investigate the truth value of compound predicates.

- A *tautology* is a proposition that is always TRUE, and a *contradiction* is a proposition that is always FALSE.

- A *rewrite rule* is a tautology that has the form of an equivalence.

- You can use rewrite rules to derive new rewrite rules without using truth tables.

Exercises

1. Which of these predicates are propositions?

   a. The sun is made of orange juice

   b. $y + x > y$

   c. There exists a database management system that is truly relational

   d. If you are not female you must be male

   e. 5 is an even number

2. Express the logical connectives AND and OR in terms of the NAND connective, as defined in Table 1-9.

3. Show that the rewrite rules in Table 1-13 are correct, by setting up a truth table for each of them or by using the rewrite rules you checked earlier during this exercise.

4. Show that the following important rewrite rules concerning the implication are correct:

   a. $(P \Rightarrow Q) \Leftrightarrow (\neg Q \Rightarrow \neg P)$

   b. $(P \Leftrightarrow Q) \Leftrightarrow ((P \Rightarrow Q) \wedge (Q \Rightarrow P))$

   c. $\neg (P \Rightarrow Q) \Leftrightarrow (P \wedge \neg Q)$

   d. $\neg (P \wedge Q) \Leftrightarrow (P \Rightarrow \neg Q)$

   e. $((P \Rightarrow Q) \wedge (P \Rightarrow \neg Q)) \Leftrightarrow \neg P$ (the absurdity rule)

5. Look at the following predicates, and check whether they are tautologies:

   a. $P \Rightarrow (P \wedge Q)$

   b. $P \Rightarrow (P \vee Q)$

   c. $(P \wedge Q) \Rightarrow P$

   d. $(P \vee Q) \Rightarrow P$

   e. $(P \wedge (P \Rightarrow Q)) \Rightarrow Q$

   f. $(P \Rightarrow Q) \Rightarrow (P \wedge Q)$

   g. $(P \wedge Q) \Rightarrow (P \Rightarrow Q)$

   h. $((P \Rightarrow Q) \wedge (Q \Rightarrow R)) \Rightarrow (P \Rightarrow R)$

   i. $(P \Rightarrow R) \Rightarrow ((P \Rightarrow Q) \wedge (Q \Rightarrow R))$

   j. $(P \vee Q) \Leftrightarrow (\neg P \Rightarrow Q)$

   k. $(P \vee Q \vee R) \Leftrightarrow ((\neg P \wedge \neg Q) \Rightarrow R)$

   l. $(P \vee Q \vee R) \Leftrightarrow (\neg P \Rightarrow (Q \vee R))$

   m. $P \vee (Q \wedge R) \Leftrightarrow (\neg P \Rightarrow Q) \vee (\neg P \Rightarrow R)$

   n. $P \vee (Q \wedge R) \Leftrightarrow (\neg P \Rightarrow Q) \wedge (\neg P \Rightarrow R)$

CHAPTER 2

Set Theory: Introduction

This chapter is about set theory. Set theory provides an excellent language to reliably describe complex database designs, data retrieval, and data manipulation. Set theory is reliable because it is both precise and powerful; this will become clear from Chapter 5 onwards. As explained before, you'll need to exercise some patience: Chapters 1 through 4 first lay down the foundation.

In the section "Sets and Elements," the concepts of a *set* and an *element* of a set are introduced. In the section "Methods to Specify Sets," you'll see how you can specify sets using the *enumerative*, *predicative*, or *substitutive* method.

You probably remember your math teacher drawing pictures on the blackboard while explaining sets; the third section introduces these so-called *Venn diagrams*. Venn diagrams can be useful as graphical illustrations when you're working with multiple sets. However, note that Venn diagrams are "just" pictures, just like the well-known entity-relationship diagrams are pictures that you can draw for database designs. They are often imprecise, they always leave out important details, and they can even be "misleading by suggestion." Nevertheless, when used with caution, they can be quite helpful.

The section "Cardinality and Singleton Sets" discusses the *cardinality* of a set and introduces the concept of a *singleton* set.

Then we'll discuss *subsets* and their most important properties in the section "Subsets," followed by the well-known set operators *union*, *intersection*, and (*symmetric*) *difference* in the section "Union, Intersection, and Difference." In the same section we'll explore *disjoint* sets— that is, sets with an empty intersection.

The section "Powersets and Partitions" introduces two slightly more advanced set theory concepts: *powersets* and *partitions*. These two concepts are quite useful in database modeling, as you'll see in later chapters.

Ordered pairs $(x;y)$ have a first coordinate x and a second coordinate y. In the section "Ordered Pairs and Cartesian Product," we'll explore sets of ordered pairs and the *Cartesian product* of two sets. As you'll find out in Chapter 4, we'll use sets of ordered pairs to define (binary) relations and functions, which in turn will be used to define tables and databases— so we're getting closer and closer to the application of the mathematics.

The section "Sum Operator" introduces the sum operator.

Note You should be familiar with logic, as explained in the previous chapter. In the treatment of set theory, we'll frequently use logic connectives to define the various set-theory concepts.

You'll find a "Chapter Summary" at the end of the chapter, followed by an "Exercises" section. We strongly advise you to spend sufficient time on these exercises before moving on to other chapters.

Sets and Elements

Set theory is about sets, obviously. And there we are, faced with our first problem: what exactly *is* a set? A set is a collection of objects, and those objects are called the *elements* of the set. In mathematics, we like to be precise—so we want formal definitions of all terms we use. Just like in geometry, we all have a common understanding of what a *point* is, but providing a formal definition of a point turns out to be difficult. That's why we declare them as *primitive terms*; that is, they are just given, and you don't need to define them. Probably the best definition of a set is the one given by Definition 2-1.

■Definition 2-1: Set A set is fully characterized by its distinct elements, and nothing else but these elements.

As a rather obvious but important consequence, no two distinct sets contain the same elements; moreover:

- The elements of a set don't have any ordering

- Sets don't contain duplicate elements

Two sets, say A and B, are the same if each element of A is also an element of B and each element of B is also an element of A.

Note that elements of a set can be any type of object. They can even be sets on their own; you'll see numerous examples of sets containing sets as elements in the remainder of this book.

Set theory has a mathematical symbol $\in$ that is used to state that some object is an element of some set. The following expression states that object x is an element of set S:

x $\in$ S

The negation of this, saying that x is not an element of S, is expressed as follows:

x $\notin$ S

This latter expression is shorthand for the negation of the former expression:

x $\notin$ S $\Leftrightarrow$ ¬(x $\in$ S)

Table 2-1 lists these and some other commonly used set-theory symbols.

Table 2-1. *Set-Theory Symbols*

Symbol	Meaning
∈	Is an element of
∉	Is *not* an element of
Z	The set of all positive and negative integers, including value zero
N	The set of natural numbers; that is, integers greater than or equal to zero
∅	The empty set

N and **Z** are examples of sets from regular arithmetic; following are some other examples:

- The set, say P, of all prime numbers less than 20:

    P := {2,3,5,7,11,13,17,19}

- The set, say W, of the seven names of the days of the week:

    W := {'sunday','monday', 'tuesday','wednesday','thursday','friday','saturday'}

Here we use the enumerative method of specifying a set: listing all elements, separated by commas, between braces. This and some other methods of specifying a set are introduced in the next section.

The empty set symbol ∅ represents a set that has no elements. {} is also used for the representation of the empty set.

As soon as you have given your sets a name, as we did for the preceding two sets P and W, you can write expressions such as the following:

    -5 ∉ **N**
    -6 ∈ **Z**
    '4'∉ **N**
    'thursday' ∈ W
    x ∈ P

Note that the first four expressions are in fact propositions; all of them have truth value TRUE, by the way. The last one is a predicate (assuming x represents a numeric variable).

You can try to keep your expressions readable by adopting certain standards; for example, it's common practice to use *lowercase* naming for elements and *uppercase* naming for sets. However, note that this is a naming convention only; you cannot draw any conclusions from the fact that an identifier name is spelled in uppercase or lowercase. Consider the following expression:

    X ∈ Y

This expression is defined *only* if Y represents (or refers to) a set; otherwise, it is an undefined, meaningless, or ill-formed formula. That is, if Y doesn't refer to a set, you cannot say whether the statement is TRUE or FALSE. On the other hand, both X and Y could refer to sets, because sets may contain sets as elements. Check out the following three examples:

$3 \in 5$ is neither TRUE nor FALSE; it is a *meaningless* expression

$1 \in \{1,2\}$ is TRUE and $2 \in \{1,2\}$ is TRUE

$\{1,2\} \in \{1,2\}$ is FALSE

$\{1,2\} \in \{\{1,2\},3\}$ is TRUE

To clarify the last example being a TRUE proposition, let's give the set at the right-hand side a name:

```
S := {{1,2},3}
```

Then set S contains two elements: the first element is set $\{1,2\}$ and the other element is the numeric value 3. Therefore, the statement $\{1,2\} \in \{\{1,2\},3\}$ is a TRUE proposition.

Methods to Specify Sets

So far, you have already seen several examples of sets; with the exception of sets **Z** and **N**, they all used the *enumerative* method to specify their elements, listing all their elements as a comma-separated list enclosed in braces. The other methods we'll discuss in this section are based on a given set and use predicates to derive new sets.

Enumerative Method

Enumeration (literally, to name one by one) is by far the simplest set specification method; you list all elements of a set between braces (also known as accolades) separated by commas. See Listing 2-1 for some examples.

Listing 2-1. *Enumerative Set Specification Examples*

```
E1 := {1,3,5,7,9}
E2 := {'a',2,'c',4}
E3 := {8,6,{8,6}}
```

Note that in mathematics, elements of the same set don't need to be of the same type; for example, set E2 in Listing 2-1 contains a mixture of numbers and characters.

Note also that the order in which you specify the elements of a set is irrelevant; moreover, repeating the same element more than once is not forbidden but meaningless. Therefore, the following three sets are equal:

$$\{1,2\} = \{2,1\} = \{1,2,1\}$$

The disadvantage of the enumerative method to specify sets becomes obvious as soon as the number of elements of the set increases; it takes a lot of time to write them all down, and the expressions become too long.

Predicative Method

For a large set, an alternative way to specify the set is the *predicative* method. Let S be a given set (for instance the set of natural numbers), and let P(x) be a given predicate with exactly one parameter named x *of type* S (that is, the elements in S constitute the values that parameter x is allowed to take). Then, the following definition of a set, called E4, is a valid one:

```
E4 := { x∈S | P(x) }
```

This method also uses braces to enclose the set specification (just like the enumerative method) but now you specify a vertical bar symbol (|) somewhere between the braces. This vertical bar should be read as "... *such that...*" or "... *for which the following is true:...*"

At the right-hand side of the vertical bar you specify a *predicate*, and at the left-hand side you specify a *set* from which to choose values for the parameter involved in the predicate. The preceding syntax should be read as follows: "The set E4 consists of all elements x of S for which the predicate P(x) becomes TRUE."

See Listing 2-2 for some examples of using this method (assume EMP represents some set containing "employee records," loosely speaking). The first example uses the mod (modulo) function, which might be unfamiliar for you; it returns the remainder of division of the first argument by the second argument.

Listing 2-2. *Predicative Set Specification Examples*

```
E5 := { x∈Z | mod(x,2) = 0 ∧ x² ≤ 169}
E6 := { e∈EMP | e(JOB) = 'SALESREP'}
```

Set E5 has as its elements all even integers (zero remains after division by two) whose quadratic is less than or equal to 169. Set E6 has as its elements all employee records whose JOB value equals 'SALESREP'.

Substitutive Method

The third method to specify sets is the *substitutive* method. See Listing 2-3 for some examples of using this method.

Listing 2-3. *Substitutive Set Specification Examples*

```
E7 := { x² - 1 | x∈N }
E8 := { (e(HIRED)-e(BORN)) | e∈EMP }
```

The preceding specification for set E7 should be read as follows: "The set E7 consists of all $x^2 - 1$ values where x is an element of **N**." In general, the left-hand side of both set specifications (E7 and E8) now contains an *expression*; the right-hand side after the vertical bar tells you from which set you must choose the values for x to substitute in that expression.

Hybrid Method

Optionally, the right-hand side can be followed by a predicate that has x as a parameter. This enables you to specify set E4 also, as follows:

```
E4 := { x | x∈S ∧ P(x) }
```

The left-hand side now contains just x, instead of some expression using x. Often it is convenient to use a hybrid combination of the predicative and the substitutive method for a set specification. Take a look at the example in Listing 2-4.

Listing 2-4. *Hybrid Set Specification Example*

$$E9 := \{ x^2 - 1 \mid x \in \mathbf{N} \wedge mod(x,3) = 1 \}$$

Formally, this is a contraction of the following specification of set E9 consisting of two steps, using an intermediate set definition T1:

$$T1 := \{ x \in \mathbf{N} \mid mod(x,3) = 1 \}$$ (Using the predicative method first)

$$E9 := \{ x^2 - 1 \mid x \in T1 \}$$ (Followed by the substitutive method)

Of course, we don't formally split up set definitions like this. The predicative, substitutive, and hybrid methods all have in common that they allow you to use a *given set* and *predicates* in cases where using the enumerative method would become too labor intensive. For every set you want to specify, you just select the most appropriate specification method. In this book, the hybrid method will be the main method used to specify large sets.

Venn Diagrams

Venn diagrams (named after the Scottish professor John Venn) are *pictures* of sets. They can help you visualize the relationships between multiple sets. However, keep in mind that Venn diagrams are "just" pictures; they can also be confusing and even misleading. You probably remember Venn diagrams from the math lessons during your school days. See Figure 2-1 for Venn diagram examples showing the three sets E1, E2, and E3 from Listing 2-1.

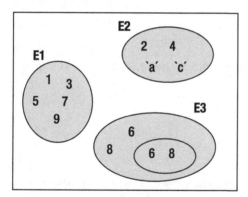

Figure 2-1. *Venn diagram examples*

The Venn diagram of set E3 is already confusing, because it contains the numbers 8 and 6 twice; moreover, it isn't immediately obvious that set E3 contains three elements. It isn't clear how you should represent an element that is a set itself in a Venn diagram. Evidently set E3 is not suited to be represented as a Venn diagram. And if you want to investigate the empty set, you face the tough problem of how to draw an empty set in a Venn diagram. As long as you keep their limitations in mind, Venn diagrams can be quite helpful. In the rest of this chapter, they'll be used to clarify various set-theory concepts.

Cardinality and Singleton Sets

Sets can be *finite* and *infinite*; however, when dealing with databases all your sets are finite by definition. For every finite set S, the *cardinality* is defined as the number of elements of S. A common notation for the cardinality of a set S is |S|, where you put the name (or specification) of the set between vertical bars. However, in this book we prefer to use the # symbol, as used in Definition 2-2, to denote the cardinality operator, because we use the vertical bar already quite heavily in predicative and substitutive set specifications.

Definition 2-2: Cardinality of a Set The cardinality of a (finite) set S is the number of elements in S, denoted by #S.

Note There is also a cardinality concept for infinite sets, but that won't be discussed in this book.

Listing 2-5 shows some examples of sets and their cardinality.

Listing 2-5. *Cardinality Examples*

```
#{1,2,3} = 3
#{{1,2,3}} = 1
#{1,3,2,3} = 3
#{{1,3},{2,3}} = 2
#∅ = 0
#{∅} = 1
```

Note the subtle difference between the first and second example. The third example shows that duplicates are not counted as separate elements; the last example shows that the set consisting of the empty set is not empty—it contains a single element, namely the empty set.

Singleton Sets

Listing 2-5 shows two examples of sets with cardinality one—the second and the last example. Sets with exactly one element are called a *singleton* (see Definition 2-3).

Definition 2-3: Singleton A singleton is a set with exactly *one* element.

Note that a singleton is still a set; therefore, {42} is *not* the same as 42. {42} is a set and 42—its only element—is an integer value. Be careful; it is a common mistake to mix up a singleton set with the element it contains.

The Choose Operator

We introduce a special operator that allows you to "extract" or "choose" the single element from a singleton set. In this book we use the symbol ⌐ for this operator; for example:

$$⌐\{5\} = 5$$
$$⌐\{\{5,6\}\} = \{5,6\}$$

For singleton sets, you could consider the choose operator as an "unbracer," enabling you to write expressions that would otherwise be somewhat more awkward. The ⌐ operator always expects a singleton set as its operand; therefore, the following expression is an ill-formed, meaningless formula:

$$⌐\{5,6\}$$

The operand here is not a singleton, but a set with a cardinality of 2.

Subsets

The concept of a *subset* is rather intuitive, so let's start with the definition right away, as shown in Definition 2-4, which also introduces the reverse concept: a *superset*.

Definition 2-4: Subset and Superset A is a subset of B (B is a superset of A) if every element of A is an element of B. The notation is $A \subseteq B$.

Note that this definition does not exclude the possibility that sets A and B are equal; the symbol we use for subsets ($\subseteq$) actually suggests this possibility explicitly. If you want to exclude the possibility of equality, you should use the special subset flavor with its corresponding symbol, as shown in Definition 2-5.

Definition 2-5: Proper Subset/Superset A is a proper subset of B, B is a proper superset of A (notation: $A \subset B$) $\Leftrightarrow$ A is a subset of B and $A \neq B$.

You can use the diagonal stroke as a negation; for example, $A \not\subset B$ means that A is *not* a proper subset of B. Apart from this $\not\subset$ symbol with a built-in negation, you can always use a separate negation symbol to write a logically equivalent statement, as follows:

$$A \not\subset B \Leftrightarrow \neg(A \subset B)$$

See Listing 2-6 for some examples of propositions about subsets; check out for yourself that they are all TRUE.

Listing 2-6. *Examples of Subset Propositions That Are True*

$\{1,2\} \subseteq \{1,2,3\}$
$\{1,2\} \subset \{1,2,3\}$
$\{1,2,3\} \not\subset \{1,2,3\}$
$\{1,2,3\} \subseteq \{1,2,3\}$
$\varnothing \subseteq \{1,2,3\}$

The last two examples of Listing 2-6 are interesting, because they illustrate the following two important properties of subsets:

- Every set is a subset of itself: $A \subseteq A$

- The empty set is a subset of every set: $\varnothing \subseteq A$

Two more subset properties worth mentioning here are the following ones:

- Transitivity: $((A \subseteq B) \wedge (B \subseteq C)) \Rightarrow (A \subseteq C)$

- Equality: $(A = B) \Leftrightarrow ((A \subseteq B) \wedge (B \subseteq A))$

Union, Intersection, and Difference

You can apply various operations on sets. The most well-known set operators are *union, intersection*, and *difference*. For the difference operator, we have two flavors: the regular difference and the symmetric difference. The formal definitions and the corresponding mathematical symbols for these four operators are shown in Table 2-2.

Table 2-2. *Common Set Operators*

Name	Symbol	Definition
Union	$\cup$	$A \cup B = \{ x \mid x \in A \vee x \in B \}$
Intersection	$\cap$	$A \cap B = \{ x \mid x \in A \wedge x \in B \}$
Difference	$-$	$A - B = \{ x \mid x \in A \wedge x \notin B \}$
Symmetric difference	$\div$	$A \div B = (A - B) \cup (B - A)$

Figure 2-2 shows corresponding Venn diagrams; the gray areas indicate the union, intersection, difference, and symmetric difference of the two sets A and B.

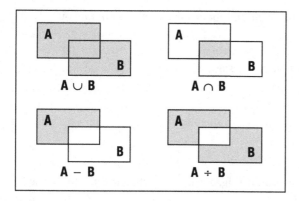

Figure 2-2. *Venn diagram of the union, intersection, and difference*

Let's look at an example. Suppose the following two sets A and B are given:

```
A := {1,3,5}
B := {3,4,5,6}
```

Then the union, intersection, difference, and symmetric difference of A and B are as follows:

```
A ∪ B = { x | x∈A ∨ x∈B } = {1,3,4,5,6} = areas I, II and III
A ∩ B = { x | x∈A ∧ x∈B } = {3,5} = area II
A − B = { x | x∈A ∧ x∉B } = {1} = area I
B − A = { x | x∈B ∧ x∉A } = {4,6} = area III
A ÷ B = ( A−B ) ∪ ( B−A ) = {1,4,6} = areas I and III
```

Figure 2-3 shows a Venn diagram visualizing the various areas (mentioned earlier) that correspond to the preceding expressions.

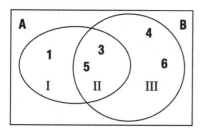

Figure 2-3. *Venn diagram of A (set {1,3,5}) and B (set {3,4,5,6})*

An important property of operators in general is the *closure property*. An operator is said to be closed over some given set, if every operation on elements of that given set always results in an(other) element of that same set.

The set operators introduced in this section always result in sets. Union, intersection, and (symmetric) difference are said to be *closed over sets*. The next section will discuss a few more properties of the set operators.

Properties of Set Operators

Just like we investigated various properties of the logical connectives in the previous chapter, we can do the same for set operators. Table 2-3 shows some conclusions you can draw about the properties of the four set operators.

Table 2-3. *Properties of Set Operators*

Property	Set Operators
Commutativity	$A \cup B = B \cup A$ $A \cap B = B \cap A$ $A \div B = B \div A$
Associativity	$(A \cup B) \cup C = A \cup (B \cup C)$ $(A \cap B) \cap C = A \cap (B \cap C)$
Distributivity	$A \cup (B \cap C) = (A \cup B) \cap (A \cup C)$ $A \cap (B \cup C) = (A \cap B) \cup (A \cap C)$

Note that the regular difference operator is *not* commutative.

If you draw a Venn diagram with three sets A, B, and C, you can illustrate the associative and distributive properties of the union and the intersection intuitively (see Table 2-3), as shown in Figure 2-4.

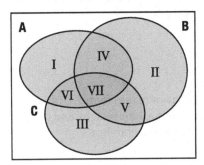

Figure 2-4. *Venn diagram to illustrate associativity and distributivity*

As you can see, with three sets (A, B, C) you already have seven different areas in your Venn diagram. Let's check the following distributive property: $A \cap (B \cup C) = (A \cap B) \cup (A \cap C)$.

```
A: I            + IV    + VI + VII    A∩B:        IV      + VII
B∪C: II + III + IV + V + VI + VII    A∩C:             VI + VII
--------------------------------    --------------------------
A∩(B∪C):        IV    + VI + VII    (A∩B)∪(A∩C): IV + VI + VII
```

Set Operators and Disjoint Sets

This section explores how the set operators introduced in the previous section behave under special circumstances; namely, if the intersection of the two operands is the empty set. First, we introduce a new term to indicate that situation. See Definition 2-6 for a definition of disjoint sets.

■**Definition 2-6: Disjoint Sets** Two given sets, say A and B, are disjoint $\Leftrightarrow$ A $\cap$ B = $\varnothing$.

Two sets are called disjoint if and only if they have no elements in common; that is, if and only if their intersection is the empty set. Listing 2-7 shows some properties of disjoint sets, apart from the fact that their intersection is the empty set by definition.

Listing 2-7. *Some Properties of Two Disjoint Sets A and B*

```
A - B = A
A ÷ B = A ∪ B
#A + #B = #(A ∪ B)
```

■**Note** If you want to draw a Venn diagram to visualize how set operators behave on disjoint sets, you must make sure that the two figures representing those disjoint sets do *not* overlap; that is, there should be no intersecting area II like the one containing elements 3 and 5 in Figure 2-3.

Set Operators and the Empty Set

As another special case, it's always a good idea to check the behavior of the *empty set*, because we want it to behave just like any other set. So let's see how the union, intersection, and difference set operators behave if the empty set is involved as one of their operands:

```
A ∪ Ø = { x | x∈A ∨ x∈Ø } = A
A ∩ Ø = { x | x∈A ∧ x∈Ø } = Ø
A - Ø = { x | x∈A ∧ x∉Ø } = A
Ø - A = { x | x∈Ø ∧ x∉A } = Ø
A ÷ Ø = ( A-Ø ) ∪ ( Ø-A ) = A ∪ Ø = A
```

In other words, a union with the empty set doesn't add anything. Every intersection with the empty set is empty because there are no common elements; the difference and the symmetric difference don't take any elements out, so they don't change anything either.

The following logical equivalence is also a tautology—that is, it is a rewrite rule:

$$(((A - B) = \varnothing) \wedge ((B - A) = \varnothing)) \Leftrightarrow (A = B)$$

You can prove this equivalence in two steps, with the following reasoning:

- If A - B is the empty set, then you can show that A is a subset of B;

- if B - A is also the empty set, then you can also show that B is a subset of A;

- but then A must be equal to B.

The proof of the other direction of the equivalence is trivial; if A and B are equal, then A − B and B − A are obviously the empty set.

Powersets and Partitions

Powersets and partitions are two more advanced set theory concepts. Let's start with the definition of the important concept of the powerset, as shown in Definition 2-7.

Definition 2-7: Powerset The powerset of a given set S (notation: $\wp$ S) is the set consisting of all possible subsets of S.

Now let's look at an example. Suppose the following two sets are given:

```
V := {1,2,3}
W := {1,{2,3},4}
```

Then the powerset of V looks like this:

```
℘V = { ∅
     , {1},{2},{3}
     , {1,2},{1,3},{2,3}
     , {1,2,3}
     }
```

And the powerset of W looks like this:

```
℘W = { ∅
     , {1},{{2,3}},{4}
     , {1,{2,3}},{1,4},{{2,3},4}
     , {1,{2,3},4}
     }
```

Note that the set V itself is an element of the powerset of V, and the empty set too—which we already mentioned as being two important properties of subsets. Check for yourself that the following propositions are all TRUE, based on the same two sets V and W:

```
{2,3} ∈ ℘V
{2,3} ∈ W
{1,{2,3}} ∈ ℘W
℘∅ = {∅}
```

Note The empty set is an element of every powerset; this means that the powerset of even the empty set is *not* empty, as illustrated by the last proposition in the preceding example.

Listing 2-8 shows two properties related to powersets.

Listing 2-8. *Powerset Properties*

```
( A ∈ ℘B ) ⇔ ( A ⊆ B )
( #A = n ) ⇔ ( #℘A = 2ⁿ )
```

The first logical equivalence follows immediately from the definition of the powerset; the second one becomes clear if you consider that for every possible subset, each element of A can be *selected* as an element or can be *left out*—that is, for every element of A you have two choices. Therefore, if set A contains n elements, the total number of possible subsets becomes 2^n (2 power n), the two extreme subsets being the empty set (n times "left out") and the set itself (n times "selected"). See also the earlier example of set V, containing three elements ($\{1,2,3\}$), and its powerset $℘V$, containing eight elements.

The concept of a powerset is one of two key stepping stones that will be used in Part 2 of this book, when we'll introduce the concept of a *database universe* as a formal definition for a database design. The second key concept, which will be introduced in Chapter 4, is the concept of a *generalized product* of a set function.

Union of a Set of Sets

Before we discuss the concept of partitions in the next section, we first introduce a slightly more convenient flavor of the union operator. Although the union operator is *dyadic* (that is, it accepts two operands), it often occurs that you want to "union" several sets, not just two; for example:

A1 ∪ A2 ∪ A3 ∪ ... ∪ An

To save a lot of typing (repeating the union symbol each time), we introduce a special *monadic* notation (accepting only one operand) for the union operator, as shown in Definition 2-8.

■Definition 2-8: Monadic Union Operator If A is a set consisting of sets, then

∪A := { x | x is an element of some element of A }.

You see what this definition does? The result of the union ∪A contains all elements x that occur in some set, say Ai, which is an element of A. Remember, for this definition to be valid, every element of set A must be a set.

If you look at the following examples, you'll see that this "union of a set of sets" is indeed a more powerful and generic union operator than the dyadic one we used so far, because now you can produce the union of any number of sets with a convenient shorthand notation. In these examples, S and T represent a set:

```
∪{S} = S
∪{S,T} = S∪T
∪∅ = ∅
∪℘S = S
```

If you don't understand these equalities at first sight, you might want to check them against the formal Definition 2-8. Take a look at the following rather simple example; you can see that this operator acts as a "brace remover:"

Suppose: S := {{1,2,3},{2,3,4},{4,5,6}} (a set consisting of sets)

Then: ∪S = {1,2,3,4,5,6}

Partitions

Now that we've introduced the union of a set of sets, we can define *partitions* as shown in Definition 2-9.

Definition 2-9: Partition If S is a non-empty set, then P is a partition of S if P is a set consisting of mutually disjoint non-empty subsets of S for which the union equals S.

Or, described in a more formal way, you could use the following equation:

```
(P is a partition of S ) ⇔ ( P ⊆ ℘S-{∅} ) ∧
                           ( let A,B∈P then (A≠B ⇒ (A∩B)=∅) ) ∧
                           ( ∪P = S )
```

This definition states the following:

- P is a proper subset of the powerset ℘S (because *the empty set is excluded*).

- Any two elements of the partition must be *disjoint*.

- The *union* of partition P must result in the original set S.

If you want to think in terms of Venn diagrams, a partition is simply a matter of segmenting the original set in a number of non-empty non-overlapping pieces, as illustrated in Figure 2-5. Suppose S := {1,2,3,4,5,6,7,8,9} and P := {{1},{2,4},{3,6,7},{5},{8,9}}. Then every element of S occurs in precisely one element of partition P.

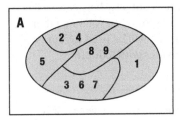

Figure 2-5. *Venn diagram of partition P*

Let's look at another rather simple numeric example:

Suppose: T := {1,2,3}

Then the sets P1 through P5 are all the possible partitions of T:

P1 := {{1},{2},{3}}
P2 := {{1,2},{3}}
P3 := {{1,3},{2}}
P4 := {{2,3},{1}}
P5 := {{1,2,3}}

Note that the last example shows that in general {S} is always a partition of S. Always? Even if S is the empty set? Check this statement carefully against the definition of a partition; this check is left as an exercise at the end of this chapter.

Ordered Pairs and Cartesian Product

If a set contains two elements, the order of those two elements is irrelevant. For example, the set {1,2} is identical to the set {2,1}. On the other hand, in geometry we normally represent points with x and y coordinates, where the order of the coordinates is important. If you swap the x and y coordinates of a given point, assuming they are not the same value, you end up with a different point.

Ordered Pairs

This section introduces the concept of ordered pairs, allowing you to make the distinction in the order of two values that are paired together. We use a special notation for this, as shown in Definition 2-10.

■**Definition 2-10: Ordered Pair** An ordered pair is a pair of elements, say a and b, for which the order is important. The notation is (a;b).

The concept of an ordered pair is important in this book. That's not only because we'll use ordered pairs to introduce the Cartesian product operator; but moreover, we will need them to introduce binary relations and functions in Chapter 4, which in turn will be used to represent *tuples* (we note now that this word is pronounced such that it rhymes with "couples").

■**Note** Generally a comma is used as the serialization operator for the elements of an ordered pair. An ordered pair would be depicted as (a,b). However, because the comma is already heavily used to separate the elements of an enumeratively specified set, this book uses the semicolon to separate the elements of an ordered pair. It makes various expressions easier to read.

The two elements of an ordered pair are also referred to as the first and second *coordinates* of the ordered pair. Because the order of the coordinates of an ordered pair is important, the following two properties hold:

$$(a \neq b) \Leftrightarrow (\ (a;b) \neq (b;a)\ )$$
$$(\ (a;b) = (c;d)\ ) \Leftrightarrow (\ (a = c) \wedge (b = d)\ )$$

The second property in the preceding equation is also known as the "equality axiom." Using De Morgan's rewrite rules you can also specify this axiom as follows:

$$(\ (a;b) \neq (c;d)\ ) \Leftrightarrow (\ (a \neq c) \vee (b \neq d)\ )$$

Note Just like elements in a set, the two values that are paired together in an ordered pair can be of arbitrary complexity. For example, $(A; \{1,2,3\})$ is a valid ordered pair. This pair has A as its first coordinate and the set $\{1,2,3\}$ as its second coordinate.

We introduce operators π_1 and π_2 to retrieve the first and second coordinates from an ordered pair. For a given ordered pair—say $(a;b)$—the first coordinate can be retrieved using the expression $\pi_1(a;b)$, which results in a, and the second coordinate via expression $\pi_2(a;b)$, which equals b.

Cartesian Product

The Cartesian product of two given sets can now be defined using ordered pairs, as shown by Definition 2-11.

Definition 2-11: Cartesian Product The Cartesian product of two given sets A and B, notation A×B, equals $\{\ (a;b)\ |\ a \in A \wedge b \in B\ \}$.

That is, the Cartesian product A×B is the set of all ordered pairs you can construct by choosing a first coordinate from set A and a second coordinate from set B. Let's look at an example. Suppose the following sets are given:

```
A := {1,2,3}
B := {3,4}
```

Then

```
A×B = { (1;3), (1;4)
      , (2;3), (2;4)
      , (3;3), (3;4) }
```

And

$$B{\times}A = \{ \ (3;1), \ (3;2), \ (3;3)$$
$$, \ (4;1), \ (4;2), \ (4;3) \ \}$$

This example clearly shows that A×B is in general *not* the same as B×A. In other words, the Cartesian product operator is not commutative. You can even prove that in case A×B and B×A are the same, A and B must be equal (and vice versa):

$$(\ A{\times}B = B{\times}A \ ) \Leftrightarrow (\ A = B \ )$$

Note also that the two example sets A and B contain *numbers* as their elements, while the results of both Cartesian products contain *ordered pairs*. In this regard, the Cartesian product clearly differs from the operators we discussed before. The union, intersection, and difference operators all repeat (or leave out) elements of their operands; they don't create new types of elements.

Because the Cartesian product produces every possible combination of two coordinates from the two finite input sets, the following property is also rather intuitive (also see the preceding example):

$$\#A{\times}B = \#A * \#B$$

The cardinality of a Cartesian product is equal to the product of the cardinalities of the two operands. Last but not least, let's not forget to check the empty set:

$$A{\times}\varnothing = \varnothing{\times}A = \varnothing$$

Sum Operator

We conclude this introductory chapter on set theory by establishing the sum operator (see Definition 2-12). With the sum operator, you can evaluate a numeric expression for every element in a given set and compute the sum of all these evaluations.

■**Definition 2-12: Sum Operator (SUM)** The sum of a numeric expression $f(x)$, where x is chosen from a given set S, is denoted as follows:

$$(\ SUM \ x \in S: \ \ f(x) \ )$$

For every element x that can be chosen from set S, the sum operator evaluates expression $f(x)$ and computes the sum of all such evaluations. In case S represents the empty set, then (by definition) the sum operator returns the numeric value 0.

Here are a few examples:

$$(\ SUM \ x \in \{ \ -1, \ 2, \ 5 \ \}: x \ )$$
$$(\ SUM \ x \in \{ \ -1, \ 2, \ 5 \ \}: 1 \ )$$
$$(\ SUM \ n \in \{ \ x | \ x \in \mathbf{N} \wedge x \leq 4 \ \}: 2{*}n \ )$$
$$(\ SUM \ p \in \{ \ (A;1), \ (B;1), \ (C;5) \ \}: \pi_2(p) \ )$$

The first example sums values -1, 2, and 5. This results in 6. The second example is a somewhat elaborate way to compute the cardinality of the set { -1, 2, 5 }; it sums value 1 for every element in this set and results in 3. The third example computes the sum 2*0 + 2*1 + 2*2 + 2*3 + 2*4 and results in 20. The fourth example computes 1 + 1 + 5, resulting in 7.

Some Convenient Shorthand Set Notations

We use some (finite) sets frequently in the database world: dates, numbers, and strings. There-fore, we introduce the set specification shorthand listed in Table 2-4.

Table 2-4. *Some Convenient Set Specification Shorthand*

Shorthand	Definition
date	{ d | d is a date between January 1, 4712 BC and December 31, 4712 AD }
number(p,s)	{ n | n is a valid number with precision p and scale s }
varchar(n)	{ s | s is a string with at least 1 and at most n characters }
[n..m]	{ x∈$\mathbf{Z}$ | x ≥ n ∧ x ≤ m }

As you can see, this shorthand shows a rather obvious resemblance with the common data types that are supported by SQL database management systems. For the date shorthand, the boundaries defined are those that are implemented by at least one common DBMS ven-dor. The last shorthand in Table 2-4 allows you to specify closed intervals of integers.

Chapter Summary

This section provides a summary of this chapter, formatted as a bulleted list. You can use it to check your understanding of the various concepts introduced in this chapter before continu-ing with the exercises in the next section.

- Sets are fully characterized by their elements and nothing but their elements.

- You can specify sets by *enumeration*, by using the *predicative* method, by using the *substitutive* method, or a mixture of the predicative and substitutive methods.

- *Venn diagrams* are pictures of sets, and as such can provide a visual aid when working with sets; however, keep their limitations in mind.

- The number of elements of a finite set is known as its *cardinality*. We use the symbol # to represent the cardinality operator.

- A set with precisely one element is known as a *singleton*; for singletons we can use the "choose" operator (⨆) to unpack the singleton element.

- A is a *subset* of B if every element of A is also an element of B; the notation is A⊆B. If A is also not equal to B, it is called a proper subset of B (the notation is A⊂B).

- Every set is a subset of itself, and the empty set is a subset of every set.

- The most common set operators are *union, intersection,* and (*symmetric*) *difference.*

- Two sets are called *disjoint* if their intersection is the empty set.

- The *powerset* $\wp V$ of a set V is the set consisting of all possible subsets of V. If V contains n elements, then the powerset $\wp V$ contains 2^n elements (including the empty set and V itself).

- The *union of a set of sets* is a generalization of the dyadic union operator, allowing you to produce the union of an arbitrary number of sets.

- A *partition* of a non-empty set S is a set of mutually disjoint, non-empty subsets of S for which the union equals S.

- An *ordered pair* (a;b) consists of two coordinates, a and b, for which the order is important; in other words, ((a;b) = (c;d)) ⇔ (a = c ∧ b = d).

- The π_1 and π_2 operators enable you to retrieve the first and second coordinates from an ordered pair.

- The *Cartesian product* of two sets is the set consisting of all possible ordered pairs you can construct by choosing a first coordinate from the first set and a second coordinate from the second set.

- The *sum* operator enables you to compute the sum of a given expression across a given set.

Exercises

1. Suppose the following set is given: A := {1,2,3,4,5}

   Which of the following expressions are TRUE?

   a. 3 ∈ A

   b. 3 ⊂ A

   c. ∅ ⊆ A

   d. ∅ ∈ A

   e. {2} ⊂ A

   f. {3,4} ∈ A

   g. {3,4} ⊂ A

   h. {{3,4}} ⊄ A

   i. #{{3,4}} = 2

j. $\varnothing \in \{\varnothing\}$

k. $\varnothing \subset \varnothing$

l. $\varnothing \in \{0\}$

m. $\{1,2,3,\varnothing\} = \{1,2,3\}$

2. Give an enumerative specification of the following sets:

   a. $\{ 2x - 1 \mid x \in \mathbf{N} \wedge 1 < x < 6 \} = \dots$

   b. $\{ y \mid y \in \mathbf{N} \wedge y = y+1 \} = \dots$

   c. $\{ z \mid z \in \mathbf{N} \wedge z = 2*z \} = \dots$

3. Give a formal (predicative) specification for the following sets:

   a. The set of all quadratics of the natural numbers

   b. The set of all even natural numbers

   c. The set of all ordered pairs with natural number coordinates such that the sum of both coordinates does not exceed 10

4. Draw a Venn diagram of the following three sets:

   A := $\{1,2,4,7,8\}$
   B := $\{3,4,5,7,9\}$
   C := $\{2,4,5,6,7\}$

   Enumerate the elements of the following set expressions:

   a. $B \cup \varnothing$

   b. $B \cup \{\varnothing\}$

   c. $A - (B - C)$

   d. $(A - B) - C$

   e. $B \div C$

   f. $A - B \cap C$

5. Which of the following seven sets are equal?

   A := $\varnothing$
   B := $\{0\}$
   C := $\{\varnothing\}$
   D := $\{\{\varnothing\}\}$
   E := $\{ x \in \mathbf{N} \mid x = x+1 \}$
   F := $\{ x \in \mathbf{N} \mid x = 2x \}$
   G := $\{ x \in \mathbf{N} \mid x = x^2 \}$

6. Suppose the following set is given:

S := {1,2,3,{1,2},{1,3}}

Which of the following expressions are TRUE?

   a. {1,2} ⊂ S

   b. {1,2} ∈ S

   c. {1,2} ∈ ℘S

   d. {2,3} ⊂ S

   e. {2,3} ∈ S

   f. {2,3} ∈ ℘S

   g. {1} ∉ ℘S

   h. {∅,S} ⊆ ℘S

   i. {∅} ∈ ℘℘S

   j. #℘℘S = 25

   k. ∪S = {1,2,3}

   l. {{1,2,3},{{1,2}},{{1,3}}} is a partition of S

Evaluate the following set expressions:

   m. #S = ...

   n. { x∈ ℘S | #x = 2 } = ...

   o. S − ∅ = ...

   p. ∅ − S = ...

   q. S ∩ ∅ = ...

7. Continuing with the example set S of the previous exercise, which connection symbols can you substitute for the ellipsis character (...) in the first column of the following table, in such a way that it becomes a TRUE proposition?

Expression	=	≠	⊂	⊄	∈	∉
∅ ... ∅						
∅ ... {∅}						
{∅} ... {∅}						
{∅} ... {{∅}}						
1 ... S						
{1} ... S						
{1,2} ... S						

Expression	=	≠	⊂	⊄	∈	∉
{1,2,3} ... S						
{1,2,{1,2}} ... S						
{1,{1}} ... S						
∅ ... S						
{∅} ... S						
#S ... S						

8. Suppose you have three sets A, B, and C, satisfying the following conditions:

   #(A∩B) = 11
   #(A∩C) = 12
   #(A∩B∩C) = 5

   What is the minimum cardinality of set A?

9. The following two sets are given:

   S := {1,2,3,4,5}
   T := {6,7,{6,7}}

   Evaluate the following expressions:

   a. ∪{S,T} = ...

   b. ℘S − S = ...

   c. ℘T − T = ...

   d. T − ℘T = ...

   e. #∪℘S = ...

CHAPTER 3

Some More Logic

As announced in Chapter 1's introduction, this third chapter about logic continues where the first one stopped.

In the section "Algebraic Properties," we'll revisit rewrite rules to focus on certain algebraic properties of our logical connectives: identity, commutativity, associativity, distributivity, reflexivity, transitivity, idempotence, double negation, and absorption.

In the section "Quantifiers," we'll explore quantification. Quantification over a set is a powerful concept to bind parameters, and as such it's important in data management. The two most important quantifiers are the *universal* quantifier (represented by the symbol ∀ and read "for all") and the *existential* quantifier (represented by the symbol ∃ and read "there exists"). Once these two quantifiers are introduced, we'll identify some important rewrite rules concerning quantifiers. We'll also investigate quantification over the empty set, which is often misunderstood and therefore a source of confusion.

The section "Normal Forms" discusses normal forms in logic—not to be confused with normal forms of data (defined for database design purposes). Normal forms can help you to structure your predicates. We'll explore the following two normal forms for predicates:

- *Conjunctive* normal form is a predicate rewritten in the format of an iterated AND.

- *Disjunctive* normal form is a predicate rewritten in the format of an iterated OR.

After the "Chapter Summary," there's another section with exercises, focusing on quantifiers and normal forms. We again strongly advise you to spend sufficient time on these exercises before moving on to other chapters.

This chapter ends the formal treatment of logic; Chapter 4 will continue with more set theory.

Algebraic Properties

From regular mathematics, we know that arithmetic operations such as sum and product have certain properties, such as those shown in Listing 3-1.

Listing 3-1. *Examples of Properties for Sum and Product*

```
-(-x) = x
x+y = y+x
(x+y)+z = x+(y+z)
x*(y+z) = (x*y)+(x*z)
```

Such arithmetic properties are referred to as *algebraic* properties. Logical connectives also have similar algebraic properties. Table 1-13 in Chapter 1 showed 19 rewrite rule examples, subdivided in certain categories. The names of those categories refer to algebraic properties; they are important enough to justify giving them more attention, so the following sections discuss them in more detail, while adding more properties.

Identity

Just as the numeric value 1 is the identity under regular multiplication (a multiplication of any given number by 1 will result in that given number), and 0 is the identity under regular addition (0 added to any number results in that number), you also have similar identities in logic, which are shown in Listing 3-2.

Listing 3-2. *Identities*

```
P ∧ TRUE ⇔ P
P ∨ FALSE ⇔ P
P ∧ FALSE ⇔ FALSE
P ∨ TRUE ⇔ TRUE
```

The first expression states that TRUE is the identity with respect to AND. The second states that FALSE is the identity with respect to OR. The last two expressions are also known as the two *boundedness* identities; they state that anything ANDed with FALSE is FALSE and anything ORed with TRUE is TRUE.

Commutativity

An operator (or a connective) is *commutative* if and only if it is dyadic and its left and right operands can be interchanged without affecting the result. Listing 3-3 shows the commutative properties of some logic operators.

Listing 3-3. *Commutative Properties*

```
( P ∧ Q ) ⇔ ( Q ∧ P )
( P ∨ Q ) ⇔ ( Q ∨ P )
( P ⇔ Q ) ⇔ ( Q ⇔ P )
```

Conjunction, disjunction, and equivalence are commutative connectives.

Associativity

If you want to repeat the same dyadic operator on a series of operands and it doesn't matter in which order you process the occurrences of the operator, the operator is *associative*. Note the parentheses in the propositional forms shown in Listing 3-4.

Listing 3-4. *Associative Properties*

```
( ( P ∧ Q ) ∧ R ) ⇔ ( P ∧ ( Q ∧ R ) )
( ( P ∨ Q ) ∨ R ) ⇔ ( P ∨ ( Q ∨ R ) )
```

Conjunction and disjunction are associative. Associativity is the reason why you often see that parentheses are left out in expressions with iterated conjunctions or disjunctions that involve more than two operands.

Distributivity

Just like commutativity and associativity, you probably remember *distributivity* from regular arithmetic, typically expressed as a formula like the following, which was shown at the beginning of this section:

    a*(b+c) = (a*b) + (a*c)

This algebraic property shows a certain relationship between addition and multiplication; in regular arithmetic, multiplication distributes over addition. In logic, something similar holds for the relationship between conjunction and disjunction, as shown in Listing 3-5.

Listing 3-5. *Distributive Properties*

```
( P ∨ ( Q ∧ R ) ) ⇔ ( ( P ∨ Q ) ∧ ( P ∨ R ) )
( P ∧ ( Q ∨ R ) ) ⇔ ( ( P ∧ Q ) ∨ ( P ∧ R ) )
```

As these tautologies demonstrate, conjunction is distributive over disjunction and vice versa. Note that in regular arithmetic, addition does *not* distribute over multiplication.

Reflexivity

The regular equality is an example of a *reflexive* operator; x = x is TRUE for any x (regardless of the type of x). In logic, the implication and equivalence connectives are reflexive, because the predicates shown in Listing 3-6 are always TRUE.

Listing 3-6. *Reflexive Properties*

```
P ⇔ P
P ⇒ P
```

Transitivity

The regular equality is *transitive*, as expressed by the following formula:

    ((x = y) ∧ (y = z)) ⇒ (x = z)

Conjunction, implication, and equivalence are transitive in logic, as shown in Listing 3-7.

Listing 3-7. *Transitive Properties*

```
( ( P ∧ Q ) ∧ ( Q ∧ R ) ) ⇒ ( P ∧ R )
( ( P ⇒ Q ) ∧ ( Q ⇒ R ) ) ⇒ ( P ⇒ R )
( ( P ⇔ Q ) ∧ ( Q ⇔ R ) ) ⇒ ( P ⇔ R )
```

Note that the disjunction is not transitive: (P ∨ Q) ∧ (Q ∨ R) does *not* imply P ∨ R.

De Morgan Laws

The laws of De Morgan (1806–1871) are quite useful for manipulating expressions involving negation, and are shown in Listing 3-8.

Listing 3-8. *De Morgan Laws*

$$\neg(\ P \lor Q\ ) \Leftrightarrow (\ \neg P \land \neg Q\ )$$
$$\neg(\ P \land Q\ ) \Leftrightarrow (\ \neg P \lor \neg Q\ )$$

Using plain English, these laws describe that "the negation of a disjunction equals the conjunction of the negations (of the operands)" and vice versa "the negation of a conjunction equals the disjunction of the negations."

Idempotence

Some (dyadic) operators have the property that if their operands are equal, then their result is equal to this operand. The operands are said to be *idempotent* under the operator. In logic, propositions are idempotent under disjunction and conjunction, as shown in Listing 3-9.

Listing 3-9. *Idempotence Properties*

$$(\ P \land P\ ) \Leftrightarrow P$$
$$(\ P \lor P\ ) \Leftrightarrow P$$

Double Negation (or Involution)

If you apply the negation twice, you should get back the original operand. In other words, the negation operates as the complement, as shown in Listing 3-10.

Listing 3-10. *Double Negation*

$$\neg\neg P \Leftrightarrow P$$

Absorption

The absorption properties are not so well known and might be a little difficult to understand at first glance. They are listed in Listing 3-11.

Listing 3-11. *Absorption Properties ("P Absorbs Q")*

$$(\ P \lor (\ P \land Q\ )\ ) \Leftrightarrow P$$
$$(\ P \land (\ P \lor Q\ )\ ) \Leftrightarrow P$$

The first absorption rule states that in a disjunction of two predicates (say R1 $\lor$ R2) where one of the disjuncts (say the right one R2) is *stronger* than the other disjunct (R1), then R2 may be left out without affecting the truth value of the predicate.

■**Note** Recall from the section "Predicate Strength" in Chapter 1 that a predicate R2 is stronger than a predicate R1 if and only if R2 ⇒ R1. In the first absorption rule, the right disjunct P ∧ Q is always stronger than P (left disjunct), because the predicate (P ∧ Q) ⇒ P is a tautology.

Similarly, the second absorption rule states that in a conjunction of two predicates, say R1 ∧ R2, where one of the conjuncts (say the right one R2) is *weaker* than the other conjunct (R1), then R2 may be left out without affecting the truth value of the predicate.

The proof of the two absorption equivalences is left as an exercise at the end of this chapter.

Quantifiers

Chapter 1 clarified the difference between propositions and predicates. It talked about how you can turn a predicate into a proposition. There are two ways to achieve that goal:

- By providing values for the parameters in the predicate

- By binding the parameters in the predicate through quantification

The first method is straightforward and is explained in Chapter 1; this section explains the second method.

To use quantification for this goal, you must first define which set of possible values a parameter of the predicate, say x, is allowed to choose its values from. Through quantification over this set of possible values, you can then say something about *how many* of those possible values have a certain property (this is, where the predicate is turned into a proposition). For example, you could say that there are precisely 42 values for x with a certain property. However, the two most common quantifying statements are as follows:

- There exists a value for x for which it is TRUE that, [declarative sentence with x].

- For all values for x it is TRUE that, [declarative sentence with x].

The first statement says something about the existence of at least one value; therefore it's referred to as *existential* quantification. The second statement is known as *universal* quantification because you say something about all elements of a given set. You can represent the existential and universal quantifiers with two symbols, as you can see in Table 3-1.

Table 3-1. *The Existential and Universal Quantifiers*

Symbol	Description
∃	Existential quantifier (There exists . . .)
∀	Universal quantifier (For all . . .)

Let P(x) and Q(y) be given predicates with parameters x and y, respectively. Let set A be a given set representing the possible values for parameter x, and set B the same for y. The general syntax for expressions using quantification is shown in Listing 3-12.

Listing 3-12. *General Quantifier Syntax*

```
∃x∈A: P(x)
∀y∈B: Q(y)
```

The meaning of these two expressions is defined as follows:

- There exists a value in set A that will transform predicate P(x) into a TRUE proposition when that value is provided as the value for parameter x of predicate P(x).

- For all values in set B, predicate Q(y) will transform into a TRUE proposition when such value is provided as the value for parameter y of predicate Q(y).

Note Whether these two quantified expressions are TRUE obviously depends on the sets involved (A and B) and the given predicates, P(x) and Q(y).

GENERAL QUANTIFIER SYNTAX

The general existential and universal quantifier syntax introduced in Listing 3-12 is actually shorthand syntax. That syntax relies on set theory (it uses the 'is element of' operator). Pure logicians don't need set theory to express quantifications. In fact, set theory is an offshoot of logic. From a logician's viewpoint, a set represents the extension of some predicate. For example, the set A might represent the extension of the predicate A(x) that has the form "x is a <whatever A means>". How does set A represent predicate A(x)? By being the set that holds every object that, when substituted for x in A(x), yields a TRUE proposition. The example that's given in the text regarding lying mathematicians would be expressed as ∀x: "x is a mathematician" ⇒ "x is a liar". General syntax equivalent to the shorthand syntax introduced in Listing 3-12, and *not* depending on set theory, would now be ∃x: "x is a <whatever A means>" ⇒ P(x) and ∀y: "y is a <whatever B means>" ⇒ Q(y), respectively. Because most practical cases of quantified predicates are precisely of the form "if x is a . . . then P(x)", it's customary to use the shorthand notation that relies on set theory.

We can now revisit an example proposition that was given in the section "Propositions and Predicates" in Chapter 1: all mathematicians are liars. This proposition is actually a universal quantification. Following is a formal way of specifying this predicate:

```
∀x∈M: "x is a liar"
```

Here M represents the set of all persons who are mathematicians. This set is used to quantify over the predicate "x is a liar"—a predicate that contains one parameter named x. This quantification binds parameter x (it supplies values for this parameter). The resulting quantification is now a proposition; it effectively doesn't have a parameter anymore.

Look at the following three examples (using the set of natural numbers that was introduced in Chapter 2):

∃x∈ **N**: x < 42
∀y∈ **N**: y/2 ∈ **N**
∀z∈ **N**: z ≥ 0

The first and third predicate (more precisely, propositions, because they effectively don't have a parameter) are TRUE, the second one is FALSE. To show that the first one—an existential quantification—is TRUE, it's sufficient to give a single example. In this case, we must supply a single natural number for x that is smaller than 42; for example, 41 is a natural number less than 42. To show a universal quantification is FALSE (the second one), it's sufficient to give a single counter example; for example, 3 (an odd number) divided by 2 results in 1.5 (one and a half), which is not a natural number. For the third statement, you'll have to check all natural numbers and come up with a single natural number not greater than or equal to zero, to show that the proposition is FALSE. Of course, you'll never find such a number. The smallest natural number is 0 (zero)—which is greater than or equal to 0—therefore, the predicate is TRUE for all natural numbers.

When a parameter of a predicate gets bound by a quantifier, the *name* of the parameter becomes free to choose. Let's clarify this with an example. Consider the predicate "x lives in Utrecht". This predicate has one parameter that happens to have been named x. Let's now define a new proposition by universally quantifying this predicate across set {Toon, Lex, Chris, Cary, Hugh} as follows:

∀x∈ {Toon, Lex, Chris, Cary, Hugh}: "x lives in Utrecht"

It's probably not too difficult to see that this proposition is equivalent to the following compound proposition (a conjunction with five conjuncts):

"Toon lives in Utrecht"
∧ "Lex lives in Utrecht"
∧ "Chris lives in Utrecht"
∧ "Cary lives in Utrecht"
∧ "Hugh lives in Utrecht"

You should realize that the original name of the parameter (x) doesn't influence the meaning of the universal quantification that constitutes our new proposition. If you replace parameter x with a parameter named y—both at the quantifier and inside the predicate that is quantified—you'll end up with a proposition that's logically equivalent to the preceding conjunction of five conjuncts:

∀y∈ {Toon, Lex, Chris, Cary, Hugh}: "y lives in Utrecht"

You can choose names of bound parameters in quantifications (both universal and existential) arbitrarily. Sometimes it's convenient to pick a different name for such a parameter to avoid confusion.

Because a quantified expression, like the preceding examples, is a predicate, it's perfectly valid to use such an expression as a component of a *compound* predicate. That is, you can combine quantified expressions with other predicates by using the logical connectives introduced in Chapter 1. For example, the following two expressions are valid predicates (in fact, both are propositions):

(∀x∈ A: x > 0) ∧ (∃y∈ B: y < 10)
¬(∀z∈ A: z > 10) ⇒ (∃x∈ A: x < 11)

Quantifiers and Finite Sets

Although databases grow larger and larger these days, they are always finite by definition—as opposed to sets in mathematics, which are sometimes infinite. If you work with finite sets only, you can always treat the existential and universal quantifiers as iterated OR and iterated AND constructs, respectively. Iteration is done over all elements of the set from which the quantifier parameter is drawn; for each element value, the occurrences of the variable inside the predicate are replaced by that value. This alternative way of interpreting quantified expressions might help when you investigate their truth values.

For example, suppose P is the set of all prime numbers less than 15:

    P := {2,3,5,7,11,13}

Then these two propositions

    ∃x∈P: x > 12
    ∀y∈P: y > 3

are logically equivalent with the following two propositions:

Iterate x over all elements in P: 2>12 ∨ 3>12 ∨ 5>12 ∨ 7>12 ∨ 11>12 ∨ 13>12

Iterate y over all elements in P: 2>3 ∧ 3>3 ∧ 5>3 ∧ 7>3 ∧ 11>3 ∧ 13>3

You could now manually compute the truth value of both predicates. If you evaluate the truth value of every disjunct, the first proposition becomes FALSE ∨ FALSE ∨ ... ∨ FALSE ∨ TRUE, which results in TRUE. If you do the same for the conjuncts of the second proposition, you get FALSE ∧ FALSE ∧ TRUE ∧ ... ∧ TRUE, which results in FALSE.

Quantification Over the Empty Set

The empty set (∅) contains no elements. Because it still is a set, you can quantify over the empty set. The following two expressions are valid propositions:

    ∃x∈∅: P(x)
    ∀y∈∅: Q(y)

But what does it mean to say that there exists an element x in the empty set for which P(x) holds? Clearly, the empty set has no elements. Therefore, regardless of the involved predicate P, whenever we propose that there's such an element in the empty set, we must be stating something that's unmistakably FALSE, because it's impossible to choose an element from the empty set.

The second proposition—universal quantification over the empty set—is less intuitive. By treating universal quantification as an iterated AND, you'll notice that a universal quantification over the empty set delivers no conjunct. Such quantification adds no predicate at all, and can therefore be considered the weakest predicate possible, which is TRUE (recall the paragraph on predicate strength in the "Truth Tables" section in Chapter 1). As you'll see when we discuss some additional rewrite rules regarding the negation of quantifiers in the section "Negation of Quantifiers," it makes complete sense. Table 3-2 lists these two important rewrite rules regarding quantification over the empty set.

Table 3-2. *Quantification Over the Empty Set—Rewrite Rules*

Quantification	Evaluates to
$(\exists x \in \varnothing: P(x))$	FALSE, regardless of predicate $P(x)$
$(\forall y \in \varnothing: Q(y))$	TRUE, regardless of predicate $Q(y)$

Nesting Quantifiers

Quantifiers can be nested. That is, you can use multiple quantifiers in a single predicate. Let's look at an example first. Suppose the following two sets are given:

```
S := {1,2,3,4}
T := {1,2}
```

Now look at the following four (very similar) propositions:

- $(\forall x \in S: (\exists y \in S: y = x))$ (For all x in S there exists a y in S for which y = x)

- $(\exists y \in S: (\forall x \in S: y = x))$ (There exists a y in S for which all x in S y = x)

- $(\forall x \in S: (\exists y \in T: y = x))$ (For all x in S there exists a y in T for which y = x)

- $(\forall x \in T: (\exists y \in S: y = x))$ (For all x in T there exists a y in S for which y = x)

If you compare the first two propositions, you'll see that they refer to the set S only; moreover, the two quantifiers are interchanged. In the last two examples, the two sets S and T are interchanged. Now if you check these propositions against the given two sets to investigate their truth value, you can draw the following conclusions:

- The first proposition is obviously TRUE, because you can simply choose the same value for y as the one you chose for x.

- The second proposition is FALSE; there is no such value y. As soon as you've bound variable y by selecting a value, there is only one choice for x (namely the same value).

- The third proposition is FALSE too; the counter examples are x = 3 and x = 4.

- The last proposition is TRUE, because T is a subset of S.

Interchanging Nested Quantifiers

From the first two examples in the previous section, you can draw this important conclusion: sometimes you can safely interchange nested quantifiers in your expressions, but sometimes you can't—without changing the meaning of the expression.

Caution Nested quantifications cannot always be interchanged without risk.

You can safely interchange two successive quantifiers in a formula if the following two conditions are met:

- Both quantifications are of the *same type*; that is, they must be either both universal or both existential.

- None of the sets over which you quantify is dependent on the variable bound to the other set; that is, the set for the inner quantifier is not influenced by the value you choose for the variable in the outer quantifier.

For example, the following two expressions are tautologies:

$\forall x \in A: \ \forall y \in B: \ P(x,y) \ \Leftrightarrow \ \forall y \in B: \ \forall x \in A: \ P(x,y)$
$\exists x \in A: \ \exists y \in B: \ Q(x,y) \ \Leftrightarrow \ \exists y \in B: \ \exists x \in A: \ Q(x,y)$

However, these two *are not* tautologies:

$\forall x \in A: \ \exists y \in B: \ P(x,y) \ \Leftrightarrow \ \exists y \in B: \ \forall x \in A: \ P(x,y)$
$\forall x \in A: \ \forall y \in (B \cup \{x\}): \ Q(x,y) \ \Leftrightarrow \ \forall y \in (B \cup \{x\}): \ \forall x \in A: \ Q(x,y)$

The last example is rather tricky; remember from Chapter 2, the symbol $\cup$ stands for the union operator. So as soon as you have chosen a value for x, you add that value to set B before you try to find a value y for which $Q(x,y)$ is TRUE. Note that the expression even becomes illegal if you interchange the quantifiers, because now you have a reference to the variable x in $\forall y \in (B \cup \{x\})$ before x is introduced in the second quantifier. To be more precise, the expression is not illegal, but rather confusing. If you bind a variable by quantification, the scope of that variable is the quantified expression; the variable is *unknown* outside the quantified expression. In other words, in the expression $\forall y \in (B \cup \{x\}): \ \forall x \in A: \ Q(x,y)$ the first x is not the same as the other ones. So, you might as well say $\forall y \in (B \cup \{x\}): \ \forall z \in A: \ Q(z,y)$. But then, this expression is not a proposition but a predicate, because it contains a free variable x.

Abbreviation of Consecutive Nested Quantifiers

If you have two consecutive quantifiers of the *same* type over the *same* set, it's common to abbreviate your formulas as follows:

$\exists x \in N: \ \exists y \in N: \ x + y > 42$

The preceding existential quantification over the same set becomes

$\exists x, y \in N: \ x + y > 42$

And likewise for universal quantification:

$\forall x \in N: \ \forall y \in N: \ x + y > 42$

The preceding universal quantification over the same set becomes

$\forall x, y \in N: \ x + y > 42$

Distributive Properties of Quantifiers

Listing 3-13 shows the distributive properties of the universal and existential quantifiers.

Listing 3-13. *Distributive Properties of Quantifiers*

(∃x∈ S: P(x) ∨ Q(x)) ⇔ ((∃x∈ S: P(x)) ∨ (∃x∈ S: Q(x)))
(∀x∈ S: P(x) ∧ Q(x)) ⇔ ((∀x∈ S: P(x)) ∧ (∀x∈ S: Q(x)))
(∃x∈ S: P(x) ∧ Q) ⇔ ((∃x∈ S: P(x)) ∧ Q)
(∀x∈ S: P(x) ∨ Q) ⇔ ((∀x∈ S: P(x)) ∨ Q)

Note that in the last two examples in Listing 3-13, predicate Q is not written as Q(x); this denotes that predicate Q does not have a parameter x. You can use the last two logical equivalences only if x does *not* occur as a parameter in predicate Q; for example:

(∀y∈ S: (∃x∈ S: x>10 ∧ y<5))
⇔ (∀y∈ S: (∃x∈ S: x>10) ∧ y<5)
⇔ (∀y∈ S: (∃x∈ S: x>10)) ∧ (∀y∈ S: y<5)

By the way, do you see that the left conjunct in the last equation is of the form (∀y∈ S: Q)? More specifically, it represents a universal quantification over a proposition; it doesn't quantify over a predicate whose parameter gets bound by the quantifier. Something similar can occur with an existential quantification. Take a look at Listing 3-14, which introduces two rewrite rules for these situations.

Listing 3-14. *Rewrite Rules for Quantification Over Propositions*

(∀x∈ S: P) ⇔ ((S = ∅) ∨ P)
(∃x∈ S: Q) ⇔ ((S ≠ ∅) ∧ Q)

Here P and Q represent propositions. Using these rewrite rules, you can further rewrite the preceding example into the following expression:

((S = ∅) ∨ (∃x∈ S: x>10)) ∧ (∀y∈ S: y<5)

Negation of Quantifiers

If you use the negation connective in combination with a universal quantifier, the following happens:

1. ¬(∀x∈ S: P(x)) means that P is *not* TRUE for all elements x of S.

2. Therefore, there must be (at least) one value for which P is not TRUE; in other words:

(∃x∈ S: ¬P(x))

Likewise, adding the negation to an existential quantification results in the following:

1. ¬(∃x∈ S: P(x)) means that there is no element x of S for which P is TRUE.

2. Therefore, P must be FALSE for all values x in S; in other words:

(∀x∈ S: ¬P(x))

So we have two important quantifier rewrite rules, as shown in Listing 3-15.

Listing 3-15. *Rewrite Rules for Negation of Quantifiers*

```
¬( ∀x∈S: P(x) ) ⇔ ( ∃x∈S: ¬P(x) )
¬( ∃x∈S: P(x) ) ⇔ ( ∀x∈S: ¬P(x) )
```

Do you remember the discussion about quantification over the empty set in the previous section "Quantification Over the Empty Set" (see Table 3-2)? We don't want the empty set to cause any exceptions to the rules. Therefore

- Given $(∃x∈\varnothing: P(x)) ⇔ \text{FALSE}$, we can transform this into $¬(∀x∈\varnothing: ¬P(x)) ⇔ \text{FALSE}$ (using the first rewrite rule in Listing 3-15)

- But then $¬¬(∀x∈\varnothing: ¬P(x)) ⇔ \text{TRUE}$ (negation of predicates at both sides of equivalence)

- So $(∀x∈\varnothing: ¬P(x)) ⇔ \text{TRUE}$, regardless of the predicate (strike out the double negation in front of the universal quantifier)

So you see it's logically correct that universal quantification over the empty set always results in TRUE, regardless of the actual predicate after the colon.

If you're still not fully convinced, here's an alternative reasoning. The universal quantifier corresponds with an iterated AND construct, as explained in the paragraph on quantifiers in section "Quantifiers and Finite Sets." Therefore, you can set up the following series of logical equivalences:

```
∀x∈S: P(x)
⇔ P(x₁) ∧ P(x₂) ∧ P(x₃) ∧ ... ∧ P(xₙ₋₁) ∧ P(xₙ)
⇔ TRUE ∧ P(x₁) ∧ P(x₂) ∧ P(x₃) ∧ ... ∧ P(xₙ₋₁) ∧ P(xₙ)
```

The prefix TRUE ∧ is allowed according to one of the "special case" rewrite rules listed in Table 1-12. As you can see, you start with a set S containing n values. Now if you start removing the elements of set S one by one, you can remove $∧ P(x_n)$ from the end, followed by $∧ P(x_{n-1})$, and so on, until you will eventually end up with the empty set—because you removed the last element of set S. However, then the equivalence is reduced to $∀x∈\varnothing: P(x)$ which is equivalent to TRUE.

Rewrite Rules with Quantifiers

The previous sections already introduced a few rewrite rules with regard to quantification. Listing 3-16 lists the most commonly used rewrite rules for quantifiers.

Listing 3-16. *Rewrite Rules With Quantifiers*

```
¬( ∃x∈S: P(x) ) ⇔ ( ∀x∈S: ¬P(x) )
¬( ∀x∈S: P(x) ) ⇔ ( ∃x∈S: ¬P(x) )
( ∃x∈S: P(x) ) ⇔ ¬( ∀x∈S: ¬P(x) )
( ∀x∈S: P(x) ) ⇔ ¬( ∃x∈S: ¬P(x) )
( ∀x∈A: ( ∀y∈B: P(x,y) ) ) ⇔ ( ∀y∈B: ( ∀x∈A: P(x,y) ) )
( ∃x∈A: ( ∃y∈B: Q(x,y) ) ) ⇔ ( ∃y∈B: ( ∃x∈A: Q(x,y) ) )
```

$$(\exists x \in S: P(x) \lor Q(x)) \Leftrightarrow ((\exists x \in S: P(x)) \lor (\exists x \in S: Q(x)))$$
$$(\forall x \in S: P(x) \land Q(x)) \Leftrightarrow ((\forall x \in S: P(x)) \land (\forall x \in S: Q(x)))$$
$$(\exists x \in S: P(x) \land Q) \Leftrightarrow ((\exists x \in S: P(x)) \land Q)$$
$$(\forall x \in S: P(x) \lor Q) \Leftrightarrow ((\forall x \in S: P(x)) \lor Q)$$
$$\neg (\forall x \in S: \forall y \in T: P(x,y)) \Leftrightarrow (\exists x \in S: \exists y \in T: \neg P(x,y))$$
$$\neg (\exists x \in S: \exists y \in T: P(x,y)) \Leftrightarrow (\forall x \in S: \forall y \in T: \neg P(x,y))$$
$$\neg (\forall x \in S: \exists y \in T: P(x,y)) \Leftrightarrow (\exists x \in S: \forall y \in T: \neg P(x,y))$$
$$\neg (\exists x \in S: \forall y \in T: P(x,y)) \Leftrightarrow (\forall x \in S: \exists y \in T: \neg P(x,y))$$

The third and fourth rewrite rules in Listing 3-16 state that you can rewrite a universal quantification into an existential quantification (with the use of a negation connective) and vice versa. This means that you don't need one of the quantifiers to express any arbitrary quantified predicate. However, it's convenient to have the two quantifiers available, because we use both in natural language.

You'll prove one of these rewrite rules in the exercises at the end of this chapter.

Normal Forms

Normal forms (also referred to as canonical forms) are often used in mathematics. The English word "normal" here is being used in the sense of conforming to a norm (that is a standard) as opposed to the meaning "usual."

Normal forms are typically used to rewrite expressions in such a way that you can solve (or further analyze) them easily. A characteristic example is the well-known normal form for quadratic equations: $ax^2 + bx + c = 0$. Once you have rewritten your quadratic equations to this format, you can use the quadratic formula to find the values for x. In logic, there are similar normal forms; we'll discuss two of them in the sections that follow. In general, normal forms are useful in automated theorem proving. The disjunctive and conjunctive normal forms discussed in the following sections are particularly useful to verify whether a predicate is a tautology or a contradiction.

■**Note** Normal forms are also useful for comparing two predicates. By rewriting two seemingly similar predicates into the same normal form, you can examine more closely what exactly the difference is between the two. Or maybe after having transformed both into a normal form, you discover that they are in fact the same predicate. This is one of the applications in Part 2 of this book when data integrity rules are specified as formal predicates.

Conjunctive Normal Form

A predicate is in *conjunctive normal form* (CNF) if it consists of one or more members separated by AND; that is, if the predicate, say P-CNF, has the following format:

    P-CNF := $C_1 \land C_2 \land C_3 \land \ldots \land C_n$

In this formula, C_1, C_2, ... C_n are known as the *conjunction members*—or just *conjuncts* for short. Each conjunction member is an iterated OR of *simple predicates* only (note that zero iteration is allowed too, which results in a conjunction member containing no invocation of OR); a simple predicate is a predicate that cannot be further decomposed into a disjunction or conjunction (that is, it cannot be a compound predicate). These simple predicates may optionally be preceded by a negation connective. Note that the set $\{\lor, \land, \lnot\}$ is functionally complete, as explained in Chapter 1; therefore, you don't need other connectives to express any arbitrary predicate. Also, as we'll demonstrate shortly, CNF is always achievable for any arbitrary predicate.

CNF in full detail looks as shown in Listing 3-17.

Listing 3-17. *Conjunctive Normal Form (CNF)*

$$P\text{-}CNF := (SP_{11} \lor SP_{12} \lor SP_{13} \lor \ldots \lor SP_{1a}) \land$$
$$(SP_{21} \lor SP_{22} \lor SP_{23} \lor \ldots \lor SP_{2b}) \land$$
$$(SP_{31} \lor SP_{32} \lor SP_{33} \lor \ldots \lor SP_{3c}) \land$$
$$\ldots \land$$
$$(SP_{n1} \lor SP_{n2} \lor SP_{n3} \lor \ldots \lor SP_{nd})$$

In Listing 3-17, each simple predicate SP_{ij} is allowed to be prefixed with a negation connective. It's easy to check whether a proposition in CNF is a tautology, because as soon as one of the conjunction members is FALSE, the proposition becomes FALSE. In other words, you can check the conjunction members one by one. Moreover, because all conjunction members of a predicate in CNF must be an iterated OR with simple predicates only, the tautology check can also be formulated as follows:

> *A CNF predicate is a tautology (always* TRUE*) if and only if each conjunction member contains a simple predicate* P *and its negation.*

Listing 3-18 shows four examples of predicates in CNF (P, Q, R, and S are simple predicates).

Listing 3-18. *Examples of Predicates in CNF*

```
P
P ∨ Q
P ∧ Q
(P ∨ Q ∨ ¬R) ∧ (P ∨ ¬R)
(P ∨ Q ∨ ¬P) ∧ (Q ∨ ¬Q) ∧ (¬R ∨ R ∨ S)
```

The first predicate has one conjunction member that consists of one simple predicate. The second predicate has one conjunction member that happens to be a disjunction of two simple predicates; the third and the fourth examples consist of two conjunction members. The fifth example is a tautology; note that the three conjunction members contain the pairs of simple predicates (P, ¬P), (Q, ¬Q), and (R, ¬R), respectively.

Disjunctive Normal Form

A predicate is in *disjunctive normal form* (DNF) if it consists of one or more members separated by OR; that is, if the predicate, say P-DNF, has the following format:

$$P\text{-}DNF := D_1 \lor D_2 \lor D_3 \lor \ldots \lor D_n$$

In this formula, D_1, D_2, ... , D_n are known as the *disjunction members*—or just *disjuncts* for short. Each disjunction member is an iterated AND with *simple predicates* only (zero iteration allowed). So DNF in full detail looks as shown in Listing 3-19.

Listing 3-19. *Disjunctive Normal Form (DNF)*

```
P-DNF := (SP₁₁ ∧ SP₁₂ ∧ SP₁₃ ∧ ...  ∧ SP₁ₐ) ∨
         (SP₂₁ ∧ SP₂₂ ∧ SP₂₃ ∧ ...  ∧ SP₂ᵦ) ∨
         (SP₃₁ ∧ SP₃₂ ∧ SP₃₃ ∧ ...  ∧ SP₃ᵧ) ∨
         ...                                   ∨
         (SPₙ₁ ∧ SPₙ₂ ∧ SPₙ₃ ∧ ...  ∧ SPₙᵈ)
```

In Listing 3-19, each SP_{ij} is allowed to be prefixed with a negation connective. Compound predicates in DNF are easy to check for contradictions. For a predicate in DNF to be a contradiction, all disjunction members must be FALSE—because the predicate is written as an iterated OR construct. Following the same reasoning as we did for predicates in CNF, we can say the following about predicates in DNF:

> *A DNF predicate is a contradiction if and only if each disjunction member contains a simple predicate P and its negation.*

See Listing 3-20 for examples of predicates in DNF.

Listing 3-20. *Examples of Predicates in DNF*

```
P ∨ Q
P ∧ Q
(P ∧ Q ∧ ¬R) ∨ (S ∧ ¬R)
(P ∧ Q ∧ ¬P) ∨ (R ∧ ¬R ∧ S)
```

The first two examples are in DNF as well as in CNF (compare Listing 3-18); the second example consists of one disjunction member that happens to be a conjunction of two simple predicates; the third and last example consists of two disjunction members. The last example is also a contradiction.

Finding the Normal Form for a Given Predicate

In this section we'll investigate how you can transform a given predicate into DNF or CNF.

Finding the DNF for a Given Predicate

There are several methods to rewrite existing predicates into DNF. Normally, you try to use existing rewrite rules to move your expression into the "right" direction until it has the desired format: an iterated OR where the disjuncts are iterated ANDs with simple predicates only.

An interesting alternative technique is based on using a truth table. For example, suppose this is the original predicate:

$$P \Rightarrow (Q \Leftrightarrow \neg P)$$

Table 3-3 shows the corresponding truth table.

Table 3-3. *Using a Truth Table to Rewrite Predicates to DNF*

P	Q	$\neg P$	$Q \Leftrightarrow \neg P$	$P \Rightarrow (Q \Leftrightarrow \neg P)$
t	t	f	f	f
t	f	f	t	t
f	t	t	t	t
f	f	t	f	t

As you can see from the last column of Table 3-3, the given predicate is TRUE for the last three truth combinations of (P,Q): $(\mathbf{t},\mathbf{f})$, $(\mathbf{f},\mathbf{t})$, and $(\mathbf{f},\mathbf{f})$. You can represent those three truth combinations with the following corresponding conjunctions:

$(\mathbf{t},\mathbf{f})$: $C_1 := P \wedge \neg Q$
$(\mathbf{f},\mathbf{t})$: $C_2 := \neg P \wedge Q$
$(\mathbf{f},\mathbf{f})$: $C_3 := \neg P \wedge \neg Q$

Now, if you combine these three conjunctions into the iterated disjunction $C_1 \vee C_2 \vee C_3$, you end up with a *rewritten predicate* in DNF that precisely represents the truth table of the original predicate:

$$(P \wedge \neg Q) \vee (\neg P \wedge Q) \vee (\neg P \wedge \neg Q)$$

If you aren't convinced, set up a truth table for the rewritten predicate and compare the result with the original predicate in Table 3-3. By the way, did you notice that the last column of Table 3-3 is identical to the definition of the NAND operator? The rewritten expression in DNF precisely represents the NAND operator; the expression is FALSE if and only if both operands are TRUE.

■**Note** This DNF rewrite algorithm using a truth table is relatively easy to automate. You could write a program that does the conversion for you, without the need for inspiration and creativity; DNF is always achievable.

FUNCTIONAL COMPLETENESS REVISITED

Do you remember the discussion of functional completeness in Chapter 1? Clearly, you can use the preceding technique to rewrite any arbitrary predicate (optionally containing any nonstandard connectives from the huge set of theoretical connective possibilities) to produce a predicate in DNF. Regardless of the complexity of the original predicate and regardless of which connectives it contains, you end up with a truth table column that "represents" the truth value of the expression for all given truth value combinations of its variables. The preceding technique uses this information to generate a logically equivalent expression containing conjunctions, disjunctions, and negations only; therefore, $\{\wedge, \vee, \neg\}$ is functionally complete.

Finding the CNF for a Given Predicate

To find the CNF for a given predicate—which is also always achievable—you first apply the preceding method using the truth table to find the DNF of the predicate. You then apply the distributive laws to convert the iterated disjunction into an iterated conjunction. Here's an example derivation that converts the predicate $(P \wedge Q) \vee (R \wedge S)$, which is in DNF, into CNF:

$$(P \wedge Q) \vee (R \wedge S)$$
$$\Leftrightarrow (P \vee (R \wedge S)) \wedge (Q \vee (R \wedge S))$$
$$\Leftrightarrow (P \vee R) \wedge (P \vee S) \wedge (Q \vee R) \wedge (Q \vee S)$$

We'll revisit CNF in Part 2 of this book when we discuss specification and implementation guidelines for data integrity constraints.

Chapter Summary

This section contains a summary of the contents of this chapter, formatted as a bulleted list—just like the previous chapter. Again, if you don't feel comfortable about one of the following concepts, you might want to revisit certain chapter sections before continuing with the exercises in the next section.

- Just like regular arithmetic operators, logical connectives can also have certain *algebraic properties*, such as commutativity, associativity, distributivity, reflexivity, transitivity, idempotence, and absorption.

- You can turn predicates into propositions in two ways, one of them being by binding parameters through *quantification*.

- There are two quantifiers:

    - The *existential quantifier* allows you to express statements such as "There exists . . ." using the symbol ∃.

    - The universal quantifier allows you to express statements such as "For all . . ." using the symbol ∀.

- Because sets are *finite* by definition in databases, you can always interpret predicates with an existential quantifier over some set in the database as an iterated OR construct; similarly, you can interpret predicates with a universal quantifier as an iterated AND construct.

- Be careful when quantifying over the *empty set*. The existential quantifier will always return FALSE, regardless of the predicate, whereas the universal quantifier will always return TRUE when applied to the empty set.

- Quantifiers can be *nested*. Sometimes you can interchange quantifiers in your expressions, but in many cases you'll change the meaning of the expression. In general, you may interchange quantifiers if they are of the same type and none of the sets over which you quantify are dependent on the variable bound by the other set.

- You can apply many *rewrite rules* to quantified expressions. For example, you can always rewrite a universal quantifier expression to an existential quantifier expression, and vice versa.

- *Normal forms* are often used to rewrite expressions in such a way that you can easily solve them, automate the process of proving theorems, or investigate predicates, whether they are tautologies or contradictions. This chapter introduced two normal forms:

  - *Conjunctive normal form (CNF)*: Predicate written as iterated AND. CNF is useful when you are investigating tautologies.

  - *Disjunctive normal form (DNF)*: Predicate written as iterated OR. DNF is useful when checking for contradictions.

Exercises

1. Prove the two absorption equivalences from Listing 3-11, using a truth table:

   P ∨ (P ∧ Q) ⟺ P
   P ∧ (P ∨ Q) ⟺ P

2. The following two sets are given: A := {2,4,6,8} and B := {1,3,5,7,9}. Which of the following propositions are TRUE?

   a. ∀x∈ A: x > 1

   b. ∃x∈ B: mod(x,5) = 0

   c. ∀x∈ A: ∀y∈ B: x + y ≥ 4

   d. ∀x∈ A: ∃y∈ B: x + y = 11

   e. ∃y∈ B: ∀x∈ A: x + y = 11

   f. ∃x∈ A: ∃y∈ A: x + y = 4

   For the propositions that are FALSE, could you come up with different definitions for sets A or B in such a way that they become TRUE?

3. Give a formal representation of the following statements:

   a. Each element of A is divisible by 2.

   b. Each number in B is less than 9.

   c. A contains three different numbers of which the sum is 18.

4. Eliminate the negation from the following propositions; that is, rewrite the formal representations without using the negation symbol ($\neg$):

   a. $\neg\exists x\in A:\ x < 5$

   b. $\neg\forall x\in B:\ \mathrm{mod}(y,2)\ =\ 1$

   c. $\neg\forall x\in A:\ \exists y\in B:\ y\ -\ x\ =\ 1$

   d. $\neg\exists x,y,z\in B:\ x\ +\ y\ +\ z\ =\ 11$

5. Rewrite the following propositions to *disjunctive* normal form:

   a. $(\ P\lor Q\ )\land(\ R\lor S\ )$

   b. $\neg(\ P\Rightarrow(\ Q\land\neg R\ )\ )$

   c. $P\Leftrightarrow\neg Q$

6. Rewrite the second proposition of the previous exercise to *conjunctive* normal form:

   $\neg(\ P\ \Rightarrow\ (\ Q\ \land\ \neg R\ )\ )$

   Hint: First, try to find the DNF of the negation of the preceding predicate; when found, apply one of De Morgan's laws.

7. Prove the last rewrite rule from Listing 3-16, using other rewrite rules:

   $\neg(\ \exists x\in S:\ \forall y\in T:\ P(x,y)\ )\ \Leftrightarrow\ (\ \forall x\in S:\ \exists y\in T:\ \neg P(x,y)\ )$

8. Let S be a given finite set and P(x) a given predicate. Complete the following expressions in such a way that they are transformed into tautologies:

   a. $(\ \exists x\in S:\ P(x)\ )\Leftrightarrow\#\{\ x\ |\ x\in S\land P(x)\ \}\ \ldots$

   b. $(\ \forall x\in S:\ P(x)\ )\Leftrightarrow\#\{\ x\ |\ x\in S\land P(x)\ \}\ \ldots$

CHAPTER 4

Relations and Functions

Chapter 2 laid down the basics of set theory. This fourth chapter will build on those basics and introduce some more set-theory concepts that will be used in Part 2 of this book as tools to define a database design formally—including all constraint specifications.

In the section "Binary Relations," we'll revisit ordered pairs and the Cartesian product to introduce the concept of a *binary relation* between two sets. As you'll see, such a binary relation is in fact a subset of the Cartesian product of two sets.

The section "Functions" then introduces the important concept of a *function*. A function is a special kind of binary relation—one that conforms to certain properties. In this section we'll also establish some terminology around the (set-theory) concept of a function.

The section "Operations on Functions" revisits the union, intersection, and difference set operators and takes a closer look at how these behave when applied to functions as their operands. You'll also be introduced to a new (dyadic) set operator called *limitation* of a function.

This chapter then continues by introducing another important concept that we call a *set function*. A set function holds a special kind of ordered pair: one where the second coordinate of the pair is always a set. We'll reveal the link that a set function has with specifying a database design: it can be used to characterize an *external predicate*. An external predicate describes something about the real world that we want to represent in a database. If a set function is used for this purpose, we'll refer to it as a *characterization*. In the same section, you'll be introduced to a new monadic set operator called the *generalized product*. The generalized product takes a set function—or rather a characterization—as its operand and produces a new *set of functions*. The concept of a generalized product is the second key stepping stone (next to the concept of a powerset that was introduced in Chapter 2) that will be used in Part 2 of this book when we'll demonstrate how to define a database design formally.

We conclude this chapter with the notion of *function composition*, which will be applied in Chapter 5 (operations on tables) when we investigate the join in a formal way.

You'll find a "Chapter Summary" at the end followed by an "Exercises" section. You're strongly advised to spend sufficient time on these exercises before moving on to the other chapters.

Binary Relations

Before we start dealing with binary relations, take a look at this quote from Chapter 1:

> *The importance of data management being based on logic was envisioned by E. F. (Ted) Codd (1923–2003) in 1969, when he first proposed his famous relational model in the IBM research report "Derivability, Redundancy and Consistency of Relations Stored in Large Data Banks." The relational model for database management introduced in this research report has proven to be an influential general theory of data management and remains his most memorable achievement.*

The word *Relations*, as used by E. F. Codd in the preceding quote in the title of his research report, created the name of the general theory we now refer to as the *relational* model of data.

■**Note** It is a common misconception that the word *relational* in "the relational model of data" refers to "relationships" (many-to-one, many-to-many, and so on) that can exist between different "entity types," as you too probably have designed at some point using the pervasive design technique known as entity-relationship diagrams (ERDs). The word *relational* in "the relational model of data" has nothing to do with the R of ERD. The word refers to the *mathematical* concept of a (n-ary) relation, which is totally different from the "relationship" concept in ERD. The former is a mathematical—set-theory—concept; the latter eventually maps to certain cases of data integrity constraints (loosely speaking).

In this chapter, you'll be introduced to the set-theory concept of a relation—the meaning used by E. F. Codd. More specifically, you'll be introduced to a certain type of relation: a *binary* relation. We'll deal with relationships in the ERD sense—as data integrity constraints—in Part 2 of this book.

Ordered Pairs and Cartesian Product Revisited

Let's first recall a bit from Chapter 2. That chapter ended with the following two definitions regarding ordered pairs and the Cartesian product:

- An *ordered pair* is a pair of elements, also referred to as the *coordinates* of the ordered pair. The notation is $(a;b)$.

- The *Cartesian product* of two given sets, say A and B, is defined as follows:
  $A{\times}B = \{ \ (a;b) \ | \ a{\in}A \ \wedge \ b{\in}B \ \}$

This definition shows that the result of the Cartesian product of two given sets is in fact a set of ordered pairs. It holds every possible combination of an element from the first set and one from the second set.

Listing 4-1 illustrates the Cartesian product with an example.

Listing 4-1. *Example Cartesian Product*

```
A := {X,Y,Z}
B := {1,2}
A×B = { (X;1), (X;2), (Y;1), (Y;2), (Z;1), (Z;2) }
```

The same section of Chapter 2 also listed the following properties:

```
a≠b ⇒ (a;b)≠(b;a)
(a;b)=(c;d) ⇔ (a=c ∧ b=d)
A×B=B×A ⇔ A=B
```

These properties illustrate the following facts:

- The order of the coordinates of an ordered pair is important.

- The Cartesian product is *not* a commutative operator.

This enables us to introduce the mathematical concept of a binary relation in the next section.

Binary Relations

A *binary relation from set A to set B* is defined as a *subset of the Cartesian product A×B*. It's called a *binary* relation because it deals with two sets (A and B). Let's start with a small example, based on the same two sets in Listing 4-1:

```
A := {X,Y,Z}
B := {1,2}
```

Take a look at the set R1 shown here:

```
R1 := { (X;1), (X;2), (Y;1), (Z;2) }
```

Note that set R1 does not hold every possible combination of an element from set A and one from set B; set R1 only holds four ordered pairs as its elements. Every ordered pair is also an element of the Cartesian product of sets A and B, as shown in Listing 4-1. Formally, this can be expressed as follows:

```
( ∀p∈R1: p∈A×B )
```

This makes R1 a subset of the Cartesian product of sets A and B, and therefore a binary relation from set A to set B. Definition 4-1 illustrates another way to define a binary relation and uses the important powerset operator that was introduced in Chapter 2.

■**Definition 4-1: Binary Relation** "R is a binary relation from set A to set B" ⇔ R∈ ℘(A×B)

The powerset of a given set holds every possible subset of that set. In the preceding case, the powerset holds every possible subset of the Cartesian product of set A and set B. Consequently, every element of this powerset is a binary relation from set A to set B.

Note In the small example relation R1, every A value appears in the ordered pairs, as does every B value. This is not always true, of course. There are other binary relations from A to B where this is not the case.

You can draw a picture of a binary relation. This is done by visualizing (as in a Venn diagram) the two sets separately and connecting the paired elements of both sets with arrows. Figure 4-1 shows binary relation R1 as a picture, where the four arrows represent the ordered pairs.

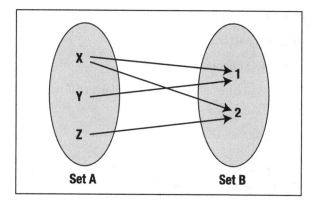

Figure 4-1. *Picture of binary relation R1*

You can instantly see in the picture of binary relation R that two arrows depart from element X of set A, and only one arrow each departs from elements Y and Z. You can also immediately see that both elements 1 and 2 of set B have two arrows arriving. In the next section, a limit will be imposed on the number of arrows departing from each element to get to the definition of a function.

Note Instead of declaring a binary relation to be *from* set A *to* set B, other textbooks might declare binary relations to be *over* set A and *on* set B.

Functions

A *function* is a binary relation that doesn't have two elements that have the same first coordinate; or said in another way, in a function two distinct ordered pairs always have different first coordinates. From the picture point of view, this limits the number of arrows departing from an element of the set at the left-hand side to one arrow at most.

Furthermore, if every element in the set at the left-hand side has exactly one arrow departing, then we say that the binary relation is a function *over* this set (at the left-hand side).

Definition 4-2 illustrates how to define this additional limitation formally. It employs the π_1 operator introduced in Chapter 2 (it selects the first coordinate of an ordered pair).

Definition 4-2: Function "F is a function over set A into set B" ⇔

$F \in \wp(A \times B) \land (\ \forall p1, p2 \in F:\ p1 \neq p2 \Rightarrow \pi_1(p1) \neq \pi_2(p2)\ ) \land \{\pi_1(p)\ |\ p \in F\ \} = A$

The second conjunct at the right-hand side of the equivalence in Definition 4-2 constitutes the additional limitation mentioned earlier: for all ordered pairs p1 and p2 that are in function F, if p1 and p2 are different pairs then they should hold different first coordinates. Put in another way (using the result of Exercise 4a of Chapter 1), if p1 and p2 have the same first coordinate then they must be the same pair. The last conjunct states that for F to be a function *over* A, every element of A must appear as a first coordinate.

Most of the time, we're interested in the fact that the first coordinates of the function originate from set A (and much less that the second coordinates originate from set B). Instead of saying that "F is a function over A into B," we say that "F is a function over A."

Now take a look at the following examples:

```
F1 := { (X;1), (X;2), (Y;1), (Z;2) }
F2 := { (X;2), (Y;1), (Z;2) }
F3 := { (X;1), (Y;1), (X;1), (Z;1) }
F4 := { (Z;2) }
F5 := ∅
F6 := { (empno;126), (ename;'Lex de Haan'), (born;'11-aug-1954') }
```

The first example F1 is not a function because it holds two distinct pairs—(X;1) and (X;2)—that have the same first coordinate X. The second binary relation F2 is indeed a function: no two distinct pairs have the same first coordinate. The third one F3 is also a function. Although two pairs are enumerated that have the same first coordinate (the first and the third pair), they are in fact the same pair. One of these pairs need not have been enumerated and can be left out without changing set F3. Example F4 is also a function, and the empty set (F5) is indeed a function too. It is a subset of the Cartesian product of any two sets (the empty set is a subset of *every* set). The additional limitation given in Definition 4-2 also holds. You might want to revisit the second rewrite rule in Table 3-2 for this. The last example binary relation F6 is a function too. Through this example, you can begin to see how functions can be used (as building blocks) to specify database designs. We'll come back to this at the end of the section "Set Functions."

We continue with the introduction of various terminologies around the set-theory concept of a function.

Domain and Range of Functions

The set of all first coordinates of a function, say F, is called the *domain* of that function; the notation is dom(F). The set of all second coordinates of a function is called the *range* of that function; the notation is rng(F). These two concepts are rather trivial; to find the domain or range of a function you simply enumerate all first or second coordinates of the ordered pairs of that function. Listing 4-2 lists the domains of the five functions F2 through F6 introduced in the preceding section.

Listing 4-2. *Domains of the Example Functions*

```
dom(F2) = dom(F3) = {X,Y,Z}
dom(F4) = {Z}
dom(F5) = Ø
dom(F6) = {empno,ename,born}
```

Listing 4-3 gives the ranges of these five functions.

Listing 4-3. *Ranges of the Example Functions*

```
rng(F2) = {1,2}
rng(F3) = {1}
rng(F4) = {2}
rng(F5) = Ø
rng(F6) = {126,'Lex de Haan','11-aug-1954'}
```

From a picture of a function, you can determine the domain and range by leaving out the elements that have no arrows departing from or arriving in them. Figure 4-2 shows a binary relation F7 from a set A := {A,B,C,D,E} to a set B := {1,2,3,4,5}. As you can see, it straightforwardly represents a function (at most one arrow departs from the elements of set A) and dom(F7) = {A,C,D,E} and rng(F7) = {2,4}.

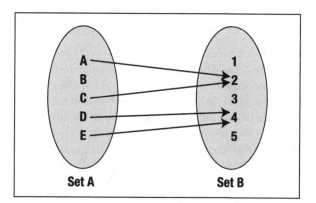

Figure 4-2. *Binary relation F7 from set A to set B*

We define a function to be *over* a set A and *into* a set B, if the following two properties hold:

- dom(F) = A

- rng(F) ⊆ B

Because F is a function over A into B, by definition the set of all first coordinates—the domain of F—is equal to A. And because every ordered pair in a function over A into B has an element of B as its second coordinate, the range of F will be a subset of set B; often it will be a proper subset of B.

Note You probably have noticed that the set-theory concept of a *domain* introduced here is quite different from the usual meaning of the word "domain" in other database textbooks. In other textbooks, a domain usually represents the set of possible values—or if you will, the type—of a "column" in a "table." In this book, there's a similar concept for that meaning of the word domain (we'll call this an *attribute value set*) that will be precisely defined in the section "Set Functions."

Given that a function never has two pairs with the same first coordinate, you can unambiguously determine the range element that is paired to a given domain element of a function (remember from every domain element exactly one arrow is departing). Mathematicians have a special way of denoting that single range element for a given domain element. If F is a function and x is an element of dom(F), then F(x) (pronounce it as "F of x," or "F applied to x") denotes the range element that is paired to x in function F. This notation is called *function application*. We'll illustrate this using function F7 introduced in Figure 4-2. Following is the formal specification of F7:

    F7 := { (A;2), (C;2), (D;4), (E;4) }

Another valid way of specifying function F7 is by using the function application notation; just specify for each domain element what its range element is:

    F7(A) = 2
    F7(C) = 2
    F7(D) = 4
    F7(E) = 4

You might already be familiar with this notation from your mathematics classes in the past. Here's a typical example specification for some function F:

    F(x) := 3x² - 2x + 1

Given function F, you'd write expressions such as F(2), which would in this case evaluate to 9 (three times four, minus two times two, plus one).

The set-theory specification of the same function F would be as follows (assuming we want to specify this function over set **Z** into set **Z**):

    F := { (x; 3x² - 2x + 1) | x∈**Z** }

Here we've used the substitutive method to specify function F in a set-theory way.

Identity Function

A function f is called the *identity function over* A if A is the domain of f, and for all elements x in set A, f of x equals x. We use the notation id(A) to represent the identity function over A. Here are a few examples:

```
id({1,2,3})           = { (1;1), (2;2), (3;3) }
id({deptno})          = { (deptno;deptno) }
id({course,startdate}) = { (course;course), (startdate;startdate) }
```

Subset of a Function

In this section, we'll briefly investigate subsets of a function. Because a function is a set, you can construct a subset of a function. Listing 4-4 provides every (proper) subset of the function F2 := { (X;2), (Y;1), (Z;2) } that was introduced in the preceding section.

Listing 4-4. *All Proper Subsets of Function F2*

```
{ (X;2), (Y;1) }
{ (X;2), (Z;2) }
{ (Y;1), (Z;2) }
{ (X;2) }
{ (Y;1) }
{ (Z;2) }
∅
```

As you can see, every proper subset of F2 is again a function. Indeed, this is a property that holds for every function. For a given function F, every proper subset of F will be a function too.

This concludes the introduction of set-theory functions. Because functions are an important concept that will be extensively used throughout the rest of this book, we offer a brief summary here.

- A function is a binary relation and therefore a *set of ordered pairs*.

- In a function *every first coordinate appears only once*.

- You can use a function to specify a certain part of a database design.

The title of this chapter was deliberately chosen to be "Relations and Functions" because we felt you should be introduced to (at least) the mathematical concept of a binary relation. The more general concept of an n-*ary* relation (that is, not just a binary one) is a cornerstone concept introduced by E. F. Codd into the database field. The concept of a binary relation is sufficient for the mathematical method to specify database designs that will be developed in this book. Other textbooks deal with—and use in their methods—the concept of an n-*ary* relation. They also use n-ary relations differently than the way this book deals with a special case of the 2-ary relation: the function. To avoid confusion from here on, this book will explicitly not use the terms *binary relation* or *relation* anymore.

Operations on Functions

Because functions are sets, you can apply the set operators—union, intersection, and difference—with functions as their operands. This section will explore the application of these set operators on functions.

Union, Intersection, and Difference

It's always interesting for mathematicians to investigate the *closure property* of an operator. In the context of this chapter, we ask ourselves whether the union, intersection, and difference operators, which are closed on sets, are also closed on functions. Or put differently, when you apply these operators on two functions, will this result in another function?

Take a look at the following example, which introduces two functions G1 and G2, and illustrates the result of the union of those two functions:

```
G1 := { (a;1), (b;2), (c;3) }
G2 := { (a;2), (d;4) }
G1 ∪ G2 = { (a;1), (b;2), (c;3), (a;2), (d;4) }
```

This example illustrates that the union of two functions does not necessarily result in a function, because the result of the union of functions G1 and G2 holds two *different* ordered pairs that have the same first coordinate: (a;1) and (a;2).

Take a look at another example:

```
G3 := { (empno;999), (ename;'Toon Koppelaars'), (born;'14-feb-1965') }
G4 := { (empno;999), (occupation;'IT architect') }
G3∪G4 = { (empno;999), (ename;'Toon Koppelaars'),
          (born;'14-feb-1965'), (occupation;'IT architect') }
```

The result of the union of functions G3 and G4 does result in a function. This is because G3(empno) = G4(empno), and empno is the only domain element that both functions have in common. In the result of the union, you don't repeat element (empno;999) twice.

It shouldn't be too difficult now to conceive of the generic property that two functions should have for the union of those two functions to result in a function. This property is called *compatibility* or *joinability* of two functions. Definition 4-3 formally specifies this particular property.

■Definition 4-3: Compatible (Joinable) Functions "Function F is compatible with function G" ⇔
(∀c∈(dom(F)∩dom(G)): F(c)=G(c))

Two functions are compatible if and only if for every first coordinate that the two functions have in common (that is, that can be chosen from the intersection of the domains of both functions), the corresponding second coordinates match. Only if two functions are compatible will the union of those two functions result in another function.

Note that Definition 4-3 considers two functions that have no first coordinate in common always to be compatible. As the following example illustrates, the union of two such functions is indeed a function:

```
G5 := { (deptno;1), (dname;'Natural Join'), (location;'Utrecht') }
G6 := { (invoice;'inv123'), (amount;3500) }
G5 ∪ G6 = { (deptno;1), (dname;'Natural Join'), (location;'Utrecht'),
            (invoice;'abc123'), (amount;3500) }
```

If two functions have no first coordinate in common, then the union of those two functions won't hold two different ordered pairs with the same first coordinate. In fact, this is a property that is always true for two functions with no common first coordinate(s). However, in practice such unions will be meaningless.

Now let's take a look at the intersection of two functions and reuse the example functions G1 through G6 for this:

```
G1 ∩ G2 = ∅
G3 ∩ G4 = { (empno;999) }
G5 ∩ G6 = ∅
```

The intersection of functions G1 and G2 is empty; there is no ordered pair that is an element of both G1 and G2. The intersection of functions G3 and G4 is precisely the singleton ordered pair for which the first coordinate appears in the intersection of dom(G3) and dom(G4) (coordinate empno), and the property G3(empno) = G4(empno) holds. Finally, the intersection of functions G5 and G6 is empty; although these two functions are compatible, there is no first coordinate that they have in common, let alone an ordered pair.

The result of an intersection of two functions will always be another function. A simple way to understand this is to realize that the intersection of any two given *sets* will always be a subset of both given sets; let A and B be two sets, then $(A ∩ B) ⊆ A$ and $(A ∩ B) ⊆ B$. The intersection of two functions will be a subset of both two functions, and therefore a function (recall the section "Subset of a Function," with Listing 4-4).

The difference of two functions will always be a function. This is due to the same reasoning as with the intersection of two functions. The difference of set A and set B—A minus B—will always be a subset of set A.

Limitation of a Function

In Part 2 of this book, we'll often be interested in a subset of a given function. Instead of all ordered pairs, we'll only want to consider those ordered pairs whose first coordinate can be chosen from some given subset of the domain of the function. This leads us to the concept of a *limitation* of a function. Definition 4-4 defines the concept of a limitation of a function.

■**Definition 4-4: Limitation of a Function** Let F be a function and A a set. The limitation of function F on set A; notation F↓A is defined as follows:

$$F↓A := \{ p \mid p∈F ∧ π_1(p)∈A \}$$

The limitation of a function F on set A is the subset of F that only holds those ordered pairs for which the first coordinate is an element of set A. Let's illustrate this with a few examples in Listing 4-5. The aforementioned function G5 is reused in this listing.

Listing 4-5. *Example Limitations of Functions*

```
{ (X;2), (Y;1) }↓{X} = { (X;2) }
{ (X;2), (Z;2) }↓{Z} = { (Z;2) }
{ (X;2), (Z;2), (Y;1) }↓{X,Y,Z} = { (X;2), (Z;2), (Y;1) }
G5↓{dname,location} = { (dname;'Natural Join'), (location;'Utrecht') }
G5↓∅=∅
```

Note that a limitation of a function *always* results in another function; if you limit on the empty set the result is the empty function.

With the availability of this limitation operator, you're able to give an alternative definition for compatibility of two functions; that is, the property two functions should have in order for the union of those two functions to result in another function. See Definition 4-5 for this alternative definition.

Definition 4-5: Alternative Definition for Compatibility (Joinability) of Functions Using Limitation "Function F is compatible with function G" ⇔ F↓(dom(F)∩dom(G)) = G↓(dom(F)∩dom(G))

Two functions are compatible (joinable) if, when limited to the intersection of their domains, these resulting limitations are equal.

Set Functions

Another concept that we'll need in Part 2 of this book is the concept of a *set function*. Set functions will be used as the foundation for the definition of a *database universe*: a formal specification of a database design that will be introduced in Part 2.

As you know by now, a function is a set of ordered pairs, and an ordered pair is a pair of two elements for which the order is significant.

Note No limitations have been put on the type of an element that is allowed to appear as a coordinate of an ordered pair. They can be of arbitrary complexity. For instance, coordinates are allowed to be sets.

A set function is a function in which every ordered pair holds a set as its second coordinate. Definition 4-6 formally defines this concept.

Definition 4-6: Set Function "F is a set function" ⇔ F is a function and $(\forall c \in \text{dom}(F): F(c)$ is a set)

As you can read from this definition, a set function is a function in which every range element is a set (possibly the empty set). Listing 4-6 provides various examples of set functions.

Listing 4-6. *Example Set Functions*

```
H1 := { (X;{1,2,3,4,5}), (Y;{1,2,3,4}) }
H2 := { (X;{1,2}), (Z;{3,4}) }
H3 := { (company;{'Natural Join','Centraal Boekhuis','Oracle','Remmen & De Brock'})
       , (location;{'Utrecht','Culemborg','De Meern','Eindhoven'}) }
H4 := { (empno;[1..99])
       , (ename;varchar(10))
       , (born;date)
       , (job;{'CLERK','SALESMAN','TRAINER','MANAGER','PRESIDENT'})
       , (salary;[1000..4999]) }
```

The first example H1 is a function (no first coordinate appears more than once). It is a set function because both H1(X) and H1(Y) evaluate to set values; {1,2,3,4,5} and {1,2,3,4}, respectively. The second example, function H2, is also a set function because H2(X) = {1,2} and H2(Z) = {3,4}.

Characterizations

You can consider set function H3 to enumerate, through the first coordinates of its ordered pairs, two aspects of a company: the name of the company (coordinate company) and the location of the company (coordinate location). Such first coordinates are referred to as *attributes*. Attached to these attributes are the value sets—as second coordinates of the ordered pairs—that could be considered to represent the set of possible values for these attributes of a company. Equally, you can consider set function H4 to characterize an employee. Note that the definition of H4 uses some of the set specification shorthand that was introduced in Table 2-3.

A set function is called a *characterization* when you use it to describe something in the real world by listing the relevant attributes in combination with the set of admissible values for each attribute. The relevant attributes are the first coordinates of the ordered pairs, and the sets of admissible values are their respective second coordinates.

We'll refer to the first coordinates of the ordered pairs of a characterization as the *attributes* of the characterization, and we'll refer to the second coordinates of the ordered pairs of a characterization as the *attribute value sets* for the attributes of the characterization.

As mentioned earlier, set function H4 can be considered a characterization representing the attributes of an employee. In this case, you'd only be interested in representing each employee's number (attribute empno), name (attribute ename), birth date (attribute born), occupation (attribute job), and salary (attribute salary).

External Predicates

There's another way of looking at characterizations. They can be considered to characterize a predicate in the real world; the characterization introduces the (names of the) parameters of the predicate and the corresponding value sets from which these parameters can take their values. For instance, characterization H4 characterizes the following predicate:

```
Employee ENAME is assigned employee number EMPNO, is born at date BORN,
holds position JOB, and has a monthly salary of SALARY dollars.
```

This predicate has five parameters (ENAME, EMPNO, BORN, JOB, SALARY) that correspond to the five first coordinates in H4. The predicate is a natural language sentence describing the meaning and correlation of the involved attributes. In Part 2 of this book, a characterization will be at the basis of a table design. The predicate characterized by the characterization of a table design represents the user-understood meaning of that table design. Such a predicate is referred to as the *external predicate* of that table.

The Generalized Product of a Set Function

Having introduced set functions, we can now establish the concept of a *generalized product* of a set function (at first sight, frequently considered a complex concept). The generalized product takes a set function as its operand and produces a new *set of functions*.

The generalized product operator is a second key stepping stone, next to the powerset operator that was introduced in Chapter 2. Using these two set operators, we'll be able to construct *value sets* that are usually fairly large, sets of *tuples* (introduced hereafter), sets of *tables* (introduced in Chapter 5), and a set of *database states* (introduced in Chapter 5). In Chapter 7, we'll demonstrate a method that involves defining these value sets as building blocks for a formal specification of a database design.

The generalized product of a set function F, with the notation $\prod(F)$, generates a set with all *possible* functions that have the same domain as F, and for which the ordered pairs (in these functions) have a second coordinate that is *chosen from (that is, is an element of) the relevant set that was attached to the same first coordinate in F*. Definition 4-7 formally defines the generalized product operator.

Definition 4-7: Generalized Product of a Set Function Let F be a set function. The generalized product of F, notation $\prod(F)$, is defined as follows:

$$\prod(F) = \{ f \mid f \text{ is a function} \land \text{dom}(f) = \text{dom}(F) \land (\forall c \in \text{dom}(f): f(c) \in F(c)) \}$$

The last conjunct inside this definition specifies that every function generated by this operator has second coordinates that are elements of the relevant set (second coordinate) in the set function. Listing 4-7 gives a few examples that will quickly illustrate the effect this operator has when you apply it to a set function. Set functions H2 and H3 from the previous section are reused in this listing.

Listing 4-7. *Example Applications of the Generalized Product*

```
Π({ (a;{1,2,3}), (b;{4,5}) }) =
          { {(a;1), (b;4)}
          , {(a;1), (b;5)}
          , {(a;2), (b;4)}
          , {(a;2), (b;5)}
          , {(a;3), (b;4)}
          , {(a;3), (b;5)} }
Π(H2) = { {(X;1), (Z;3)}
          , {(X;1), (Z;4)}
          , {(X;2), (Z;3)}
          , {(X;2), (Z;4)} }
Π(H3) = { {(company;'Natural Join'), (location;'Utrecht')}
          , {(company;'Natural Join'), (location;'Culemborg')}
          , {(company;'Natural Join'), (location;'De Meern')}
          , {(company;'Natural Join'), (location;'Eindhoven')}
          , {(company;'Centraal Boekhuis'), (location;'Utrecht')}
          , {(company;'Centraal Boekhuis'), (location;'Culemborg')}
          , {(company;'Centraal Boekhuis'), (location;'De Meern')}
          , {(company;'Centraal Boekhuis'), (location;'Eindhoven')}
          , {(company;'Remmen & De Brock'), (location;'Utrecht')}
          , {(company;'Remmen & De Brock'), (location;'Culemborg')}
          , {(company;'Remmen & De Brock'), (location;'De Meern')}
          , {(company;'Remmen & De Brock'), (location;'Eindhoven')}
          , {(company;'Oracle'), (location;'Utrecht')}
          , {(company;'Oracle'), (location;'Culemborg')}
          , {(company;'Oracle'), (location;'De Meern')}
          , {(company;'Oracle'), (location;'Eindhoven')} }
```

The first example applies the generalized product to set function $\{(a;\{1,2,3\}),$ $(b;\{4,5\})\}$. Let's call this set function S1. The domain of S1 is $\{a,b\}$. The *set of functions* that results from the application of the generalized product on S1 holds six elements, each of which is a function. The first one enumerated is function $\{(a;1), (b;4)\}$. Let's call this function f1. Function f1 has the same domain as the set function S1:

$$dom(S1) = dom(f1) = \{a,b\}$$

Note also that the following propositions hold: $f1(a) \in S1(a)$ and $f1(b) \in S1(b)$. The first proposition evaluates to $1 \in \{1,2,3\}$, which is true, and the second evaluates to $4 \in \{4,5\}$, which is also true. The conjunction of these two propositions corresponds to the universal quantification in Definition 4-7. In the same way, you can verify that the other five functions listed in the first example comply with Definition 4-7.

The second example holds four functions in the resulting set. Again, you can see that the domain of each of these functions equals $\{X,Z\}$, which is equivalent to $dom(H2)$.

In the third example, the generalized product applied to characterization H3 results in a set of 16 functions. Every function can be considered to represent an actual possible company based on the example characterization for companies, H3.

We'll refer to the functions in the result set of the generalized product of a set function as *tuples*. Note that such set functions will typically signify a characterization. The elements of a tuple—the ordered pairs—are called the *attribute-value pairs* of the tuple. In a relational database design, a tuple represents a proposition in the real world (see the sidebar "Closed World Assumption").

Do you see how the cardinality of the resulting sets in Listing 4-7 can be computed?

```
#∏({ (a;{1,2,3}), (b;{4,5}) }) = #{1,2,3} * #{4,5} = 3 * 2 = 6
#∏(H2) = #H2(X) * #H2(Z) = #{1,2} * #{3,4} = 2 * 2 = 4
#∏(H3) = #H3(company) * #H3(location) = 4 * 4 = 16
```

The cardinality of the generalized product of a set function is equal to the product of the cardinalities of all range elements of the set function.

CLOSED WORLD ASSUMPTION

Every tuple in the result set of the generalized product of a characterization can be considered to denote a proposition in the real world. The proposition denoted by a given tuple is the proposition that is formed by instantiating the external predicate, characterized by the characterization, using the attribute values of the tuple.

For instance, tuple { (empno;100), (ename;'Smith'), (born;'14-feb-1965'), (job;'MANAGER'), (salary;5000) } denotes proposition "Employee Smith is assigned employee number 100, is born at date 14-feb-1965, holds position MANAGER, and has a monthly salary of 5000 dollars."

One of the principles in the relational model for database management is that if a given tuple appears in a table design, then we assume that the proposition denoted by that tuple is currently a true proposition in the real world. The other way around, if a given tuple that could appear in the table design, but currently does not appear, then we assume that the proposition denoted by that tuple is a false proposition in the real world. This principle is referred to as the "Closed World Assumption;" tuples held in a database design describe all, and only, currently true propositions in the real world.

A Preview of Constraint Specification

Recall function H4 defined in Listing 4-6:

```
H4 = { (empno;[1..99])
     , (ename;varchar(10))
     , (born;date)
     , (job; {'CLERK','SALESMAN','TRAINER','MANAGER','PRESIDENT'})
     , (salary;[1000..4999]) }
```

You can consider ∏(H4) as the set that has every *possible* representation of an employee—or instantiation of the external predicate, if you will—based on the attributes and corresponding attribute value sets given by characterization H4. This set holds a lot of tuples, yet it still has a finite cardinality because every range element of set function H4 is a finite set.

■Note For simplicity, we assume that only characters a through z (both lowercase and uppercase) are used for the varchar(n) set shorthand, which gives us 52 characters. The cardinality of date follows from its definition that was given in Table 2-3.

Following are the cardinalities of these range elements:

```
#[1..99] = 99
#varchar(10) = 52¹⁰ + 52⁹ + 52⁸ + ... + 52¹ = 7516865509350965246
#date = 3442447
#{'CLERK','SALESMAN','TRAINER','MANAGER','PRESIDENT'} = 5
#[1000..4999] = 4000
```

In Part 2 we'll develop a variety of value sets that can be considered the type of certain variables. For tuple variables, we won't be interested in the set that holds every *possible* tuple—based on H4—but rather in the set that holds every *admissible* tuple (admissible given certain rules in the real world); this is a certain *subset* of $\prod$(H4). For instance, the following rules may be applicable to employees:

- A CLERK has a salary of less than 2500.

- A PRESIDENT has a salary of more than 4000.

You can define the set of admissible tuples by first creating the set of all possible tuples and then narrowing down this set by specifying the rules (as predicates) to which every tuple should conform. All ingredients for doing so have now been presented. Take a look at the specification of the following set (named t-emp):

$$t\text{-emp} := \{ \ t \ | \ t \in \prod(H4) \ \wedge \ (\ t(job)='CLERK' \ \Rightarrow \ t(salary)<2500 \ )$$
$$\wedge \ (\ t(job)='PRESIDENT' \ \Rightarrow \ t(salary)>4000 \ ) \ \}$$

In this example, we start combining the logic introduced in Chapters 1 and 3 with the set theory introduced in Chapter 2 and this chapter. Set t-emp is a subset of $\prod$(H4); only those (possible) tuples that satisfy the two additional predicates given inside the set specification are in set t-emp. These predicates are the formal representation of the two informally described rules.

Function Composition

One final concept, *function composition*, needs to be introduced before you can finally move on to Part 2 of this book and see the full application of all mathematical concepts introduced in the first four chapters. You can use function composition to *rename attributes* of tuples; this is something you'll occasionally need to apply when using the *join* (to be introduced in Part 2), union, intersection, or difference operators.

Function composition is about applying two functions, serially, one after the other. Given some domain element, you first apply one function that results in a range element. You then apply the second function on this resulting range element. You can find a formal definition for function composition in Definition 4-8.

Definition 4-8: Function Composition Let A, B, and C be sets. Let f be a function over A into B. Let g be a function over rng(f) into C.

The composition of functions f and g, notation g◊f (pronounced as "g of f" or "g after f"), is defined as follows: g◊f := { (a; g(f(a)) | a∈dom(f) ∧ f(a)∈dom(g) }

As you can see from the definition, the composition of two functions results in another set of ordered pairs. In fact, it results in another function because the domain of g◊f is equal to dom(f), and only one pair per domain element of function f is introduced in the composition g after f.

Let's illustrate function composition with an example. Listing 4-8 introduces two functions, f and g, and shows the result of applying g after f (derived in three steps).

Listing 4-8. *Example Functions f and g, and Their Function Composition g After f*

```
f := { (num;empno), (name;ename), (occup;job) }
g := { (empno;999), (ename;'Smith'), (job;'Trainer') }
g◊f = { (num;g(f(num))), (name,g(f(name))), (occup;g(f(occup))) }
    = { (num;g(empno)), (name;g(ename)), (occup;g(job))
    = { (num;999), (name;'Smith'), (occup;'Trainer') }
```

This example specifically shows you how function composition can be employed to rename attributes of a given tuple (in this case function g). In this example, f is the renaming function and g is the tuple for which the attributes get renamed according to f.

The application of the first function (f) performs the renaming of the first coordinates (attribute empno is renamed to num, ename is renamed to name, and job is renamed to occup), and the application of the second function (g) reattaches the second coordinates to the renamed attributes.

Note If the renaming function holds fewer attributes than the tuple whose attributes are being renamed, then in effect, you are at the same time performing a function limitation too. For instance, if f (from Listing 4-8) would be equal to {(num;empno)}, then g◊f results in {(num;999)}.

You can also draw a picture of function composition. Figure 4-3 shows a picture of the function composition of functions f and g, introduced in Listing 4-8.

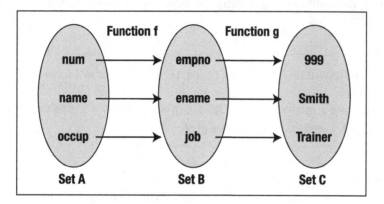

Figure 4-3. *Function composition g◊f*

You can immediately see from this picture that coordinate num maps to range element 999, coordinate name maps to 'Smith', and coordinate occup maps to 'Trainer'.

Chapter Summary

This section provides a summary of this chapter, formatted as a bulleted list. You can use it to check your understanding of the various concepts introduced in this chapter before continuing with the exercises in the next section.

- A *binary relation* from set A to set B is defined as a subset of the Cartesian product A×B. Formally, "R is a binary relation from set A to set B" ⇔ R∈ ℘(A×B).

- A *function* is a binary relation where no first coordinate appears more than once. Formally, "F is a function over A into B" ⇔ F∈ ℘(A×B) ∧ (∀p1,p2∈ F: p1≠p2 ⇒ π_1(p1)≠ π_1(p2)) ∧ { π_1(p) | p∈F } = A.

- The set of all first coordinates of a function F is referred to as the *domain* of function F. The notation is dom(F). Therefore, if F is a function over A into B, then dom(F) = A.

- The set of all second coordinates of a function F is referred to as the *range* of function F. The notation is rng(F). Therefore, if F is a function over A into B, then rng(F) ⊆ B.

- If F is a function and x is an element of dom(F), then F(x) (the application of F to x) denotes the range element that is paired to x in function F.

- Every subset of a function is a function.

- Two functions are *compatible* (or *joinable*) if and only if for every first coordinate that the two functions have in common, the corresponding second coordinates match. Only if two functions are compatible will the union of those two functions be a function.

- The *limitation* of a function F to set A is the subset of F that only holds those ordered pairs for which the first coordinate is an element of set A. The notation is F↓A.

- A *set function* is a function in which every element (an ordered pair) holds a set as its second coordinate.

- If a set function is used to represent the aspects of something in the real world that we want to capture, then we refer to such a set function as a *characterization*. The domain elements of a characterization are called the *attributes* of the characterization. The range elements are called the *attribute value sets* of these attributes.

- The *generalized product* of a set function F, with the notation $\Pi(F)$, generates a set with all possible functions that have the same domain as F, and for which the ordered pairs have a second coordinate that is chosen from the corresponding set attached to the same first coordinate in F.

- The elements in a generalized product of a characterization can be considered to represent propositions in the real world and are referred to as *tuples*.

- The first coordinates of the ordered pairs in a tuple are referred to as the *attributes* of that tuple.

- The *function composition* of two given functions f and g, notation g◊f (g after f), can be used to rename the attributes of a tuple. In this case, f is the renaming function and g is the tuple for which the attributes get renamed according to f.

Exercises

1. How many distinct *binary relations* can be constructed from a given set A with cardinality 3 to a given set B with cardinality 4?

2. How many distinct *functions* can be constructed from a given set A with cardinality 3 to a given set B with cardinality 4?

3. Suppose the following sets are given:

    A := {a, b, c}
    B := {c, d, e, f}

    Which of the following sets are functions from A to B?

    a. { (a;b), (b;d) }

    b. { (c;c), (b;f), (a;f) }

    c. { (a;c), (c;f), (a;c), (b;e) }

    d. { }

    e. { (x;y) | x∈{a,b} ∧ y∈{e,f} ∧ (x=a ⇒ y=f) }

    f. { (c;b), (d;f) }

4. What is the domain of the following functions?

   a. { (X;1), (Y;1) }

   b. { (X;1), (Z;3), (X;1) }

   c. { (empno;100), (ename;'Codd'), (occupation;'mathematician') }

5. What is the range of the following functions?

   a. { (X;1), (Y;3) }

   b. { (X;1), (Y;{1}) }

   c. { (X;∅), (Z;3), (Y;(a;b)) }

   d. { (deptno;50), (dname;'Research'), (location;'London') }

6. Which of the following expressions represent functions?

   a. { (X;1), (Y;3) } ∪ { (X;1), (Z;2), (R;1) }

   b. { (X;1), (Y;3) } ∩ { (X;1), (Y;2), (X;2) }

   c. { (X;1), (Y;3) } ∪ { (X;1), (X;2) }

   d. { (X;1), (Y;2) } ∩ { (X;1), (Y;2), (X;2) }↓{Y}

   e. { p | p∈{X,Y}×{1,2} ∧ (π_1(p)=Y ⇒ π_2(p)=2) }↓{Y}

7. Give the result sets for the following expressions using the enumerative method:

   a. Π{ (a;{1}), (b;{1,2}) }

   b. Π{ (a;{1,2,3,4}), (b;{5,6,7,8}), (d;∅), (e;{9,10}) }

   c. { t | t∈Π{(a;{1,2,3,4}), (b;{5,6,7,8})} ∧ t(a)+t(b)<8 }

   d. { f | f∈Π{(X;{1,2}), (Y;{1,2,3})} ∧ #rng(f)=1 }

8. Given the following function

   f := { (ean;9786012), (descr;'A very nice book')
       , (price;24.99), (category;A) }

   Provide the result sets for these expressions:

   a. f↓{ean,price}

   b. f↓dom(f)

   c. f↓{descr}

   d. f↓{description}

   e. rng(f↓{ean,price,category})

9. Given the following characterization

```
F := { (ean;num(7,0))
     , (descr;varchar(10))
     , (price;[1..99])
     , (stock;[0..10])
     , (category;{A,B,C}) }
```

Which of the following tuples is an element of set $\Pi(F)$?

a. `{ (ean;123), (stock;9), (category;C), (descr;'Nice article'), (price;10) }`

b. `{ (price;1), (category;A), (stock;11), (descr;'Fine book') (ean;987403) }`

c. `{ (ean;4572), (descr;'Book 4572'), (price;79), (stock;4), (category;A) }`

d. `{ (ean;4572), (descr;'Book 4572'), (stock;6), (price;0) }`

Give the result for the following expressions:

e. `#F`

f. `F↓{price,stock}`

g. `F(stock)×F(category)`

10. Given the following two functions

```
f := { (empno;103), (ename;'Tedesco'), (deptno;11) }
g := { (eno;103), (ename;'Tedesco'), (dno;11) }
```

Specify function h that renames the empno attribute in f to eno and the deptno attribute to dno. Formally, specify function h such that `(f◊h) = g`.

11. Given the following sets

```
E := { { (empno;103), (ename;'Tedesco'), (mgrno;104), (deptno;10) }
     ,{ (empno;104), (ename;'Rhodes'), (mgrno;106), (deptno;10) }
     ,{ (empno;105), (ename;'Sparks'), (mgrno;106), (deptno;20) }
     ,{ (empno;106), (ename;'Weiss'), (mgrno;102), (deptno;10) } }
D := { { (deptno;10), (dname;'Gaming') }
     ,{ (deptno;20), (dname;'Sales') }
     ,{ (deptno;30), (dname;'Research') } }
f := { (empno;mgrno) }
```

Investigate the truth value of these two propositions:

a. `{ e◊f | e ∈ E} = { e↓{empno} | e ∈ E }`

b. `{ e↓{deptno} | e ∈ E } ⊂ { d↓{deptno} | d ∈ D }`

PART 2

■■■

The Application

You have reached the part of the book where the mathematical foundation laid down in the first four chapters will be applied. In particular, you'll see how this can be applied to *specify database designs*.

Chapter 5 will start with some important stepping stones. We'll familiarize you with how to formally specify a *table* and a *database state*. This chapter will also formally introduce you to the most common table operators: *union, intersection, difference, projection, restriction, join, attribute renaming, extension,* and *aggregation*.

Chapter 6 will introduce you to the concepts of *tuple, table,* and *database predicates*. We'll use these types of predicates to specify the *data integrity constraints* of a database design. This chapter will also explore some predicate *patterns* that often play a role in database designs.

Chapter 7 builds on the previous two chapters and introduces a formal methodology to fully specify a database design. Such a specification is referred to as a *database universe*. This methodology was originally developed in the 1980s jointly by Bert De Brock and Frans Remmen at the Computer Science department of the Eindhoven University of Technology. We'll define an extensive example database design using this methodology.

Chapter 8 introduces you to the concept of a *transaction universe*. You can use this concept to further specify the semantics of a database design. A database universe holds the majority of constraints involved in a database design: *static constraints*. A transaction universe allows you to specify a different class of constraints referred to as *dynamic constraints*; they limit the transactions allowed on grounds other than the static constraints.

Chapter 9 deals with data retrieval. By means of a *query*, you retrieve data from a database. We'll introduce you to a formal way of specifying a query. This chapter will also be the first chapter that employs SQL to demonstrate the application of the mathematics introduced in this book further, by giving lots of examples.

Chapter 10 introduces a formal way of specifying a *transaction*. Like Chapter 9, it gives various examples to demonstrate this, both formally and by using SQL expressions.

CHAPTER 5

Tables and Database States

From this chapter onward we'll assume that you're thoroughly familiar with all terminology introduced in Part 1 of this book. Only if we deem it necessary will we make explicit references back to where specific terminology was first introduced and defined.

We'll start with an introduction of various interrelated terms that are used in this chapter and the other chapters of Part 2 that follow.

In Part 1 we hinted that a table can be considered a set of functions. In this chapter we'll demonstrate this in detail. The section "Formal Specification of a Table" shows how you can formally represent a *table*. It also introduces a *shorthand notation* for a table and defines what's called the *heading* of a table. We'll familiarize you with a method to formally specify— in a predicative way—a table given a characterization. You already saw a preview of this in Chapter 4.

The section "Database States" deals with formally specifying a *database state*. The database state that is the current value of the database variable holds all tables of a database. This section also defines the concept of a *database skeleton*.

The section "Operations on Tables" discusses various common table operators: *union, intersection, difference, projection, restriction, join, attribute renaming, extension,* and *aggregation*. These operators take tables as their operands and produce another table.

You'll find a "Chapter Summary" at the end, followed by an "Exercises" section.

Terminology

This section introduces various interrelated terms that we'll use in the chapters of Part 2. Because some of these terms might have a meaning to you that differs from the one we intend to use in this book, or because some of these terms are new to you, we decided to introduce them here in advance. This introduction is informal. Two of these terms (*database design* and *table design*) were already used in Chapter 4. Some of the terms are formal terms; we'll specify these precisely in this part of the book.

Note You might find the informal introduction of some of these terms somewhat vague. If so, then don't worry about it now. Just start reading the chapters of Part 2 and revisit this informal introduction of the terms later.

Database Design

Database design is the informal term for the blueprint of a set of data structures that are used to store business data, including the integrity requirements of this data. In this book, these blueprints will always be relational designs; they will conform to the relational model of data. Among other things, this implies that the aforementioned data structures are *table data structures*; that is, the data is stored via *tables* (using the meaning of a *table* as introduced hereafter).

We'll often use a business term to indicate what particular database design we're talking about; for instance, the HR (human resources) database design, or the education department database design.

Note The other meaning often attributed to database design is the *process* of developing such a blueprint. This process includes activities such as requirements analysis, conceptual database design, logical database design, and physical database design. Using this other meaning, you can say that this book refers to a database design as the end result of the logical database design (process). In Part 3 (Chapter 11) we'll look into the physical database design using an SQL DBMS.

Database Variable

Database variable is an implementation term. It is a variable (that is, a holder for a value) that is capable of storing actual values for the data structures described by a *database design*. In Chapter 7 we'll provide a mathematical treatment of the type of—or value set for—a database variable. This value set is referred to as the *database universe*. At any given point in time and space, a database variable will hold an element of this value set as its current value. The elements of a *database universe* are referred to as *database states*. Note that a database consists of exactly one *database variable*. In a sense, that variable *is* the database.

Like every variable, the *database variable* will have a name, allowing us to talk about it without knowing which database state it currently holds.

Note An SQL DBMS does not supply the concept of a database variable. Instead, SQL DBMS vendors have implemented the concept of table variables. A table variable can hold a table as its value; in an SQL DBMS you create one through the `create table` statement. In these DBMSes, a database design is implemented by creating as many table variables as the database design has table structures, and defining their respective types (instead of defining just one database variable and defining its type).

Database Universe

Database universe is a formal term. It is the mathematical construct used to formally specify the *table data structures* and integrity requirements of a *database design*. A *database universe* is the main part of the formal specification of a *database design*; it precisely describes the data values (tables) that we allow to be stored by the *table data structures*. Chapter 7 will establish the formal definition of a *database universe*; for now just think of it as a set of all values that we allow for a given *database variable* to hold over the course of time.

We'll often use a shorthand name for a given *database universe* (just symbols) for convenience of reference in the text.

Database State

Database state is a formal term. It is a mathematical construct used to formally specify a value that can be held by a *database variable*. This chapter will establish the formal definition of a *database state*. We'll often use a shorthand name for a given *database state* for convenience of reference in the text.

Database

Database is an informal term for the actual (business) data that is stored in a computer in a structured way (that is, conforming to the database design). Abstractly, a *database* is the current value of the *database variable*; it is the informal term for *database state*.

Database Management System (DBMS)

A *DBMS* is a computer program used to manage, query, and update the value of a *database variable*.

Table Design

Table design is the informal term for the blueprint of one of the *table data structures* of a *database design*. A relational *database design* typically consists of several *table designs* and a set of constraints (see Chapter 7) addressing the integrity requirements for the database. It is often convenient to talk about a single *table design*, and for this reason we'll use a business term to indicate what particular *table design* we're talking about; for instance, the employee *table design*, or the department *table design*.

Table Structure

Table structure, short for *table data structure*, is an implementation term. It is used to refer to the data structure that implements a specific *table design*. As mentioned before in the implementation of a *database design*, you are accustomed to using SQL table variables to implement the separate *table data structures*. You could regard a *table structure* as a table variable. However, we deliberately do not use the term table variable in this book; the methodology developed in this book only knows the concept of a *database variable*. A *table structure* can be considered a specific subsection of the *database variable*: the subsection that holds the current *table* for only one of the involved *table designs*.

In Chapter 10 we'll discuss a formal way of specifying updates (value changes) of a *database variable*; we consider updating just one of the *table structures* of a database as an update of the *database variable*. However, when explaining our formal methodology we'll often conveniently use the term *table structure* as if it were a separately addressable (table) variable, and we'll even give such a *table data structure* a name—as we would give a name to a table variable—enabling us to talk about it without knowing which value is currently held by the data structure.

Table

Table is a formal term. It is a mathematical construct used to formally specify a value that can be held by a *table structure* that implements a specific *table design* (or if you will, a value that can be held by a table variable). We'll formally establish this term in the next section. We'll often use a shorthand name for a given *table* for convenience of reference in the text.

Tables

In Chapter 4 you saw that you can use a tuple (a set of ordered pairs) to describe a true proposition in the real world. For instance, the tuple { (empno;100), (ename;'Smith'), (job;'MANAGER') } might represent this proposition: "Employee with number 100 has name Smith and is employed as a MANAGER." In this section we'll build on this use of tuples and introduce you to a formal way of specifying a table.

Formal Specification of a Table

A table represents many (zero or more) true propositions of the same kind. If you can use a tuple to represent a single proposition, then evidently a table can be regarded as a *set of tuples*. Take a look at the set of tuples, which we have named T1, in Listing 5-1.

Listing 5-1. *A Set of Tuples*

```
T1 :=
{ { (partno;1), (name;'hammer'),      (instock;22), (price;10) }
 ,{ (partno;2), (name;'screwdriver'), (instock;19), (price;5)  }
 ,{ (partno;3), (name;'axe'),         (instock;0),  (price;30) }
 ,{ (partno;4), (name;'saw'),         (instock;4),  (price;15) }
 ,{ (partno;5), (name;'wrench'),      (instock;7),  (price;20) }
 ,{ (partno;6), (name;'scissors'),    (instock;32), (price;5)  } }
```

Set T1 contains six tuples; in other words, six functions (recall that a tuple can be regarded as a function). All six functions have the same domain: {partno,name,instock,price}. We'll refer to a set of functions that all share the same domain as a *table*.

The tuples in T1 represent six propositions. They can be regarded as instantiations of the following external predicate, for instance: "The part with part number partno is named name, instock items of it are currently held in stock, and its price is price."

■Note The English word "table" here is being used in a different sense than its normal meaning (two-dimensional picture of columns and rows). In this book we'll use *table* to denote a set of functions. However, you'll see that a table is usually *represented* in columns and rows.

Definition 5-1 describes the concept of a *table* in a formal way. It uses the concept of "a function over a given set" (see Definition 4-2).

■**Definition 5-1: Table** If T and H are sets, then "T is a table over H" ⇔ (∀t∈T: t is a function over H).

This definition is generic in the sense that no restrictions are imposed upon the elements of set H. However, in practice we'll only be interested in those cases where H is a set of names representing attributes.

Table T1 can be considered a *parts table*. It is a table over {partno,name,instock,price}, consisting of six tuples, each representing information about a different part. It holds for each such part the part number, its name, how many items of the part are in stock, and the price of the part.

Here are a few more examples:

```
T2 := { { (X;2), (Y;1) }, { (Y;8), (X;0) }, { (Y;10), (X;5) } }
T3 := { { (partno;3), (name;'hammer') }, { (pno;4), (pname;'nail') } }
T4 := { { (empno;105), (ename;'Mrs. Sparks'), (born;'03-apr-1970') }
       ,{ (empno;202), (ename;'Mr. Tedesco') } }
```

T2 is indeed a table. It holds three functions, all of which share the domain {X,Y}. It is a table over {X,Y}. Note that the order of the pairs (inside the functions) doesn't matter. T3 is not a table. It is a set of functions; however, the domain of the first function is {partno,name}, which differs from the domain of the second function: {pno,pname}. Likewise, T4 is also not a table. It is a set of functions; however, the domain of the first function is {empno, ename, born}, which differs from the domain of the second function: {empno,ename}.

An element of a table is a function, and each such function is referred to specifically as a *tuple*. In Chapter 4 you were introduced to this term when we introduced the generalized product of a characterization (see the section "The Generalized Product of a Set Function"). The generalized product of a characterization is in fact a table; it holds functions, all of which share the same domain.

A table is a set, and the elements of this set are tuples. By the definition of a set, this implies that every tuple is unique within that set; no tuple can appear more than once in the same table.

If T is a table over H, then every proper, non-empty subset of T (containing fewer tuples than T) is of course also a table over H.

Even the empty set (∅) is a table. In fact, under Definition 5-1 (which quantifies over the elements in the table), the empty set is a table *over any set*. You might want to revisit the rewrite rules in Table 3-2 for this.

■**Note** The empty set is often used as the initial state for a given table structure.

Shorthand Notation

Writing down a table using the formal enumerative method as introduced in Listing 5-1 is quite elaborate. For every tuple that's an element of the table, you're essentially repeating the (shared) domain as the first coordinates of the ordered pairs. To avoid this repetition, it's common to draw a picture of a table. In this picture you list the names of the attributes of the tuples only once (as column headers) and under those you then list the attribute values for every tuple (one per row). Figure 5-1 shows this shorthand notation of a *table*. It does so for table T1 introduced in Listing 5-1.

partno	name	instock	price
1	'hammer'	22	10
2	'screwdriver'	19	5
3	'axe'	0	30
4	'saw'	4	15
5	'wrench'	7	20
6	'scissors'	32	5

Figure 5-1. *Shorthand notation for table T1*

As you can see, this looks like a table in *the common language sense* (a two-dimensional picture of columns and rows). But remember, a *table*—in this book—is a set of functions. This has two important implications. First, this means that the order in which functions are enumerated is arbitrary; it does not matter. And second, the order in which the ordered pairs are enumerated (within a tuple) does not matter either. Therefore, in the preceding shorthand notation, the order of the column headers (left to right) and the order of the rows (top to bottom) don't matter.

Note In the shorthand notation, an ordering to the attributes has been introduced because the order of attribute values in each tuple now has to correspond to the ordering of the column headings.

The shorthand notation demonstrates some other terminology that is often used when dealing with tables. As you can see, table T1 is a table over {partno,name,instock,price}. This shared domain of the tuples in T1 is referred to as the *heading* of table T1 (see Definition 5-2).

Definition 5-2: Heading of a Table   If "T is a table over H" then H is referred to as the heading of T.

We'll often use the shorthand notation in the remainder of this book to illustrate a particular table. However, you should never forget that it is only a shorthand notation. In this book, a table is formally defined as a set of functions, all of which share the same domain.

This formal definition of a table enables you to deal with operations on tables (later in this chapter) and data integrity predicates (discussed in the next chapter) in a clear and formal way too.

Table Construction

You can construct a table from a given set function by applying the generalized product to it. Let's demonstrate this with an example. Listing 5-2 displays a set function called F1.

Listing 5-2. *Set Function F1*

```
F1 := { (X; {0,1,2})
       ,(Y; {0,1,2})
       ,(Z; {-1,0,1}) }
```

The generalized product of set function F1 will result in a set of twenty-seven functions (three times three times three). Listing 5-3 shows this result.

Listing 5-3. *The Generalized Product of Set Function F1*

```
∏(F1) :=
    { { (X;0), (Y;0), (Z;-1) }, { (X;0), (Y;0), (Z;0) }, { (X;0), (Y;0), (Z;1) }
    , { (X;0), (Y;1), (Z;-1) }, { (X;0), (Y;1), (Z;0) }, { (X;0), (Y;1), (Z;1) }
    , { (X;0), (Y;2), (Z;-1) }, { (X;0), (Y;2), (Z;0) }, { (X;0), (Y;2), (Z;1) }
    , { (X;1), (Y;0), (Z;-1) }, { (X;1), (Y;0), (Z;0) }, { (X;1), (Y;0), (Z;1) }
    , { (X;1), (Y;1), (Z;-1) }, { (X;1), (Y;1), (Z;0) }, { (X;1), (Y;1), (Z;1) }
    , { (X;1), (Y;2), (Z;-1) }, { (X;1), (Y;2), (Z;0) }, { (X;1), (Y;2), (Z;1) }
    , { (X;2), (Y;0), (Z;-1) }, { (X;2), (Y;0), (Z;0) }, { (X;2), (Y;0), (Z;1) }
    , { (X;2), (Y;1), (Z;-1) }, { (X;2), (Y;1), (Z;0) }, { (X;2), (Y;1), (Z;1) }
    , { (X;2), (Y;2), (Z;-1) }, { (X;2), (Y;2), (Z;0) }, { (X;2), (Y;2), (Z;1) } }
```

In this result set, every function has the same domain {X,Y,Z}; the result set is therefore a table over {X,Y,Z}. Now take a look at the following, more realistic, example. Listing 5-4 shows a characterization of a part. For a part, the attributes of interest are the number of the part (partno), its name (name), the quantity in stock of this part (instock), and the part's price (price).

Listing 5-4. *Characterization of a Part*

```
chr_PART := { (partno;   [1..999])
             ,(name;     varchar(12))
             ,(instock;  [0..99])
             ,(price;    [1..500]) }
```

The generalized product of chr_PART is a rather large table; it contains all *possible* tuples that can be generated using the given attribute-value sets that are introduced in the definition of chr_PART. Note that every tuple inside table T1—introduced at the beginning of this chapter—is an element of $\prod$(chr_PART). This makes T1 a subset of $\prod$(chr_PART).

Note Every subset of $\prod$(chr_PART)—not just T1—is a table over {partno,name,instock,price}.

In fact, every tuple in table T1 is an element of the following set (named T2) that is based on $\prod$(chr_PART):

$$T2 := \{ \ t \ | \ t \in \prod(chr\_PART) \ \wedge \ (\ t(price) \geq 20 \Rightarrow t(instock) \leq 10 \ )$$
$$\wedge \ (\ t(price) \leq 5 \Rightarrow t(instock) \geq 15 \ )$$
$$\}$$

Inside the definition of T2, two predicates are introduced that condition the contents of T2. The first condition states that if the price of a part is 20 or more, then the quantity in stock for this part should be 10 or less. The second condition states that if the price of a part is 5 or less, then the quantity in stock for this part should be 15 or more. T2—a table over {partno,name,instock,price}—will hold all and only those tuples of $\prod$(chr_PART) for which both these two conditions are true. Note that because $\prod$(chr_PART) will hold many tuples that violate one or both of these conditions, T2 is a proper subset of $\prod$(chr_PART). Because all tuples of T1 conform to these two conditions, T1 is a subset of T2. In fact, it is a proper subset of T2.

In Chapter 7 we'll revisit this way of defining T2; that is, taking the generalized product of a characterization and "plugging in" additional predicates.

Database States

A database is a representation of the state of affairs of some organization. It consists of a table for every kind of proposition about this organization that we would like to record in the database. This section introduces you to a formal way of specifying a database via a *database state*.

Formal Representation of a Database State

Let's consider a simple database design involving two table structures: one for employees and one for departments. Take a look at tables EMP1 and DEP1, which are displayed in Figures 5-2 and 5-3.

empno	ename	job	sal	deptno
101	'Chris'	'MANAGER'	7900	10
102	'Kathy'	'TRAINER'	6000	12
103	'Thomas'	'CLERK'	2100	10
104	'David'	'TRAINER'	5600	10
105	'Renu'	'CLERK'	3000	12
106	'Bob'	'MANAGER'	8500	10
107	'Sue'	'CLERK'	2700	12

Figure 5-2. *Example employee table EMP1*

deptno	dname	loc	salbudget
10	'RESEARCH'	'DENVER'	50000
11	'SALES'	'DENVER'	20000
12	'SUPPORT'	'LOS ANGELES'	40000
13	'SALES'	'SAN FRANCISCO'	20000

Figure 5-3. *Example department table DEP1*

Let's assume that tables EMP1 and DEP1 represent the current state of the employee and department table structures, respectively. We can formally specify the *database state* consisting of tables EMP1 and DEP1 as a function. In this function, the first coordinates of the ordered pairs represent the table structure *names* and the second coordinates hold the (current) *values*—tables EMP1 and DEP1—for these table structures. Listing 5-5 gives the formal specification of this example database state.

Listing 5-5. *The Database State DBS1 Holding Tables EMP1 and DEP1*

```
DBS1 :=
  { (EMPLOYEE;
    { {(empno;101),(ename;'Chris'), (job;'MANAGER'),(sal;7900),(deptno;10)}
     ,{(empno;102),(ename;'Kathy'), (job;'TRAINER'),(sal;6000),(deptno;12)}
     ,{(empno;103),(ename;'Thomas'),(job;'CLERK'),  (sal;2100),(deptno;10)}
     ,{(empno;104),(ename;'David'), (job;'TRAINER'),(sal;5600),(deptno;10)}
     ,{(empno;105),(ename;'Renu'),  (job;'CLERK'),  (sal;3000),(deptno;12)}
     ,{(empno;106),(ename;'Bob'),   (job;'MANAGER'),(sal;8500),(deptno;10)}
     ,{(empno;107),(ename;'Sue'),   (job;'CLERK'),  (sal;2700),(deptno;12)} }
```

```
        )
        ,(DEPARTMENT;
          { {(deptno;10),(dname;'RESEARCH'),(loc;'DENVER'),        (salbudget;50000)}
          ,{(deptno;11),(dname;'SALES'),    (loc;'DENVER'),        (salbudget;20000)}
          ,{(deptno;12),(dname;'SUPPORT'),  (loc;'LOS ANGELES'),   (salbudget;40000)}
          ,{(deptno;13),(dname;'SALES'),    (loc;'SAN FRANCISCO'),(salbudget;20000)} }
        )
    }
```

Note We could have also listed DBS1 to equal the set {(EMPLOYEE;EMP1), (DEPARTMENT;DEP1)}.

Database state DBS1 is a function containing just two ordered pairs. The first coordinate of the first ordered pair listed is EMPLOYEE (the name we chose for the employee table structure), and the corresponding second coordinate is table EMP1. Likewise, in the second ordered pair you'll notice that we chose DEPARTMENT as the name for the department table structure. In this case, the second coordinate is table DEP1.

Given this definition of function DBS1, you can now—using function application—refer to expressions such as DBS1(EMPLOYEE), which denotes table EMP1, and DBS1(DEPARTMENT), which denotes table DEP1.

Database Skeleton

To specify a database state, you not only need actual tables (EMP1 and DEP1 in the preceding example), but you also need to decide upon *names* for the table structures (EMPLOYEE and DEPARTMENT in the preceding example).

You probably won't be surprised by now that the formal specification of a database design (which we'll demonstrate in Chapter 7) also holds the specification of a characterization for every table design involved. You choose the names of the attributes involved in a table design when you specify the characterization for that table design.

A *database skeleton* collects all these names—for the table structures and the involved attributes—into a single formal structure. A database skeleton is a set function with an ordered pair for every table structure. Every first coordinate introduces the table structure name, and the second coordinate introduces the set of names of the involved attributes.

Listing 5-6 displays the database skeleton for the employee/department database design introduced in the previous section.

Listing 5-6. *The Database Skeleton SK1*

```
SK1 :=
  { (EMPLOYEE;   {empno,ename,job,sal,deptno} )
   ,(DEPARTMENT; {deptno,dname,loc,salbudget} ) }
```

As you can see, set function SK1 introduces the names EMPLOYEE and DEPARTMENT for the table structures involved in the employee/department database design, and it attaches the set of names of the relevant attributes to them.

Note You should carefully choose the names introduced by the database skeleton, because they not only constitute the vocabulary between you (the database professional) and your customer (the users), they are also the first stepping stone to understanding the meaning (semantics) of a database design. You'll see in the following chapters that data integrity constraints form a further important stepping stone for the understanding of the semantics of the database design.

Operations on Tables

This section covers some important table operators. *You will apply these operators when specifying queries and transactions (Chapters 9 and 10), or certain types of predicates (Chapters 6, 7, and 8).*

We'll first take a look at the well-known set operators *union, intersection,* and *difference.* Next we'll investigate the *projection* and *restriction* of a table, followed by the *join*—an important operator in the database field—and closely related to the join, the *attribute renaming* operator. Finally, we'll deal with *extension* and *aggregation.*

Union, Intersection, and Difference

Because tables are sets, you can apply the well-known set operators, union, intersection, and difference, with tables as their operands. This section will explore the application of these set operators on tables.

We'll use three example tables, named E1, E2, and E3, in the following sections. Figure 5-4 displays these tables.

E1

EMPNO	ENAME	JOB
101	Anne	TRAINER
102	Thomas	SALESMAN
103	Lucas	PRESIDENT

E2

EMPNO	ENAME	JOB
102	Thomas	SALESMAN
104	Pete	MANAGER

E3

E#	NAME	JOB	SAL
101	Anne	TRAINER	3000
102	John	MANAGER	5000

Figure 5-4. *Example tables E1, E2, and E3*

As you can see, E1 and E2 are both tables over {EMPNO,ENAME,JOB}, and E3 is a table over {E#,NAME,JOB,SAL}. All three tables represent information about employees. For E3, some of the names of the attributes were chosen differently, and E3 holds additional information (the salary). Employee 102 occurs in both table E1 and table E2 (with the same attribute values). Employee 101 occurs in both table E1 and table E3.

Union

As you probably know, the union of two sets holds all objects that are either an element of the first set, or an element of the second set, or an element of both. Here is the union of tables E1 and E2, denoted by E1∪E2:

```
E1∪E2 =
    { {(EMPNO;101), (ENAME;'Anne'),   (JOB;'TRAINER')  }
    ,{(EMPNO;102), (ENAME;'Thomas'), (JOB;'SALESMAN') }
    ,{(EMPNO;103), (ENAME;'Lucas'),  (JOB;'PRESIDENT')}
    ,{(EMPNO;104), (ENAME;'Pete'),   (JOB;'MANAGER')  } }
```

The union of E1 and E2 is a table over {EMPNO,ENAME,JOB}. It holds four tuples, not five, because the tuple of employee 102 is a member of both sets.

Now take a look at the union of tables E1 and E3 (E1∪E3):

```
E1∪E3 =
    { {(EMPNO;101), (ENAME;'Anne'),   (JOB;'TRAINER')              }
    ,{(EMPNO;102), (ENAME;'Thomas'), (JOB;'SALESMAN')             }
    ,{(EMPNO;103), (ENAME;'Lucas'),  (JOB;'PRESIDENT')            }
    ,{(E#;101),    (NAME;'Anne'),    (JOB;'TRAINER'),  (SAL;3000)}
    ,{(E#;102),    (NAME;'John'),    (JOB;'MANAGER'),  (SAL;5000)} }
```

This result is a set of functions, but it clearly isn't a table; not all the functions in this result set share the same domain.

Remember the closure property (in the section "Union, Intersection, and Difference" in Chapter 2)? We're only interested in those cases where the union of two tables results in another table. The union operator is evidently not closed over tables in general. It's only closed over tables if the operands are tables *that have the same heading*. If the operands of the union operator are non-empty tables over different headings, then the resulting set won't be a table.

Note the special case where the empty table is involved as an operand. The union of a given table with the empty table (∅) always results in the given table; because ∅ is a table over any heading, the closure property holds.

Intersection

The intersection of two sets holds all objects that are an element of the first set *and* an element of the second set. Here's the intersection of tables E1 and E2 (E1∩E2):

```
E1∩E2 = { {(EMPNO;102), (ENAME;'Thomas'), (JOB;'SALESMAN')} }
```

The intersection of E1 and E2 is a table. It's probably not difficult to see that the intersection of two tables with the same heading will always result in another table. Note that the intersection is also closed over tables when the operands are tables over *different* headings.

However, the intersection is useless in these cases, because it then always results in the empty table; you might want to check this by investigating the intersection of E1 and E3 (tables with different headings).

You can meaningfully intersect tables E1 and (part of) E3, but first you'd have to *transform* one of these in such a way that it has the same heading as the other table. The concepts that enable you to do so have all been introduced in Chapter 4: function limitation and function composition.

Take a look at the following definition for table E4. It renames attributes E# and NAME of table E3.

```
E4 := { e◊{(EMPNO;E#),(ENAME;NAME),(JOB;JOB),(SAL;SAL)} | e∈E3 }
```

Set E4 is a table over {EMPNO,ENAME,JOB,SAL}. We used function composition (◊; see Definition 4-8) to rename two attributes. Attribute E# is renamed to EMPNO and attribute NAME is renamed to ENAME. The other two attributes (JOB and SAL) are left untouched.

Next we need to get rid of the extra SAL attribute (which is also not part of the heading of E1). For this we use function limitation (↓, see Definition 4-4). Take a look at the definition of E5:

```
E5 := { e↓{EMPNO,ENAME,JOB} | e∈E4 }
```

E5 equals the following set:

```
{ {(EMPNO;101), (ENAME;'Anne'), (JOB;'TRAINER')}
 ,{(EMPNO;102), (ENAME;'John'), (JOB;'MANAGER')} }
```

The intersection of E5 with E1 has now become meaningful, and results in the following set:

```
E5∩E1 = { {(EMPNO;101), (ENAME;'Anne'), (JOB;'TRAINER')} }
```

Last, we note the special case where the empty table is involved as an operand. The intersection of a given table with the empty table always results in the empty table.

Difference

The difference of two sets holds all objects that are an element of the first set and that are *not* an element of the second set. Here is the difference of tables E1 and E2 (E1–E2):

```
E1–E2 =
    { {(EMPNO;101), (ENAME;'Anne'),   (JOB;'TRAINER')  }
     ,{(EMPNO;103), (ENAME;'Lucas'),  (JOB;'PRESIDENT')} }
```

Again, as you can see, the result is a table over {EMPNO,ENAME,JOB}. The difference of two tables with the same heading always produces another table. Like the intersection, the difference operator is also closed over tables when the operands are tables over *different* sets. However, here too, in these cases the difference is useless because it always results in the first table; the second table cannot have tuples that are in the first table (due to the different headings). Hence, tuples will never be "removed" from the first set.

Because the difference operator is not commutative, we note the two special cases when the empty set is involved as an operand (in contrast with the preceding intersection and union). Let T be a given table; then T–∅ always results in a given table T, and ∅–T always results in the empty table.

Projection

Another important table operator that needs to be introduced is the *projection* of a table on a given set. The projection of a given table—say T—on a given set—say B—performs the *limitation* of every tuple in T on set B. We use symbol ⇓ to denote projection. The projection operator can be viewed as a version of the limitation operator that has been lifted to the table level. Definition 5-3 formally defines this operator.

■Definition 5-3: Projection of a Table Let T be a set of functions and B a set. The projection of T on B, notation T⇓B, is defined as follows:

T⇓B := { t↓B | t∈T }

The projection of T on B holds every function in T limited to B. Although the preceding definition describes the projection for each set of functions T and each set B, we are mainly (but not exclusively) interested in those cases in which T is a table, and moreover in which B is a (non-empty) proper subset of the heading of such a table.

Let's take a look at an example to illustrate the concept of projection. Listing 5-7 introduces table T3. It holds five tuples with domain {empno,ename,salary,sex,dno}.

Listing 5-7. *Table T3*

```
T3 := { {(empno;10), (ename;'Thomas'),    (salary;2400), (sex;'male'),   (dno;1)}
       ,{(empno;20), (ename;'Lucas'),     (salary;3000), (sex;'male'),   (dno;1)}
       ,{(empno;30), (ename;'Aidan'),     (salary;3000), (sex;'male'),   (dno;2)}
       ,{(empno;40), (ename;'Keeler'),    (salary;2400), (sex;'male'),   (dno;1)}
       ,{(empno;50), (ename;'Elizabeth'), (salary;5600), (sex;'female'), (dno;2)} }
```

Here's the result of the projection of T3 on {salary,sex}, denoted by T3⇓{salary,sex}:

```
T3⇓{salary,sex} =
    { {(salary;2400), (sex;'male')}
    , {(salary;3000), (sex;'male')}
    , {(salary;5600), (sex;'female')} }
```

Note that the projection of T3 on {salary,sex} results in another table: a table over {salary,sex}. This table has only three elements, whereas T3 has five elements. The first and the fourth tuple enumerated in the definition of T3 result in the same (limited) function, as do the second and the third function enumerated in T3. Therefore, only three tuples remain in the resulting set of this projection.

You can now specify E5 introduced in the section "Intersection" with E4⇓{EMPNO,ENAME,JOB}.

Restriction

Tables typically hold many tuples. Often you're only interested in some of these tuples: tuples that have a certain property. You want to look at a *subset* of the tuples in the given table. You can derive a subset of a given table through *table restriction*. This operator does not require a new mathematical symbol; you can simply use the predicative method to specify a new set of tuples (that is, a new table) that's based on the given table.

Using the employee table T3 from Listing 5-7, let's assume you want to restrict that table to only male employees who have a salary greater than 2500. Here is how you would specify that (we have named this result T4):

T4 := { e | e∈T3 ∧ e(sex)='male' ∧ e(salary)>2500 }

Table T4 has two tuples: the ones representing employees 'Lucas' and 'Aidan', who are the only male employees in T3 that earn more than 2500.

The specification of T4 is an example of a simple case of table restriction, and one you will use a lot. Here is the general pattern for this kind of restriction:

{ t | t∈T ∧ P(t) }

In this expression, T represents the table that is being restricted and P(t) represents a predicate with one parameter of some tuple type. Predicate P can be a simple predicate or a compound predicate (that is, one that involves logical connectives). This predicate will typically have expressions that involve function application using argument t; for each tuple of T you can decide if it remains in the result set by inspecting one or more attribute values of (only) that tuple.

Restrictions of a table can be a bit more complex. For instance, let's assume that we want to restrict table T3 to only the male employee who earns the most (among all males) and the female employee who earns the most (among all females). A way to specify this restriction of T3, which we will name T5, is as follows:

T5 := { e | e∈T3 ∧ ¬(∃e2∈T3: e2(sex)=e(sex) ∧ e2(sal)>e(sal)) }

Table T5 will have every tuple (say e) of T3 for which there is no other tuple in T3 (say e2), such that e and e2 match on the sex attribute, and the sal value in e2 is greater than the sal value in e. Note that this particular restriction actually results in a table of three tuples; there are two male employees in T3 who both earn the most.

This more complex case of restricting a table conforms to another pattern that is often applied. Here is the general pattern for this kind of restriction:

{ t | t∈T ∧ P(t,T) }

In this pattern, P(t,T) represents a predicate with two parameters. The first parameter takes as a value a tuple from table T, and the second one takes as a value the actual table T. For each tuple of T, you decide if it remains in the result set, not only by inspecting one or more attribute values of that tuple, but also by inspecting other tuples in the same table.

Restrictions can also involve other tables (other than the table being restricted). Say we have a table named D1 over {dno,dname,loc}, representing a department table (with the obvious semantics). Let's assume that we want to restrict table T3 to only the male employees who earn more than 2500 and who are employed in a department that is known in D1 and located in San Francisco ('SF'). A way to specify this restriction of T3 is as follows:

{ e | e∈T3 ∧ e(sex)='male' ∧ e(sal)>2500 ∧
        (∃d∈D1: e(dno)=d(dno) ∧ d(loc)='SF') }

This case of restricting a table conforms to the following pattern:

$$\{ \ t \ | \ t \in T \ \wedge \ P(t,S) \ \}$$

Here S represents some given table (that differs from T). For each tuple of T, you now decide if it remains in the result set by not only inspecting one or more attribute values of that tuple, but also by inspecting tuples in another table.

As you'll understand by now, there are many more ways to perform a restriction of a given table; any number of other tables (including the table being restricted) could be involved.

In practice it's also generally possible to specify such a restriction on a table that is the result of a join (see the next section).

Join

In a database you'll often find that two tables are related to each other through some attribute (or set of attributes) that they share. If this is the case, then you can meaningfully combine the tuples of these tables.

This combining of tuples is done via the *compatibility* concept of two tuples (you might want to go back to Definition 4-3 and refresh your memory). Every tuple from the first table is combined with the tuple(s) from the second table that are *compatible* with this tuple. Let's demonstrate this with an example. Figures 5-5 and 5-6 introduce table T6 (representing employees) and table T7 (representing departments).

empno	ename	job	sal	deptno
101	'Chris'	'MANAGER'	7900	10
102	'Kathy'	'TRAINER'	6000	12
103	'Thomas'	'CLERK'	2100	10
104	'David'	'TRAINER'	5600	10
105	'Renu'	'CLERK'	3000	12
106	'Bob'	'MANAGER'	8500	10
107	'Sue'	'CLERK'	2700	12

Figure 5-5. *Example table T6*

deptno	dname	loc	salbudget
10	'RESEARCH'	'DENVER'	50000
11	'SALES'	'DENVER'	20000
12	'SUPPORT'	'LOS ANGELES'	40000
13	'SALES'	'SAN FRANCISCO'	20000

Figure 5-6. *Example table T7*

You can combine tuples from tables T6 and T7 that correspond on the attributes that they share, in this case the deptno attribute. The resulting table from this combination has as its heading the union of the heading of T6 and the heading of T7.

Figure 5-7 displays the result of such a combination of tables T6 and T7.

empno	ename	job	sal	deptno	dname	loc	salbudget
101	'Chris'	'MANAGER'	7900	10	'RESEARCH'	'DENVER'	50000
102	'Kathy'	'TRAINER'	6000	12	'SUPPORT'	'LOS ANGELES'	40000
103	'Thomas'	'CLERK'	2100	10	'RESEARCH'	'DENVER'	50000
104	'David'	'TRAINER'	5600	10	'RESEARCH'	'DENVER'	50000
105	'Renu'	'CLERK'	3000	12	'SUPPORT'	'LOS ANGELES'	40000
106	'Bob'	'MANAGER'	8500	10	'RESEARCH'	'DENVER'	50000
107	'Sue'	'CLERK'	2700	12	'SUPPORT'	'LOS ANGELES'	40000

Figure 5-7. *Table T8, the combination of tables T6 and T7*

You can formally specify this table in a predicative way as follows:

$\{ \ e \cup d \ | \ e \in T6 \ \wedge \ d \in T7 \ \wedge \ e(deptno) = d(deptno) \ \}$

Every tuple from T6 is combined with the tuples in T7 that have the same deptno value. This combining of tuples of two "related" tables is known as the *join* of two such tables. Definition 5-4 formally defines this operator.

■**Definition 5-4: The Join of Two Tables** Let R and T be two (not necessarily distinct) tables. The join of R and T (notation R⊗T) is defined as follows:

R⊗T := { r∪t | r∈R ∧ t∈T ∧ "r and t are compatible" }

The join of two tables, say R and T, will hold the union of every pair of tuples r and t, where r is a tuple in R, and t is a tuple in T, such that the union of r and t is a function (compatibility concept). With this definition, you can now specify T8 (from Figure 5-7) as T6⊗T7.

The set of attributes that two tables, that are being joined, have in common is referred to as the set of *join attributes*. We will also sometimes say that two tuples are *joinable*, instead of saying that they are compatible.

As mentioned at the end of the previous section on restriction, you'll often restrict the join of two tables. For example, here is the restriction of the join of tables T6 and T7 to only those tuples that represent clerks located in Denver:

{ t | t∈T6⊗T7 ∧ t(job)='CLERK' ∧ t(loc)='DENVER' }

Note that Definition 5-4 is not restricted to those cases in which the operands actually have at least one attribute in common. You're allowed to join two tables for which the set of join attributes is empty (the compatibility concept allows for this); in this case every tuple from the first table is compatible with every tuple from the second table (this follows from Definition 4-3). You are then in effect combining every tuple of the first table with every tuple of the second table. This special case of a join is also referred to as a *Cartesian join*.

In general, a Cartesian join is of limited practical use in data processing. A Cartesian join that involves a table of cardinality one is reasonable and sometimes useful. Here is an example of such a Cartesian join:

T7⊗{ { (maxbudget;75000) } }

This expression joins every tuple of T7 with every tuple of the right-hand argument of the join operator, which is a table over {maxbudget}. It effectively *extends* every department tuple of T7 with a new attribute called maxbudget. This Cartesian join is in fact a special case of *table extension*, which will be treated shortly hereafter in the section "Extension."

Note also an opposite special case of a Cartesian join, in which you join two tables that share the same heading. That is, the set of join attributes equals this shared heading. In such a join you are in effect intersecting these two tables. This makes the intersection a special case of the join (and therefore a redundant operator).

Attribute Renaming

Sometimes two tables are related to each other such that joining these two tables makes sense. However, the names of the attributes with which the joining should be performed don't match; the set of join attributes is the empty set. In these cases, the join operator won't work as intended; it will perform a Cartesian join. The way a join is defined requires the names of the intended join attributes to be the same. For instance, suppose the deptno attribute in the preceding table T7 was named dept#. Performing the join of T6 and T7—T6⊗T7—would then result in a Cartesian join of T6 and T7. To fix this, you must first either rename attribute deptno in T6 to dept#, or rename attribute dept# in T7 to deptno.

Also, sometimes performing the intersection, union, or difference of two tables makes sense; however, the headings of the two tables differ, not in cardinality, but in the names of the attributes. To fix this too, you must first rename attributes of the tables involved such that they have equal headings.

For this, we introduce the *attribute renaming* operator; Definition 5-5 formally defines this operator.

■**Definition 5-5: The Attribute Renaming Operator** Let T be a table and f be a function. The renaming of attributes in T according to f (notation T◊◊f) is defined as follows:

T◊◊f := { t◊f | t∈T }.

You can view the attribute renaming operator as a version of the function composition operator that has been lifted to the table level.

Using this operator, we can rename attribute deptno in T6 to dept# as follows:

T6◊◊{(empno;empno),(ename;ename),(job;job),(sal;sal),(dept#;deptno)}

Note that the renaming function f holds an ordered pair for every attribute in the heading of T6. All second coordinates in the ordered pairs represent the current attribute names of the table. Only if an attribute needs to be renamed do the first and second coordinates of the ordered pair differ; the first coordinate will have the new name for the attribute.

Extension

Sometimes you want to add attributes to a given table. You want to introduce new attributes to the heading of the table, and supply values for these new attributes for every tuple in the table. Performing this type of operation on a table is referred to as *extending the table*, or performing *table extension*. Table extension does not require a new mathematical symbol; you can simply use the predicative method to specify a new set of tuples (that is, a new table) that's based on the given table.

Let's take a look at an example of table extension. Figure 5-8 shows two tables. The one at the left is a table over {empno, ename}; it is the result of projecting table T6 (see Figure 5-5) on {empno, ename}. We'll name this table T9. The one at the right (T10) represents the extension of T9 with the attribute initial. For every tuple, the value of this attribute is equal to the first character of the value of attribute ename.

■**Note** We'll be using a function called substr to yield a substring from a given string. The expression substr(<some string value>,n,m) represents the substring of <some string value> that starts at position n and is m characters long. For instance, the expression substr('I like this book',13,4) is equal to the string value 'book'.

T9	empno	ename	T10	empno	ename	initial
	101	'Chris'		101	'Chris'	'C'
	102	'Kathy'		102	'Kathy'	'K'
	103	'Thomas'		103	'Thomas'	'T'
	104	'David'		104	'David'	'D'
	105	'Renu'		105	'Renu'	'R'
	106	'Bob'		106	'Bob'	'B'
	107	'Sue'		107	'Sue'	'S'

Figure 5-8. *Example of extending a table with a new attribute*

Given table T9, you can formally specify table T10 as follows:

```
T10 := { e ∪ { (initial;substr(e(ename),1,1)) } | e∈T9 }
```

For every tuple, say e, in T9, table T10 holds a tuple that is represented by the following expression:

```
e ∪ { (initial;substr(e(ename),1,1)) }
```

This expression adds an attribute-value ordered pair to tuple e. The attribute that is added is `initial`. The value attached to this attribute is `substr(e(ename),1,1)`, which represents the initial of value e(ename).

Here's another example. Figure 5-9 shows two tables. The one at the left (T11) represents a department table over {deptno,dname}. The one at the right (T12) is the extension of T11 with an `emps` attribute. For each tuple, the `emps` attribute represents the number of employees found in table T6 (see Figure 5-5) that are assigned to the department represented by the tuple.

T11

deptno	dname
10	'RESEARCH'
11	'SALES'
12	'SUPPORT'
13	'SALES'

T12

deptno	dname	emps
10	'RESEARCH'	4
11	'SALES'	0
12	'SUPPORT'	3
13	'SALES'	0

Figure 5-9. *Another example of extending a table with a new attribute*

Given table T11 and T6, you can formally specify table T12 as follows:

```
T12 := { d ∪ { (emps;#{ e | e∈T6 ∧ e(deptno)=d(deptno)}) } | d∈T11 }
```

Here we've used the cardinality operator (symbol #) to count the number of employees in each department.

Aggregation

Aggregate operators operate on a set. They yield a (numeric) value by aggregation, of some expression, over all elements in the set. There are five common aggregate operators: *sum*, *average, count, minimum*, and *maximum*.

You were introduced to the sum operator in Chapter 2; you might quickly want to revisit Definition 2-12. You can apply the sum operator to a table. Here is an example. Given table T6 (see Figure 5-5), here is an expression yielding the sum of all salaries of employees working for the research department (deptno=10):

```
(SUM x∈{ t | t∈T6 ∧ t(deptno)=10 }: x(sal))
```

The resulting value of the preceding sum aggregation is 24100. Now take a look at the following expression that again uses table T6:

```
{ e1 ∪ {(sumsal;(SUM x∈{ e2 | e2∈T6 ∧ e2(deptno)=e1(deptno) }: x(sal)))}
                                                    | e1 ∈ T6⇓{deptno} }
```

Here we first project T6 on {deptno} and then extend the resulting table with a sumsal attribute. For every tuple in this resulting table, we determine the value of this new attribute by computing the sum of the salaries of all employees who work in the department corresponding to the department represented by the tuple. Figure 5-10 shows the result of this expression.

deptno	sumsal
10	24100
12	11700

Figure 5-10. *Sum of T6, salaries per department*

We don't need to introduce a new definition for the count operator. We can simply use the set-theory symbol # (cardinality) to count the elements of a set. You already saw an example of this in the preceding "Extension" section; the formal specification of T12 is an example of the count aggregate operator.

Definition 5-6 defines the average aggregate operator.

Definition 5-6: The Average Operator (AVG) The average of an expression $f(x)$, where x is chosen from a given, non-empty set S, and f represents an arbitrary numeric function over x, is denoted as follows:

$(AVG \ x \in S: \ f(x))$

For every element x that can be chosen from set S, the average operator evaluates expression $f(x)$ and computes the average of all such evaluations. Note that this operator is not defined in case S is the empty set.

In the same way as earlier, Definition 5-7 defines the maximum (MAX) and minimum (MIN) aggregate operators.

Definition 5-7: The Maximum (MAX) and Minimum (MIN) Operators The maximum and minimum of an expression $f(x)$, where x is chosen from a given, non-empty set S, and f represents an arbitrary numeric function over x, are respectively denoted as follows:

$(MAX \ x \in S: \ f(x))$ and $(MIN \ x \in S: \ f(x))$

For every element x that can be chosen from set S, the maximum and minimum operators evaluate expression $f(x)$ and compute the maximum, or respectively the minimum, of all such evaluations. Note that these operators are also not defined in case S is the empty set.

Next to the (*number valued*) aggregate operators discussed so far, two other aggregate operators are worth mentioning. They are *truth-valued* aggregate operators; they yield TRUE or FALSE. You've already been introduced to these two in Chapter 3; they are the existential quantification and the universal quantification. They yield a Boolean value by instantiating some predicate over all elements in a set (used as the arguments) and computing the truth value of the combined disjunction or conjunction, respectively, of all resulting propositions.

We conclude this chapter with a few examples that again use T6. Listing 5-8 displays expressions involving these operators and also supplies the values that they yield.

Listing 5-8. *Example Expressions Involving AVG, MAX, and MIN*

```
/* Minimum salary of employees working in department 10 */
(MIN x ∈ { e |e∈T6 ∧ e(deptno)=10 }: x(sal))
   = 2100
/* (rounded) Average salary of all employees */
(AVG x∈T6 : x(sal))
   = 5114
/* Table over {deptno,minsal,maxsal} representing the minimum and maximum
   salary per department (number) */
{ e1 ∪ { (minsal; (MIN x ∈ { e2 |e2∈T6 ∧ e2(deptno)=e1(deptno) }: x(sal))),
```

```
        (maxsal; (MAX x ∈ { e2 |e2∈T6 ∧ e2(deptno)=e1(deptno) }: x(sal))) }
        | e1∈T6⇓{deptno} }
= { {(deptno;10), (minsal;2100), (maxsal;8500)}
  , {(deptno;12), (minsal;2700),  (maxsal;6000)} }
```

Chapter Summary

This section provides a summary of this chapter, formatted as a bulleted list. You can use it to check your understanding of the various concepts introduced in this chapter before continuing with the exercises in the next section.

- A *table* can formally be represented as a set of functions, all of which share a common domain; you can specify this set by writing down all involved functions in the *enumerative way*.

- The elements of a table are referred to as tuples; the ordered pairs of a tuple are called *attribute-value pairs*.

- The shared domain of all tuples in a table is referred to as the *heading* of the table.

- We usually draw a table as a *two-dimensional picture* of rows and columns (shorthand notation). The column header represents the heading of the table and the rows represent the tuples of the table.

- The order in which tuples are drawn (shorthand notation) or enumerated (set-theory notation) doesn't matter. Neither do the order of the columns or the order of the attribute-value pairs matter.

- The generalized product of a characterization will result in a table. You can use this as the given set to specify tables in a *predicative way*, by adding predicates you further constrain the content of the set.

- A *database state*, containing x tables, can formally be represented as a function containing x ordered pairs. In every ordered pair, the first coordinate represents the name of a table structure and the second coordinate represents the current table for that table structure.

- A *database skeleton* formally describes the structure of a database design. It introduces the table structure names and the names of all attributes involved in the database design.

- Because tables are sets, you can apply the well-known set operators *union* (∪), *intersection* (∩), and *difference* (–) with tables as their operands.

- You can use the *projection* operator (⇓) to *limit* all tuples to a given subset of the heading of the table.

- You can select a subset of the tuples from a given table by specifying, in a predicative way, a new set based on the given table. The predicates that you add in such a predicative specification are said to perform a table *restriction*.

- The *join* operator (⊗) combines *compatible* tuples from two given tables. Because it is based on the compatibility concept, it requires the attributes that are to be used for this combination to have matching names.

- The *attribute renaming* operator (◊◊) enables you to selectively rename one or more attributes in the heading of a table. You can use it to ensure that attributes of two tables have matching names, prior to performing the join of these two tables.

- You can use *table extension* to add new attributes to a table (including their values for every tuple).

- The five aggregate operators—*sum, count, average, maximum,* and *minimum*—enable you to compute a value by aggregation over all elements in a given set.

Exercises

Figure 5-11 introduces three tables P, S, and SP, which will be used in the exercises.

P

partno	pname	price
101	'Desktop'	2000
102	'Printer'	400
103	'Laptop'	2900
104	'Router'	250

S

suppno	sname	location
1	'PC&Co'	DALLAS
2	'HW Supply'	NEW YORK

SP

partno	suppno	available	reserved
101	1	200	10
102	1	150	0
101	2	0	200
104	1	20	5
103	2	50	75
106	2	80	30

Figure 5-11. *Example tables P, S, and SP*

1. Check for each of the following expressions whether it represents a table, and if so, over which set?

   a. P∪S

   b. P∩S

   c. $(P\Downarrow\{partno\}) \cup (SP\Downarrow\{partno\})$

   d. S-SP

   e. $P\cup\emptyset$

2. Formally specify a table that is based on characterization chr_PART, in which

   a. A hammer always costs more than 250.

   b. A part that costs less than 400 cannot be a drill.

   c. For parts 10, 15, and 20 there are never more than 42 items in stock.

3. Evaluate the following expressions.

   ```
   E1 := P∪{ {(partno;201)} }
   E2 := P∪{ {(partno;201),(price;35),(pname;'Optical mouse')} }
   E3 := S-{ {(location;'DALLAS')} }
   E4 := S-{ s | s∈S ∧ (∃sp∈SP: sp(suppno) = s(suppno) ∧ sp(available)>150) }
   E5 := SP-{ sp | sp∈SP ∧ ¬(∃p∈P: p(partno)=sp(partno)) }
   ```

4. Evaluate the following expressions.

   ```
   E6 := S⊗SP
   E7 := P⊗SP
   E8 := S⊗P
   E9 := S⊗(P⊗SP)
   E10 := SP⊗(S⇓{suppno,location})
   E11 := (SP∞{(suppno;suppno),(partno;partno),(reserved;available),
       (available;reserved)})⇓{suppno,reserved}
   ```

5. Give an informal description of the following propositions and evaluate their truth
   values.

   ```
   P1 := ( ∀p1∈P: ( ∀p2∈P: p1(partno) ≠p2(partno) ) )
   P2 := ( ∀p1∈P: ( ∀p2∈P: p1<>p2 ⇒ p1(partno) ≠p2(partno) ) )
   P3 := ( ∀sp∈SP: ( ∃p∈P: sp(partno) = p(partno) ) )
   P4 := { s(suppno)| s∈S } = { sp(suppno) | sp∈SP }
   P5 := P⇓{partno} = SP⇓{partno}
   P6 := ( ∀sp1∈SP: sp1(available)=0 ⇒
           ( ∃sp2∈SP: sp2(partno)=sp1(partno) ∧ sp2(suppno)≠sp1(suppno) ∧
                       sp2(available)>0 ) )
   P7 := (P⊗SP)⇓{partno,pname,price} = P
   ```

6. What is the result of the projection of a given table on the empty set?

7. Given table T6 (see Figure 5-5), what values do the following two expressions yield?

   ```
   (SUM x∈{ t | t∈T6 ∧ t(deptno)=10 }: x(sal))
   (SUM x∈{ t(SAL) | t∈T6 ∧ t(deptno)=10 }: x)
   ```

   Explain the difference between these two expressions.

CHAPTER 6

Tuple, Table, and Database Predicates

This chapter introduces the concepts of a *tuple*, a *table*, and a *database predicate* (using the meaning of *predicate* that was established in Chapter 1). You can use tuple, table, and database predicates to describe the data integrity constraints of a database design. The goal of this chapter is to establish these three different classes of predicates—which jointly we'll refer to as *data integrity predicates*—and to give ample examples of predicates within each class.

Note We introduce data integrity predicates in this chapter and show that they hold for a certain argument (value). Of course, we aren't interested in this incidental property (whether a predicate is TRUE for one given value); they should hold for value *spaces* (that is, they should constitute a structural property). This will be further developed in Chapter 7.

A data integrity predicate deals with data. We classify data integrity predicates into three classes by looking at the scope of data that they deal with. In increasing scope, a predicate can deal with a *tuple*, a *table*, or a *database state*.

The section "Tuple Predicates" establishes the concept of a *tuple predicate*. This type of data integrity predicate has a single parameter of type tuple. You can use it to accept or reject a tuple (loosely speaking, a set of attribute values).

The next section, "Table Predicates," will introduce you to *table predicates*. A table predicate deals with a table, and consequently has a single parameter of type table. We'll use them to accept or reject a table (a set of tuples).

We familiarize you with the concept of *database predicates* in the section "Database Predicates." Database predicates deal with database states. We'll use them to accept or reject a database state (loosely speaking, a set of tables).

■**Note** There is a reason why this book discerns between these three classes of data integrity predicates. In Chapter 7 you'll study a formal methodology of specifying a database design and learn that this methodology uses a *layered* approach. Every layer (three in total) introduces a class of constraints: tuple, table, and database constraints, respectively. You'll specify these constraints through data integrity predicates.

The section "Common Patterns of Table and Database Predicates" will explore five data integrity predicate *patterns* that often play a role in a database design: *unique identification, subset requirement, specialization, generalization*, and *tuple-in-join* predicates.

In a database design you always (rare cases excluded) encounter data integrity constraints that are based on unique identification and subset requirement predicates. You'll probably identify these two predicate patterns with the relational concepts of unique and foreign key constraints, respectively. The specialization and generalization predicate patterns will probably remind you of the ERD concepts of a subtype and a supertype. The tuple-in-join predicate pattern involves a join between two or more tables, and is at the basis of a type of constraint that is also often encountered in database designs.

As usual, you'll find a "Chapter Summary" at the end, followed by an "Exercises" section.

Tuple Predicates

Let's explain right away what a *tuple predicate* is and then quickly demonstrate this concept with a few examples. A *tuple predicate* is a predicate with one parameter. This parameter is of type tuple. Listing 6-1 displays a few examples of tuple predicates.

Listing 6-1. *Tuple Predicate Examples*

```
P0(t) := ( t(sex) ∈ {'male', 'female'} )
P1(t) := ( t(price) ≥ 20 ⇒ t(instock) ≤ 10 )
P2(t) := ( t(status) = 'F' ∨ ( t(status) = 'I' ∧ t(total) > 0 ) )
P3(t) := ( t(salary) < 5000 ∨ t(sex) = 'female' )
P4(t) := ( t(begindate) < t(enddate) )
```

Predicate P0 states that the sex attribute value of a tuple should be 'male' or 'female'. Predicate P1 states that if the price (attribute) value of a tuple is greater than or equal to 20, then the instock (attribute) value should be 10 or less. P2 states that the status value is either F or it is I, but then at the same time the total value should be greater than 0. Predicate P3 states that salary should be less then 5000 or sex is female. Finally, predicate P4 states that the begindate value should be less than enddate.

We'll use a tuple predicate (in Chapter 7) to accept or reject a given tuple. If the predicate—when instantiated with a given tuple as the argument—turns into a FALSE proposition, then we will reject the tuple; otherwise, we will accept it. In the latter case, we say that the given tuple *satisfies the predicate*. In the former case, the tuple *violates the predicate*.

Again, let's demonstrate this with a few example tuples (see Listing 6-2).

Listing 6-2. *Example Tuples t0 Through t6*

```
t0 := { (empno;101), (begindate;'01-aug-2005'), (enddate;'31-mar-2007') }
t1 := { (price;30), (instock;4) }
t2 := { (partno;101), (instock;30), (price;20), (type;'A') }
t3 := { (status;'F'), (total;20) }
t4 := { (total;50) }
t5 := { (salary;6000), (sex;'male'), (name;'Felix') }
t6 := { (salary;5000), (sex;'female') }
```

Instantiating predicate P0 with tuple t5—rendering expression P0(t5)—results in the proposition 'male'∈{'male', 'female'}, which is a TRUE proposition, and we say that t5 satisfies P0. Instantiating predicate P1 with tuple t1—expression P1(t1)—results in the proposition $30 \geq 20 \Rightarrow 4 \leq 10$. This is also a TRUE proposition; therefore t1 satisfies P1. Check for yourself that the following propositions are TRUE propositions: P0(t6), P2(t3), P3(t6), P4(t0). The following are FALSE propositions: P1(t2), P3(t5).

Note that we cannot instantiate a tuple predicate with just any tuple. For instance, instantiating predicate P2 with tuple t4 cannot be done because t4 lacks a status attribute. This brings us to the concept of a *tuple predicate over a set*.

We call predicate P1 a tuple predicate *over* {price,instock}; the components of this predicate assume that there is a price and an instock attribute available within the tuple that is provided as the argument. In the same way that predicate P0 is a tuple predicate over {sex}, P2 is a tuple predicate over {status,total}, P3 is a tuple predicate over {salary,sex}, and P4 is a tuple predicate over {begindate,enddate}. In general, if a given predicate, say P(t), is a predicate over some set A, then we can only meaningfully instantiate predicate P with tuples whose domain is a superset of A. For instance, the domain of t5—{salary,sex,name}—is a (proper) superset of {salary,sex}. Therefore, we can instantiate predicate P3—a predicate over {salary,sex}—with t5.

As you can see by the examples given, a tuple predicate is allowed to be compound; that is, one that involves logical connectives. The components of this predicate typically compare the attribute values of the tuple supplied as the argument with certain given values.

We need to make two more observations with regards to tuple predicates. The first one deals with the number of attributes involved in the predicate. Note that predicate P0 only references the sex attribute; it is a tuple predicate over a singleton.

We consider a tuple predicate—say P(t)—over a singleton—say A—a degenerate case of a tuple predicate. In Chapter 7, and also later on in Chapter 11, we'll deal with such a degenerate case of a tuple predicate as a condition on the attribute value set of attribute ↲A (see the section "The Choose Operator" in Chapter 2 to refresh your mind on the choose operator ↲).

■**Note** The *layered approach* (mentioned in the second note of this chapter's introduction) requires that tuple predicates over a singleton are specified in a different layer than the tuple predicates over a set (say A) where the cardinality of A is two or more.

Second, tuple predicates shouldn't be decomposable into multiple conjuncts. In Chapters 7 and 11, we'll require that a tuple predicate when written in conjunctive normal form (CNF) will consist of only one conjunct. If the CNF version of the predicate has more than one conjunct, then we are in fact dealing with multiple (as many conjuncts as there are) potential tuple predicates.

Predicate P2 from Listing 6-1 violates this second observation; it has more than one conjunct in CNF. Here is predicate P2 rewritten into CNF (you can quickly achieve this by using the distribution rewrite rules):

```
P2(t) := ( (t(status)='F' ∨ t(status)='I') ∧ (t(status)='F' ∨ t(total)>0) )
```

Predicate P2 has two conjuncts in CNF; therefore, we're dealing with two tuple predicates. We'll name them P2a and P2b, respectively:

```
P2a(t) := ( t(status)='F' ∨ t(status)='I' )
P2b(t) := ( t(status)='F' ∨ t(total)>0 )
```

As you can see, predicate P2a is a tuple predicate over singleton {status}. Therefore, according to our first observation, P2a is a degenerate case of a tuple predicate. We have broken down what seemed like a tuple predicate, P2, into a combination of a (simpler) tuple predicate P2b and a condition on the attribute value set of the status attribute (P2a).

Table Predicates

In the previous section you were introduced to a certain type of predicate: the tuple predicate. In this section we'll introduce you to the concept of a *table predicate*. Table predicates deal with *multiple tuples* within a single table. They are predicates that have a single parameter of type table. Listing 6-3 displays a few examples of table predicates.

Listing 6-3. *Table Predicate Examples*

```
P5(T) := ¬( ∃t1,t2∈T: t1≠t2 ∧ t1(partno)=t2(partno) )
P6(T) := ( (Σt∈T: t(instock)*t(price)) ≤ 2500 )
P7(T) := ( ∀t1∈T: t1(instock)=0 ⇒
              (∃t2∈T: t2(partno) ≠t1(partno) ∧ t2(name)=t1(name) ∧ t2(instock)>0 ))
```

Predicate P5 states that there are no two distinct tuples (parts) in table T such that they have the same partno value. Assuming predicate P6 also deals with parts tables, it states— loosely speaking—that the total stock value represented by the parts table T does not exceed 2500. Predicate P7 states that whenever a certain part is out of stock, then there should be a different part (one with a different part number) that has the same name and is still in stock.

Note It's important that you (the database professional) can render these formal specifications into informal representations, and vice versa. You'll see more examples of this in the sections that follow.

In the same way as with tuple predicates, we say that P5 is a table predicate over {partno}, P6 is a table predicate over {instock,price}, and P7 is a table predicate over {instock,partno, name}.

Now take a look at table PAR1 in Figure 6-1.

partno	name	instock	price
1	'hammer'	22	10
2	'screwdriver'	19	5
3	'axe'	0	30
4	'saw'	4	15
5	'wrench'	7	20
6	'scissors'	32	5

Figure 6-1. *Table PAR1*

PAR1 is a table over {partno,name,instock,price}. This is a superset of all sets that P5, P6, and P7 are table predicates over; we can therefore meaningfully supply PAR1 as an argument to these predicates.

As you've probably already noticed, PAR1 satisfies predicate P5; there are no two different parts in PAR1 that have the same partno value. The total stock value represented by PAR1 is 675, which is less than 2500, so PAR1 also satisfies P6. However, it violates predicate P7; part 3 is out of stock but there isn't a different part with the same name (axe) that's in stock.

In the remainder of this book, we'll consider a table predicate a degenerate case of a table predicate if it can be rewritten into a predicate with the following pattern:

P(T) := (∀t∈T: Q(t))

Here Q(t) represents a tuple predicate. If a table predicate is of the preceding form, then we consider it a *tuple predicate in disguise*. In the next chapter, we'll specify these degenerate cases of table predicates differently than the other table predicates; in fact, for these cases we'll specify tuple predicate Q(t) in a different *layer* than the other table predicates, and table predicate P(T) is discarded as a table predicate.

A degenerate case of a table predicate disguising a tuple predicate would be this:

P(T) := (∀t∈T: t(price) ≥ 20 ⇒ t(instock) ≤ 10)

This is the table predicate variation of tuple predicate P1(t) from Listing 6-1 that we won't allow as a table predicate.

Note Predicate P7 is indeed a table predicate, though you might at first sight think that it fits the preceding pattern. It actually does not; it is of the form (∀t∈T: Q(t,T)), which is a different pattern.

Without loss of generality we will also—just like tuple predicates—confine our attention to table predicates consisting of a single conjunct. If you can rewrite a given table predicate $P(T)$ into an expression of the form $Q(T) \wedge R(T)$, then you are in fact dealing with two table predicates. Here is an example to illustrate this:

$$(\ \forall t1 \in T: \ t1(instock) > 100 \ \Rightarrow$$
$$(\ (\forall t2 \in T: \ t2(partno) \neq t1(partno) \ \Rightarrow \ t2(name) \neq t1(name))$$
$$\wedge$$
$$t1(price)? < 200$$
$$)$$
$$)$$

This predicate states that if for a given part we have more than 100 items in stock, then there should not exist another part that has the same name, nor should the price of the given part be equal to 200 or more. This table predicate is of the following form:

$$(\ \forall t \in T: \ Q1(t) \ \Rightarrow \ (\ Q2(t,T) \wedge Q3(t) \ ) \ )$$

Using the following rewrite rule

$$(\ A \Rightarrow (B \wedge C) \ ) \ \Leftrightarrow \ (\ (A \Rightarrow B) \wedge (A \Rightarrow C) \ )$$

together with the distributive property of a universal quantification (see Listing 3-12), you can rewrite this into a conjunction of two predicates:

$$(\ \forall t \in T: \ Q1(t) \ \Rightarrow \ Q2(t,T) \ )$$
$$\wedge$$
$$(\ \forall t \in T: \ Q1(t) \ \Rightarrow \ Q3(t) \ )$$

This shows that you're dealing with two predicates. The first conjunct is indeed a table predicate, and the second one is actually a tuple predicate in disguise!

We conclude this section on table predicates with another example introducing three more table predicates. Listing 6-4 first introduces characterization chr_EMP that models an employee.

Listing 6-4. *Characterization chr_EMP*

```
chr_EMP := { (empno;   [100..999])
           ,(ename;   varchar(20))
           ,(job;     {'MANAGER','CLERK','TRAINER'} )
           ,(sal;     [2000..9000])
           ,(deptno; [10..99]) }
```

For an employee, the employee number (empno), its name (ename), the employee's job (job), the salary (sal), and the number (deptno) of the department that employs the employee are the relevant attributes that are captured by this characterization. Using this characterization, you can generate an employee table by choosing a subset from $\prod(chr\_EMP)$. Such a table can be provided as the argument to a table predicate. Listing 6-5 introduces three table predicates that can accept a table over dom(chr_EMP) through parameter T.

Listing 6-5. *More Table Predicate Examples*

```
P8(T)  := ¬( ∃e1,e2∈T: ( (e1(job)='MANAGER' ∧ e2(job)='TRAINER') ∨
                           (e1(job)='TRAINER' ∧ e2(job)='CLERK'  ) ) ∧
                         e1(sal) ≤ e2(sal) )
P9(T)  := ( ∀d∈T⇓{deptno}: #{ e2| e2∈T ∧ e2(deptno)=d(deptno) } ≥  3 )
P10(T) := ( ∀d∈T⇓{deptno}: ( Σe2∈{ e| e∈T ∧ e(deptno)=d(deptno) }: e2(sal) )
                         ≤ 40000 )
```

Table predicate P8 states that managers earn more than trainers, and trainers earn more than clerks. Predicate P9 states that every department should have at least three employees. Predicate P10 states that departmental salary budgets cannot exceed 40000.

Figure 6-2 displays an example subset of ∏(chr_EMP) named EMP1.

empno	ename	job	sal	deptno
101	'Chris'	'MANAGER'	7900	10
102	'Kathy'	'TRAINER'	6000	12
103	'Thomas'	'CLERK'	2100	10
104	'David'	'TRAINER'	5600	10
105	'Renu'	'CLERK'	3000	12
106	'Bob'	'MANAGER'	8500	10
107	'Sue'	'CLERK'	2700	12

Figure 6-2. *Example table EMP1*

Verify for yourself that EMP1 is indeed a subset of ∏(chr_EMP) and that it satisfies predicates P8, P9, and P10.

■Note Given the attribute value set for attribute sal in characterization chr_EMP, the last table predicate P10 (assuming it can be considered a data integrity constraint) implies that there can never be more than 20 employees in a single department, because 20 times 2000 (minimum salary possible) equals 40000 (maximum departmental salary budget). During information analysis, it's often quite useful to confront end users with such *derivable* statements. It can act as a double check for the data integrity constraints already established, or likely, it will get you more information that the end user didn't tell you yet.

Database Predicates

We continue now by further increasing the scope of data that a predicate deals with. After tuple predicates (scope of data is a tuple) and table predicates (scope of data is a table), the next level up is predicates that deal with *multiple tables*. We'll call this kind of predicate a *database predicate*. A database predicate has one parameter of type database state.

To show a few examples of predicates that deal with a database state, we first introduce a department characterization alongside the earlier introduced employee characterization. Listing 6-6 defines characterization chr_DEPT that models a department.

Listing 6-6. *Characterization chr_DEPT*

```
chr_DEPT := { (deptno;      [10..99])
            ,(dname;      varchar(20))
            ,(loc;        {'LOS ANGELES','SAN FRANCISCO','DENVER'} )
            ,(salbudget;  [25000..50000]) }
```

For a department, the department number (deptno), its name (dname), the department's location (loc), and the salary budget (salbudget) are the relevant attributes this characterization captures.

Figure 6-3 displays an example department table that we name DEP1.

deptno	dname	loc	salbudget
10	'RESEARCH'	'DENVER'	50000
11	'SALES'	'DENVER'	20000
12	'SUPPORT'	'LOS ANGELES'	40000
13	'SALES'	'SAN FRANCISCO'	20000

Figure 6-3. *Example table DEP1*

Check that table DEP1 is a subset of $\prod$(chr_DEPT) and that it satisfies the table predicates shown in Listing 6-7.

Listing 6-7. *Two Example Table Predicates*

```
P11(T) := ¬( ∃d1,d2∈ T: d1≠d2 ∧d1(deptno)=d2(deptno) )
P12(T) := ( ∀d1,d2∈ T: d1≠d2 ⟹ d1↓{dname,loc}≠d2↓{dname,loc} )
```

Table predicate P11 states that there cannot be two different departments that share the same department number. P12 states that two different departments either have different names or different locations (or both).

By the way, do you see that these two predicates are of the same form? You can transform predicate P11 into a universal quantification using rewrite rules, as follows:

$$\neg(\ \exists d1,d2 \in T:\ d1 \neq d2\ \wedge\ d1(deptno) = d2(deptno)\ )$$
$$\Leftrightarrow\ (\ \forall d1,d2 \in T:\ \neg(\ d1 \neq d2\ \wedge\ d1(deptno) = d2(deptno)\ )\ )$$
$$\Leftrightarrow\ (\ \forall d1,d2 \in T:\ \neg(d1 \neq d2)\ \vee\ \neg(d1(deptno) = d2(deptno))\ )$$
$$\Leftrightarrow\ (\ \forall d1,d2 \in T:\ \neg(d1 \neq d2)\ \vee\ d1(deptno) \neq d2(deptno)\ )$$
$$\Leftrightarrow\ (\ \forall d1,d2 \in T:\ d1 \neq d2\ \Rightarrow\ d1(deptno) \neq d2(deptno)\ )$$

Here we have used a rewrite rule that transforms an existential quantifier into a universal quantifier, a De Morgan Law, and a rewrite rule that transforms disjunction into implication. Predicates P11 and P12 are both of the form of one of the common patterns of data integrity predicates that we'll treat in the next section.

You can now construct a database state, say S1, as follows:

```
S1 := { (employee;EMP1), (department;DEP1) }
```

In this expression, EMP1 and DEP1 represent the tables that were introduced in Figures 6-2 and 6-3. You can also represent database state S1 in this way (see Figure 6-4).

S1 =

{ (employee;

empno	ename	job	sal	deptno
101	'Chris'	'MANAGER'	7900	10
102	'Kathy'	'TRAINER'	6000	12
103	'Thomas'	'CLERK'	2100	10
104	'David'	'TRAINER'	5600	10
105	'Renu'	'CLERK'	3000	12
106	'Bob'	'MANAGER'	8500	10
107	'Sue'	'CLERK'	2700	12

)

, (department;

deptno	dname	loc	salbudget
10	'RESEARCH'	'DENVER'	50000
11	'SALES'	'DENVER'	20000
12	'SUPPORT'	'LOS ANGELES'	40000
13	'SALES'	'SAN FRANCISCO'	20000

)

}

Figure 6-4. *Database state S1*

S1 represents a database state over the skeleton { (employee;{empno,ename,job,sal, deptno}), (department;{deptno,dname,loc,salbudget}) }. As a reminder from the previous chapter, you can write expressions such as S1(employee) and S1(department), which respectively evaluate to EMP1 (the employee table from Figure 6-2) and DEP1 (the department table from Figure 6-3).

Now let's take a look at database predicates P13 and P14 in Listing 6-8. Remember parameter S represents a database state.

Listing 6-8. *Two Example Database Predicates*

```
P13(S) := { e(deptno)| e∈S(employee) } ⊆ { d(deptno)| d∈S(department) }
P14(S) := ( ∀d∈S(department):
                ( Σe2∈{ e1| e1∈S(employee) ∧ e1(deptno)=d(deptno) }: e2(sal) )
                ≤ d(salbudget) )
```

Predicate P13 states that every employee is employed within a department that is known in the department table.

This type of database predicate (the set of values of a specified attribute of one table forms a subset of the set of values of a specified attribute of another table) is commonly found in database designs and will be treated in more detail in the next section. Supplying database state S1 as the argument to predicate P13 results in the following proposition:

$$\{10,12\} \subseteq \{10,11,12,13\}$$

This is a TRUE proposition. The set of numbers at the left-hand side is a subset of the set of numbers at the right-hand side. Again we say that database state S1 satisfies (does not violate) database predicate P13. A somewhat more succinct way to specify predicate P13 is as follows:

```
P13(S) := S(employee)⇓{deptno} ⊆ S(department)⇓{deptno}
```

We now use table projection. Supplying state S1 as the value for the parameter results in this proposition:

```
{ {(deptno;10)}, {(deptno;12)} } ⊆
{ {(deptno;10)}, {(deptno;11)}, {(deptno;12)}, {(deptno;13)} }
```

This is again a TRUE proposition. The set of two functions at the left-hand side is a subset of the set of four functions at the right-hand side.

Predicate P14 states that the sum of the salaries of all employees in the employee table that work in a particular department should not exceed the salary budget for that department as found in the department table. Database state S1 also satisfies P14.

As with tuple and table predicates, some cases of database predicates are considered degenerate cases. If a database predicate, say P, can be rewritten into a predicate with the following pattern, we consider the database predicate a degenerate case:

```
P(S) := Q(S(T))
```

If a database predicate is of the preceding form, then it involves only one table structure. In the right-hand side expression, T represents one of the table structure names in a database state S. S(T) then represents the corresponding table, and Q represents a table predicate. Database predicates that involve just one table structure (in the preceding case, T) are considered degenerate. These degenerate cases are in fact disguising a table predicate. In the next chapter we'll require for these cases that Q is introduced as a table predicate and that database predicate P is discarded.

Without loss of generality, we again confine our attention to database predicates that cannot be decomposed into multiple conjuncts. If you can rewrite a given database predicate P(S) into an expression of the form Pa(S) ∧ Pb(S), then you are in fact dealing with two database predicates.

A Few Remarks on Data Integrity Predicates

We conclude the introduction of the preceding three classes of data integrity predicates with a few observations.

As you've seen through the various examples, we can elegantly use tuple, table, and database predicates to formally define the conditions (business rules) that are part of the real world and that need to be reflected somehow in the specification of a database design. The predicate class (tuple, table, or database) to which a business rule maps is fully dependent on the given database skeleton of the database design. For instance, predicate P8 (see Listing 6-5) is a *table predicate* because all the information to formally specify the business rule that managers earn more than trainers, and trainers earn more than clerks, is available within the employee table structure. Now, if for some reason a separate table structure, say trainer, was introduced to hold all trainer information (rendering employee to hold only manager and clerk information), then this real-world constraint would map to a *database predicate* involving both table structures employee and trainer.

You might have a question regarding the way we've introduced data integrity predicates in this chapter. In the various examples you've seen, we've employed these predicates to show whether a given tuple, table, or database state satisfies them. However, when formally specifying a database design, we aren't interested in a single database state (or table or tuple). We are interested in a *database state space*: a set that holds all values that we allow for our database. We intend to mathematically model such a database state space that represents the *value set* for a database variable (this will be done in Chapter 7). When we do so, we'll use the three classes of data integrity predicates introduced in this chapter, in a sophisticated manner such that they represent data integrity constraints that play a role at the database state space level.

Common Patterns of Table and Database Predicates

This section will establish five common patterns of table and database predicates: *unique identification* predicates, *subset requirement* predicates, *specialization* predicates, *generalization* predicates, and *tuple-in-join* predicates. These five patterns of data integrity predicates are common in database designs and are therefore important enough to justify a separate section dealing with them.

Unique Identification Predicate

We've mentioned before that every tuple that is an element of a given table is unique within that table. The attribute *values* make a tuple unique inside a table, not its attributes. Often it doesn't take all attribute values to identify a tuple uniquely in a table; a proper subset of the attribute values suffices. The way this property can be stated for a certain table is through a special kind of table predicate called a *unique identification* predicate. A unique identification predicate is a table predicate as defined in Definition 6-1.

■Definition 6-1: Unique Identification Predicate Let T be a table and let A be a given non-empty subset of the heading of T. A table predicate is a unique identification predicate if it is of the following form (or can be rewritten into this form):

$$(\ \forall t_1,t_2 \in T: \ t_1{\downarrow}A{=}t_2{\downarrow}A \ \Rightarrow \ t_1{=}t_2 \ )$$

We say that A *is uniquely identifying in* T.

A unique identification predicate states that if any two tuples in a table have the same attribute values on a given subset of the attributes, then they must be the same tuple. Using rewrite rules introduced in Part 1 of this book, you can also express a unique identification predicate in the forms listed in Listing 6-9.

Listing 6-9. *Other Manifestations of Unique Identification Predicates*

$$(\ \forall t_1,t_2 \in T: \ t_1{\neq}t_2 \ \Rightarrow \ t_1{\downarrow}A{\neq}t_2{\downarrow}A \ )$$
$$(\ \forall t_1,t_2 \in T: \ t_1{=}t_2 \ \lor \ t_1{\downarrow}A{\neq}t_2{\downarrow}A \ )$$
$$\neg(\ \exists t_1,t_2 \in T: \ t_1{\neq}t_2 \ \land \ t_1{\downarrow}A{=}t_2{\downarrow}A \ )$$

The first form listed might be a more intuitive formal version of the unique identification predicate; two different tuples in a table must differ on the given subset of attributes. Predicate P12 in Listing 6-7 was written in this form; it states that {dname,loc} is uniquely identifying in table T. Predicate P11 in the same listing is also a unique identification predicate. It is written in the third form displayed in Listing 6-9 and states that {deptno} is uniquely identifying in table T. The first predicate in Listing 6-3 also uses this form.

Given that a set A is uniquely identifying in table T (with heading H), then every subset of H that is a proper *superset* of A is of course also uniquely identifying in table T. In a unique identification predicate, you want to specify an *irreducible* subset A of heading H that is uniquely identifying in table T.

■Note There can be more than one such irreducible subset of H that is uniquely identifying in a table. Listing 6-7 shows two distinct subsets—{deptno} and {dname,loc}—that are both considered to be uniquely identifying in a department table.

If you choose a reducible subset of H, then the resulting unique identification predicate is too weak. The weakest unique identification predicate would be that the heading of T (the largest possible superset) is uniquely identifying in table T. In fact, this wouldn't add any constraint at all on the set of tuples that is admissible for table T; as mentioned at the beginning of this section, we already know that tuples are unique within a table.

You can also conclude this by taking a more formal approach. Take a look what happens if you substitute the heading of T for set A in the unique identification predicate pattern:

$$(\ \forall t_1,t_2 \in T: \ t_1{\downarrow}dom(t_1){=}t_2{\downarrow}dom(t_2) \ \Rightarrow \ t_1{=}t_2 \ )$$

Note that if t is an element of T, then you can refer to the heading of T via expression dom(t): the domain of tuple t. Using the rewrite rule t↓dom(t) = t (the restriction of a tuple to all its attributes is the same as the tuple itself), we can rewrite the preceding predicate into this:

(∀t1,t2∈T: t1=t2 ⇒ t1=t2)

The predicate is now a tautology; it is always TRUE, irrespective of the value of T. Therefore it doesn't constrain T in any way at all.

Note We are deliberately not talking about *keys* in this section. In Chapter 7 we will define, for every table structure in a database design, the set of admissible tables—referred to as *the table universe*—for that table structure. When defining a table universe, we will ensure that every table (in the universe) satisfies one or more unique identification predicates. We then say that a set of uniquely identifying attributes constitutes a *key* in the table universe.

Subset Requirement Predicate

The different table structures that you capture in a database design are not all independent of each other. Many *pairs* of these table structures have a relationship that is referred to as a *subset requirement*. Definition 6-2 defines the concept of a subset requirement predicate. The structure of the predicate in this definition shows why it is referred to as a subset requirement.

Definition 6-2: Subset Requirement Predicate   Let T1 and T2 be tables and let A be a given subset of the heading of T1 as well as a subset of the heading of T2. We refer to a database predicate as a subset requirement predicate if it is of the following form:

{ t1↓A | t1∈T1 } ⊆ { t2↓A | t2∈T2 }

We say that *A in T1 references A in T2.*

Let's demonstrate this with tables EMP1 and DEP1 (see Figures 6-2 and 6-3). If we substitute EMP1 for T1, DEP1 for T2, and {deptno} for A, we end up with the following expression:

{ t1↓{deptno} | t1∈EMP1 } ⊆ { t2↓{deptno} | t2∈DEP1 }

This evaluates to the following expression:

{ {(deptno;10)}, {(deptno;12)} } ⊆
{ {(deptno;10)}, {(deptno;11)}, {(deptno;12)}, {(deptno;13)} }

This is a TRUE proposition; every department number in EMP1 also appears in DEP1.

If the cardinality of A equals 1 (that is, if A represents a singleton), then we will often use function application instead of function limitation to specify a subset requirement predicate. Using the preceding example, we would write this:

{ t1(deptno) | t1∈ EMP1 } ⊆ { t2(deptno) | t2∈ DEP1 }

This subset requirement is analogous to predicate P13 in Listing 6-8.

A subset requirement predicate is often accompanied by a unique identification predicate. Using the names from Definition 6-2, you'll often encounter that "A is uniquely identifying in T2;" in the preceding example {deptno} is indeed uniquely identifying in DEP1. This is not mandatory; the example database design that will be given in Chapter 7 actually has a subset requirement where the accompanying unique identification predicate is absent.

When using function limitation to specify a subset requirement, you must sometimes apply function composition to rename one or more attributes in one of the tables involved. Let's illustrate this through an example. Take a look at table DEP2, displayed in Figure 6-5, which very much resembles table DEP1.

dno	dname	loc	salbudget
10	'RESEARCH'	'DENVER'	50000
11	'SALES'	'DENVER'	20000
12	'SUPPORT'	'LOS ANGELES'	40000
13	'SALES'	'SAN FRANCISCO'	20000

Figure 6-5. *Example table DEP2*

Table DEP2 differs from table DEP1 in that the attribute used to hold the department number is now named dno instead of deptno. You can express a subset requirement from EMP1 (see Figure 6-2) to DEP2 using function application, as follows:

{ e(deptno)| e∈ EMP1 } ⊆ { d(dno)| d∈ DEP2 }

However, if you want to specify this subset requirement using function limitation, you must first either rename the deptno attribute in table EMP1 into dno, or rename the dno attribute in table DEP2 into deptno. Here is the specification for this subset requirement, where the attribute renaming is applied to EMP1 tuples:

{ e◊{(dno;deptno)} | e∈ EMP1 } ⊆ { d↓{dno}| d∈ DEP2 }

In this expression, the function {(dno;deptno)} represents an attribute renaming function. It renames the deptno attribute in tuples from table EMP1 to dno.

■**Note** In this case the renaming function performs a tuple limitation too (see the note in the section "Function Composition" in Chapter 4).

By using the more elaborate function limitation as opposed to the function application that was used in Listing 6-8, you are able to express subset requirements that involve multiple attributes of both involved tables at the same time. The database design that will be introduced in Chapter 7 has an example subset requirement that involves multiple attributes.

A subset requirement predicate usually involves two *different* table structures, and therefore represents a database predicate. However, this need not always be the case; sometimes they involve just one table structure. In these cases, they represent a table predicate. For instance, assume that table EMP1 is extended with a mgr (manager) attribute that holds the employee number of the manager of the employee. You would require that every manager number that appears in EMP1 also appears as an employee number in EMP1. Formally, you can express this as a subset requirement:

{ t1(mgr) | t1∈EMP1 } ⊆ { t2(empno) | t2∈EMP1 }

You might even require that every manager number that appears in EMP1 also appears as an employee number in a certain *restriction* of EMP1. Perhaps the referenced tuples must each have a JOB value indicating that the employee in question is indeed a manager. Formally, you can express this as follows:

{ t1(mgr) | t1∈EMP1 } ⊆ { t2(empno) | t2∈EMP1 ∧ t2(job)='MANAGER' }

We consider the preceding expression also a subset requirement.

Subset requirements can be visualized by a picture. You can draw a picture for a subset requirement "A in T1 references A in T2" by drawing two rectangles (or some other shape)—one for T1 and one for T2—and connecting the two rectangles with a directed arrow going from T1 to T2. The arrow represents that every tuple in table T1 references at least one tuple in table T2. Figure 6-6 shows the subset requirement from EMP1 to DEP2.

Figure 6-6. *Visualization of subset requirement from EMP1 to DEP2*

Note that this picture of a subset requirement doesn't tell you what the involved attributes are at both sides of the arrow, nor if any attribute renaming is involved. It is *just a picture* and should always be accompanied by the formal predicate that tells you exactly what the intended meaning of the arrow is.

Sometimes you know that the subset requirement is actually a *proper* subset requirement. Suppose you want to specify the requirement that the set of department numbers found in an employee table is a proper subset of the set of department numbers found in a department table. You can specify this database predicate as follows:

P15a(D,E) := { e(deptno)| e∈E } ⊂ { d(dno)| d∈D }

In this book, we'll call this special case a subset requirement too. Another way of dealing with this is to still use the subset operator (instead of the proper subset) and to specify a second database predicate that expresses the existence of at least one department number in the department table that does not appear in the employee table. The following database predicate P15b does just that:

P15b(D,E) := (∃d∈D: (∀e∈E: e(deptno)≠d(deptno)))

Tables EMP1 (employee) and DEP2 (department) conform to both database predicate P15a and P15b. At other times you know that the subset requirement is actually an *equality* requirement. Suppose you want to specify the requirement that every department must have employees. You can specify this as follows:

P16a(D,E) := { e(deptno)| e∈E } = { d(dno)| d∈D }

In this book we'll call this special case a subset requirement too. Again, another way of dealing with this is to use the subset operation (instead of the equality) and to add a second integrity constraint that expresses the existence of at least one employee for every department. Database predicate P16b expresses just that:

P16b(D,E) := (∀d∈D: (∃e∈E: e(deptno)=d(deptno)))

By the way, do you see that predicate P15b is just the negation of predicate P16b? This is because these two special cases—proper subset and equality—are mutually exclusive.

■**Note** These variations of subset requirements in conjunction with unique identification predicates of the tables involved in the subset requirements are mathematical counterparts of various relationships found in entity relationship diagrams.

Specialization Predicate

Take a look at table TRN1 displayed in Figure 6-7.

empno	certified
102	20-MAY-2006
104	01-OCT-2005

Figure 6-7. *Table TRN1*

The propositions regarding tables EMP1 and TRN1 listed in Listing 6-10 are TRUE propositions.

Listing 6-10. *Propositions Regarding Tables EMP1 and TRN1*

```
P7 := {empno} is uniquely identifying in TRN1
P8 := { e↓{empno}| e∈EMP1 ∧ e(job)='TRAINER' } = { t↓{empno}| t∈TRN1 }
```

> **Note** We have formally defined what we mean by saying that *a set is uniquely identifying in a table*. So P7 is indeed a formal specification.

It follows from proposition P7 that the uniquely identifying attributes of tables TRN1 and EMP1 are the same. Proposition P8 states that the employee numbers of trainers in table EMP1 equal the employee numbers found in table TRN1 (loosely speaking). Note the *equality*. For every trainer that can be found in table EMP1, you can find a related tuple in table TRN1. And vice versa, for every tuple in TRN1 you can find a trainer in EMP1.

Table TRN1 can be considered to hold additional information regarding trainers (and only trainers): the date on which they got certified (again loosely speaking).

This type of circumstance is often found in database designs; for a certain subset of tuples in a given table—specifiable through some predicate (in the preceding case e(job)='TRAINER')—additional information is found in another given table where both tables share the same uniquely identifying attributes. In this case, table TRN1 is referred to as a *specialization* of table EMP1. Definition 6-3 formally specifies this concept.

> **Definition 6-3: Specialization Predicate** Let T1 and T2 be tables and let A be a given subset of the heading of T1 as well as a subset of the heading of T2. Let P be a tuple predicate. We refer to a database predicate as a specialization predicate if it is of the following form:
>
> { t1↓A | t1∈T1 ∧ P(t1) } = { t2↓A | t2∈T2 }
>
> We say that *T2 is a specialization of T1*.

You'll usually find that set A is uniquely identifying in both tables T1 and T2. In the example from Listing 6-10, you saw that {empno} is uniquely identifying in both EMP1 and TRN1.

A given table can have more than one specialization. Assume that you want to hold additional information for managers too; for instance, the agreed yearly bonus for a manager. For the sake of this example, assume that trainers and clerks do not have a yearly bonus, only managers do. Take a look at table MAN1 (see Figure 6-8) that holds the yearly bonus for managers; it is also a specialization of EMP1.

empno	ybonus
101	16000
106	17000

Figure 6-8. *Table MAN1*

The following proposition holds between tables EMP1 and MAN1. It is of the form introduced in Definition 6-3.

$$\{ \ e\!\downarrow\!\{empno\}| \ \ e \in EMP1 \ \wedge \ e(job)='MANAGER' \ \} = \{ \ t\!\downarrow\!\{empno\}| \ \ t \in MAN1 \ \}$$

In the next section we'll discuss a concept that is related to specializations.

Generalization

If a given table T has multiple specializations, say tables S1 through Sn (n>1), such that for every tuple in T there exists exactly one related tuple in exactly one of the specializations, then we say that "table T is a *generalization* of tables S1 through Sn."

Let's build on the example of the previous section. Suppose you also want to hold additional information for clerks; for instance, the type of contract they have (full time or part time) and the manager that they report to. Table CLK1, shown in Figure 6-9, is a specialization of table EMP1 that holds this extra information for clerks.

empno	contract	manager
103	'fulltime'	106
105	'parttime'	106
107	'parttime'	101

Figure 6-9. *Table CLK1*

Specializations TRN1, MAN1, and CLK1 now have seven tuples in total. For every tuple in table EMP1—there are seven—there exists exactly one tuple in exactly one of the tables TRN1, MAN1, or CLK1. This makes table EMP1 a generalization of tables TRN1, MAN1, and CLK1.

Note By the way, you can now also specify a subset requirement (involving the manager attribute of CLK1) from CLK1 to EMP1. This is left as an exercise at the end of the chapter.

In a generalization table, you'll often find a specific attribute that determines in which specialization table the additional information can be found. In the example used, this attribute is the job attribute. For the tuples in table EMP1 that have job='TRAINER', additional information is found in specialization TRN1. For tuples with job='MANAGER', additional information can be found in table MAN1, and for tuples with job='CLERK', additional information can be found in table CLK1. Such an attribute in a generalization table is referred to as the *inspection attribute*.

Note that an inspection attribute is a redundant attribute; that is, its value can be derived from other tuples. For a given tuple of EMP1, a corresponding tuple exists in either TRN1, MAN1, or CLK1. You can directly deduce the job value of the EMP1 tuple from where this corresponding tuple appears; its value should be 'TRAINER', 'MANAGER', or 'CLERK', respectively.

In general, you shouldn't introduce data redundancy in a database design; it forces you to maintain the redundancy whenever you update data that determines the redundant data. Or, viewed from a database design perspective, it forces you to introduce a constraint that imposes the data redundancy. However, an inspection attribute is very helpful when specifying a generalization property in a database design (there is an exercise on this at the end of this chapter).

Tuple-in-Join Predicate

Often two tables are related through a subset requirement. When two tables are thus related, the need to join them arises often, for obvious reasons. You can join tuples from tables EMP1 and DEP1 that correspond on the attributes that are involved in the subset requirement between these two tables, in this case the deptno attribute. The resulting table from this combination will have as its heading the union of the heading of EMP1 and the heading of DEP1.

Figure 6-10 displays the result of such a combination of tables EMP1 and DEP1.

empno	ename	job	sal	deptno	dname	loc	salbudget
101	'Chris'	'MANAGER'	7900	10	'RESEARCH'	'DENVER'	50000
102	'Kathy'	'TRAINER'	6000	12	'SUPPORT'	'LOS ANGELES'	40000
103	'Thomas'	'CLERK'	2100	10	'RESEARCH'	'DENVER'	50000
104	'David'	'TRAINER'	5600	10	'RESEARCH'	'DENVER'	50000
105	'Renu'	'CLERK'	3000	12	'SUPPORT'	'LOS ANGELES'	40000
106	'Bob'	'MANAGER'	8500	10	'RESEARCH'	'DENVER'	50000
107	'Sue'	'CLERK'	2700	12	'SUPPORT'	'LOS ANGELES'	40000

Figure 6-10. *Table EMPDEP1, the join of tables EMP1 and DEP1*

Every tuple in table EMPDEP1 is called a *tuple in the join* of EMP1 and DEP1. *Tuple-in-join predicates* are tuple predicates dealing with these tuples in a join; the joined tuple is the parameter for the tuple predicate. Here is an example of a tuple predicate regarding EMPDEP1:

($\forall t \in$ EMPDEP1: t(sal)$\leq$t(salbudget)/5)

This proposition states that all tuples in EMPDEP1—the join of EMP1 and DEP1—have a sal attribute value that doesn't exceed 20 percent of the salbudget attribute value. In this proposition the expression t(sal)$\leq$t(salbudget)/5 represents the tuple predicate. If you express this proposition not in terms of table EMPDEP1, but in terms of the two tables that are joined—EMP1 and DEP1—you'll end up with a proposition looking like this:

($\forall e \in$ EMP1: ($\forall d \in$ DEP1: e(deptno)=d(deptno) $\Rightarrow$ e(sal)$\leq$d(salbudget)/5))

It states that no employee can earn more than a fifth of the departmental salary budget (of the department where he or she is employed). Another way of formally specifying this is as follows:

$$(\ \forall t \in EMP1 \otimes DEP1: \ t(sal) \leq t(salbudget)/5 \ )$$

In this proposition, the expression $t(sal) \leq t(salbudget)/5$ represents a tuple predicate that constrains the tuples in the join. This predicate pattern is commonly found in database designs and is referred to as a *tuple-in-join predicate*. Definition 6-4 formally specifies it.

■Definition 6-4: Tuple-in-Join Predicate Let T1 and T2 be tables and P a tuple predicate. A predicate is a tuple-in-join predicate if it is of the following form:

$$(\ \forall t \in T1 \otimes T2: \ P(t) \ )$$

We say that *P constrains tuples in the join of T1 and T2.*

In the preceding definition, you will typically find that tables T1 and T2 are related via a subset requirement that involves the join attributes.

Listing 6-11 demonstrates two more instantiations of a tuple-in-join predicate involving tables EMP1 and DEP1.

Listing 6-11. *More Tuple-in-Join Predicates Regarding Tables EMP1 and DEP1*

```
P9  := ( ∀e∈ EMP1: ( ∀d∈ DEP1: e↓{deptno}=d↓{deptno} ⇒
                     (d(loc)='LOS ANGELES'⇒ e(job)≠'MANAGER') ) )
P10 := ( ∀e∈ EMP1: ( ∀d∈ DEP1: e↓{deptno}=d↓{deptno} ⇒
                     (d(loc)='SAN FRANCISCO'⇒ e(job)∈{'TRAINER','CLERK'}) ) )
```

P9 states that managers cannot be employed in Los Angeles. P10 states that employees working in San Francisco must either be trainers or clerks. Given the sample values EMP1 and DEP1 in Figure 6-10 both propositions are TRUE; there are no managers working in Los Angeles and all employees working in San Francisco—there are none—are either trainers or clerks.

In this section, we've defined the tuple-in-join predicate to involve only two tables. However, it is often meaningful to combine three or even more tables with the join operator. Of course, tuples in these joins can also be constrained by a tuple predicate. Here is the pattern of a tuple-in-join predicate involving three tables (T1, T2, and T3):

$$(\ \forall t1 \in T1: (\ \forall t2 \in T2: (\ \forall t3 \in T3: (t1 \downarrow A = t2 \downarrow A \ \wedge \ t2 \downarrow B = t3 \downarrow B) \ \Rightarrow P(t1 \cup t2 \cup t3) \ ) \ ) \ )$$

In this pattern, A represents the set of join attributes for tables T1 and T2, and B represents the set of join attributes for tables T2 and T3. Predicate P represents a predicate whose argument is the tuple in the join. In the next chapter, you'll see examples of tuple-in-join predicates involving more than two tables.

Chapter Summary

This section provides a summary of this chapter, formatted as a bulleted list. You can use it to check your understanding of the various concepts introduced in this chapter before continuing with the exercises in the next section.

- A *tuple predicate* is a predicate with one parameter of type tuple. It can be used to accept (or reject) tuples based on the combination of attribute values that they hold.

- A *table predicate* is a predicate with one parameter of type table. It can be used to accept (or reject) tables based on the combination of tuples that they hold.

- A *database (multi-table) predicate* is a predicate with one parameter of type database state. It can be used to accept (or reject) database states based on the combination of tables that they hold.

- Five patterns of table and database predicates are commonly found in database designs: *unique identification, subset requirement, specialization, generalization,* and *tuple-in-join* predicates.

- A *unique identification* predicate is a table predicate of the following form (T represents a table): ($\forall t_1, t_2 \in T$: $t_1{\downarrow}A = t_2{\downarrow}A \Rightarrow t_1 = t_2$).

  In this expression, A represents the set of attributes that uniquely identify tuples in table T.

- A *subset requirement* predicate is a predicate of the following form (T1 and T2 represent tables): { $t_1{\downarrow}A$ | $t_1 \in T_1$ } $\subseteq$ { $t_2{\downarrow}A$ | $t_2 \in T_2$ }.

  In this expression, A often represents the set of attributes that uniquely identify tuples in table T2.

- A *specialization* predicate is a database predicate of the following form (T1 and T2 represent tables): { $t_1{\downarrow}A$ | $t_1 \in T_1 \wedge P(t_1)$ } = { $t_2{\downarrow}A$ | $t_2 \in T_2$ }.

  In this expression, A represents the set of attributes that uniquely identify tuples in both tables T1 and T2. Predicate P is a predicate specifying a subset of table T1. We say that "T2 is a specialization of T1." T2 is considered to hold additional information for the subset of tuples in T1 specified by predicate P.

- If a given table, say T, has more than one specialization such that for every tuple in T there exists exactly one tuple in exactly one of the specialization tables that holds additional information for that tuple, then table T is referred to as the *generalization* of the specializations.

- A *tuple-in-join* predicate is a predicate of the following form (T1 and T2 represent tables): ($\forall t_1 \in T_1$: ($\forall t_2 \in T_2$: $t_1{\downarrow}A = t_2{\downarrow}A \Rightarrow P(t_1 \cup t_2)$)).

  In this expression, A represents the set of attributes that is typically involved in a subset requirement between tables T1 and T2. Predicate P is a tuple predicate.

Exercises

1. Evaluate the truth value of the following propositions (PAR1 was introduced in Figure 6-1):

   a. ($\forall p \in$ PAR1: mod(p(partno),2)=0 $\Rightarrow$ p(price)≤15)

   b. ¬($\exists p \in$ PAR1: p(price)≠5 $\vee$ p(instock)=0)

   c. #{ p | p∈PAR1 $\wedge$ (p(instock)>10 $\Rightarrow$ p(price)≤10) } = 6

2. Let A be a subset of the heading of PAR1. Give all possible values for A such that "A is uniquely identifying in PAR1" (only give the smallest possible subsets).

3. Specify a subset requirement predicate from CLK1 and EMP1 stating that the manager of a clerk must be an employee whose job is 'MANAGER'.

4. Formally specify the fact that table EMP1 is a generalization of tables TRN1, MAN1, and CLK1.

5. In EMP1 the job attribute is a (redundant) inspection attribute. Formally specify the fact that EMP1 is a generalization of TRN1, MAN1, and CLK1 given that EMP1 does *not* have this attribute.

6. Using rewrite rules for implication and quantifiers that have been introduced in Part 1, give at least three alternative formal expressions for proposition P12.

7. Using the semantics introduced by tables EMP1 and CLK1, give a formal specification for the database predicate "A manager of a clerk must work in the same department as the clerk."

   Is this proposition TRUE for tables EMP1 and CLK1?

8. Using the semantics introduced by tables DEP1, EMP1, and CLK1, give a formal specification for the database predicate "A manager of a clerk must work in a department that is located in Denver."

   Is this proposition TRUE for these tables?

CHAPTER 7

Specifying Database Designs

In this chapter, we'll give a demonstration of how you can formally specify a database design. Formalizing a database design specification has the advantage of avoiding any ambiguity in the documentation of not only the database structure but, even more importantly, of all involved data integrity constraints.

Note Within the IT industry, the term *business rules* is often used to denote what this book refers to as *data integrity constraints*. However, because a clear definition of what exactly is meant by business rules is seldom given, we cannot be sure about this. In this book, we prefer not to use the term business rules, but instead use data integrity constraints. In this chapter, we'll give a clear definition of the latter term.

We'll give the formal specification of a database design by defining the data type of a database variable. This data type—essentially a set—holds all admissible database states for the database variable and is dubbed the *database universe*.

You'll see that a database universe can be constructed in a phased (layered) manner, which along the way provides us with a clear classification schema for data integrity constraints.

First, you define what the vocabulary is. What are the things, and aspects of these things in the real world, that you want to deal with in your database? Here you specify a name for each table structure that is deemed necessary, and the names of the attributes that the table structure will have. We'll introduce an example database design to demonstrate this. The vocabulary is formally defined in what is called a *database skeleton*. A good way to further explain the meaning of all attributes (and their correlation) is to provide the *external predicate* for each table structure; this is a natural language sentence describing the meaning and correlation of the involved attributes.

Given the database skeleton, we then define for each attribute the set of admissible attribute values. This is done by introducing a *characterization* for each table structure. You were introduced to the concept of a characterization in Chapter 4.

You'll then use these characterizations as building blocks to construct the set of admissible tuples for each table. This is called a *tuple universe*, and includes the formal specification of *tuple constraints*.

Then, you'll use the tuple universes to build the set of admissible tables for each table structure. This set is called a *table universe*, and can be considered the data type of a table variable. The definition of a table universe will include the formal specification of the relevant *table constraints*.

The last section of this chapter shows how you can bring together the table universes in the definition of the set of admissible database states, which was the goal set out for this chapter: to define a database universe. In this phase you formally specify the *database (multi-table) constraints*.

Because the example database universe presented in this chapter has ten table structures, we'll introduce you to ten characterizations, ten tuple universes, and ten table universes. This, together with the explanatory material provided, makes this chapter a rather big one. However, the number of examples should provide you with a solid head start to applying the formal theory, and thereby enable you to start practicing this methodology in your job as a database professional. You can find a version of this example database design specification that includes the design's bare essentials in Appendix A.

After the "Chapter Summary" section, a section with exercises focuses primarily on changing or adding constraint specifications in the various layers of the example database universe introduced in this chapter.

Documenting Databases and Constraints

Because you're reading this book, you consider yourself a database professional. Therefore, it's likely that the activity of specifying database designs is part of your job. You'll probably agree that the process of designing a database roughly consists of two major tasks:

1. Discovering the things in the real world for which you need to introduce a table structure in your database design. This is done by interviewing and communicating with the users and stakeholders of the information system that you're trying to design.

2. Discovering the data integrity constraints that will control the data that's maintained in the table structures. These constraints add meaning to the table structures introduced in step one, and will ultimately make the database design a satisfactory fit for the reality that you're modeling.

The application of the math introduced in Part 1 of this book is primarily geared to the second task; it enables you to formally specify the data integrity constraints. We're convinced that whenever you design a database, you should spend the biggest part of time on designing the involved data integrity constraints. Accurately—that is, unambiguously—documenting these data integrity constraints can spell the difference between your success and failure.

Still, today documenting data integrity constraints is most widely done using natural language, which often produces a quick dive into ambiguity. If you use plain English to express data integrity constraints, you'll inevitably hit the problem of *how the English sentence maps, unambiguously, into the table structures*. Different programmers (and users alike) will interpret such sentences differently, because they all try to convert these into something that will map into the database design. Programmers then code *their* perception of the constraint (not necessarily the specifier's).

The sections that follow will demonstrate that the logic and set theory introduced in Part 1 lends itself excellently to capturing database designs with their integrity constraints in a formal manner. Formal specifications of data integrity constraints tell you exactly how they map into the table structures. You'll not only avoid the ambiguity mentioned earlier, but moreover you'll get a clear and expert view of the most important aspect of a database: all involved data integrity constraints.

Note Some of you will be surprised, by the example that follows, of how much of the overall specification of an information system actually sits in the specification of the database design. A lot of the "business logic" involved in an information system can often be represented by data integrity constraints that map into the underlying table structures that support the information system.

The Layers Inside a Database Design

Having set the scene, we'll now demonstrate how set theory and logic enable you to get a clear and professional view of a database design and its integrity constraints. The next two sections introduce you (informally) to a particular way of looking at the quintessence of a database design. This view is such that it will enable a layered set-theory specification of a database design.

Top-Down View of a Database

A database (state) at any given point in time is essentially a set of tables. Our database, or rather our database variable, holds the current database state. In the course of time, transactions occur that assign new database states to the database variable. We need to specify the set of all *admissible database states* for our database variable. This set is called the *database universe*, and in effect defines the data type for the database variable. Viewed top down, within the database universe for a given database design that involves say n table structures, you can observe the following:

- Every database state is an admissible set of n tables (one per table structure), where

- every table is an admissible set of tuples, where

- every tuple is an admissible set of attribute-value pairs, where

- every value is an admissible value for the given attribute.

Because all preceding layers are sets, you can define them all mathematically using set theory. Through logic (by adding embedded predicates) you define exactly what is meant by *admissible* in each layer; here the data integrity constraints enter the picture.

So how do you specify, in a formal way, this set called the database universe? This is done in a bottom-up approach using the same layers introduced earlier. First, you define what your vocabulary is: what are the things, and aspects of them in the real world, that you want to deal with in your database? In other words, what table structures do you need, and what attributes does each table structure have? This is formally defined in what is called a *database skeleton*.

For each attribute introduced in the database skeleton, you then define the set of admissible attribute values. You've already been introduced to this; in this phase all *characterizations* (one per table structure) are defined.

You then use the characterizations as building blocks to build (define) for each table structure the *set of admissible tuples*. This involves applying the generalized product operator (see Definition 4-7) and the introduction of tuple predicates. The set of admissible tuples is called a *tuple universe*.

You can then use the tuple universes to build for each table structure the *set of admissible tables*, which is called a *table universe*. You'll see how this can be done in this chapter; it involves applying the powerset operator and introducing table predicates.

In the last phase you define the set of admissible database states—the database universe—using the previously defined table universes.

This methodology of formally defining the data type of a database variable was developed by the Dutch mathematician Bert De Brock together with Frans Remmen in the 1980s, and is an elegant method of accurately defining a database design, including all relevant data integrity constraints. The references *De grondslagen van semantische databases* (Academic Service, 1990, in Dutch) and *Foundations of Semantic Databases* (Prentice Hall, 1995) are books written by Bert De Brock in which he introduces this methodology.

Classification Schema for Constraints

In this bottom-up solid construction of a database universe, you explicitly only allow sets of admissible values at each of the levels described earlier. This means that at each level these sets must satisfy certain data integrity constraints. The constraints specify which sets are valid ones; they condition the contents of the sets. This leads straightforwardly to four classes of data integrity constraints:

- *Attribute constraints*: In fact, these are the attribute value sets that you specify in a characterization. You can argue whether the term "constraint" is appropriate here. A characterization simply specifies the attribute value set for every attribute (without further *constraining* the elements in it). However, the attribute value set does *constrain* the values allowed for the attribute.

Note We'll revisit this matter in Chapter 11 when the attribute value sets are implemented in an SQL database management system.

- *Tuple constraints*: These are the *tuple predicates* that you specify inside the definition of a tuple universe. The tuple predicates constrain combinations of values of different attributes within a tuple. Sometimes these constraints are referred to as *inter-attribute constraints*. You can specify them without referring to other tuples. For instance, here's a constraint between attributes Job and Salary of an EMP (employee) table structure: "Employees with job President earn a monthly salary greater than 10000 dollars."

- *Table constraints*: These are *table predicates* that you specify inside the definition of a table universe. The table predicates constrain combinations of different tuples within the same table. Sometimes these constraints are referred to as *inter-tuple constraints*. You can specify them without referring to other tables. For instance: "No employee can earn a higher monthly salary than his/her manager" (here we assume the presence of a Manager attribute in the EMP table structure that references the employee's manager).

- *Database constraints*: These are database predicates that you specify inside the definition of a database universe. The database predicates constrain combinations of tables for different table structures. Sometimes these constraints are referred to as inter-table constraints. You can only specify them while referring to different table structures. For instance, there's the omnipresent database constraint between the EMP and DEPT table structures: each employee must work for a known department.

These four classes of constraints accept or reject a given database state. They condition database states and are often referred to as *static* (or *state*) *constraints*; they can be checked within the context of a (static) database state. In actuality there is one more constraint class. This is the class of constraints that limit database state *transitions* (on grounds other than the static constraints). Predicates specifically conditioning database state transitions are referred to as *dynamic* (or *state transition*) *constraints*. We'll cover these separately in Chapter 8.

Because the preceding classification scheme is driven by the *scope of data* that a constraint deals with, it has the advantage of being closely related to implementation issues of constraints. When you implement a database design in an SQL DBMS, you'll be confronted with these issues, given the poor declarative support for data integrity constraints in these systems. This lack of support puts the burden upon you to develop often complex code that enforces the constraints. Chapter 11 will investigate these implementation challenges of data integrity constraints using the classification introduced here.

Specifying the Example Database Design

We'll demonstrate the application of the theory presented in Part 1 of this book through an elaborate treatment of a database design that consists of ten table structures.

We comment up front that this database design merely serves as a vehicle to demonstrate the formal specification methodology; it is explicitly not our intention to discuss *why* the design is as it is. We acknowledge that some of the assumptions on which this design is based could be questionable. Also we mention up front that this design has two hacks, probably by some of you considered rather horrible. We'll indicate these when they are introduced.

Figure 7-1 shows a diagram of the ten table structures (represented by boxes) and their mutual relationships (represented by arrows). Each of the arrows indicates a subset requirement predicate that is applicable between a pair of table structures.

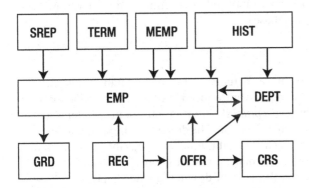

Figure 7-1. *Picture of example database*

■**Note** The majority of these arrows represent what is often called *many-to-one relationships* and will eventually end up as *foreign keys* during the implementation phase in an SQL DBMS. However, this need not always be the case, as you will see. The exact meaning of each arrow will be given in the database universe specification where each arrow translates to a database constraint.

Our database holds employees (EMP) and departments (DEPT) of a company. Some of the arrows indicate the following:

- Every employee works for a department.

- Every department is managed by an employee.

- Every employee is assigned to a salary grade (GRD).

Employee history (HIST) records are maintained for all salary and/or "works-for-department" changes; every history record describes a period during which one employee was assigned to a department with a specific salary.

We hold additional information for all sales representatives in a separate table structure (SREP). We hold additional information for employees who no longer work for the company (that is, they have been terminated or they resigned) in TERM. Note that we keep the EMP information for terminated employees. We also hold additional information for all managed employees (MEMP); that is, employees who have a manager assigned to them.

The database further holds information about courses (CRS), offerings (OFFR) of those courses, and registrations (REG) for those course offerings. Some more arrows show the following:

- An offering must be taught by a trainer who works for the company.

- An offering is for an existing course.

- A registration records an employee as an attendee for a course offering.

You now have some idea of the information we're maintaining in this database. In the next section, you'll find the *database skeleton*. As mentioned before, it introduces the names of all attributes for every table structure. Together with the table structure names, they form the vocabulary that we have available in our database design.

Database Skeleton

The names of the things in the real world that we are representing in our database design, including the names of the attributes of interest, are introduced in what is called a database skeleton. We sometimes refer to this as the *conceptual skeleton*. As you saw in Chapter 5, a database skeleton is represented as a set-valued function. The domain of the skeleton function is the set of table structure names. For each name, this function yields the set of attribute names of that table structure; that is, the heading of that table structure.

Our database skeleton DB_S for the example database design is defined in Listing 7-1. Inside the specification of DB_S you see embedded comments (/* ... */) to clarify further the chosen abbreviations for the table structure and attribute names.

Listing 7-1. *Database Skeleton Definition*

```
DB_S := { (EMP;                      -- Employees
              { EMPNO          /* Employee number              */
              , ENAME          /* Employee name                */
              , JOB            /* Employee job                 */
              , BORN           /* Date of birth                */
              , HIRED          /* Date hired                   */
              , SGRADE         /* Salary grade                 */
              , MSAL           /* Monthly salary               */
              , USERNAME       /* Username                     */
              , DEPTNO    } )  /* Department number            */
        , (SREP;                      -- Sales Representatives
              { EMPNO          /* Employee number              */
              , TARGET         /* Sales target                 */
              , COMM      } )  /* Commission                   */
        , (MEMP;                      -- Managed Employees
              { EMPNO          /* Employee number              */
              , MGR       } )  /* Manager: employee number     */
        , (TERM;                      -- Terminated Employees
              { EMPNO          /* Employee number              */
              , LEFT           /* Date of leave                */
              , COMMENTS } )   /* Termination comments         */
        , (DEPT;                      -- Departments
              { DEPTNO         /* Department number            */
              , DNAME          /* Department name              */
              , LOC            /* Location                     */
              , MGR       } )  /* Manager: employee number     */
        , (GRD;                       -- Salary Grades
              { GRADE          /* Grade code                   */
              , LLIMIT         /* Lower salary limit           */
              , ULIMIT         /* Upper salary limit           */
              , BONUS     } )  /* Yearly bonus                 */
        , (CRS;                       -- Courses
              { CODE           /* Course code                  */
              , DESCR          /* Course description           */
              , CAT            /* Course category              */
              , DUR       } )  /* Duration of course in days   */
        , (OFFR;                      -- Course Offerings
              { COURSE         /* Code of course               */
              , STARTS         /* Begin date of this offering  */
              , STATUS         /* Scheduled, confirmed, ...    */
              , MAXCAP         /* Max participants capacity    */
              , TRAINER        /* Trainer: employee number     */
              , LOC       } )  /* Location                     */
        , (REG;                       -- Course Registrations
              { STUD           /* Student: employee number     */
              , COURSE         /* Course code                  */
```

```
            , STARTS          /* Begin date course offering  */
            , EVAL      } )    /* Evaluation                  */
    , (HIST;                   -- Employee History Records
            { EMPNO           /* Employee number             */
            , UNTIL           /* History record end date      */
            , DEPTNO          /* Department number           */
            , MSAL      } ) }  /* Monthly salary              */
```

Given the database skeleton, you can now write expressions such as DB_S(DEPT), which represents the set of attribute names of the DEPT table structure. The expression denotes the set {DEPTNO, DNAME, LOC, MGR}.

With this definition of the table headings, you're now developing some more sense of what each table structure in our database design is all about—what it intends to represent. A way to clarify further the *meaning* of the table structures and their attributes is to provide the *external predicates*. An external predicate is an English sentence that involves all attributes of a table structure and supplies a statement regarding these attributes that explains their inter-connected meaning. Following is the external predicate for the EMP table structure:

> The employee with employee number **EMPNO** has name **ENAME**, job **JOB**, was born on **BORN**, is hired on **HIRED**, has a monthly salary of **MSAL** dollars within the **SGRADE** salary grade, is assigned to account **USERNAME** and works for the department with department number **DEPTNO**.

It is called *external* because a database management system cannot deal with this English sentence. It is meant for the (external) users of the system, and supplies an interpretation of the chosen names for the attributes. It is called a *predicate* because you can view this English sentence as being parameterized, where the parameters are the embedded attribute names. You can instantiate the external predicate using the tuples in the current EMP table. You do this by replacing every occurrence of an attribute name inside the sentence with the corresponding attribute value within a given tuple. The new sentence formed this way can be viewed as a proposition that can either yield TRUE or FALSE. Sentences generated in this way by the external predicate are statements about the real world represented by the table. By convention, the propositions that are constructed in this way are assumed to be TRUE. This is precisely how external predicates further clarify the meaning of your database design.

Table 7-1 lists the external predicates for all table structures introduced in the skeleton.

Table 7-1. *External Predicates*

Table	External Predicate
EMP	The employee with employee number EMPNO has name ENAME, job JOB, was born on BORN, is hired on HIRED, has a monthly salary of MSAL dollars within the SGRADE salary grade, is assigned to account USERNAME, and works for the department with department number DEPTNO.
SREP	The sales representative with employee number EMPNO has an annual sales target of TARGET dollars and a yearly commission of COMM dollars.
MEMP	The employee with employee number EMPNO is managed by the employee with employee number MGR.
TERM	The employee with employee number EMPNO has resigned or was fired on date LEFT due to reason COMMENTS.

Table	External Predicate
DEPT	The department with department number DEPTNO, has name DNAME, is located at LOC, and is managed by the employee with employee number MGR.
GRD	The salary grade with ID GRADE has a lower monthly salary limit of LLIMIT dollars, an upper monthly salary limit of ULIMIT dollars, and a maximum yearly bonus of BONUS dollars.
CRS	The course with code CODE has description DESCR, falls in course category CAT, and has a duration of DUR days.
OFFR	The course offering for the course with code COURSE that starts on STARTS, has status STATUS, has a maximum capacity of MAXCAP attendees, is offered at location LOC, and (unless TRAINER equals -1) the offering has the employee with employee number TRAINER assigned as the trainer.
REG	The employee whose employee number is STUD has registered for a course with code COURSE that starts on STARTS, and (unless EVAL equals -1) has rated the course with an evaluation score of EVAL.
HIST	At date UNTIL, for the employee whose employee number is EMPNO, either the department or the monthly salary (or both) have changed. Prior to date UNTIL, the department for that employee was DEPTNO and the monthly salary was MSAL.

■**Note** Have you spotted the two hacks? Apparently there are two sorts of offerings: offerings with a trainer assigned and offerings without one assigned. A similar remark can be made about registrations; some of them include an evaluation score for the course offering, and some of them don't. In a properly designed database, you should have *decomposed* the offering and registration table structures into two table structures each.

These external predicates give you an *informal* head start with regards to the meaning of all involved table structures and their attributes that were introduced by the database skeleton. The *exact* meaning of this example database design will become clear as we progress through all formal phases of a database universe definition in the sections that follow.

The next section will supply a characterization for each table structure introduced in the skeleton.

Characterizations

As you saw in Chapter 4, a characterization defines the attribute value sets for the attributes of a given table structure. For a given table structure, the characterization is a set-valued function whose domain is the set of attributes of that table structure. For each attribute, the characterization yields the attribute value set for that attribute. The characterizations form the base on which the next section will build the tuple universes. You'll then notice that the way these characterizations are defined here is very convenient. Take a look at Listing 7-2. It defines the characterization for the EMP table.

Note A few notes:

In defining the attribute value sets for the EMP table, we are using the shorthand names for sets that were introduced in Table 2-4.

We use chr_<table structure name> as a naming convention for the characterization of a table structure.

In the definition of chr_EMP (and in various other places) you'll see a function called upper. This function accepts a case-sensitive string and returns the uppercase version of that string.

Listing 7-2. *Characterization chr_EMP*

```
chr_EMP :=
{ ( EMPNO;    [1000..9999]                      )
, ( ENAME;    varchar(9)                        )
, ( JOB;      /* Five JOB values allowed */
              {'PRESIDENT','MANAGER','SALESREP',
               'TRAINER','ADMIN'}               )
, ( BORN;     date                              )
, ( HIRED;    date                              )
, ( SGRADE;   [1..99]                           )
, ( MSAL;     { n | n∈number(7,2) ∧ n > 0 }     )
, ( USERNAME; /* Usernames are always in uppercase */
              { s | s∈varchar(15) ∧
                    upper(USERNAME) = USERNAME } )
, ( DEPTNO;   [1..99]                           )
}
```

For every attribute of table structure EMP, function chr_EMP yields the attribute value set for that attribute. You can now write expressions such as chr_EMP(EMPNO), which represents the attribute value set of the EMPNO attribute of the EMP table structure. The expression denotes set [1000..9999].

The definition of characterization chr_EMP tells us the following:

- EMPNO values are positive integers within the range 1000 to 9999.

- ENAME values are variable length strings with at most nine characters.

- JOB values are restricted to the following five values: 'PRESIDENT', 'MANAGER', 'SALESREP', 'TRAINER','ADMIN'.

- BORN and HIRED values are date values.

- SGRADE values are positive integers in the range 1 to 99.

- MSAL values are positive numbers with precision seven and scale two.

- USERNAME values are uppercase variable length strings with at most 15 characters.

- DEPTNO values are positive integers in the range 1 to 99.

In the remainder of our database design definition, four sets will occur quite frequently: employee numbers, department numbers, salary-related amounts, and course codes. We define shorthand names (symbols for ease of reference in the text) for them here, and use these in the characterization definitions that follow.

```
EMPNO_TYP    := { n | n∈number(4,0) ∧ n > 999       }
DEPTNO_TYP   := { n | n∈number(2,0) ∧ n > 0         }
SALARY_TYP   := { n | n∈number(7,2) ∧ n > 0         }
CRSCODE_TYP  := { s | s∈varchar(6)  ∧ s = upper(s) }
```

Listings 7-3 through 7-11 introduce the characterization for the remaining table structures. You might want to revisit Table 7-1 (the external predicates) while going over these characterizations. Embedded comments clarify attribute constraints where deemed necessary.

Listing 7-3. *Characterization chr_SREP*

```
chr_SREP :=
{ ( EMPNO;   EMPNO_TYP      )
            /* Targets for sales reps are five digit numbers */
, ( TARGET; [10000..99999] )
, ( COMM;   SALARY_TYP     )
}
```

Listing 7-4. *Characterization chr_MEMP*

```
chr_MEMP :=
{ ( EMPNO;  EMPNO_TYP )
, ( MGR;    EMPNO_TYP )
}
```

Listing 7-5. *Characterization chr_TERM*

```
chr_TERM :=
{ ( EMPNO;     EMPNO_TYP   )
, ( LEFT;      date        )
, ( COMMENTS; varchar(60) )
}
```

Listing 7-6. *Characterization chr_DEPT*

```
chr_DEPT :=
{ ( DEPTNO; DEPTNO_TYP                                      )
, ( DNAME;  { s | s∈varchar(12) ∧ upper(DNAME) = DNAME } )
, ( LOC;    { s | s∈varchar(14) ∧ upper(LOC) = LOC }      )
, ( MGR;    EMPNO_TYP                                      )
}
```

Listing 7-7. *Characterization chr_GRD*

```
chr_GRD :=
{ ( GRADE;  { n | n∈number(2,0) ∧ n > 0 } )
, ( LLIMIT; SALARY_TYP                     )
, ( ULIMIT; SALARY_TYP                     )
, ( BONUS;  SALARY_TYP                     )
}
```

Listing 7-8. *Characterization chr_CRS*

```
chr_CRS :=
{ ( CODE;  CRSCODE_TYP      )
, ( DESCR; varchar(40)      )
           /* Course category values: Design, Generate, Build */
, ( CAT;   {'DSG','GEN','BLD'} )
           /* Course duration must be between 1 and 15 days */
, ( DUR;   [1..15]          )
}
```

Listing 7-9. *Characterization chr_OFFR*

```
chr_OFFR :=
{ ( COURSE; CRSCODE_TYP            )
, ( STARTS; date                  )
           /* Three STATUS values allowed: Scheduled, Confirmed, Canceled */
, ( STATUS; {'SCHD','CONF','CANC'} )
           /* Maximum course offering capacity; minimum = 6 */
, ( MAXCAP; [6..100]              )
           /* TRAINER = -1 means "no trainer assigned" */
, ( TRAINER; EMPNO_TYP ∪ { -1 }    )
, ( LOC;    varchar(14)           )
}
```

Listing 7-10. *Characterization chr_REG*

```
chr_REG :=
{ ( STUD;   EMPNO_TYP   )
, ( COURSE; CRSCODE_TYP )
, ( STARTS; date        )
  /* -1: too early to evaluate (course is in the future) */
  /* 0: not evaluated by attendee */
  /* 1-5: regular evaluation values (from 1=bad to 5=excellent) */
, ( EVAL;   [-1..5]     )
}
```

Listing 7-11. *Characterization chr_HIST*

```
chr_HIST :=
{ ( EMPNO;   EMPNO_TYP  )
, ( UNTIL;   date       )
, ( DEPTNO;  DEPTNO_TYP )
, ( MSAL;    SALARY_TYP )
}
```

Note that in Listing 7-9 the attribute value set for attribute TRAINER includes a special value -1 next to valid employee numbers. This value represents the fact that no trainer has been assigned yet. In our formal database design specification method, there is no such thing as a NULL, which is a "value" commonly (mis)used by SQL database management systems to indicate a missing value. There are no missing values inside tuples; they always have a value attached to every attribute. Characterizations specify the attribute value sets from which these values can be chosen. So, to represent a "missing trainer" value, you must explicitly include a value for this fact inside the corresponding attribute value set. Something similar is specified in Listing 7-10 in the attribute value set for the EVAL attribute.

■**Note** Appendix F will explicitly deal with the phenomenon of NULLs. Chapter 11 will revisit these -1 values when we sort out the database design implementation issues and provide guidelines.

The specification of our database design started out with a skeleton definition and the external predicates for the table structures introduced by the skeleton. In this section you were introduced to the characterizations of the example database design. Through the attribute value sets, you are steadily gaining more insight into the meaning of this database design. The following section will advance this insight to the next layer: the tuple universes.

Tuple Universes

A tuple universe is a (non-empty) set of tuples. It is a very special set of tuples; this set is meant to hold only tuples that are admissible for a given table structure. You know by now that tuples are represented as functions. For instance, here is an example function tdept1 that represents a possible tuple for the DEPT table structure:

    tdept1 := {(DEPTNO;10), (DNAME;'ACCOUNTING'), (LOC;'DALLAS'), (MGR;1240)}

As you can see, the domain of tdept1 represents the set of attributes for table structure DEPT as introduced by database skeleton DB_S.

    dom(tdept1) = {DEPTNO, DNAME, LOC, MGR} = DB_S(DEPT)

And, for every attribute, tdept1 yields a value from the corresponding attribute value set, as introduced by the characterization for the DEPT table structure:

- tdept1(DEPTNO) = 10, which is an element of chr_DEPT(DEPTNO)

- tdept1(DNAME) = 'ACCOUNTING', which is an element of chr_DEPT(DNAME)

- tdept1(LOCATION) = 'DALLAS', which is an element of chr_DEPT(LOCATION)

- tdept1(MGR) = 1240, which is an element of chr_DEPT(MGR)

Here's another possible tuple for the DEPT table structure:

tdept2 := {(DEPTNO;20), (DNAME;'SALES'), (LOC;'HOUSTON'), (MGR;1755)}

Now consider the set {tdept1, tdept2}. This is a set that holds two tuples. Theoretically it could represent the tuple universe for the DEPT table structure. However, it is a rather small tuple universe; it is very unlikely that it represents the tuple universe for the DEPT table structure. The tuple universe for a given table structure should hold *every* tuple that we allow (admit) for the table structure.

■**Note** Tuples tdept1 and tdept2 are functions that share the same domain. This is a requirement for a tuple universe; all tuples in the tuple universe share the same domain, which in turn is equal to the heading of the given table structure.

You have already seen how you can generate a set that holds every possible tuple for a given table structure using the characterization of that table structure (see the section "Table Construction" in Chapter 5). If you apply the generalized product to a characterization, you'll end up with a set of tuples. This set is not just any set of tuples, but it is precisely the set of *all possible* tuples based on the attribute value sets that the characterization defines.

Let us illustrate this once more with a small example. Suppose you're designing a table structure called RESULT; it holds average scores for courses followed by students that belong to a certain population. Here's the external predicate for RESULT: "The rounded average score scored by students of population POPULATION for course COURSE is AVG_SCORE." Listing 7-12 defines the characterization chr_RESULT for this table structure.

Listing 7-12. *Characterization chr_RESULT*

```
chr_RESULT :=
{ ( POPULATION; {'DP','NON-DP'}            )
  /* DP = Database Professionals, NON-DP = Non Database Professionals */
, ( COURSE;     {'set theory','logic'}   )
, ( AVG_SCORE;  {'A','B','C','D','E','F'} )
}
```

The three attribute value sets represent the attribute constraints for the RESULT table structure. If you apply the generalized product $\prod$ to chr_RESULT, you get the following set of possible tuples for the RESULT table structure:

```
Π(chr_RESULT) =
    { { (POPULATION; 'DP'),     (COURSE; 'set theory'), (AVG_SCORE; 'A') }
    , { (POPULATION; 'DP'),     (COURSE; 'set theory'), (AVG_SCORE; 'B') }
    , { (POPULATION; 'DP'),     (COURSE; 'set theory'), (AVG_SCORE; 'C') }
    , { (POPULATION; 'DP'),     (COURSE; 'set theory'), (AVG_SCORE; 'D') }
    , { (POPULATION; 'DP'),     (COURSE; 'set theory'), (AVG_SCORE; 'E') }
    , { (POPULATION; 'DP'),     (COURSE; 'set theory'), (AVG_SCORE; 'F') }
    , { (POPULATION; 'DP'),     (COURSE; 'logic'),      (AVG_SCORE; 'A') }
    , { (POPULATION; 'DP'),     (COURSE; 'logic'),      (AVG_SCORE; 'B') }
    , { (POPULATION; 'DP'),     (COURSE; 'logic'),      (AVG_SCORE; 'C') }
    , { (POPULATION; 'DP'),     (COURSE; 'logic'),      (AVG_SCORE; 'D') }
    , { (POPULATION; 'DP'),     (COURSE; 'logic'),      (AVG_SCORE; 'E') }
    , { (POPULATION; 'DP'),     (COURSE; 'logic'),      (AVG_SCORE; 'F') }
    , { (POPULATION; 'NON-DP'), (COURSE; 'set theory'), (AVG_SCORE; 'A') }
    , { (POPULATION; 'NON-DP'), (COURSE; 'set theory'), (AVG_SCORE; 'B') }
    , { (POPULATION; 'NON-DP'), (COURSE; 'set theory'), (AVG_SCORE; 'C') }
    , { (POPULATION; 'NON-DP'), (COURSE; 'set theory'), (AVG_SCORE; 'D') }
    , { (POPULATION; 'NON-DP'), (COURSE; 'set theory'), (AVG_SCORE; 'E') }
    , { (POPULATION; 'NON-DP'), (COURSE; 'set theory'), (AVG_SCORE; 'F') }
    , { (POPULATION; 'NON-DP'), (COURSE; 'logic'),      (AVG_SCORE; 'A') }
    , { (POPULATION; 'NON-DP'), (COURSE; 'logic'),      (AVG_SCORE; 'B') }
    , { (POPULATION; 'NON-DP'), (COURSE; 'logic'),      (AVG_SCORE; 'C') }
    , { (POPULATION; 'NON-DP'), (COURSE; 'logic'),      (AVG_SCORE; 'D') }
    , { (POPULATION; 'NON-DP'), (COURSE; 'logic'),      (AVG_SCORE; 'E') }
    , { (POPULATION; 'NON-DP'), (COURSE; 'logic'),      (AVG_SCORE; 'F') }
    }
```

In this set of 24 tuples, the previously defined attribute constraints will hold. However, no restrictions exist in this set with regards to *combinations* of attribute values of different attributes inside a tuple. By specifying *inter-attribute*—or rather, *tuple constraints*—you can restrict the set of possible tuples to the set of *admissible* tuples for the given table.

Suppose that you do not allow average scores D, E, and F for database professionals, nor average scores A and B for non-database professionals (regardless of the course). You can specify this by the following definition of tuple universe tup_RESULT; it formally specifies two *tuple predicates*:

```
tup_RESULT :=
    { r | r∈Π(chr_RESULT) ∧
        /* ============================ */
        /* Tuple constraints for RESULT */
        /* ============================ */
        /* Database professionals never score an average of D, E or F */
        r(POPULATION)='DP'  ⇒ r(AVG_SCORE)∉{'D','E','F'} ∧
        /* Non database professionals never score an average of A or B */
        r(POPULATION)='NON-DP' ⇒ r(AVG_SCORE)∉{'A','B'}
    }
```

The tuple predicates introduced by the definition of a tuple universe are referred to as *tuple constraints*. You can also specify set tup_RESULT in the enumerative way.

■Note The original set of 24 possible tuples has now been reduced to a set of 14 admissible tuples. Ten tuples did not satisfy the tuple constraints that are specified in `tup_RESULT`.

```
{ { (POPULATION; 'DP'),     (COURSE; 'set theory'), (AVG_SCORE; 'A') }
, { (POPULATION; 'DP'),     (COURSE; 'set theory'), (AVG_SCORE; 'B') }
, { (POPULATION; 'DP'),     (COURSE; 'set theory'), (AVG_SCORE; 'C') }
, { (POPULATION; 'DP'),     (COURSE; 'logic'),      (AVG_SCORE; 'A') }
, { (POPULATION; 'DP'),     (COURSE; 'logic'),      (AVG_SCORE; 'B') }
, { (POPULATION; 'DP'),     (COURSE; 'logic'),      (AVG_SCORE; 'C') }
, { (POPULATION; 'NON-DP'), (COURSE; 'set theory'), (AVG_SCORE; 'C') }
, { (POPULATION; 'NON-DP'), (COURSE; 'set theory'), (AVG_SCORE; 'D') }
, { (POPULATION; 'NON-DP'), (COURSE; 'set theory'), (AVG_SCORE; 'E') }
, { (POPULATION; 'NON-DP'), (COURSE; 'set theory'), (AVG_SCORE; 'F') }
, { (POPULATION; 'NON-DP'), (COURSE; 'logic'),      (AVG_SCORE; 'C') }
, { (POPULATION; 'NON-DP'), (COURSE; 'logic'),      (AVG_SCORE; 'D') }
, { (POPULATION; 'NON-DP'), (COURSE; 'logic'),      (AVG_SCORE; 'E') }
, { (POPULATION; 'NON-DP'), (COURSE; 'logic'),      (AVG_SCORE; 'F') }
}
```

Note that the former specification of `tup_RESULT`, using the predicative method to specify a set, is highly preferred over the latter enumerative specification, because it explicitly shows us what the tuple constraints are (and it is a shorter definition too; much shorter in general).

Now let's continue with our example database design. Take a look at Listing 7-13, which defines tuple universe `tup_EMP` for the `EMP` table structure of the example database design.

Listing 7-13. *Tuple Universe tup_EMP*

```
tup_EMP :=
{ e | e∈ Π(chr_EMP) ∧
      /* ========================== */
      /* Tuple constraints for EMP */
      /* ========================== */
      /* We hire adult employees only */
      e(BORN) + 18 ≤ e(HIRED) ∧
      /* Presidents earn more than 120K */
      e(JOB) = 'PRESIDENT' ⇒ 12*e(MSAL) > 120000 ∧
      /* Administrators earn less than 5K */
      e(JOB) = 'ADMIN' ⇒ e(MSAL) < 5000
}
```

■Note In this definition, we assume that addition has been defined for values of type date (see Table 2-4), enabling us to add years to such a value.

Are you starting to see how this works? Tuple universe tup_EMP is a subset of Π(chr_EMP). All tuples that do not satisfy the tuple constraints (three in total) specified in the definition of tup_EMP are left out. You can use any of the logical connectives introduced in Table 1-2 of Chapter 1 in conjunction with valid attribute expressions to formally specify tuple constraints.

Note that all ambiguity is ruled out by these formal specifications:

- By "adult," the age of 18 or older is meant. The ≤ symbol implies that the day someone turns 18 he or she can be hired.

- The "K" in 120K and 5K (in the comments) represents the integer 1000 and not 1024. The salaries mentioned (informally by the users and formally inside the specifications) are actually the monthly salary in the case of a CLERK and the yearly salary in the case of a PRESIDENT. This could be a habit in the real world, and it might be wise to reflect this in the formal specification too. Of course, you can also specify the predicate involving the PRESIDENT this way: e(JOB) = 'PRESIDENT' ⇒ e(MSAL) > 10000.

Listings 7-14 through 7-22 introduce the tuple universes for the other table structures in our database design. You'll find embedded informal comments to clarify the tuple constraints. Note that tuple constraints are only introduced for table structures GRD, CRS, and OFFR; the other table structures happen to have no tuple constraints.

Listing 7-14. *Tuple Universe tup_SREP*

```
tup_SREP :=
{ s | s∈Π(chr_SREP) /* No tuple constraints for SREP */ }
```

Listing 7-15. *Tuple Universe tup_MEMP*

```
tup_MEMP :=
{ m | m∈Π(chr_MEMP) }
```

Listing 7-16. *Tuple Universe tup_TERM*

```
tup_TERM :=
{ t | t∈Π(chr_TERM) }
```

Listing 7-17. *Tuple Universe tup_DEPT*

```
tup_DEPT :=
{ d | d∈Π(chr_DEPT) }
```

Listing 7-18. *Tuple Universe tup_GRD*

```
tup_GRD :=
{ g | g∈Π(chr_GRD) ∧
      /* Salary grades have a "bandwidth" of at least 500 dollars */
      g(LLIMIT) ≤ g(ULIMIT) - 500 ∧
```

```
        /* Bonus must be less than lower limit */
        g(BONUS) < g(LLIMIT)
}
```

Listing 7-19. *Tuple Universe tup_CRS*

```
tup_CRS :=
{ c | c∈Π(chr_CRS) ∧
        /* Build courses never take more than 5 days */
        c(CAT) = 'BLD' ⇒ c(DUR) ≤ 5
}
```

Listing 7-20. *Tuple Universe tup_OFFR*

```
tup_OFFR :=
{ o | o∈Π(chr_OFFR) ∧
        /* Unassigned TRAINER allowed only for certain STATUS values */
        o(TRAINER) = -1 ⇒ o(STATUS)∈{'CANC','SCHD'}
}
```

Listing 7-21. *Tuple Universe tup_REG*

```
tup_REG :=
{ r | r∈Π(chr_REG) }
```

Listing 7-22. *Tuple Universe tup_HIST*

```
tup_HIST :=
{ h | h∈Π(chr_HIST) }
```

Listing 7-20 defines when the special -1 value is allowed for the TRAINER attribute; confirmed offerings (STATUS = 'CONF') must have an employee number assigned as the trainer.

This concludes the tuple universe layer of our example database design. Through the specification of the tuple constraints, you've gained more insight into the meaning of this database design. The next section continues the construction of the database design's specification, by advancing to the *table universe* layer. As you'll see, this involves the application of more set-theory and logic concepts that were introduced in Part 1 of this book.

Table Universes

You can use a tuple universe to build a *set of admissible tables* (we'll demonstrate this shortly). Such a set is called a *table universe*. Every element in a table universe is an admissible table for the corresponding table structure.

A tuple universe is a set of tuples *and can be considered a table too*. It is a rather large set of tuples, because it has every tuple that can be built using the characterization and taking into consideration the tuple constraints. We've mentioned before that a tuple universe can be considered the largest table for a given table structure.

Every subset of a tuple universe is a table too. In fact, if you would construct a set that holds every subset of a tuple universe, then this set would contain lots of tables; every *possible* table for a given table structure would be in this set. Do you remember, from Part 1 of this book, how to construct the set of all subsets of a given set? The powerset operator does just that. The powerset of a tuple universe can be considered the set of all possible tables for a given table structure.

■**Note** You might want to revisit the section "Powersets and Partitions" in Chapter 2, and refresh your memory regarding the powerset operator.

In a similar way as tuple universes are defined, you can restrict the powerset of a tuple universe to obtain the set of *admissible* tables. You can add *table predicates* (constraining combinations of tuples) to discard possible tables that were generated by the powerset operator, but that do not reflect a valid representation of the real world. Table predicates that are used to restrict the powerset of a tuple universe are referred to as *table constraints*.

Let's illustrate all this using the RESULT table structure that was introduced in the previous section. The powerset of tuple universe tup_RESULT results in a set that holds every possible RESULT table. There are lots of tables in this set. To be precise, because the cardinality of tup_RESULT is 14, there are exactly 16384 (2 to the 14th power) possible tables. These are far too many to list in the enumerative way. Figure 7-2 displays just one of these tables (an arbitrarily chosen subset of tup_RESULT). Let's name this table R1.

POPULATION	COURSE	AVG_SCORE
NON-DP	logic	F
DP	logic	C
DP	set theory	C
NON-DP	set theory	D
NON-DP	set theory	E
DP	logic	A
DP	set theory	B
DP	set theory	A
DP	logic	B
NON-DP	set theory	F
NON-DP	logic	D

Figure 7-2. *A possible table for a RESULT named R1*

Table R1 is a subset of tup_RESULT. It holds 11 distinct tuples. Because these tuples originate from the tuple universe, all of them are admissible tuples; they satisfy the tuple constraints, and every attribute holds an admissible value.

Now assume that the following (informally specified) data integrity constraints play a role in a table for the RESULT table structure:

- The combination of attributes POPULATION and COURSE is uniquely identifying in a RESULT table (constraint P1).

- A RESULT table is empty or it holds exactly four tuples: one tuple for every combination of POPULATION and COURSE (constraint P2).

- The average score (AVG_SCORE) of the logic course is always higher than the average score of the set theory course; score A is the highest, F the lowest (constraint P3).

- Non-database professionals always have a lower average score than database professionals (constraint P4).

▪Note Some of these integrity constraints are rather contrived. Their sole purpose in this example is to bring down the number of tables in the table universe of the RESULT table structure to such an extent that it becomes feasible to enumerate all admissible tables.

In Listing 7-23 you can find these four constraints formally specified as table predicates, using the names P1 through P4 introduced earlier. To be able to compare average scores in these specifications, we introduce a function f, which is defined as follows:

$$f := \{ \ ('A';6), \ ('B';5), \ ('C';4), \ ('D';3), \ ('E';2), \ ('F';1) \ \}$$

This enables us to compare, for instance, scores B and E. Because $f(B)=5$ and $f(E)=2$ (and $5>2$), we can say that B is a higher score than E.

Listing 7-23. *Table Predicates P1, P2, P3, and P4*

```
P1(T) := ( ∀r1,r2∈T: r1↓{POPULATION,COURSE} = r2↓{POPULATION,COURSE} ⇒ r1 = r2 )
P2(T) := ( #T = 0 ∨ #T = 4 )
P3(T) := ( ∀r1,r2∈T: ( r1(POPULATION) = r2(POPULATION) ∧
                       r1(COURSE) = 'logic' ∧ r2(COURSE) = 'set theory' )
                  ⇒ f(r1(AVG_SCORE)) > f(r2(AVG_SCORE)) )
P4(T) := ¬( ∃r1,r2∈T: r1(POPULATION) = 'NON-DP' ∧ r2(POPULATION) = 'DP' ∧
                      f(r1(AVG_SCORE)) ≥ f(r2(AVG_SCORE)) )
```

Table predicate P1 is one of the common types of data integrity predicates that were introduced in the section "Unique Identification Predicate" in Chapter 6.

Table predicate P2 is rather simple; the cardinality of the table should be either zero or four. Here is an alternative way to specify this: $\#T \in \{0,4\}$.

As you can see, table predicate P3 specifies that the average score for the logic course should always be higher than the average score for the set theory course *within a population*.

The first conjunct in the universal quantification—r1(POPULATION) = r2(POPULATION)—speci-fies this. A user can take for granted that the average scores for logic are always higher than those for set theory, *within a given population*, but fail to mention this explicitly (as was done in the preceding informal specification) when conveying the requirement informally.

Table predicate P4 unambiguously specifies that the "lower average score" mentioned in the informal specification is meant to be irrespective of the course; there is no conjunct r1(COURSE) = r2(COURSE) inside the existential quantification.

You can instantiate predicates P1 through P4 using table R1 that was introduced in Figure 7-2. Check for yourself that table R1 violates predicates P1, P2, and P3, and that it satisfies predicate P4.

```
P1(R1) = false
P2(R1) = false
P3(R1) = false
P4(R1) = true
```

With these formal table predicate specifications you can now define the table universe for the RESULT table structure. Take a look at Listing 7-24, which formally specifies table universe tab_RESULT using tuple universe tup_RESULT and table predicates P1, P2, P3, and P4.

Listing 7-24. *Specification of Table Universe tab_RESULT*

```
tab_RESULT :=
{ R | R∈ ℘(tup_RESULT) ∧ P1(R) ∧ P2(R) ∧ P3(R) ∧ P4(R)
}
```

tab_RESULT holds every subset of tup_RESULT that satisfies all four table predicates; obvi-ously table R1 is not an element of tab_RESULT. The table predicates restrict the powerset of a tuple universe and are therefore referred to as *table constraints*.

■**Note** If a unique identification predicate constitutes a table constraint (as does P1 in the preceding case), then the set of uniquely identifying attributes is commonly referred to as a *key* for the given table structure. In this case {POPULATION,COURSE} is a key for the RESULT table structure.

Table constraints P1, P2, P3, and P4 are contrived such that they significantly bring down the total number of tables from the original 16384 possible tables generated by the powerset; in fact, only 13 admissible tables remain in this table universe. Listing 7-25 displays an enu-merative specification of table universe tab_RESULT.

Listing 7-25. *Enumerative Specification of Table Universe tab_RESULT*

```
tab_RESULT :=
{ ∅
, { { (POPULATION;'DP'),      (COURSE;'set theory'), (AVG_SCORE;'B') }
  , { (POPULATION;'DP'),      (COURSE;'logic'),      (AVG_SCORE;'A') }
  , { (POPULATION;'NON-DP'), (COURSE;'set theory'), (AVG_SCORE;'D') }
```

```
        , { (POPULATION;'NON-DP'), (COURSE;'logic'),      (AVG_SCORE;'C') } }
    , { { (POPULATION;'DP'),     (COURSE;'set theory'), (AVG_SCORE;'B') }
      , { (POPULATION;'DP'),     (COURSE;'logic'),      (AVG_SCORE;'A') }
      , { (POPULATION;'NON-DP'), (COURSE;'set theory'), (AVG_SCORE;'E') }
      , { (POPULATION;'NON-DP'), (COURSE;'logic'),      (AVG_SCORE;'C') } }
    , { { (POPULATION;'DP'),     (COURSE;'set theory'), (AVG_SCORE;'B') }
      , { (POPULATION;'DP'),     (COURSE;'logic'),      (AVG_SCORE;'A') }
      , { (POPULATION;'NON-DP'), (COURSE;'set theory'), (AVG_SCORE;'F') }
      , { (POPULATION;'NON-DP'), (COURSE;'logic'),      (AVG_SCORE;'C') } }
    , { { (POPULATION;'DP'),     (COURSE;'set theory'), (AVG_SCORE;'B') }
      , { (POPULATION;'DP'),     (COURSE;'logic'),      (AVG_SCORE;'A') }
      , { (POPULATION;'NON-DP'), (COURSE;'set theory'), (AVG_SCORE;'E') }
      , { (POPULATION;'NON-DP'), (COURSE;'logic'),      (AVG_SCORE;'D') } }
    , { { (POPULATION;'DP'),     (COURSE;'set theory'), (AVG_SCORE;'B') }
      , { (POPULATION;'DP'),     (COURSE;'logic'),      (AVG_SCORE;'A') }
      , { (POPULATION;'NON-DP'), (COURSE;'set theory'), (AVG_SCORE;'F') }
      , { (POPULATION;'NON-DP'), (COURSE;'logic'),      (AVG_SCORE;'D') } }
    , { { (POPULATION;'DP'),     (COURSE;'set theory'), (AVG_SCORE;'B') }
      , { (POPULATION;'DP'),     (COURSE;'logic'),      (AVG_SCORE;'A') }
      , { (POPULATION;'NON-DP'), (COURSE;'set theory'), (AVG_SCORE;'F') }
      , { (POPULATION;'NON-DP'), (COURSE;'logic'),      (AVG_SCORE;'E') } }
    , { { (POPULATION;'DP'),     (COURSE;'set theory'), (AVG_SCORE;'C') }
      , { (POPULATION;'DP'),     (COURSE;'logic'),      (AVG_SCORE;'A') }
      , { (POPULATION;'NON-DP'), (COURSE;'set theory'), (AVG_SCORE;'E') }
      , { (POPULATION;'NON-DP'), (COURSE;'logic'),      (AVG_SCORE;'D') } }
    , { { (POPULATION;'DP'),     (COURSE;'set theory'), (AVG_SCORE;'C') }
      , { (POPULATION;'DP'),     (COURSE;'logic'),      (AVG_SCORE;'A') }
      , { (POPULATION;'NON-DP'), (COURSE;'set theory'), (AVG_SCORE;'F') }
      , { (POPULATION;'NON-DP'), (COURSE;'logic'),      (AVG_SCORE;'D') } }
    , { { (POPULATION;'DP'),     (COURSE;'set theory'), (AVG_SCORE;'C') }
      , { (POPULATION;'DP'),     (COURSE;'logic'),      (AVG_SCORE;'A') }
      , { (POPULATION;'NON-DP'), (COURSE;'set theory'), (AVG_SCORE;'F') }
      , { (POPULATION;'NON-DP'), (COURSE;'logic'),      (AVG_SCORE;'E') } }
    , { { (POPULATION;'DP'),     (COURSE;'set theory'), (AVG_SCORE;'C') }
      , { (POPULATION;'DP'),     (COURSE;'logic'),      (AVG_SCORE;'B') }
      , { (POPULATION;'NON-DP'), (COURSE;'set theory'), (AVG_SCORE;'E') }
      , { (POPULATION;'NON-DP'), (COURSE;'logic'),      (AVG_SCORE;'D') } }
    , { { (POPULATION;'DP'),     (COURSE;'set theory'), (AVG_SCORE;'C') }
      , { (POPULATION;'DP'),     (COURSE;'logic'),      (AVG_SCORE;'B') }
      , { (POPULATION;'NON-DP'), (COURSE;'set theory'), (AVG_SCORE;'F') }
      , { (POPULATION;'NON-DP'), (COURSE;'logic'),      (AVG_SCORE;'D') } }
    , { { (POPULATION;'DP'),     (COURSE;'set theory'), (AVG_SCORE;'C') }
      , { (POPULATION;'DP'),     (COURSE;'logic'),      (AVG_SCORE;'B') }
      , { (POPULATION;'NON-DP'), (COURSE;'set theory'), (AVG_SCORE;'F') }
      , { (POPULATION;'NON-DP'), (COURSE;'logic'),      (AVG_SCORE;'E') } }
}
```

This set has 13 elements, each of which is a table. The first one represents the empty table; the other 12 all are sets of 4 tuples. You might want to validate for yourself that all these tables satisfy all four table constraints specified *and* that there are no other tables (not listed in Listing 7-25) that also satisfy all four table constraints.

In case you have some trouble reading the nested set of sets, Figure 7-3 might clarify what is going on. It shows another way to specify table universe tab_RESULT using the shorthand notation for tables.

tab-RESULT=

{ {}

POPULATION	COURSE	AVG_SCORE
DP	set theory	B
DP	logic	A
NON-DP	set theory	D
NON-DP	logic	C

POPULATION	COURSE	AVG_SCORE
DP	set theory	B
DP	logic	A
NON-DP	set theory	E
NON-DP	logic	C

POPULATION	COURSE	AVG_SCORE
DP	set theory	B
DP	logic	A
NON-DP	set theory	F
NON-DP	logic	C

POPULATION	COURSE	AVG_SCORE
DP	set theory	B
DP	logic	A
NON-DP	set theory	E
NON-DP	logic	D

POPULATION	COURSE	AVG_SCORE
DP	set theory	B
DP	logic	A
NON-DP	set theory	F
NON-DP	logic	D

POPULATION	COURSE	AVG_SCORE
DP	set theory	B
DP	logic	A
NON-DP	set theory	F
NON-DP	logic	E

POPULATION	COURSE	AVG_SCORE
DP	set theory	C
DP	logic	A
NON-DP	set theory	E
NON-DP	logic	D

POPULATION	COURSE	AVG_SCORE
DP	set theory	C
DP	logic	A
NON-DP	set theory	F
NON-DP	logic	D

POPULATION	COURSE	AVG_SCORE
DP	set theory	C
DP	logic	A
NON-DP	set theory	F
NON-DP	logic	E

POPULATION	COURSE	AVG_SCORE
DP	set theory	C
DP	logic	B
NON-DP	set theory	E
NON-DP	logic	D

POPULATION	COURSE	AVG_SCORE
DP	set theory	C
DP	logic	B
NON-DP	set theory	F
NON-DP	logic	D

POPULATION	COURSE	AVG_SCORE
DP	set theory	C
DP	logic	B
NON-DP	set theory	F
NON-DP	logic	E

}

Figure 7-3. *Enumerative specification of tab_RESULT using table shorthand notation*

Note In general, table universes hold far too many elements to enumerate them.

Let's now continue with the specification of our example database design. Take a look at Listing 7-26, which shows the definition of table universe tab_EMP for the EMP table structure. This definition formally specifies four table constraints for EMP. Some informal clarification is embedded as comments.

Listing 7-26. *Table Universe tab_EMP*

```
tab_EMP :=
{ E | E∈ ℘(tup_EMP) ∧
      /* EMPNO uniquely identifies an employee tuple */
      ( ∀e1,e2∈E: e1(EMPNO) = e2(EMPNO) ⟹ e1 = e2 )
      ∧
      /* USERNAME uniquely identifies an employee tuple */
      ( ∀e1,e2∈E: e1(USERNAME) = e2(USERNAME) ⟹ e1 = e2 )
      ∧
      /* At most one president allowed */
      #{ e | e∈E ∧ e(JOB) = 'PRESIDENT' } ≤ 1
      ∧
      /* A department that employs the president or a manager */
      /* should also employ at least one administrator        */
      ( ∀d∈E⇓{DEPTNO}:
        ( ∃e2∈E: e2(DEPTNO) = d(DEPTNO) ∧ e2(JOB) ∈ {'PRESIDENT','MANAGER'} )
          ⟹
        ( ∃e3∈E: e3(DEPTNO) = d(DEPTNO) ∧ e3(JOB) = 'ADMIN' )
      )
}
```

The first two constraints are unique identification predicates; the EMPNO attribute is uniquely identifying in an EMP table, as is the USERNAME attribute.

The specification of the third constraint constructs the subset of tuples that have the value PRESIDENT for the JOB attribute and restricts the cardinality of this set to 1 at most. This reflects the real-world requirement that there cannot be more than one president.

The last table constraint states that if there exists a PRESIDENT or a MANAGER in a *given* department, then there exists an ADMIN in the *same* department. The outer universal quantification supplies all departments for which to perform this check. Note that the informal embedded specification of this constraint might imply that this constraint is a multi-table constraint involving not just the EMP table structure but also the DEPT table structure. Take a look at the following database predicate named P that accepts two parameters: a department table (parameter D) and an employee table (parameter E).

```
P(D,E) :=
  ( ∀d∈D:
      ( ∃e2∈E: e2(DEPTNO) = d(DEPTNO) ∧ e2(JOB) ∈ {'PRESIDENT','MANAGER'} )
        ⟹
      ( ∃e2∈E: e3(DEPTNO) = d(DEPTNO) ∧ e3(JOB) = 'ADMIN' )
  )
```

This predicate closely follows the informal specification: it quantifies over all departments and states that if the department employs a PRESIDENT or a MANAGER, then the department should employ an ADMIN. Note that only the DEPTNO attribute of parameter D is used. The corresponding predicate inside the definition of tab_EMP quantifies over all available DEPTNO values inside the EMP table and then states the same. Because a DEPTNO attribute is available in the EMP table structure (and, as we shall see later, it always identifies a valid department), this constraint can be specified as a table constraint.

■**Caution** It is not uncommon that constraints that are, in fact, table constraints are specified as database (multi-table) constraints. This can also happen one phase earlier: tuple constraints that are specified as table constraints. This refers back to the comments we made in Chapter 6 when we mentioned terms such as "tuple predicate in disguise." In the database design specification methodology introduced in this book, you should always try to specify constraints *at the earliest possible phase*: attribute value sets first, then tuple constraints, then table constraints, and finally database constraints. Not only will this result in a clear view of your database design, but also will it aid in your effort to implement it (covered in Chapter 11).

Here is an alternative (equivalent) formal specification for the third table constraint of EMP that might be easier to understand, and clearly shows that there is no need to involve the DEPT table structure:

```
( ∀e2∈E: e2(JOB) ∈ {'PRESIDENT','MANAGER'}
        ⇒
        ( ∃e3∈E: e3(DEPTNO) = e2(DEPTNO) ∧ e3(JOB) = 'ADMIN' )
)
```

This predicate states that for all employee tuples that represent a PRESIDENT or a MANAGER, there should exist an employee tuple that represents an ADMIN working in the same department. You probably intuitively feel that this formal specification is equivalent, and therefore represents the same constraint. In fact, it can formally be *proven* that it is equivalent to the formal specification of this constraint inside tab_EMP. However, this requires the development of more rewrite rules regarding quantifications, which is beyond the scope of this book.

Listings 7-27, 7-28, and 7-29 define the table universes for the SREP, MEMP, and TERM table structures. As you can see, they all have a unique identification constraint and no other table constraints.

Listing 7-27. *Table Universe tab_SREP*

```
tab_SREP :=
{ S | S∈ ℘(tup_SREP) ∧
      /* EMPNO uniquely identifies a tuple */
      ( ∀s1,s2∈S: s1(EMPNO) = s2(EMPNO) ⇒ s1 = s2 )
}
```

Listing 7-28. *Table Universe tab_MEMP*

```
tab_MEMP :=
{ M | M∈ ℘(tup_MEMP) ∧
      /* EMPNO uniquely identifies a tuple */
      ( ∀m1,m2∈M: m1(EMPNO) = m2(EMPNO) ⇒ m1 = m2 )
}
```

Listing 7-29. *Table Universe tab_TERM*

```
tab_TERM :=
{ T | T∈ ℘(tup_TERM) ∧
        /* EMPNO uniquely identifies a tuple */
        ( ∀t1,t2∈T: t1(EMPNO) = t2(EMPNO) ⇒ t1 = t2 )
}
```

The table universe for DEPT (shown in Listing 7-30) introduces two unique identification constraints. Next to {DEPTNO}, the set of attributes {DNAME,LOC} is also uniquely identifying in a DEPT table.

Listing 7-30. *Table Universe tab_DEPT*

```
tab_DEPT :=
{ D | D∈ ℘(tab_DEPT) ∧
        /* Department number uniquely identifies a tuple */
        ( ∀d1,d2∈D: d1(DEPTNO) = d2(DEPTNO) ⇒ d1 = d2 )
        ∧
        /* Department name and location uniquely identify a tuple */
        ( ∀d1,d2∈D:
          d1↓{DNAME,LOC} = d2↓{DNAME,LOC} ⇒ d1 = d2 )
        ∧
        /* You cannot manage more than two departments */
        ( ∀m∈D⇓{MGR}: #{ d | d∈D ∧ d(MGR) = m(MGR) } ≤ 2 )
}
```

The second unique identification constraint states that there cannot be two departments that have the same name and that are located in the same location; department names are unique within a location. The third table constraint is a formal representation of the constraint that no employee can manage more than two departments. It states that for every department manager, the cardinality of the set of departments managed by him/her is less than or equal to two.

Listing 7-31 shows the table universe definition for the GRD table structure.

Listing 7-31. *Table Universe tab_GRD*

```
tab_GRD :=
{ G | G∈ ℘(tup_GRD) ∧
        /* Salary grade code uniquely identifies a tuple */
        ( ∀g1,g2∈G: g1(GRADE) = g2(GRADE) ⇒ g1 = g2 )
        ∧
        /* Salary grade lower limit uniquely identifies a tuple */
        ( ∀g1,g2∈G: g1(LLIMIT) = g2(LLIMIT) ⇒ g1 = g2 )
        ∧
        /* Salary grade upper limit uniquely identifies a tuple */
        ( ∀g1,g2∈G: g1(ULIMIT) = g2(ULIMIT) ⇒ g1 = g2 )
        ∧
        /* A salary grade overlaps with at most one (lower) grade */
```

```
    ( ∀g1∈G:
      ( ∃g2∈G:  g2(LLIMIT) < g1(LLIMIT) )
        ⇒
      #{ g3 | g3∈G ∧ g3(LLIMIT) < g1(LLIMIT) ∧
                     g3(ULIMIT) ≥ g1(LLIMIT) ∧
                     g3(ULIMIT) < g1(ULIMIT) } = 1
    )
}
```

As you can see, this table universe specifies three unique identification constraints for GRD. The fourth table constraint specifies that there cannot be a salary gap between the ULIMIT salary and the LLIMIT salary of two consecutive salary grades. This is done by requiring that for every tuple (say g1) for which there exists a tuple that corresponds to a lower salary grade (say g2), there should exist a tuple (say g3) that corresponds to a lower salary grade and that overlaps with the salary range of tuple g1. In fact, there should exist exactly one such g3, thereby covering every salary by at most two salary grades. The formal specification states exactly what is meant and leaves no room for ambiguity.

Listings 7-32 and 7-33 define the table universes for the CRS and OFFR table structures. As you can see, only unique identification constraints are involved.

Listing 7-32. *Table Universe tab_CRS*

```
tab_CRS :=
{ C | C∈ ℘(tup_CRS) ∧
      /* Course code uniquely identifies a tuple */
      ( ∀c1,c2∈C: c1(CODE) = c2(CODE) ⇒ c1 = c2 )
}
```

Listing 7-33. *Table Universe tab_OFFR*

```
tab_OFFR :=
{ O | O∈ ℘(tup_OFFR) ∧
      /* Course code and begin date uniquely identify a tuple */
      ( ∀o1,o2∈O:
        o1↓{COURSE,STARTS} = o2↓{COURSE,STARTS} ⇒ o1 = o2 )
      ∧
      /* Begin date and (known) trainer uniquely identify a tuple */
      ( ∀o1,o2∈{ o | o∈O ∧ o(TRAINER) ≠ -1 }:
        o1↓{STARTS,TRAINER} = o2↓{STARTS,TRAINER} ⇒ o1 = o2 )
}
```

The second table constraint is sort of a special case of a unique identification constraint. The set {STARTS,TRAINER} is uniquely identifying within *a subset of* an OFFR table. This constraint states that a trainer cannot engage more than one course offering per start date. There can certainly be multiple course offerings starting at the same date that have no trainer assigned to them yet; hence the exclusion of offerings with no assigned trainer in the universal quantification.

■Note There is obviously a wider limitation here that involves the full duration of an offering: trainers cannot engage another offering for the duration of an assigned offering. This involves the duration of the corresponding course (attribute DUR in the CRS table structure). Therefore, it is a multi-table constraint and will be specified in the next phase (database universe).

Listing 7-34 defines table universe tab_REG for the REG table structure.

Listing 7-34. *Table Universe tab_REG*

```
tab_REG :=
{ R | R∈ ℘(tup_REG) ∧
      /* Attendee and begin date uniquely identify a tuple */
      ( ∀r1,r2∈R:
        r1↓{STARTS,STUD} = r2↓{STARTS,STUD} ⇒ r1 = r2 )
      ∧
      /* Offering is evaluated by all attendees, or it is too early to */
      /* evaluate the offering */
      ( ∀r1,r2∈R:
        ( r1↓{COURSE,STARTS} = r2↓{COURSE,STARTS} )
          ⇒
        ( ( r1(EVAL) = -1 ∧ r2(EVAL) = -1 ) ∨
          ( r1(EVAL) ≠ -1 ∧ r2(EVAL) ≠ -1 )
        ) )
}
```

Do you notice that the first table constraint does *not* state {COURSE,STARTS,STUD} is uniquely identifying with a REG table? Considering that REG is a "child table" of CRS, you would typically expect COURSE to be part of the set of attributes. However, in the real world we don't allow students to register for two offerings that start at the same date, whatever courses are involved in these offerings. Therefore, the reduced set {STARTS,STUD} is uniquely identifying in a REG table. Here too there is a wider limitation involving the duration of a course that will be specified in the definition of the database universe later on.

The second table constraint states that within the registrations of a course offering, either all evaluations (still) hold value -1, or all of them hold a value that differs from -1. Note that (quoting from the embedded comment) "evaluated by all attendees" includes the special value 0. The idea here is that near the end of the course offering, the trainer explicitly changes—in a single transaction—all evaluation values from -1 (too early to evaluate) to 0 (not evaluated). The students then evaluate the offering individually, each in their own transaction. As you'll see in the next chapter, you can formally specify this intended behavior through a dynamic (state transition) constraint.

Listing 7-35 defines the last table universe (tab_HIST) regarding the HIST table structure.

Listing 7-35. *Table Universe tab_HIST*

```
tab_HIST :=
{ H | H∈ ℘(tup_HIST) ∧
      /* Employee number and history end date uniquely identify a tuple */
      ( ∀h1,h2∈H: h1↓{EMPNO,UNTIL} = h2↓{EMPNO,UNTIL} ⇒ h1 = h2 )
      ∧
      /* Either department number or monthly salary (or both) */
      /* must have changed between two consecutive history records */
      ( ∀h1,h2∈H:
        ( h1(EMPNO) = h2(EMPNO) ∧
          h1(UNTIL) < h2(UNTIL) ∧
          ¬ ( ∃h3∈ T: h3(EMPNO) = h1(EMPNO) ∧
                      h3(UNTIL) > h1(UNTIL) ∧
                      h3(UNTIL) < h2(UNTIL) )
        ) ⇒
        ( h1(MSAL) ≠ h2(MSAL) ∨ h1(DEPTNO) ≠ h2(DEPTNO) )
      )
}
```

The first (unique identification) table constraint states that there can be at most one history record per employee per date. The second table constraint states that two consecutive history records (for the same employee) cannot have both an unchanged monthly salary and an unchanged department number; at least one of these attributes must have a different value. The way the table predicate specifies this is by universally quantifying over all pairs of HIST tuples (h1 and h2); if such a pair involves two consecutive HIST tuples for the same employee, then either the MSAL or the DEPTNO attribute values must differ. The fact that two HIST tuples are consecutive is specified by the existential quantification: there should not exist another (third) HIST tuple (h3) for the same employee that "sits in between" the other two tuples.

Again, the formal specification for this constraint leaves no room for ambiguity.

This concludes the treatment of the table universes of the example database design. The next section moves on the definition of the database universe. This definition will build on the table universes and will formally specify the database constraints.

Database Universe

You have now reached the last stepping stone (phase) of this book's formal methodology to specify a database design. As with the other phases, it continues to build on the sets specified in the previous phase.

You can use the table universes to build a *set of admissible database states* (we'll demonstrate this shortly). Such a set is called a *database universe*. Every element in the database universe is an admissible database state for the database design.

At the beginning of this chapter, we said, "Every database state is an admissible set of n tables (one per table structure)." Of course, this was loosely speaking. The way you formally represent a database state was introduced in Chapter 5; it is a function where every first element of a pair is a table structure name and every second element of a pair is a table. As you'll see, this way of representing a database state is convenient; we can easily construct functions such as this using the already defined table universes.

Let's illustrate this with the RESULT table structure that was used in the previous sections. Because this section is about database constraints, we first introduce a second table structure to go along with the RESULT table structure. Let's assume the existence of a LIMIT table structure. Here's the external predicate for LIMIT: "Average score SCORE is not allowed for population POPULATION." The idea is that the tuples in LIMIT limit the admissible tables for RESULT. We'll specify precisely how they do so later on, by a database constraint.

Listing 7-36 specifies characterization chr_LIMIT, tuple universe tup_LIMIT, and table universe tab_LIMIT.

Listing 7-36. *Specifications for chr_LIMIT, tup_LIMIT, and tab_LIMIT*

```
chr_LIMIT :=
{ ( POPULATION; {'DP','NON-DP'} )
, ( SCORE;      {'A','F'}       )
}
tup_LIMIT :=
{ l | l∈Π(chr_LIMIT) ∧
      l(POPULATION) = 'DP' ⇒ l(SCORE) = 'A' ∧
      l(POPULATION) = 'NON-DP' ⇒ l(SCORE) = 'F'
}
tab_LIMIT :=
{ L | L∈ ℘(tup_LIMIT) ∧
      ( ∀l1,l2∈L: l1(POPULATION) = l2(POPULATION) ⇒ l1 = l2 )
}
```

The tuple and table universes for LIMIT are rather small sets. Here is an enumerative specification for both of them:

```
tup_LIMIT = { { (POPULATION;'DP')    , (SCORE;'A') }
            , { (POPULATION;'NON-DP'), (SCORE;'F') } }
tab_LIMIT = { ∅
            , { { (POPULATION;'DP')    , (SCORE;'A') } }
            , { { (POPULATION;'NON-DP'), (SCORE;'F') } }
            , { { (POPULATION;'DP')    , (SCORE;'A') }
              , { (POPULATION;'NON-DP'), (SCORE;'F') } }
            }
```

As you can see, there are only four admissible LIMIT tables: the empty table, two tables with one tuple, and one table with two tuples.

■**Note** The unique identification table constraint in the specification of tab_LIMIT is in fact redundant. It is implied by the tuple constraints and the characterization.

Figure 7-4 displays tab_LIMIT using the shorthand notation for tables.

tab_LIMIT=

{ { }

POPULATION	SCORE
DP	A

,

POPULATION	SCORE
NON-DP	F

,

POPULATION	SCORE
DP	A
NON-DP	F

}

Figure 7-4. *Enumerative specification of tab_LIMIT using table shorthand notation*

Given these two table structures, we can now take a look at a database state. Figure 7-5 displays a database state, named DBS1, that involves the RESULT and LIMIT table structures.

DBS1=

{ (RESULT;

POPULATION	COURSE	AVG_SCORE
DP	set theory	B
DP	logic	A
NON-DP	set theory	D
NON-DP	logic	C

)

, (LIMIT ;

POPULATION	SCORE
DP	A

)

}

Figure 7-5. *Database state DBS1*

As you can see, it is a function that holds two pairs. The first ordered pair holds—as the second coordinate—an admissible RESULT table (that is, an element of tab_RESULT). Likewise, the second ordered pair holds an admissible LIMIT table (that is, an element of tab_LIMIT). These tables are accessible via their table structure names: the values appearing as the first coordinates, RESULT and LIMIT. Using the definition of DBS1, you can write expressions such as DBS1(RESULT) and DBS1(LIMIT), which yield the displayed RESULT and LIMIT tables, respectively.

Now take a look at the following *set* function named DBCHR:

```
DBCHR := { (RESULT; tab_RESULT), (LIMIT; tab_LIMIT) }
```

Set function DBCHR is called a *database characterization*. It characterizes a database in that it introduces the names of the table structures that are involved in a database design and attaches to them the relevant table universes (the sets that hold the admissible tables for each table structure).

Note Database state DBS1 is an element of $\prod$(DBCHR). DBS1 has the same domain as function DBCHR, and every second coordinate of DBS1 is an element chosen from the respective set (tab_RESULT and tab_LIMIT) that appears as the second coordinate in DBCHR.

You can construct a set that holds all possible database states for the result/limit database design, by taking the generalized product of set function DBCHR:

```
DB_U1 := { dbs | dbs∈ ∏(DBCHR) }
```

In set DB_U1, every element dbs is a possible database state given the table universes tab_RESULT and tab_LIMIT. The generalized product operator generates every possible combination of a RESULT table and a LIMIT table; there are 52 combinations in total (#tab_RESULT times #tab_LIMIT).

Now, finally database constraints enter the picture. You can restrict set DB_U1 by adding *database predicates* inside the specification. Take a look at Listing 7-37, which introduces set DB_U2.

Listing 7-37. *Database Universe DB_U2*

```
DB_U2 :=
{ dbs | dbs∈ ∏(DBCHR) ∧
            ( ∀r∈ db(RESULT),l∈ db(LIMIT):
                   r(POPULATION) = l(POPULATION) ⇒ r(AVG_SCORE) ≠ l(SCORE) ) }
```

The specification of DB_U2 contains one database predicate. It states that if there is a limit regarding database professionals, then there cannot be a result with an average score of A for database professionals (regardless of the course), and if there is a limit regarding non-database professionals, then there cannot be a result with an average score of F for non-database professionals.

This database predicate discards possible database states that were generated by the generalized product operator, but that do not reflect admissible representations of our real world. Database predicates that constrain the elements in a database universe are called *database constraints*.

Note Given the database constraint of universe DB_U2, state DBS1 shown in Figure 7-5 is not an admissible state (that is, DB_U2∉ DBS1); the RESULT table holds a tuple that has an average score of A for database professionals. This is not allowed given the contents of the LIMIT table in database state DBS1. In universe DB_U2, the database constraint will discard a total of 26 (possible) database states. You might want to verify this for yourself.

We'll often specify the database constraints in a slightly different manner. Instead of specifying a database predicate with one parameter of type database state, we'll specify them with two or more parameters of type table. To illustrate this, here is an alternative manner of defining database universe DB_U2:

DB_U2 := { dbs | dbs∈∏(DBCHR) ∧ PDC1(dbs(RESULT),dbs(LIMIT)) }

Inside this definition, we instantiate a predicate named PDC1 that accepts two tables as its arguments. It is defined as follows (R and L represent parameters of type table):

PDC1(R,L) := (∀r∈R,l∈L:
                    r(POPULATION) = l(POPULATION) ⇒ r(AVG_SCORE) ≠ l(SCORE)
)

These two definitions together form an equivalent specification to the one given in Listing 7-37. This way of specifying shows immediately how many tables are involved in each database constraint, and inside the database predicate you can use the table parameters directly instead of having to invoke the database state with a certain table structure name.

Let's now continue with the example database design and define its database universe, thereby formally specifying all database constraints. We start by defining the database characterization. Take a look at Listing 7-38, which holds the definition for DB_CHREX.

Listing 7-38. *Database Characterization DB_CHREX*

```
DB_CHREX :=
{ ( EMP;   tab_EMP  )
, ( SREP;  tab_SREP )
, ( MEMP;  tab_MEMP )
, ( TERM;  tab_TERM )
, ( DEPT;  tab_DEPT )
, ( GRD;   tab_GRD  )
, ( CRS;   tab_CRS  )
, ( OFFR;  tab_OFFR )
, ( REG;   tab_REG  )
, ( HIST;  tab_HIST )
}
```

Set function DB_CHREX introduces ten table aliases and attaches to each of them the relevant table universe that was specified in the previous phase. The generalized product of DB_CHREX will produce a set with many possible database states. Our database universe DB_UEX, which is defined in Listing 7-39, establishes 36 database constraints. They are specified by name only in this definition. In the sections that follow, you'll find the formal specification for each of these named constraints.

Listing 7-39. *Database Universe DB_UEX*

```
DB_UEX :=
{ dbs | dbs∈Π(DB_CHREX) ∧
  /* ========================================= */
  /* Start of Subset Requirement Constraints */
  /* ========================================= */
  PSSR1(dbs(EMP),dbs(DEPT))  ∧ PSSR2(dbs(DEPT),dbs(EMP))   ∧
  PSSR3(dbs(MEMP),dbs(EMP))  ∧ PSSR4(dbs(TERM),dbs(EMP))   ∧
  PSSR5(dbs(EMP),dbs(GRD))   ∧ PSSR6(dbs(OFFR),dbs(CRS))   ∧
  PSSR7(dbs(OFFR),dbs(DEPT)) ∧ PSSR8(dbs(OFFR),dbs(EMP))   ∧
  PSSR9(dbs(REG),dbs(EMP))   ∧ PSSR10(dbs(REG),dbs(OFFR))  ∧
  PSSR11(dbs(HIST),dbs(EMP)) ∧ PSSR12(dbs(HIST),dbs(DEPT)) ∧
  /* ================================= */
  /* Start of Specialization Constraints */
  /* ================================= */
  PSPEC1(dbs(EMP),dbs(SREP)) ∧ PSPEC2(dbs(EMP),dbs(MEMP))  ∧
  /* ================================= */
  /* Start of Tuple-in-Join Constraints */
  /* ================================= */
  PTIJ1(dbs(EMP),dbs(GRD))             ∧ PTIJ2(dbs(EMP),dbs(TERM))            ∧
  PTIJ3(dbs(SREP),dbs(EMP),dbs(MEMP))  ∧ PTIJ4(dbs(EMP),dbs(MEMP))            ∧
  PTIJ5(dbs(EMP),dbs(DEPT))            ∧ PTIJ6(dbs(EMP),dbs(HIST))            ∧
  PTIJ7(dbs(TERM),dbs(HIST))           ∧ PTIJ8(dbs(EMP),dbs(REG))             ∧
  PTIJ9(dbs(TERM),dbs(REG),dbs(CRS))   ∧
  PTIJ10(dbs(EMP),dbs(REG),dbs(OFFR),dbs(CRS)) ∧
  PTIJ11(dbs(EMP),dbs(OFFR))           ∧ PTIJ12(dbs(TERM),dbs(OFFR),dbs(CRS)) ∧
  PTIJ13(dbs(REG),dbs(OFFR))           ∧ PTIJ14(dbs(OFFR),dbs(CRS))           ∧
  PTIJ15(dbs(EMP),dbs(REG),dbs(OFFR),dbs(CRS))                                ∧
  /* ================================= */
  /* Start of Other Database Constraints */
  /* ================================= */
  PODC1(dbs(TERM),dbs(MEMP))                       ∧ PODC2(dbs(TERM),dbs(DEPT)) ∧
  PODC3(dbs(OFFR),dbs(DEPT),dbs(EMP),dbs(CRS))     ∧ PODC4(dbs(OFFR),dbs(REG))  ∧
  PODC5(dbs(OFFR),dbs(REG))                        ∧ PODC6(dbs(OFFR),dbs(REG))  ∧
  PODC7(dbs(OFFR),dbs(REG),dbs(EMP))
}
```

As you'll see, the majority of the database constraints are based on one of the common types of predicates that were introduced in the section "Common Patterns of Table and Database Predicates" in Chapter 6; there are 12 *subset requirement*, two *specialization*, and 15 *tuple-in-join* constraints in this database universe definition. Finally, there are seven "other" (that is, not of a common type) database constraints. Most database constraints only involve a pair of table structures; however, some tuple-in-join and "other" database constraints involve more than two table structures.

In the remaining part of this section, you'll find the formal specification of all database constraints, whose names were introduced in the definition of DB_UEX. For our convenience, the names for the table parameters in each of these predicates are the same as the names of the relevant table structures that are involved in the predicate. As you can see inside the specification of DB_UEX, the database predicates are instantiated by providing the relevant tables as the arguments.

Listing 7-40 shows database predicates PSSR1 through PSSR12, which represent the subset requirements in the example database design.

Listing 7-40. *The Subset Requirements of DB_UEX*

```
PSSR1(EMP,DEPT) :=
    /* Employee works for a known department */
    { e(DEPTNO) | e∈EMP } ⊆ { d(DEPTNO) | d∈DEPT }
PSSR2(DEPT,EMP) :=
    /* Dept mgr is a known employee, excluding admins and president */
    { d(MGR)    | d∈DEPT } ⊆
    { e(EMPNO) | e∈EMP ∧ e(JOB) ∉ {'ADMIN','PRESIDENT'} }
PSSR3(MEMP,EMP) :=
    /* Employees can report to a president or a manager only */
    { m(MGR)    | m∈MEMP } ⊆
    { e(EMPNO) | e∈EMP ∧ e(JOB) ∈ {'PRESIDENT','MANAGER' } }
PSSR4(TERM,EMP) :=
    /* A termination is for a known employee; not everyone has left */
    { t(EMPNO) | t∈TERM } ⊂ { e(EMPNO) | e∈EMP }
PSSR5(EMP,GRD) :=
    /* Employee has a known salary grade */
    { e(SGRADE) | e∈EMP } ⊆ { g(GRADE) | g∈GRD }
PSSR6(OFFR,CRS) :=
    /* Course offering is for a known course */
    { o(COURSE) | o∈OFFR } ⊆ { c(CODE) | c∈CRS }
PSSR7(OFFR,DEPT) :=
    /* Courses take place in locations where we have a department */
    { o(LOC) | o∈OFFR } ⊆ { d(LOC) | d∈DEPT }
PSSR8(OFFR,EMP) :=
    /* Trainer of course offering is a known trainer */
    { o(TRAINER) | o∈OFFR ∧ o(TRAINER) ≠ -1 } ⊆
    { e(EMPNO) | e∈EMP ∧ e(JOB) = 'TRAINER' }
PSSR9(REG,EMP) :=
    /* Course registration is for a known employee */
    { r(STUD) | r∈REG } ⊆ { e(EMPNO) | e∈EMP }
PSSR10(REG,OFFR) :=
    /* Course registration is for a known course offering */
    { r↓{COURSE,STARTS} | r∈REG } ⊆ o↓{COURSE,STARTS} | o∈OFFR }
PSSR11(HIST,EMP) :=
    /* History record is for a known employee */
    { h(EMPNO) | h∈HIST } ⊆ { e(EMPNO)} | e∈EMP }
PSSR12(HIST,DEPT) :=
    /* History record is for a known department */
    { h(DEPTNO) | h∈HIST } ⊆ { d(DEPTNO)} | d∈DEPT }
```

Most subset requirements are straightforward; PSSR1, 5, 6, 9, 10, 11, and 12 all state that every tuple in the first argument is related to some tuple in the second argument.

You'll probably find PSSR7 a bit unusual. It states that {LOC} in OFFR references {LOC} in DEPT. Usually, given such a subset requirement, {LOC} would be uniquely identifying in DEPT; however, this is not the case here. This means that an OFFR tuple might be related to more than one DEPT tuple.

Note Apparently the example database design does not need to hold information with regards to locations, other than the name of a location. If that were the case, then a separate table structure, say with alias LOC, would have been introduced to hold location information. Also, two subset requirements, one from DEPT to LOC and one from OFFR to LOC, would have been introduced.

Predicates PSSR2 and PSSR3 state that every tuple in the first parameter value is related to some tuple in *a subset of* the second parameter value; the set specified at the right-hand side denotes a table restriction in these cases.

Predicate PSSR8 states that every tuple in *a subset of* the first parameter value is related to some tuple in *a subset of* the second parameter value; the sets specified at both sides denote table restrictions.

Finally, you might have noticed that inside predicate PSSR4 the *proper* subset operator is used; this ensures that not every employee has been terminated (at least one employee still works for the company).

You can find the definitions for the specialization constraints PSPEC1 and PSPEC2 in Listing 7-41.

Listing 7-41. *The Specializations of DB_UEX*

```
PSPEC1(EMP,SREP) :=
    /* Salesreps have a target and a commission */
    { e(EMPNO) | e∈EMP ∧ e(JOB) = 'SALESREP' } =
    { s(EMPNO) | s∈SREP }
PSPEC2(EMP,MEMP) :=
    /* Everybody, excluding presidents, is a managed employee */
    { e(EMPNO) | e∈EMP ∧ e(JOB) ≠ 'PRESIDENT' } =
    { m(EMPNO) | m∈MEMP }
```

Predicate PSPEC1 specifies that you can find additional information for sales representatives (and no other employees) in the SREP table structure; only sales representatives have a target and a commission. Predicate PSPEC2 specifies that for all employees excluding presidents, additional information can be found in the MEMP table structure; here the employee number of the employee that acts as the manager is maintained.

Note We say that SREP and MEMP are *specializations* of EMP.

Listing 7-42 shows database predicates PTIJ1 through PTIJ15 that represent the tuple-in-join constraints in the example database design.

Listing 7-42. *The Tuple-in-Join Constraints of DB_UEX*

```
PTIJ1(EMP,GRD) :=
    /* Monthly salary must fall within assigned salary grade */
    ( ∀e∈ EMP, g∈ GRD:
        e(SGRADE) = g(GRADE) ⟹ ( g(LLIMIT) ≤ e(MSAL) ∧ e(MSAL) ≤ g(ULIMIT) ) )
PTIJ2(EMP,TERM) :=
/* Leave date must fall after hire date */
    ( ∀e∈ EMP, t∈ TERM:
        e(EMPNO) = t(EMPNO) ⟹ e(HIRED) < t(LEFT) )
PTIJ3(SREP,EMP,MEMP) :=
    /* Salesreps cannot earn more than the employee they report to */
    ( ∀s∈ SREP, es∈ EMP, m∈ MEMP, em∈ EMP:
      ( s(EMPNO)=es(EMPNO) ∧ es(EMPNO)=m(EMPNO) ∧ m(MGR) = em(EMPNO) )
        ⟹
      ( es(MSAL) + s(COMM)/12 < em(MSAL) ) )
PTIJ4(EMP,MEMP) :=
    /* Non-salesreps cannot earn more than the employee they report to */
    ( ∀e∈ EMP, m∈ MEMP, em∈ EMP:
      (e(EMPNO)=m(EMPNO) ∧ m(MGR) = em(EMPNO) ∧ e(JOB) ≠ 'SALESREP')
        ⟹
      ( e(MSAL) < em(MSAL) ) )
PTIJ5(EMP,DEPT) :=
    /* Department manager must work for department he/she manages */
    ( ∀e∈ EMP, d∈ DEPT:
        e(EMPNO) = d(MGR) ⟹ e(DEPTNO) = d(DEPTNO) )
PTIJ6(EMP,HIST) :=
    /* No history records allowed at or before hire date */
    ( ∀e∈ EMP, h∈ HIST:
        e(EMPNO) = h(EMPNO) ⟹ e(HIRED) < h(UNTIL) )
PTIJ7(TERM,HIST) :=
    /* No history records allowed at or after leave date */
    ( ∀t∈ TERM, h∈ HIST:
        t(EMPNO) = h(EMPNO) ⟹ t(LEFT) > h(UNTIL) )
PTIJ8(EMP,REG) :=
    /* You cannot register for offerings in 1st four weeks on the job */
    ( ∀e∈ EMP, r∈ REG:
        e(EMPNO) = r(STUD) ⟹ e(HIRED) + 28 ≤ r(STARTS) )
PTIJ9(TERM,REG,CRS) :=
    /* You cannot register for offerings given at or after leave date */
    ( ∀t∈ TERM, r∈ REG, c∈ CRS:
      ( t(EMPNO) = r(STUD) ∧ r(COURSE) = c(CODE) )
        ⟹
      ( t(LEFT) ≥ r(STARTS) + c(DUR) ) )
PTIJ10(EMP,REG,OFFR,CRS) :=
```

```
        /* You cannot register for overlapping course offerings */
        ( ∀e∈EMP, r1,r2∈REG, o1,o2∈OFFR, c1,c2∈CRS:
          ( e(EMPNO)             = r1(STUD)              ∧
            r1↓{COURSE,STARTS} = o1↓{COURSE,STARTS} ∧
            o1(COURSE)           = c1(CODE)             ∧
            e(EMPNO)             = r2(STUD)             ∧
            r2↓{COURSE,STARTS} = o2↓{COURSE,STARTS} ∧
            o2(COURSE)           = c2(CODE)
          ) ⇒
          ( o1↓{COURSE,STARTS} = o2↓{COURSE,STARTS} ∨
            o1(STARTS) ≥ o2(STARTS) + c2(DUR)          ∨
            o2(STARTS) ≥ o1(STARTS) + c1(DUR) ) )
PTIJ11(EMP,OFFR) :=
        /* Trainer cannot teach courses before hire date */
        ( ∀e∈EMP, o∈OFFR:
          e(EMPNO) = o(TRAINER) ⇒ e(HIRED) ≤ o(STARTS) )
PTIJ12(TERM,OFFR,CRS) :=
        /* Trainer cannot teach courses at or after leave date */
        ( ∀t∈TERM, o∈OFFR, c∈CRS:
          ( t(EMPNO) = o(TRAINER) ∧ o(COURSE) = c(CODE) )
          ⇒
          ( t(LEFT) ≥ o(STARTS) + c(DUR)                ) )
PTIJ13(REG,OFFR) :=
        /* Trainer cannot register for offerings taught by him/herself */
        ( ∀r∈REG, o∈OFFR:
          r↓{COURSE,STARTS} = o↓{COURSE,STARTS} ⇒
          r(STUD) ≠ o(TRAINER) )
PTIJ14(OFFR,CRS) :=
        /* Trainer cannot teach different courses simultaneously */
        ( ∀o1,o2∈OFFR, c1,c2∈CRS:
          ( o1(TRAINER) = o2(TRAINER) ∧
            o1(COURSE)  = c1(CODE)    ∧
            o2(COURSE)  = c2(CODE)
          ) ⇒
          ( o1↓{COURSE,STARTS} = o2↓{COURSE,STARTS} ∨
            o1(STARTS) ≥ o2(STARTS) + c2(DUR)          ∨
            o2(STARTS) ≥ o1(STARTS) + c1(DUR) ) )
PTIJ15(EMP,REG,OFFR,CRS) :=
        /* Employee cannot register for course offerings that overlap */
        /* with another course offering where he/she is the trainer */
        ( ∀e∈EMP, r∈REG, o1,o2∈OFFR, c1,c2∈CRS:
          ( e(EMPNO)   = r(STUD)                        ∧
            r↓{COURSE,STARTS} = o1↓{COURSE,STARTS} ∧
            o1(COURSE) = c1(CODE)                        ∧
            e(EMPNO)   = o2(TRAINER)                     ∧
            o2(COURSE) = c2(CODE)
          ) ⇒
```

$$(\ o1\downarrow\{COURSE,STARTS\} = o2\downarrow\{COURSE,STARTS\} \ \lor$$
$$o1(STARTS) \geq o2(STARTS) + c2(DUR) \qquad \lor$$
$$o2(STARTS) \geq o1(STARTS) + c1(DUR) \ ) \ )$$

Predicates PTIJ1 to PIJ15 all limit the tuples that are allowed in some join. Most of these joins involve only two table structures. Five predicates (PTIJ3, PTIJ9, PTIJ10, PTIJ12, PTIJ15) limit the tuples in joins that involve more than two table structures. Let's take a closer look at those five.

Predicate PTIJ3 joins an SREP tuple (variable s) with its related EMP tuple (variable es), continues to join this EMP tuple with its related MEMP tuple (variable m), and finally joins this MEMP tuple with its related EMP tuple (variable em). All tuples that are in this join across four tables (note that EMP is joined twice) are constrained by the predicate es(MSAL) + s(COMM)/12 < em(MSAL). This states that the monthly salary of the sales representative, increased with a twelfth of his/her commission, should be less than the monthly salary of the employee that is managing this sales representative. By the way, this managing employee cannot be a sales representative—which might have required adding a twelfth of a commission at the right-hand side of the smaller-than symbol too—due to subset requirement PSSR3.

Predicate PTIJ9 joins a TERM tuple (t) directly with a REG tuple (r) and continues to join the REG tuple with its related CRS tuple (c).

■Note A few notes:

The join from TERM to REG is not done "via EMP." Because TERM is a specialization of EMP, you can join TERM directly to any other table structure that EMP can join to using the EMPNO attribute.

The join from REG to CRS is not done "via OFFR." From the two subset requirements PSSR6 and PSSR10, you can deduce that {CRS} in REG references {CODE} in CRS (a subset requirement between REG and CRS), and you can thus join REG directly to CRS in the way shown.

Tuples in this join are constrained by the predicate t(LEFT) ≥ r(STARTS) + c(DUR). Do you notice that this formal specification somewhat differs from the embedded informal comment? The formal specification involves the CRS table structure too, or rather its DUR attribute. Here's a more correct informal explanation of this constraint: an employee cannot register for a course offering that starts at or after his or her leave date, nor can an employee be terminated during a course offering that he or she is attending as a student.

Now you're going down a path that is often hard to avoid when you try to describe database constraints informally: you start talking in terms of transactions that are not allowed given the constraint. This is what just happened earlier: you cannot *insert* an OFFR tuple given a certain TERM tuple, and vice versa, you cannot insert a TERM tuple given a certain OFFR tuple. With the increasing scope of data covered by a constraint, it becomes increasingly more difficult to informally—using a natural language—state *the what* of a constraint without alienating yourself from your customer. You often must dive into *the how* of a constraint. In your communication with the end users, this is not a bad thing; you start communicating in terms of *how* the system will behave (what transactions it will not accept given the constraint), and end users typically understand this. Your formal specification is the basis from which you can generate this behavior (we will deal with this in detail in Chapter 11). For instance, you might want to briefly mention to the user that given this constraint, the duration of a course cannot be increased (updated) given certain circumstances.

Predicate PTIJ10 joins an EMP tuple with two related REG tuples (r1 and r2), continues to join each of these two REG tuples with their related OFFR tuple (o1 and o2), and finally joins the two OFFR tuples with their related CRS tuple (c1 and c2). Tuples in this join are constrained by the following predicate:

```
o1↓{COURSE,STARTS} = o2↓{COURSE,STARTS} ∨
o1(STARTS) ≥ o2(STARTS) + c2(DUR)         ∨
o2(STARTS) ≥ o1(STARTS) + c1(DUR)
```

This predicate states that if the join doesn't involve the same two OFFR tuples, then offering o1 must start after offering o2 ends, or vice versa.

Predicate PTIJ12 is the "trainer" version of PTIJ9. Instead of joining TERM via REG (using the STUD attribute) to CRS, predicate PTIJ12 joins TERM via OFFR (using the TRAINER attribute) to CRS and limits the resulting tuples in the join in the same way.

Predicate PTIJ15 joins an EMP tuple to a CRS tuple via REG and OFFR (representing the student that attends a course offering), and continues to join that same EMP tuple to a CRS tuple via OFFR (representing the trainer that gives an offering). It then restricts the tuples in this join in the same way as predicate PTIJ10 does.

You might have noticed a correlation between predicates PTIJ15 and PTIJ13; we will deal with this in an exercise at the end of this chapter.

Listing 7-43 shows database predicates PODC1 through PODC7, which represent the remaining seven other database constraints in the example database design.

Listing 7-43. *The "Other" Database Constraints of DB_UEX*

```
PODC1(TERM,MEMP) :=
    /* Active employee cannot be managed by terminated employee */
    { t1(EMPNO) | t1∈TERM } ∩
    { m(MGR) | m∈MEMP ∧
                ¬ ( ∃t2∈TERM: t2(EMPNO) = m(EMPNO) ) } = ∅
PODC2(TERM,DEPT) :=
    /* Department cannot be managed by a terminated employee */
    { t(EMPNO) | t∈TERM } ∩ { d(MGR) | d∈DEPT } = ∅
PODC3(OFFR,DEPT,EMP,CRS) :=
    /* At least half of the course offerings taught by a trainer */
    /* must be at home base */
    ( ∀e1∈{ o1(TRAINER) | o1∈OFFR ∧ o1(STATUS) ≠ 'CANC' }:
    ( Σt∈{ o2∪c2| d2∈DEPT ∧ e2∈EMP ∧ o2∈OFFR ∧ c2∈CRS ∧
                    e2(EMPNO)  = e1         ∧
                    e2(EMPNO)  = o2(TRAINER) ∧
                    e2(DEPTNO) = d2(DEPTNO)  ∧
                    o2(COURSE) = c2(CODE)    ∧
                    o2(STATUS) ≠ 'CANC'      ∧
                    o2(LOC)    = d2(LOC)
            } : t(DUR)
      ) ≥
```

```
    ( Σt∈{ o3∪c3| d3∈DEPT ∧ e3∈EMP ∧ o3∈OFFR ∧ c3∈CRS ∧
                    e3(EMPNO)  = e1             ∧
                    e3(EMPNO)  = o3(TRAINER) ∧
                    e3(DEPTNO) = d3(DEPTNO) ∧
                    o3(COURSE) = c3(CODE)      ∧
                    o3(STATUS) ≠ 'CANC'        ∧
                    o3(LOC)    ≠ d3(LOC)
            } : t(DUR) ) )
PODC4(OFFR,REG) :=
    /* Offerings with 6+ registrations must have status confirmed */
    ( ∀o∈OFFR:
      #{ r | r∈REG ∧
             r↓{COURSE,STARTS} = o↓{COURSE,STARTS} } ≥ 6
        ⇒
      o(STATUS) = 'CONF' )
PODC5(OFFR,REG) :=
    /* Number of registrations cannot exceed maximum capacity of offering */
    ( ∀o∈OFFR:
      #{ r | r∈REG ∧
             r↓{COURSE,STARTS} = o↓{COURSE,STARTS} } ≤ o(MAXCAP) )
PODC6(OFFR,REG) :=
    /* Canceled offerings cannot have registrations */
    ( ∀o∈OFFR: o(STATUS) = 'CANC'
                  ⇒
                  ¬( ∃r∈REG: r↓{COURSE,STARTS} = o↓{COURSE,STARTS} ) )
PODC7(OFFR,REG,EMP) :=
    /* You are allowed to teach a certain course only if: */
    /* 1. You have been employed for at least one year, or */
    /* 2. You have attended that course first and the trainer of that */
    /*    course offering attends your first teach as participant */
    ( ∀o1∈OFFR:
      /* If this is the 1st time this trainer gives this course ... */
      ( ¬∃o2∈OFFR:
          o1↓{COURSE,TRAINER} = o2↓{COURSE,TRAINER} ∧
          o2(STARTS) < o1(STARTS)
      ) ⇒
    (/* then there should be an attendee in the classroom ... */
       ( ∃r1∈REG:
            r1↓{COURSE,STARTS} = o1↓{COURSE,STARTS} ∧
            /* who has given this course at an earlier date ... */
            ( ∃o3∈OFFR:
              o3(TRAINER) = r1(STUD)  ∧
              o3(COURSE) = o1(COURSE) ∧
              o3(STARTS) < o1(STARTS) ∧
       /* and *that* course was attended by the current trainer */
              ( ∃r2∈REG:
                o3↓{COURSE,STARTS} = r2↓{COURSE,STARTS} ∧
```

```
            r2(STUD) = o1(TRAINER)
   ) ) ) ∨
/* or, this trainer has been employed for at least one year */
   ( ⌐{ e(HIRED) | e∈EMP ∧ e(EMPNO) = o1(TRAINER) } <
      o1(STARTS) - 365 ) ) )
```

Predicate PODC1 states that the intersection of two sets should be the empty set. The first set holds all employee numbers of terminated employees. The second set holds all employee numbers of employees who manage an active (that is, not terminated) employee. By specifying that the intersection of these two sets is empty, you represent the informal requirement that an active employee cannot be managed by a terminated employee.

In the same way, predicate PODC2 represents the informal requirement that a department is managed by an active employee.

Predicate PODC3 universally quantifies over all employee numbers of employees that act as the trainer of some offering that has not been canceled. For each such employee number, it builds the set of (not canceled) OFFR tuples joined with their related CRS tuple, where the trainer of the offering equals the given employee (number), and the location of the offering is equal to the location of the department in which the given employee works. It then sums the DUR attribute values of all tuples in this set. The (summed) duration of offerings for the given trainer where the offering was given—at a location that differs from the trainer's department location—is determined in the same way. For every given trainer, the former sum cannot be less than the latter sum.

Of course, this is not the way you communicate with your users. You stick to the English sentence provided by them (see the embedded comments in the code) and verify the meaning of the terminology that they use in that sentence. The verb "taught" in "taught by a trainer" clearly means that the offering must have status scheduled or confirmed; canceled offerings are not to be considered. It appears that counting offerings involves the duration of the offering. Finally, an offering is considered to be "at home base" if its location is the same as the location of the department that employs the trainer.

Note Constraint PODC3 requires that attribute LOC of the OFFR table structure can (meaningfully) be compared to attribute LOC of the DEPT table structure. Constraint PSSR7 has been introduced to ensure exactly this requirement.

Predicate PODC4 states that offerings for which six or more students have registered must have status confirmed. It does this by inspecting the cardinality of the set that holds all registrations that are related to a given offering. If this cardinality is six or more, then the status of the given offering must be confirmed.

The structure of predicate PODC5 is similar to the structure of PODC6. It universally quantifies over all offerings, and requires that the number of related registrations for the given offering cannot exceed the maximum capacity of the given offering.

■**Note** The combination of predicates PODC4 and PODC5 imply that it would be useless to allow an offering to have a maximum capacity of less than six; such an offering could never reach status confirmed. This is exactly why the attribute value set of attribute MAXCAP starts at value six (see Listing 7-9).

Predicate PODC6 states that registrations for canceled offerings cannot exist. Consequently, whenever an offering gets canceled, all related registrations are to be removed.

Predicate PODC7 constitutes the *pièce de résistance* of our example database universe. It requires that the first-time offering of every course taught by a trainer satisfies a certain condition. If the given trainer of such an offering has not been employed for at least one year, then this given trainer must have attended a prior offering of the same course, and the trainer of that prior course offering must attend such a first-time offering taught by a given trainer. Predicate PODC7 explicitly holds additional comments to guide you through its formal specification.

When you try to read and understand a complex predicate such as PODC7, it's useful to first study the top-down structure of the predicate. In this case, the structure of the predicate is as follows:

$$(\ \forall o1 \in OFFR: \ P1(o1,OFFR) \ \Rightarrow \ (\ P2(o1,OFFR,REG) \ \lor \ P3(o1,EMP) \ )$$

Predicate PODC7 is a universal quantification over all offerings, and states that if some condition (P1) that involves the given offering and other offerings is TRUE, then a disjunction of two conditions (P2 and P3) should hold. Condition P1 states that the given offering is the first-time offering. Condition P2 involves the given offering, other offerings, and registrations; it states the complex requirement with regards to the prior offering that must have been attended by the trainer of the given offering. Condition P3 involves the given offering and employees; it states that the trainer of the given offering has been employed for at least one year.

■**Note** Constraint PODC7 implies that the very first offering given for every course must be given by a trainer that has been employed for at least one year. Evidently it takes at least a year to develop the material and reach the skill level necessary to offer a course.

This concludes the demonstration of how to formally specify a relational database design. You have seen how you can use set theory, in combination with logic, to produce a rock-solid database design specification. The method demonstrated also gives us a good and clear insight into the relevant constraints that play a role in the various layers of such a database design.

Chapter Summary

This section provides a summary of this chapter, formatted as a bulleted list. It provides a high-level overview of the material discussed in this chapter.

- Database designs are often documented using the natural language. The major part of these design documents consists of the constraint specifications that will make the database design a satisfactory fit for the real world.

- If you use plain English to express data integrity constraints, you will inevitably hit the problem of how English sentences map, unambiguously, into the table structures.

- You can use set theory to formally specify a database design in a layered (phased) manner. By formalizing your database design specification, you will eliminate all ambiguity—especially the ambiguity surrounding the constraints.

- In the first phase, you specify a set function for every table structure. This set function introduces the attribute names for the table structure and attaches the relevant attribute value set to each of them. These set functions are called *characterizations*.

- In the second phase, you specify for every table structure a set of tuples called the *tuple universe*. It holds admissible tuples for the table structure. You can construct a tuple universe by taking the generalized product of a characterization and restricting this result by specifying tuple predicates. These tuple predicates are called *tuple constraints*.

- In the third phase, you specify for every table structure a set of tables called the *table universe*. It holds admissible tables for the table structure. You can construct a table universe by taking the powerset of a tuple universe and restricting this result by specifying table predicates. These table predicates are called *table constraints*.

- In the last phase, you specify a set of database states called the *database universe*. It holds the admissible database states for the database being specified. You can construct a database universe by first defining a *database characterization*. A database characterization arranges all table universes into a single set function. You can construct the database universe by taking the generalized product of the database characterization and restricting this result by specifying database predicates. These database predicates are called *database constraints*.

- This formal model is *your*—the database professional's—reference of the database design. Users should never be confronted with this formalism. You can use an external predicate, in conjunction with the tuple constraints, to convey the meaning of the attributes of each table structure. Often you should explain table and database constraints to users by talking about the implications they have on the behavior of the system. Finally, by using rewrite rules to rewrite the predicates that constitute the constraints, you can find alternative, informal ways to discuss the relevant constraints with users.

Exercises

1. Rewrite table predicate P3 (see Listing 7-23) into a negation of an existential quantification.

2. One of your colleagues suggests that the following tuple predicate should be added to the specification of tuple universe tup_OFFR:

   $$o(STATUS)='CONF' \Rightarrow o(TRAINER) \neq -1$$

   What is your response?

3. Modify the specification of table universe tab_MEMP so that it includes a constraint that states that no manager can directly manage more than ten employees.

4. In table universe tab_GRD, there is currently no limit to the number of salary grades that are allowed to overlap with one another. Add a table constraint that ensures that a salary value falls within at most two salary grades.

5. Write down database state DBS1 using the longhand notation for tables.

6. Within the context of universe DB_U2, what are the admissible RESULT tables that can be combined with the following LIMIT table?

   ```
   { { (POPULATION;'DP'), (SCORE;'A') },
     { (POPULATION;'NON-DP'), (SCORE;'F') } }.
   ```

7. Database constraint PTIJ5 implies that no employee can manage more than one department. This renders the third table constraint of table universe tab_DEPT useless: it can never be violated given PTIJ5.

   a. Change the specification of the database constraint PTIJ5 such that if the employee manages two departments, then one of those must be the department in which the employee is employed.

   b. Add a new constraint stating that if an employee manages two departments, then these two departments must be at the same location.

8. Predicate PODC6 is a disguised tuple-in-join predicate. Can you provide the alternative formal specification that follows the structure of a tuple-in-join predicate?

9. The example database design deliberately does not have a constraint stating that cycles are not allowed in the hierarchy of managed employees. This is because other constraints prevent such cycles from ever happening. Do you see which ones these are?

10. Give an alternative formal specification of predicate PODC1 using quantifiers.

11. The employee with employee number 1000 has a special status within the company. Take a look at the following database constraint with regards to this employee:

```
PODC8(OFFR,REG) :=
    (∀o∈ OFFR: (∃r∈ REG: r↓{course,starts}=o↓{course,starts) ∧
                           r(stud)=1000)
            ⇒
            ( #{ r2 | r2∈REG ∧ r2↓{course,starts}=o↓{course,starts)} = 1
              ∧
              ¬(∃o2∈ OFFR: o2↓{loc,starts}=o↓{loc,starts} ∧
                             o2(course)≠o(course))
            )
    )
```

This constraint states that whenever employee 1000 is attending an offering, then no other students are allowed to attend this offering, nor can there be any other offering (for a different course) starting at the same date and location as this offering. This constraint is actually a conjunction of two constraints, where one is a (disguised) table constraint and the other a (simpler) database constraint. Find out what these two constraints are by applying various rewrite rules introduced in Part 1 of this book.

12. Take a look at the following database state, named db_empty:

```
{ ( EMP; ∅ ), ( SREP; ∅ ), ( MEMP; ∅ ), ( TERM; ∅ ), ( DEPT; ∅ ),
  ( GRD; ∅ ), ( CRS;  ∅ ), ( OFFR; ∅ ), ( REG;  ∅ ), ( HIST; ∅ ) }
```

Is state db_empty an element of database universe DB_UEX?

13. Extend the example database design with a BONUS table structure. Here's the external predicate of this table structure: "The employee with employee number EMPNO has received a bonus of AMOUNT dollars in year YEAR." The following constraints apply with regards to this new table structure:

   a. The yearly bonus cannot exceed the upper limit of the salary grade of the employee.

   b. An employee can only receive a bonus for full years of (active) employment.

   c. Sales reps do not receive bonuses.

Provide a characterization, tuple universe, and table universe for the BONUS table structure and (if necessary) modify the DB_UEX universe.

14. The president has decided that the business rule "no two offerings of the same course can start on the same day" should be relaxed to "only if two offerings of the same course take place at different locations, are they allowed to start on the same day." Analyze the impact of this change with regards to the data integrity constraints of the DB_UEX universe.

15. With a slight change to predicate PTIJ15, you can have it include the limitation imposed by predicate PTIJ13; it then implies PTIJ13, which means you can get rid of PTIJ13. Do you see how to change PTIJ15?

Specifying State Transition Constraints

In Chapter 6 you were introduced to tuple, table, and database predicates. These predicates deal with data in an increasing scope order: attribute values within a single tuple, tuples within a single table, and tables within a single database state.

The section "More Data Integrity Predicates" continues down this path of increasing scope by introducing the concept of a *state transition predicate*. A state transition predicate deals with a pair of database states that are referred to as the *begin state* and the *end state*. We'll use state transition predicates to define the admissible database state transitions (otherwise known as *transactions*) for a database design.

In the section "State Transition Constraints," you'll discover that a transaction can be modeled as ordered pair of two database states: the database state that exists at the start of the transaction, and the database state that exists at the end of the transaction, which is the state that the transaction results into.

We'll define the notion of a *state transition universe*: the set that holds all admissible transactions for a database design. To define a state transition universe, you'll define state transition predicates that represent the *state transition constraints* in the database design.

The section "State Transition Constraints" concludes with a specification of the state transition universe for the example database design that was introduced in Chapter 7; it includes seven state transition constraints for this database design. The example state transition universe is also available in Appendix A.

As usual, you'll find a "Chapter Summary" at the end, followed by an "Exercises" section.

More Data Integrity Predicates

In the previous chapter you were introduced to four classes of data integrity constraints: attribute, tuple, table, and database constraints. These four classes of constraints accept or reject a given database state. They can be checked within the context of a database state and are referred to as static constraints. In the real world there is often a requirement to prohibit certain *database state transitions* on grounds other than the static constraints. These state transition limiting constraints are referred to as *dynamic* (or *state transition*) constraints.

A Simple Example

A classical illustration of a state transition constraint is the requirement that the salary of an employee is not allowed to decrease. As you can see, this requirement cannot be checked within the context of a single database state; you require the context of a transaction that changes the state of a database. To check this requirement, you need to inspect the salary values in the database state that exists at the start of the transaction (its *begin state*), as well as inspect the salary values in the database state that exists at the end of the transaction (its *end state*).

Note You'll see shortly that we'll use these two database states—the begin state and the end state—to characterize a transaction.

Let's demonstrate this with an example using the database design that was introduced in the previous chapter. Figure 8-1 shows two employee tables E1 and E2.

E1

empno	ename	job	born	hired	sgrade	msal	deptno
101	'Chris'	'MANAGER'	22-02-1970	01-03-2001	7	8200	10
102	'Kathy'	'TRAINER'	06-12-1966	01-03-2001	5	6000	12
103	'Thomas'	'ADMIN'	25-07-1999	01-03-2001	2	2100	10
104	'David'	'TRAINER'	05-08-1964	01-03-2001	4	5600	10
105	'Renu'	'ADMIN'	20-01-1968	01-03-2001	2	3000	12

E2

empno	ename	job	born	hired	sgrade	msal	deptno
101	'Chris'	'MANAGER'	22-02-1970	01-03-2001	8	7900	10
102	'Kathy'	'TRAINER'	06-12-1966	01-03-2001	5	6000	12
103	'Thomas'	'ADMIN'	25-07-1999	01-03-2001	2	2100	10
104	'David'	'TRAINER'	05-08-1964	01-03-2001	4	5600	10
105	'Renu'	'ADMIN'	20-01-1968	01-03-2001	2	4000	12

Figure 8-1. *Tables E1 and E2*

These two tables differ only in three attribute values.

Let's assume that a given transaction, say TX1, starts off in a begin state that contains E1 and results in an end state that contains E2. As you can see in Figure 8-1, TX1 has apparently decreased the salary of employee 101 (from 8200 to 7900), and also changed the employee's salary grade. TX1 has also increased the salary of employee 105 (from 3000 to 4000). Transaction TX1 has not changed the salary of all other employees.

■**Note** Obviously, TX1 violates the state transition constraint stating that salaries are not allowed to be decreased.

Now let's investigate how you can formally specify that the salary of an employee is not allowed to decrease. Transaction TX1 violates this state transition requirement because there exists a combination of an employee tuple (say e1) in E1 and an employee tuple (say e2) in E2 that both concern the same employee—that is, that correspond on the empno attribute—and are such that the msal value in e2 is lower than the msal value in e1.

Assume that dbs1 is the begin state of transaction TX1 and dbs2 is its end state. Note that this means that the expression dbs1(EMP) evaluates to E1 and expression dbs2(EMP) evaluates to E2. Take a look at the proposition in Listing 8-1.

Listing 8-1. *A Proposition Concerning Database States dbs1 and dbs2*

```
prop1 :=
    (∀e1∈ dbs1(EMP): (∀e2∈ dbs2(EMP): e1(empno) = e2(empno) ⇒ e1(msal) ≤ e2(msal) ) )
```

This proposition states that there cannot exist a combination of a tuple in E1 and a tuple in E2 such that they correspond on the empno attribute, and the msal value in the E1 tuple is greater than the msal value in the E2 tuple. This precisely reflects our state transition requirement.

This type of transition constraint (at the attribute level) is common, and can also be specified in another way: by joining the table in the begin state with its corresponding version in the end state such that all attribute values (old and new) are available, and then restricting the attribute values in the resulting tuples in this join.

■**Note** Loosely speaking, such transition constraints can be considered *dynamic* tuple-in-join constraints.

Listing 8-2 shows an alternative way to formally specify this requirement; it joins the EMP table in the begin state (dbs1) with the EMP table in the end state (dbs2).

Listing 8-2. *Alternative Specification for Our State Transition Requirement*

```
prop2 :=
    ( ∀e∈ ((dbs1(EMP)⇓{empno,msal})◊◊{(empno;empno),(old_msal;msal)})⊗
          ((dbs2(EMP)⇓{empno,msal})◊◊{(empno;empno),(new_msal;msal)}):
          e(old_msal) ≤ e(new_msal) )
```

We now use the join operator (⊗) together with table projection (⇓) and attribute renaming (◊◊). In this specification both E1 and E2 are first projected on the empno and msal attributes. Then the msal attribute in (the projection of) E1 is renamed to old_msal, and the msal attribute in (the projection of) E2 is renamed to new_msal. The resulting two tables can now be joined with the join operator. The table resulting from this join is a table over heading {empno,old_msal,new_msal}. For all tuples in this table, the old_msal value should be smaller than or equal to the new_msal value.

Figure 8-2 clarifies the preceding explanation by displaying the intermediate tables and the final table resulting from the subexpressions inside prop2.

E1⇓{empno,msal}

empno	msal
101	8200
102	6000
103	2100
104	5600
105	3000

E2⇓{empno,msal}

empno	msal
101	7900
102	6000
103	2100
104	5600
105	4000

E1⇓{empno,msal}◊◊
{(empno;empno), (old_msal;msal)}

empno	old_msal
101	8200
102	6000
103	2100
104	5600
105	3000

E2⇓{empno,msal}◊◊
{(empno;empno), (new_msal;msal)}

empno	new_msal
101	7900
102	6000
103	2100
104	5600
105	4000

Resulting Table

empno	old_msal	new_msal
101	8200	7900
102	6000	6000
103	2100	2100
104	5600	5600
105	3000	4000

Figure 8-2. *Intermediate tables and final table for expression prop2*

State Transition Predicates

Continuing from Chapter 6 where the concepts of a *tuple, table*, and *database predicate* were introduced, we now further increase the scope of data that a data integrity predicate can deal with by defining the notion of a *state transition predicate*.

State transition predicates deal with *a pair of database states*. These predicates have two parameters, both of type database state; the first parameter is referred to as the begin state and the second parameter the end state. In the next section, we'll use state transition predicates to define the admissible state transitions for a database design. Only those transactions, whose begin and end state transform all state transition predicates into true propositions, are considered valid (or admissible) transactions.

Note that the propositions in Listings 8-1 and 8-2 also deal with a pair of database states: the two given database states dbs1 and dbs2. Now take a look at the state transition predicates in Listing 8-3. These are the "predicate versions" of the propositions in Listings 8-1 and 8-2.

Listing 8-3. *Two State Transition Predicates*

```
STP1(B,E) := ( ∀e1∈B(EMP), e2∈E(EMP): e1(empno)=e2(empno) ⇒ e1(msal) ≤ e2(msal) )
STP2(B,E) := ( ∀e∈((B(EMP)⇓{empno,msal})◊◊{(empno;empno),(old_msal;msal)})⊗
                    ((E(EMP)⇓{empno,msal})◊◊{(empno;empno),(new_msal;msal)}):
                 e(old_msal) ≤ e(new_msal) )
```

When you supply database states dbs1 and dbs2 as values for parameters B and E, respectively, then these state transition predicates will transform into the propositions listed in Listings 8-1 and 8-2.

```
STP1(dbs1,dbs2) = prop1
STP2(dbs1,dbs2) = prop2
```

We require that state transition predicates cannot be decomposed into multiple conjuncts, just like tuple, table, and database predicates. If you can rewrite a given state transition predicate ST(B,E) into an expression of the form STa(B,E) ∧ STb(B,E), then you are in fact dealing with two state transition predicates.

In the remainder of this book, we'll also require that a state transition predicate—say ST(B,E)—cannot be rewritten into a predicate of either of the following two forms:

```
P(B)
P(E)
```

In these expressions, P represents a database predicate; that is, a predicate that inspects a single database state (either B or E in the preceding cases). This means that we require a state transition predicate to involve at least one table from the begin state as well as at least one table from the end state. That's because, if the predicate involves only tables from one database state (either the begin or the end state), then the predicate will reflect a static constraint, not a state transition constraint.

As you'll see in the examples given in the next section, state transition predicates typically involve the tables from the begin and end states of the same table structure. Instead of specifying a state transition predicate with two parameters of type database state, we'll often specify them with two or more parameters of type table. To illustrate this, Listing 8-4 respecifies the state transition predicates of Listing 8-3 in this way. Parameters EMPB and EMPE are of type table; the idea is for parameter EMPB to accept the employee table state that exists at the beginning of a transaction, and for parameter EMPE to accept the employee table state that exists at the end of a transaction.

Listing 8-4. *Alternative Specification of State Transition Predicates STP1 and STP2*

```
STP1(EMPB,EMPE) :=
    ( ∀e1∈EMPB, e2∈EMPE: e1(empno) = e2(empno) ⇒ e1(msal) ≤ e2(msal) )
STP2(EMPB,EMPE) :=
    ( ∀e∈((EMPB⇓{empno,msal})◊◊{(empno;empno),(old_msal;msal)})⊗
          ((EMPE⇓{empno,msal})◊◊{(empno;empno),(new_msal;msal)}):
          e(old_msal) ≤ e(new_msal) )
```

In the next section, we'll use state transition predicates to formally specify the state transition constraints for a database design.

State Transition Constraints

In this section we'll introduce you to the concept of a *state transition universe*. The state transition constraints will be specified as embedded state transition predicates in the formal definition of a state transition universe.

State Transition Universe

To formally specify the state transition constraints for a database design, we'll specify the *set of all admissible transactions* for the database design. You can model a transaction as an ordered pair of its begin and end states; the first coordinate in the ordered pair represents the begin state, and the second coordinate of the ordered pair represents the end state.

You can then specify the *set of all admissible transactions* as a set of such ordered pairs. Every ordered pair in this set is of the form (B;E), where both B and E represent a valid database state (that is, they are elements of the database universe for the database design). This set of ordered pairs is called the *state transition universe*. If (B;E) is an element of the state transition universe, then the transaction that transforms state B into state E is allowed.

To illustrate this, let's assume you need to specify a state transition universe for some database design whose database universe only has four database states. We'll name these database states s1 through s4. Let's further assume that you only allow a transaction if it implements one of the following state transitions:

```
s1 to s2
s1 to s3
s1 to s4
s2 to s3
s2 to s4
s3 to s4
s4 to s1
```

In this database design, only the preceding seven distinct transactions are allowed. You can visualize these seven transactions through a *directed graph* on the four database states. Figure 8-3 illustrates this way of looking at a state transition universe.

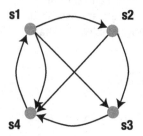

Figure 8-3. *Representing a state transition universe through a directed graph*

Listing 8-5 shows a set-theory way to specify this state transition universe; every arrow in the directed graph maps to an ordered pair.

Listing 8-5. *State Transition Universe Containing Seven Transactions*

```
{ (s1;s2), (s1;s3), (s1;s4)
 ,(s2;s3), (s2;s4)
 ,(s3;s4)
 ,(s4;s1) }
```

Of course, for real-world database designs you can't specify a state transition universe in this enumerative way, due to the vast amount of transactions that would need to be enumerated. You'll have to resort to the predicative way of specifying the set of admissible transactions.

You can formally specify a state transition universe for a given database design in a predicative way by first constructing the Cartesian product of the database universe with itself. This Cartesian product holds every possible transition from an admissible database state to another admissible database state (modeled as an ordered pair).

■**Note** If the database universe for a given database design has cardinality n, then a total of n*n distinct transactions can be identified. However, state transition constraints won't allow all of these.

By specifying state transition predicates, you can then narrow down this set of possible transitions to a set that only holds admissible transitions. Listing 8-6 shows the specification template for a state transition universe.

Listing 8-6. *State Transition Universe Specification Template*

```
STU := { TX | TX∈DBU×DBU ∧
              STC1(π₁(TX),π₂(TX)) ∧ STC2(π₁(TX),π₂(TX)) ∧ ... ∧ STCn(π₁(TX),π₂(TX)) }
```

In this template, DBU represents the relevant database universe and STC1, STC2, . . . , STCn represent state transition predicates. Expression $\pi_1(TX)$ represents the begin state of TX, and $\pi_2(TX)$ represents the end state of TX. We say that state transition predicates STC1 through STCn are the *state transition constraints* of STU.

Another way of defining state transition universe STU is as follows:

```
{ (B;E) | B∈DBU ∧ E∈DBU ∧
          STC1(B,E) ∧ STC2(B,E) ∧ ... ∧ STCn(B,E) }
```

This set holds all ordered pairs (B;E) where B and E represent admissible database states. The ordered pairs where states B and E satisfy all state transition constraints represent admissible transactions.

Completing the Example Database Design

Let's now demonstrate all this by specifying state transition constraints for the example database design that was introduced in the previous chapter. Listing 8-7 introduces the formal specification of state transition universe ST_UEX. As you can see, it builds on the DB_UEX database universe that was specified in Chapter 7. The definition of ST_UEX introduces the state transition constraints for our example database design. This definition specifies them by name only. In Listing 8-8, you'll find the formal specification for each of these named constraints.

■**Note** In Listing 8-7 we are specifying the state transition predicates in the alternative way: as predicates with parameters of type table.

Listing 8-7. *State Transition Universe ST_UEX*

```
ST_UEX := { (b;e) | b∈DB_UEX ∧ e∈DB_UEX ∧
                ∧ STC1(b(EMP),e(EMP))
                ∧ STC2(b(OFFR),e(OFFR))
                ∧ STC3(b(OFFR),e(OFFR))
                ∧ STC4(b(HIST),e(HIST))
                ∧ STC5(b(HIST),b(EMP),e(HIST),e(EMP))
                ∧ STC6(b(REG),e(REG))
                ∧ STC7(b(REG),e(REG)) }
```

State transition constraint STC1 involves the employee table structure. Constraints STC2 and STC3 involve the offering table structure. Constraint STC4 involves the history table structure. Constraint STC5 involves two table structures: history and employee. Finally, constraints STC6 and STC7 involve the registration table structure.

Listing 8-8 supplies the formal definitions for these seven state transition constraints. You'll find an elaboration on each of these in the following section.

■**Note** Often, state transition constraints inspect more than just the begin and end state of a transaction. Other data items available within the context of a transaction—and typically offered by most DBMSes—are the current system date/time (environment variable sysdate) and the username of the currently logged in user (environment variable user). Requirements that need to reference any of these *transactional environment variables* will always map to state transition constraints. Static constraints inherently cannot reference the context of a transaction. Constraints STC5 and STC7 specified in Listing 8-8 are examples of this fact; both reference variable sysdate.

Listing 8-8. *The Seven State Transition Constraints of ST_UEX*

```
STC1(EMPB,EMPE) :=
    /* Monthly salary can only increase */
    ( ∀e1∈EMPB, e2∈EMPE: e1(EMPNO) = e2(EMPNO) ⇒ e1(MSAL) ≤ e2(MSAL) )
STC2(OFFRB,OFFRE) :=
    /* New offerings must start with status SCHED */
    ( ∀o1∈OFFRE⇓{COURSE,STARTS} − OFFRB⇓{COURSE,STARTS}:
        ⅃{ o2(STATUS) | o2∈OFFRE ∧ o2↓{COURSE,STARTS} = o1↓{COURSE,STARTS} }
      = 'SCHD' )
STC3(OFFRB,OFFRE) :=
    /* Valid offering status transitions are: */
    /* SCH -> CONF, SCH -> CANC, CONF -> CANC */
    ( ∀o1∈OFFRB, o2∈OFFRE:
        (o1↓{COURSE,STARTS} = o2↓{COURSE,STARTS} ∧ o1(STATUS) ≠ o2(STATUS))
          ⇒
        (o1(STATUS);o2(STATUS)) ∈
          { ('SCHD';'CONF'), ('SCHD';'CANC'), ('CONF';'CANC') } )
STC4(HISTB,HISTE) :=
    /* No updates allowed to history records */
    ( ∀h1∈HISTB, h2∈HISTE:
        h1↓{EMPNO,UNTIL} = h2↓{EMPNO,UNTIL}
          ⇒
        ( h1(DEPTNO) = h2(DEPTNO) ∧ h1(MSAL) = h2(MSAL) ) )
STC5(HISTB,EMPB,HISTE,EMPE) :=
    /* New history records must accurately reflect employee updates */
    ( ∀h∈ (HISTE⇓{EMPNO,UNTIL} − HISTB⇓{EMPNO,UNTIL})⊗HISTE:
        h(UNTIL) = sysdate ∧
        ( ∃e1∈EMPB, e2∈EMPE:
          e1↓{EMPNO,MSAL,DEPTNO} = h↓{EMPNO,MSAL,DEPTNO} ∧
          e2(EMPNO) = h(EMPNO) ∧
          ( e2(MSAL) ≠ e1(MSAL) ∨ e2(DEPTNO) ≠ e1(DEPTNO) ) ) )
STC6(REGB,REGE) :=
    /* New registration tuples must start with EVAL = -1 */
    ( ∀r1∈ (REGE⇓{STUD,STARTS} − REGB⇓{STUD,STARTS})⊗REGE: r1(EVAL) = -1 )
STC7(REGB,REGE) :=
    /* Transitions for evaluation must be valid */
    /* and cannot occur before start date of offering */
    ( ∀r1∈REGB, r2∈REGE:
      (r1↓{STUD,STARTS} = r2↓{STUD,STARTS} ∧ r1(EVAL) ≠ r2(EVAL))
        ⇒
      ( ( r1(EVAL) = -1 ∧ r2(EVAL) = 0 ∧ r2(STARTS) ≤ sysdate ) ∨
        ( r1(EVAL) = 0 ∧ r2(EVAL) ∈ {1,2,3,4,5} ) ) )
```

State transition constraint STC1 shows yet another way to specify the classical "salary cannot be decreased" requirement. You can derive it directly from STP1 in Listing 8-4 by rewriting the existential quantifier into a universal quantifier, then applying De Morgan, and finally transforming a disjunction into an implication.

Constraints STC2 and STC3 deal with the value transitions that are allowed for the STATUS attribute in the OFFR table design. Newly inserted course offerings should always have status 'SCH' (scheduled); this is covered by STC2. The status of an existing offering is allowed to change from scheduled to 'CONF' (confirmed), or from scheduled to 'CANC' (canceled). Finally, confirmed offerings can change into canceled offerings too. These status changes are covered by STC3.

The way STC2 mandates the status value of new offerings is as follows. It first constructs the projection of the OFFR table in the end state on the uniquely identifying attributes (COURSE and STARTS). It then does the same for the OFFR table in the begin state. The difference of these two projected tables contains tuples that identify the newly inserted offerings. The universally quantified predicate then fetches—from the OFFR table in the end state—and chooses the STATUS value of such a new offering and requires it (the STATUS value) to be equal to 'SCH'.

STC3 inspects all combinations of corresponding OFFR tuples from the begin state and the end state. The combination is performed with the uniquely identifying attributes. It then requires that for every such tuple combination, either the STATUS value has not changed, or it has changed according to one of the admissible value transitions described earlier.

Another slightly different way to specify constraint STC3 is shown in Listing 8-9.

Listing 8-9. *Alternative Specification for STC3*

```
( ∀o1∈OFFRB, o2∈OFFRE:
    ( o1↓{COURSE,STARTS} = o2↓{COURSE,STARTS} ∧ o1(STATUS) ≠ o2(STATUS) )
    ⇒
    ( ( o1(STATUS) = 'SCH'  ∧ o2(STATUS) = 'CONF' ) ∨
      ( o1(STATUS) = 'SCH'  ∧ o2(STATUS) = 'CANC' ) ∨
      ( o1(STATUS) = 'CONF' ∧ o2(STATUS) = 'CANC' ) ) )
```

Here we've employed the following rewrite rule (which is left as an exercise at the end of this chapter):

$$(P \Rightarrow (Q \lor R)) \Leftrightarrow ((P \land \neg Q) \Rightarrow R)$$

In the same way as STC3, state transition constraint STC4 combines HIST tuples from the begin and the end state, and requires that neither the DEPTNO nor the MSAL attribute value has changed.

Constraint STC5 defines the semantics of the HIST table design. If a transaction changes the DEPTNO or the MSAL attribute value of an EMP tuple, then the same transaction should log a tuple that records the old values of DEPTNO and MSAL in the HIST table. This new HIST tuple should have the UNTIL attribute set to the current system date and time.

STC5 universally quantifies over all newly inserted HIST tuples and requires that within the same transaction, the DEPTNO and MSAL values should correspond with the DEPTNO and MSAL values of the matching EMP tuple found *in the begin state*. Of course, it also requires that for this particular EMP tuple *the end state* reflects a change in either the DEPTNO or MSAL attribute values (or both).

The attribute-value set of the EVAL attribute of the REG table design holds seven elements in total: -1, 0, 1, 2, 3, 4, and 5. Their meanings follow:

-1 : Too early to evaluate
 0 : Not evaluated or not yet evaluated
 1 : Really bad
 2 : Bad
 3 : Fair
 4 : Good
 5 : Excellent

The valid value transitions for an evaluation are shown in Figure 8-4.

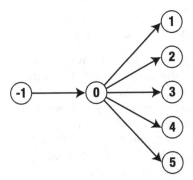

Figure 8-4. *Valid transitions for an evaluation*

New registrations must start with an evaluation value of -1 (STC6). As long as a course offering has not started yet, all evaluations should remain holding value -1; it is too early to evaluate the offering.

Once the course offering is "in session," the trainer decides when the students can evaluate the offering. This is done by setting the evaluation of all registrations for the offering to value 0. Due to the following table constraint introduced in the table universe tab_REG (see Listing 7-34), the trainer must do this within a single transaction.

```
/* Offering is evaluated, or it is too early to evaluate the offering */
( ∀r1,r2∈R:
  ( r1↓{COURSE,STARTS} = r2↓{COURSE,STARTS} )
    ⇒
  ( ( r1(EVAL) = -1 ∧ r2(EVAL) = -1 ) ∨
    ( r1(EVAL) ≠ -1 ∧ r2(EVAL) ≠ -1 )
  ) )
```

A registration value of 0 at this time represents that the student has *not yet* evaluated the offering. This transition from an evaluation value of -1 to a value of 0 is covered by the first disjunct in the conclusion of the implication in state transition constraint STC7. The disjunct also covers the fact that the transition from -1 to 0 can be done only if the offering has already started (r2(STARTS) ≥ sysdate).

Once the evaluations have been set to 0, the students can then evaluate the offering by changing the 0 into a value in the range of 1 through 5. These value transitions are covered by the second disjunct in the conclusion of the implication of STC7. A student can also choose not to evaluate at all, and have the evaluation stay at value 0 (now representing "not evaluated").

Did you notice that STC2, STC5, and STC6 demonstrate three different ways to specify a limitation on an attribute value of a newly inserted tuple? You can also write constraint STC6 the "STC2 way" or the "STC5 way"; see Listing 8-10 for this.

Listing 8-10. *Alternative Specifications for STC6*

```
STC6(REGB,REGE) :=
    ( ∀r1∈REGE⇓{STUD,STARTS} − REGB⇓{STUD,STARTS}:
        ¬{ r2(EVAL) | r2∈e(REGE) ∧ r2↓{STUD,STARTS} = r1↓{STUD,STARTS} }
        = -1 )
STC6(REGB,REGE) :=
    ( ∀r∈ (REGE⇓{STUD,STARTS} − REGB⇓{STUD,STARTS})⊗REGE: r(EVAL) = -1 )
```

If you've carefully studied the specifications in Listing 8-8, you might also have noticed that not all state transition constraints satisfy the requirement that their CNF only have one conjunct. One of the exercises in the "Exercises" section will deal with this.

We conclude this chapter by reaffirming a statement made earlier in Chapter 7: *much of the overall specification of an information system actually sits in the specification of the database design.* The concept of a state transition universe, being an integral part of the specification of a database design, demonstrates this again. "Business logic" specifically dealing with transactions can often be represented by state transition constraints, and as such this business logic should be part of a database design's specification.

Chapter Summary

This section provides a summary of this chapter, formatted as a bulleted list. You can use it to check your understanding of the various concepts introduced in this chapter before continuing with the exercises in the next section.

- Next to the four classes of constraints introduced earlier (attribute, tuple, table, and database constraints), there is a fifth class of constraints called the *state transition constraints*.

- These constraints limit transactions that are allowed within the database design. *State transition predicates* are the basis of state transition constraints.

- State transition constraints are predicates that reference a pair of database states as their parameters, one database state representing the *begin state* of a transaction, and the other representing the *end state* of the transaction.

- Typical examples for state transition constraints are limitations on the values allowed for attributes of newly inserted tuples, or limitations on value transitions (updates) of an attribute whose value set represents a set of codes.

- State transition constraints are specified as part of the specification of the *state transition universe* for a database design. This is the set representing all admissible transactions for a database design.

- State transition (contrary to static) constraints may reference *transactional environment variables* offered by the DBMS. Typical examples of these variables are the system date and time (denoted by sysdate) and the currently logged in user (denoted by user).

Exercises

1. Prove the rewrite rule (P ⇒ (Q ∨ R)) ⇔ ((P ∧ ¬Q) ⇒ R) either by using the rewrite rules from Table 1-13 or by using a truth table.

2. Rewrite prop1 from Listing 8-1 into a universal quantification. You might find this a more intuitive specification.

3. Formally specify the state transition constraint stating that the salary of an employee can only be decreased if at the same time the salary grade for the employee is increased. Does transaction TX1 introduced in the section "More Data Integrity Predicates" violate this constraint too?

4. Give an alternative specification for state transition constraint STC2 that involves the join operator.

5. Specify a state transition constraint stating that the value of attribute HIRED for newly inserted EMP tuples cannot be more than one month after sysdate. Informally, new employees can at the soonest be registered one month prior to their first workday.

6. Can state transition constraint STC7 be decomposed into multiple conjuncts? What about STC3?

7. Specify a state transition constraint stating that new employee tuples can only be inserted by sessions that are logged in with the USERNAME of an employee that works in the HR department (DNAME = 'Human resources').

8. As explained in this chapter, the way course offerings are evaluated is that the trainer first has to enable the evaluation by resetting the evaluation attribute of all registered attendees for the offering, to value 0. After this transaction—*that has to be performed by a session of the trainer*—the attendees can evaluate the offering by changing the 0 into a value ranging from 1 to 5. *Every attendee should be allowed only to update the evaluation of his or her own registration.* Modify the specification of STC7 to reflect these additional authorization requirements.

9. Further modify STC7 such that evaluations must occur at or before the last day of the offering.

10. You need to cater for the possibility of a terminated employee to be reinstated.

    One of your colleagues suggests that in these cases the TERM tuple involved should be removed and at the same time the HIRED attribute (in the corresponding EMP tuple) updated to reflect the start of the renewed employment for the employee.

    a. Give a formal specification stating that TERM tuples can only be deleted if at the same time the HIRED attribute of the employee is updated (that is, increased to a more recent date).

    b. Do you see potential problems with this solution? Under what conditions would this solution be viable?

CHAPTER 9

Data Retrieval

By means of a *query*, you retrieve data from a database. In this chapter we'll demonstrate how you can specify a query in a formal way. To do so, we won't require the formal introduction of any new concepts; we've already presented all ingredients for specifying queries.

The section "Formally Specifying Queries" introduces you to the formal concept of a *query over a database universe*. You'll find out that you can specify a query as a set-theory expression based on a given database state. In this section, we'll also give a few simple examples to familiarize you with this formal concept of a query.

The section "Example Queries Over DB_UEX" provides example queries over DB_UEX, the example database universe that was introduced in Chapter 7. It will start out with basic queries and gradually move to more complex queries. For every query, we'll present you with multiple (equivalent) formal expressions to specify the query.

For the first time in this book, you'll see the use of SQL. Every example query will be accompanied by one or more equivalent SQL expressions. You'll discover that expressing particular queries in SQL turns out to be not so trivial.

Note We assume you have a working knowledge of SQL. It is certainly not the goal of this book to teach the SQL language (although showing both the formal and the SQL expressions alongside each other might have this as a side effect). As mentioned in the book's Introduction, the SQL expressions given in this chapter, as well as in the following two chapters, are compliant with the 10*g* release of Oracle's SQL DBMS.

As usual, you'll find a "Chapter Summary" at the end, followed by an "Exercises" section.

Formally Specifying Queries

Data retrieval is a crucial application of a database. Through queries, you can extract information that is relevant to you from the database. In this section, we'll demonstrate how you can formally specify queries.

Let's first start with a simple example. We'll use the example database design that was introduced in Chapter 7. Assume E represents the employee table in some database state of universe DB_UEX. Here's a formal specification of a query, named Q1, on E that extracts the trainers who earn more than 6000:

```
Q1(E) := { e | e∈E ∧ e(JOB)='TRAINER' ∧ e(MSAL)>6000 }
```

Query Q1 returns all employee tuples representing trainers earning more than 6000. Instead of the complete tuple, if all you were interested in was the employee number (EMPNO), name (ENAME), and salary (MSAL), of trainers earning more than 6000, then the following query (Q2) would do the job:

```
Q2(E) := { e↓{EMPNO,ENAME,MSAL} | e∈E ∧ e(JOB)='TRAINER' ∧ e(MSAL)>6000 }
```

Note Both Q1 and Q2 return a table as their result. As you'll see shortly, this is not a requirement in the formal methodology set out by this book; queries are allowed to return simple values too (for instance, a single numeric or string value). However, in practice we prefer query specifications that return tables.

As indicated through the preceding example, you can view a query as a function. In this case, you pass this function a table as its argument, and it then returns another value based on the argument. Of course, queries often involve more than just one table. In general, a query can be considered to accept a database state (our formal structure that contains all current tables) as its argument. The query can then inspect any table available within this database state to determine its return value.

Let's demonstrate this with an example too. Assume dbs represents some database state of database universe DB_UEX. Take a look at query Q3; it returns the department that employs the president (if there is one):

```
Q3(dbs) := { d | d∈dbs(DEPT) ∧
               (∃e∈dbs(EMP): e(DEPTNO)=d(DEPTNO) ∧ e(JOB)='PRESIDENT') }
```

Query Q3 inspects two tables held within state dbs; expression dbs(DEPT) denotes the department table, and expression dbs(EMP) denotes the employee table. Because the argument of the query now represents a database state, the query can inspect any table available within that state.

As this example shows us, a query can formally be considered a *function over a database universe*. In other words, a query is a function whose domain is a set of database states. For every database state, the function returns (or if you will, *computes*) some value. The result of a query can be a value of any type. Query Q3 results in a table. If there is a president, then the result will be a table with one tuple; if there is no president, then the result will be the empty table. Database queries will typically result in tables. In fact, given the query language SQL, a query always results in a table. In the formalism introduced in this book, the result of a query can be as simple as a single numeric or string value too. Here is an example. Query Q4 returns the number of employees in department 10:

```
Q4(dbs) := #{ e | e∈dbs(EMP) ∧ e(DEPTNO)=10 }
```

The result of query Q4 is a numeric value. Here is a formal specification of Q4 that returns a table:

```
Q4(dbs) := { { (DEPT_TEN_EMPS; #{ e | e∈dbs(EMP) ∧ e(DEPTNO)=10 }) } }
```

This version of Q4 returns a table over {DEPT_TEN_EMPS}. It contains one tuple, with one attribute-value pair.

The next section will present many example queries over DB_UEX to familiarize you further with formally specifying queries.

Example Queries Over DB_UEX

This section provides example queries. It starts out with basic queries and gradually moves to more complex queries. For every query, we'll present you with the following:

- An informal description for the query

- One or more formal expressions to specify the query

- One or more specifications expressed in SQL for the query

Along the way, you'll find out that it becomes increasingly more difficult to precisely specify a query informally; it becomes hard to avoid ambiguity. Also, you'll see that SQL has some shortcomings that cause difficulties when you try to translate a formal query specification directly into a SELECT expression.

Listings 9-1 through 9-11 introduce the example queries. All queries are named EXQi (*example query* i), where i represents a sequence number. In the formal specifications given for each query, dbs represents a database state of DB_UEX. The various alternative formal expressions are named FEc (*formal expression* c), where c represents a letter (a, b, c, and so on).

The SQL expressions are based on an implementation of the DB_UEX database design. We'll introduce this implementation in detail in Chapter 11. For now it suffices to mention that in the implementation of DB_UEX, every table universe is implemented one on one as an SQL table, and that NULLs (a concept not known in our formal methodology) are explicitly excluded from that implementation.

In the SQL specifications we'll use the table structure names introduced by database characterization DB_CHREX (see Listing 7-38) as the table names available for SELECT expressions. We'll name alternative SQL specifications SEr (*SQL expression* r), where r represents a Roman numeral (I, II, III, and so on).

■Note Unless pointed out in the accompanying text, there is no implied relationship between the respective formal and SQL alternative expressions that are listed for every query.

Listing 9-1 gives the data of all departments.

Listing 9-1. *Query EXQ1(dbs)*

```
FEa:   dbs(DEPT)
FEb:   { d | d∈dbs(DEPT) }
SEI:   select d.* from DEPT d
SEII:  select d.LOC, d.DEPTNO, d.DNAME, d.MGR from DEPT d
```

This query is straightforward. It retrieves the department table from given database state dbs: dbs(DEPT). Alternative FEb is a somewhat less succinct way to specify this. In SEI the star

(*) symbol is used as the shorthand to denote all attributes of the department table in this case. SEII actually lists all attributes (in some arbitrary order).

Listing 9-2 gives the job of employees who either earn more than 4800 monthly, or who are assigned to salary grade 6 or higher.

Listing 9-2. *Query EXQ2(dbs)*

```
FEa:   { e(JOB) | e∈dbs(EMP) ∧ (e(MSAL) > 4800 ∨ e(SGRADE) ≥ 6) }
FEb:   { e↓{JOB} | e∈dbs(EMP) ∧ (e(MSAL) > 4800 ∨ e(SGRADE) ≥ 6) }
FEc:   { e↓(JOB) | e∈dbs(EMP) ∧ (e(MSAL) ≤ 4800 ⇒ e(SGRADE) ≥ 6) }
FEd:   { e↓(JOB) | e∈dbs(EMP) ∧ (e(SGRADE) < 6 ⇒ e(MSAL) > 4800) }
FEe:   { e↓(JOB) | e∈dbs(EMP) ∧ ¬(e(MSAL) ≤ 4800 ∧ e(SGRADE) < 6) }
FEf:   { e↓(JOB) | e∈dbs(EMP) ∧ e(MSAL) > 4800 }
       ∪
       { e↓(JOB) | e∈dbs(EMP) ∧ e(SGRADE) ≥ 6 }
SEI:   select distinct e.JOB from EMP e where e.MSAL > 4800 or e.SGRADE >= 6
SEII:  select distinct e.JOB from EMP e where not (e.MSAL <= 4800 and e.SGRADE < 6)
SEIII: select e.JOB from EMP e where e.MSAL > 4800
       union
       select e.JOB from EMP e where e.SGRADE >= 6
```

Do you notice the subtle difference between FEa and FEb? The former results in a set of job values (that is, this is not a table); the latter results in a set of tuples (that is, a table over {JOB}), and is therefore a preferred way to formally specify EXQ2.

Alternatives FEc, FEd, and FEe are variations of FEb, where the disjunction is either rewritten into an implication or a conjunction. Alternative FEf uses the union operator; jobs of employees earning more than 4800 are unioned with jobs of employees assigned to salary grade 6 or higher.

Note The way this query is formally specified implies that we only retrieve *distinct* job values. Suppose table dbs(EMP) currently holds twenty employees, of which ten conform to the predicate "monthly salary is greater than 4800 or salary grade equals 6 or higher." If eight of those ten employees have job TRAINER and the other two have job MANAGER, then the result of FEa will be {'TRAINER', 'MANAGER'}: a set with only two, not ten, elements.

The subtle difference demonstrated by FEa and FEb cannot be expressed in SQL. Specification SEI is the SQL variation for both of these. Also note that in SQL you must add the distinct keyword to ensure that no duplicate job values appear in the query result.

Alternatives FEc and FEd cannot be directly transformed into SQL, because SQL lacks the implication operator; only disjunction, conjunction, and negation are available within SQL.

Specification SEII is the SQL version for FEe, and SEIII represents the SQL version for FEf. Note that in the latter case, the use of the keyword distinct is not necessary; SQL will always return distinct values whenever you use a set operator (union, minus, or intersect).

Listing 9-3 gives the number, name, and salary of clerks, including the lower and upper limits of the salary grade to which they are assigned.

Listing 9-3. *Query EXQ3(dbs)*

```
FEa: { e↓{EMPNO,ENAME,MSAL,LLIMIT,ULIMIT} | e∈ dbs(EMP)⊗
              (dbs(GRD)◊◊{(SGRADE;GRADE),(LLIMIT;LLIMIT),(ULIMIT;ULIMIT)}) ∧
                                                    e(JOB)='CLERK' }
SEI: select e.EMPNO, e.ENAME, e.MSAL, g.LLIMIT, g.ULIMIT
     from EMP e
         ,GRD g
     where e.SGRADE = g.GRADE
       and e.JOB = 'CLERK'
```

This query is represented by a join between the employee and salary grade tables. To be able to use the join operator, you must rename either the attribute SGRADE in the employee table, or the attribute GRADE in the salary grade table. Specification FEa performs the latter renaming. You can derive the SQL expression SEI directly from FEa.

Now you're probably thinking that the SQL expression looks much easier than the formal expression, right? This is because this example is so simple. When we get to more complicated examples, you'll see that this state of affairs ceases to apply; the SQL expressions will then become more complicated than the mathematical ones.

Listing 9-4 gives the employees (EMPNO and ENAME) who manage exactly two departments at two different locations.

Listing 9-4. *Query EXQ4(dbs)*

```
FEa:   { e↓{EMPNO,ENAME} | e∈ dbs(EMP) ∧
                           #{ d(LOC) | d∈ dbs(DEPT) ∧ d(MGR)=e(EMPNO) } = 2 }
FEb:   { e↓{EMPNO,ENAME} | e∈ dbs(EMP) ∧
                           (∃d1,d2∈ dbs(DEPT): d1(MGR)=e(EMPNO) ∧
                                               d2(MGR)=e(EMPNO) ∧
                                               d1(LOC)≠d2(LOC)) }
FEc:   { e↓{EMPNO,ENAME} | e∈ (dbs(EMP)⇓{EMPNO,ENAME})⊗
                              (dbs(DEPT)◊◊{(EMPNO;MGR),(LOC1;LOC)})⊗
                              (dbs(DEPT)◊◊{(EMPNO;MGR),(LOC2;LOC)}) ∧
                           e(LOC1)≠e(LOC2) }
SEI:   select e.EMPNO, e.ENAME
       from EMP e
       where 2 = (select count(distinct d.LOC)
                  from DEPT d
                  where d.MGR = e.EMPNO)
SEII:  select e.EMPNO, e.ENAME
       from EMP e
       where exists(select d1.*
                    from DEPT d1
                    where d1.MGR = e.EMPNO
                      and exists(select d2.*
                                 from DEPT d2
                                 where d2.MGR = e.EMPNO
                                   and d1.LOC <> d2.LOC))
```

```
SEIII: select e.EMPNO, e.ENAME
       from EMP e
       where exists(select *
                    from DEPT d1
                        ,DEPT d2
                    where d1.MGR = e.EMPNO
                      and d2.MGR = e.EMPNO
                      and d1.LOC <> d2.LOC)

SEIV:  select distinct e.EMPNO, e.ENAME
       from EMP e
           ,DEPT d1
           ,DEPT d2
       where e.EMPNO = d1.MGR
         and e.EMPNO = d2.MGR
         and d1.LOC <> d2.LOC
```

Specification FEa states that the cardinality of the set of locations of departments managed by the employee must be two. Alternative FEb achieves this requirement by existentially quantifying over two departments at different locations that are managed by the employee.

■**Note** In FEb the shorthand notation for two nested existential quantifiers over the same set is used.

You can translate both formal specifications into SQL directly. Note that in SEI you must use the distinct keyword within the count aggregate function. Specification SEII is given to demonstrate the nested use of the existential quantifier available in SQL—the expression exists(...). SEIII is a shorthand version similar to the shorthand used in formal specification FEb.

Specification FEc uses the join to locate two departments at different locations that are managed by the employee. Note that in its SQL version (SEIV), you must use the distinct keyword to prevent employees who manage two departments at different locations from appearing twice in the result set.

Listing 9-5 gives the number and name of all managed employees earning more than 90 percent of their boss's salary.

Listing 9-5. *Query EXQ5(dbs)*

FEa: { e1↓{EMPNO,ENAME} | e1∈dbs(EMP) ∧ m∈dbs(MEMP) ∧ e2∈dbs(EMP) ∧
                    e1(EMPNO) = m(EMPNO) ∧ m(MGR) = e2(EMPNO) ∧
                    e1(MSAL) > 0.9*e2(MSAL) }

FEb: { e↓{EMPNO,ENAME} | e∈ (dbs(EMP)⊗dbs(MEMP))⊗
                    (dbs(EMP)◊◊{ (MGR;EMPNO), (MGR_MSAL;MSAL) }) ∧
                    e(MSAL) > 0.9*e(MGR_MSAL) }

FEc: { e1↓{EMPNO,ENAME} | e1∈dbs(EMP) ∧
                    (∃m∈dbs(MEMP): m(EMPNO)=e1(EMPNO) ∧
```
```

$$(\exists e2 \in dbs(EMP): e2(EMPNO)=m(MGR) \wedge$$
$$e1(MSAL) > 0.9*e2(MSAL))) \}$$

```
SEI:    select e1.EMPNO, e1.ENAME
        from EMP e1, MEMP m, EMP e2
        where e1.EMPNO = m.EMPNO
          and m.MGR = e2.EMPNO
          and e1.MSAL > 0.9 * e2.MSAL
SEII:   select e1.EMPNO, e1.ENAME
        from EMP e1
        where exists (select m.*
                        from MEMP m
                      where m.EMPNO = e1.EMPNO
                        and exists (select e2.*
                                    from EMP e2
                                  where e2.EMPNO = m.MGR
                                    and e1.MSAL > 0.9 * e2.MSAL))
```

By combining every EMP tuple with the corresponding MEMP tuple (via specialization PSPEC2), and then combining the MEMP tuple back to an EMP tuple (via subset requirement PSSR3), you are able to compare the monthly salary of a managed employee with the monthly salary of his or her manager. Specification FEa achieves this by binding two tuple variables for EMP (one for the employee and one for the manager) and a tuple variable for MEMP, and then imposing the combination restrictions on those. Specification FEb does this by binding a single tuple variable that draws its values from a nested join that performs the combination. The first join combines tuples from EMP with MEMP (to find the employee number of the manager). The second join combines tuples from MEMP back to EMP (to find the salary of the manager) and requires attribute renaming.

Specification SEI represents an SQL version for FEa and FEb.

Specification FEc employs a nested existential quantification to achieve the same result. You can translate it directly into SQL (see SEII) using the support for existential quantification in SQL.

Listing 9-6 gives the code, description, and category for all courses for which every scheduled offering has a maximum capacity of fewer than ten students.

Listing 9-6. *Query EXQ6(dbs)*

FEa: $\{ c\downarrow\{CODE,DESCR,CAT\} \mid c \in dbs(CRS) \wedge$
$(\forall o \in dbs(OFFR): (o(COURSE) = c(CODE) \wedge$
$o(STATUS) = 'SCHD') \Rightarrow$
$o(MAXCAP) < 10) \}$

FEb: $\{ c\downarrow\{CODE,DESCR,CAT\} \mid c \in dbs(CRS) \wedge$
$\neg(\exists o \in dbs(OFFR): o(COURSE) = c(CODE) \wedge$
$o(STATUS) = 'SCHD' \wedge$
$o(MAXCAP) \geq 10) \}$

FEc: $\{ c\downarrow\{CODE,DESCR,CAT\} \mid c \in dbs(CRS) \wedge$
$c(CODE) \notin \{ o(COURSE) \mid o \in dbs(OFFR) \wedge$
$o(STATUS) = 'SCHD' \wedge$
$o(MAXCAP) \geq 10) \} \}$

FEd: { c↓{CODE,DESCR,CAT} | c∈dbs(CRS) ∧
                              #{ o1 | o1∈dbs(OFFR) ∧ o1(COURSE) = c(CODE) ∧
                                                     o1(STATUS) = 'SCHD' }
                              =
                              #{ o2 | o2∈dbs(OFFR) ∧ o2(COURSE) = c(CODE) ∧
                                                     o2(STATUS) = 'SCHD' ∧
                                                     o2(MAXCAP) < 10) } }

SEI: select c.CODE, c.DESC, c.CAT
        from CRS c
        where not exists (select o.*
                          from OFFR o
                          where o.COURSE = c.CODE
                          and o.STATUS = 'SCHD'
                          and o.MAXCAP >= 10)

SEII: select c.CODE, c.DESC, c.CAT
        from CRS c
        where c.CODE not in (select o.COURSE
                             from OFFR o
                             where o.STATUS = 'SCHD'
                             and o.MAXCAP >= 10)

SEIII: select c.CODE, c.DESC, c.CAT
        from CRS c
        where (select count(*)
               from OFFR o1
               where o1.COURSE = c.CODE
               and o1.STATUS = 'SCHD')
              =
              (select count(*)
               from OFFR o2
               where o2.COURSE = c.CODE
               and o2.STATUS = 'SCHD'
               and o2.MAXCAP < 10)

Specification FEa closely follows the informal description for the query. FEb is a rewritten version of FEa; the universal quantifier is rewritten into an existential quantifier. Informally it queries all courses for which there do not exist a scheduled offering with a maximum capacity of ten or more. Because the ability to rewrite predicates into equivalent predicates is extremely important, we'll demonstrate once more how this is performed in this case:

($\forall$o∈ dbs(OFFR): (o(COURSE)=c(CODE) ∧ o(STATUS)='SCHD') $\Rightarrow$ o(MAXCAP)<10)
⇔ /* **Add double negation** */
¬¬($\forall$o∈ dbs(OFFR): (o(COURSE)=c(CODE) ∧ o(STATUS) = 'SCHD') $\Rightarrow$ o(MAXCAP)<10)
⇔ /* **Bring one negation into the quantification, quantifier changes** */
¬($\exists$o∈ dbs(OFFR): ¬((o(COURSE)=c(CODE) ∧ o(STATUS)='SCHD') $\Rightarrow$ o(MAXCAP)<10))
⇔ /* **Transform implication into disjunction** */
¬($\exists$o∈ dbs(OFFR): ¬(¬(o(COURSE)=c(CODE) ∧ o(STATUS)='SCHD') ∨ o(MAXCAP)<10))
⇔ /* **Apply De Morgan, disjunction changes into conjuction** */

$$\neg(\exists o \in dbs(OFFR): \neg\neg(o(COURSE)=c(CODE) \land o(STATUS)='SCHD') \land \neg o(MAXCAP)<10)$$
$$\Leftrightarrow \text{ /* Get rid of negations */}$$
$$\neg(\exists o \in dbs(OFFR): o(COURSE)=c(CODE) \land o(STATUS)='SCHD' \land o(MAXCAP)\geq 10)$$

You'll often have to rewrite a universal quantification into an existential quantification for reasons that will soon become clear.

Specification FEc is a variation of FEb; the "not exists" is now expressed as a "not an element of" some set. FEd might seem somewhat far-fetched; only those courses are included in the query result, for which the number of scheduled course offerings equals the number of scheduled course offerings that have a maximum capacity of fewer than ten students. By imposing this restriction, you end up precisely with those courses for which every scheduled offering has a maximum capacity of fewer than ten students.

SQL lacks the possibility to express universal quantification directly.

Note Remember we are using *Oracle's version of SQL* in this book. The SQL standard offers a language construct called <quantified comparison predicate> that can be used to specify universal quantification in SQL. However, Oracle's SQL DBMS doesn't support this language construct.

For this reason, you cannot directly translate FEa into SQL; you must rewrite the universal quantification into an existential quantification (which SQL does support). Once you have done this (which is what alternative FEb is all about), you can straightforwardly compose the equivalent SQL expression for the query; see SEI. Alternative SEII closely follows FEb too, but instead of the "not exists," it employs the "not in" operator available within SQL.

Alternative SEIII is the SQL version of FEc; this way of query formulation can be considered a trick to mimic a universal quantification within SQL.

What is your opinion on courses that currently do *not* have any scheduled offering at all? Should they appear in the result set of query EXQ6, or not?

Note Remember the truth value of a universal quantification over the empty set? Such a quantification is always true, regardless of the predicate that is being quantified.

Courses with no scheduled offerings will appear in the result set of this query. Whenever you encounter a universal quantification—or a negated existential quantification—you should be aware of this consequence (warning bells should ring). Moreover, whenever the set that is quantified over can possibly be the empty set, you should double check with your customer (the end user) whether he or she is aware of this "side effect" and requires this behavior of the query.

If courses with no scheduled offerings at all should not appear in the result set of this query, then here is how you could change FEa to reflect this:

$$\{ c\!\downarrow\!\{CODE,DESCR,CAT\} \mid c\in dbs(CRS) \wedge$$
$$(\exists o\in dbs(OFFR): o(COURSE) = c(CODE) \wedge$$
$$o(STATUS) = 'SCHD') \wedge$$
$$(\forall o\in dbs(OFFR): (o(COURSE) = c(CODE) \wedge$$
$$o(STATUS) = 'SCHD') \Rightarrow$$
$$o(MAXCAP) < 10) \}$$

Adding the existential quantification now ensures that courses with no scheduled offerings won't appear in the result set.

In the next example, you'll see the use of an NVL function and the outer join syntax (+). Both constructs are available with the Oracle SQL DBMS. We'll explain their meaning directly after Listing 9-7.

Listing 9-7 gives for each department the department number, name, and number of employees working in that department, as well as the total sum of monthly salaries of employees working in that department.

Listing 9-7. *Query EXQ7(dbs)*

```
FEa:   { d↓{DEPTNO,DNAME} ∪
          { (NUM_EMP; #{ e1 | e1∈dbs(EMP) ∧ e1(deptno)=d(deptno) })
          ,(SUM_MSAL; (SUM e2∈{ e3 | e3∈dbs(EMP) ∧ e3(deptno)=d(deptno) }:
                                                        e2(MSAL)))
          }
          | d∈dbs(DEPT) }
FEb:   { d ∪
          { (NUM_EMP; #{ e1 | e1∈dbs(EMP) ∧ e1(deptno)=d(deptno) })
          ,(SUM_MSAL; (SUM e2∈{ e3 | e3∈dbs(EMP) ∧ e3(deptno)=d(deptno) }:
                                                        e2(MSAL)))
          }
          | d∈dbs(DEPT)⇓{DEPTNO,DNAME} }
SEI:   select d.DEPTNO
             ,d.DNAME
             ,(select count(*)
               from EMP e1
               where e1.deptno = d.deptno) as NUM_EMP
             ,(select nvl(sum(MSAL),0)
               from EMP e2
               where e1.deptno = d.deptno) as SUM_MSAL
       from DEPT d
SEII:  select d.DEPTNO
             ,d.DNAME
             ,count(*) as NUM_EMP
             ,sum(e.MSAL) as SUM_MSAL
       from DEPT d
            ,EMP e
       where d.DEPTNO = e.DEPTNO
       group by d.DEPTNO,d.DNAME
SEIII: select d.DEPTNO
```

```
           ,d.DNAME
           ,count(e.EMPNO) as NUM_EMP
           ,nvl(sum(e.MSAL),0) as SUM_MSA
      from DEPT d
          ,EMP e
      where d.DEPTNO = e.DEPTNO (+)
      group by d.DEPTNO,d.DNAME
```

Do you see how the additional attributes NUM_EMP and SUM_MSAL are constructed for the query result? Query EXQ5 returns a table over {DEPTNO,DNAME,NUM_EMP,SUM_MSAL}. For every tuple in dbs(DEPT), a tuple appears in the result set. The first two attributes are drawn directly from a tuple of dbs(DEPT). You specify the other two attributes (NUM_EMP and SUM_MSAL) separately and add them to the first two attributes through tuple union. You specify the value for NUM_EMP as the cardinality of the set that holds all employees for the current department. In a similar way, you specify the value for attribute SUM_MSAL by employing the SUM aggregate operator.

The difference between FEa and FEb is the "moment" at which the department tuples are limited to attributes DEPTNO and DNAME. Specification FEa performs tuple limitation in the expression before the bar (|); FEb performs table projection on the table to which variable d is bound (after the bar).

You should note the following:

- The formal specification for this query states that empty departments (the ones that do not employ any employee) will be returned in the result set.

- Both the NUM_EMP as well as the SUM_MSAL attributes have well-defined values for the empty departments. The cardinality of the empty set is well defined (it is zero), and we've defined the sum operator (see Definition 2-12) such that the sum of any expression over the empty set is equal to zero.

Let's now look at the SQL expressions SEI, SEII, and SEIII. Here is a fine example of where the can of worms (mentioned in the book's Introduction) is opened.

Specification SEI follows the formal specification for this query; subqueries are used to compute the number of employees and the sum of the salaries. However, note that SQL's count operator is defined to be zero for the empty table, but SQL's sum operator is defined to return NULL when performed over an empty table. To ensure that in the cases where the department employs no employees the SQL query will return 0 (zero) as the sum of the salaries, we have employed the dyadic NVL function. The semantics of this function are as follows: if the first argument represents a value other than NULL, then NVL returns this first argument, otherwise NVL returns the second argument.

Specification SEII is often produced for these types of questions. You perform a join from DEPT to EMP, and by grouping the rows (GROUP BY), you can compute the two aggregate attributes. However, note that this SQL query won't return empty departments, and therefore doesn't represent a correct SQL version for our original query. By the way, because this query only returns departments that employ at least one employee, the SUM aggregation will never result in NULL, and therefore you can discard the NVL.

Now, if you are a proficient SQL programmer, you probably know how to fix this, right? Specification SEIII represents the repaired version for SEII; it employs the outer join to ensure that empty departments are returned too in the result set. The addition of (+) behind e.DEPTNO changes the semantics of the original join into an outer join *from table DEPT to table EMP*. Outer joins will also return a row for the "from" table when no matching row can be found in the "to" table; an all-NULLs row will be generated and used to combine with the "from" table row.

You should be aware, though, that in the repaired query SEIII, you must now change the count(*) into—for instance—count(e.EMPNO) to have SQL return the correct value of zero employees for the NUM_EMP attribute (count(*) would have returned one for empty departments). Yes, the can of worms is wide open now.

The next query retrieves for each department the employee who has the highest salary within that department. Note that it's possible for two or more employees to have that same highest salary. Listing 9-8 gives for each department (DEPTNO and DNAME) the one or more employees (EMPNO, ENAME, and MSAL) within that department who have the highest salary.

Listing 9-8. *Query EXQ8(dbs)*

```
FEa:  { d↓{DEPTNO,DNAME} ∪
          { (RICHEMP; { e1↓{EMPNO,ENAME,MSAL} | e1∈dbs(EMP) ∧ e1(DEPTNO)=d(DEPTNO) ∧
                                          ¬(∃e2∈dbs(EMP): e2(DEPTNO)=e1(DEPTNO) ∧
                                                          e2(MSAL)>e1(MSAL)) }
          )
          }
          | d∈dbs(DEPT) }
FEb:  dbs(DEPT)⇓{DEPTNO,DNAME}⊗
          { e1↓{EMPNO,ENAME,MSAL,DEPTNO} | e1∈dbs(EMP) ∧
                                          ¬(∃e2∈dbs(EMP): e2(DEPTNO)=e1(DEPTNO) ∧
                                                          e2(MSAL)>e1(MSAL)) }
FEc:  dbs(DEPT)⇓{DEPTNO,DNAME}⊗
          { e1↓{EMPNO,ENAME,MSAL,DEPTNO} | e1∈dbs(EMP) ∧
                                          (∀e2∈dbs(EMP): e2(DEPTNO)=e1(DEPTNO) ⇒
                                                          e2(MSAL)≤e1(MSAL)) }
SEI:  select d.DEPTNO, d.DNAME
            ,cursor(select e1.EMPNO, e1.ENAME, e1.MSAL
                    from EMP e1
                    where e1.DEPTNO = d.DEPTNO
                      and not exists(select e2.*
                                     from EMP e2
                                     where e2.DEPTNO = e1.DEPTNO
                                       and e2.MSAL > e1.MSAL)) as RICHEMP
      from DEPT d
SEII: select d.DEPTNO, d.DNAME, e.EMPNO, e.ENAME, e.MSAL
      from DEPT d
          ,(select e1.EMPNO,e1.ENAME,e1.MSAL,e1.DEPTNO
            from EMP e1
            where not exists(select e2.*
                             from EMP e2
                             where e2.DEPTNO = e1.DEPTNO
                               and e2.MSAL > e1.MSAL)) e
      where d.DEPTNO = e.DEPTNO
```

Note the difference in structure of the result sets specified by FEa and FEb. Query FEa returns a table over {DEPTNO,DNAME,RICHEMP}; one tuple per department is returned (empty departments are returned too). Under attribute RICHEMP, a nested table over {EMPNO,ENAME,MSAL} is returned. Attribute RICHEMP holds the set of employee tuples (limited to three attributes) that represent the employees with the highest salary in that department. Query FEb returns a table over {DEPTNO,DNAME,EMPNO,ENAME,MSAL}. This query doesn't return empty departments. Also, if multiple employees all earn the same highest salary within a department, then the department data is repeated for these employees.

Let's clarify this further by giving example tables for dbs(DEPT) and dbs(EMP). Figure 9-1 shows projected versions of a department and an employee table in some given state dbs of DB_UEX.

DEPT

deptno	dname
10	'RESEARCH'
11	'SALES'
12	'MARKETING'

EMP

empno	ename	deptno	msal
1001	'WENDY'	10	3000
1002	'SUSAN'	10	5500
1003	'BRITNEY'	10	5500
1004	'MARIAN'	12	4500
1005	'DEBBY'	12	6200

Figure 9-1. *Example department and employee tables*

Given these two tables, version FEa for query EXQ8 would return the following set:

```
{ {(DEPTNO;10), (DNAME;'RESEARCH'),
                (RICHEMP; { {(EMPNO;1002), (ENAME;'SUSAN'),   (MSAL;5500)}
                          ,{(EMPNO;1003), (ENAME;'BRITNEY'), (MSAL;5500)} })}
 ,{(DEPTNO;11), (DNAME;'SALES'), (RICHEMP;∅)}
 ,{(DEPTNO;12), (DNAME;'MARKETING'),
                (RICHEMP; { {(EMPNO;1005), (ENAME;'DEBBY'), (MSAL;6200)} })}
}
```

Version FEb would return this set:

```
{ {(DEPTNO;10), (DNAME;'RESEARCH'), (EMPNO;1002), (ENAME;'SUSAN'),   (MSAL;5500)}
 ,{(DEPTNO;10), (DNAME;'RESEARCH'), (EMPNO;1003), (ENAME;'BRITNEY'),(MSAL;5500)}
 ,{(DEPTNO;12), (DNAME;'MARKETING'),(EMPNO;1005), (ENAME;'DEBBY'),   (MSAL;6200)}
}
```

Specification FEc once more demonstrates the rewriting of a quantifier; it differs from FEb in that the existential quantifier is rewritten into a universal quantifier.

SQL expression SEI demonstrates that a specification such as FEa can be translated directly into SQL. By using the keyword cursor, you indicate that a subquery employed within the SELECT clause can potentially return multiple rows. SQL expression SEII is a direct translation for FEb; it employs a subquery within the FROM clause.

Note In Listing 9-9 that follows, we use a function to_year in expressions FEa and FEb. This function is defined to return the year component of a given date value. In Oracle SQL, you can achieve the same through the to_char function, as demonstrated in SEI and SEII.

Listing 9-9 gives the employees (EMPNO and ENAME) who attended at least one offering of every course that was given by trainer "De Haan" (employee number 1206) in 2003.

Listing 9-9. *Query EXQ9(dbs)*

```
FEa:  { e↓{EMPNO,ENAME} | e∈dbs(EMP) ∧
                       { o(COURSE) | o∈dbs(OFFR) ∧ o(TRAINER)=1206 ∧
                                     o(STATUS)='CONF' ∧ to_year(o(STARTS))=2003 }

                       ⊆

                       { r(COURSE) | r∈dbs(REG)⊗dbs(OFFR) ∧
                                     r(STUD)=e(EMPNO) ∧ r(TRAINER)=1206 ∧
                                     r(STATUS)='CONF' ∧ to_year(r(STARTS))=2003 }
      }
FEb:  { e↓{EMPNO,ENAME} | e∈dbs(EMP) ∧
                       (∀o1∈{ o2↓{COURSE} | o2∈dbs(OFFR) ∧ o2(TRAINER)=1206 ∧
                               o2(STATUS)='CONF' ∧ to_year(o2(STARTS))=2003 }:
                           (∃r∈dbs(REG)⊗dbs(OFFR): r(COURSE)=o1(COURSE) ∧
                                     r(STUD)=e(EMPNO) ∧ r(TRAINER)=1206 ∧
                                     r(STATUS)='CONF' ∧ to_year(r(STARTS))=2003))
      }
SEI:  select e.EMPNO,e.ENAME
      from EMP e
      where 0 = (select count(*)
                   from (select o1.COURSE
                           from OFFR o1
                           where o1.TRAINER = 1206
                             and o1.STATUS = 'CONF'
                             and to_char(o1.STARTS,'YYYY') = '2003'
                         minus
                         select o2.COURSE
                           from OFFR o2
                               ,REG r
                           where o2.COURSE = r.COURSE
                             and o2.STARTS = r.STARTS
                             and r.STUD = e.EMPNO
                             and o2.TRAINER = 1206
                             and o2.STATUS = 'CONF'
                             and to_char(o2.STARTS,'YYYY') = '2003'))
```

SEII: select e.EMPNO,e.ENAME
      from EMP e
      where not exists(select o1.*
                       from (select o.COURSE
                             from OFFR o
                             where o.TRAINER = 1206
                               and o.STATUS = 'CONF'
                               and to_char(o.STARTS,'YYYY') = '2003') o1
                       where not exists(select r.*
                                        from REG r
                                            ,OFFR o2
                                        where r.COURSE = o2.COURSE
                                          and r.STARTS = o2.STARTS
                                          and r.STUD = e.EMPNO
                                          and o2.STATUS = 'CONF'
                                          and to_char(r.STARTS,'YYYY') = '2003'
                                          and r.TRAINER = 1206
                                          and r.COURSE = o1.COURSE))

Formal specification FEa queries all employees for which the set of distinct courses given by De Haan in 2003 is a subset of the set of courses for which an offering (taught by De Haan) was attended by the employee in 2003. Note that for an employee to have attended a course offering, the following must be true:

1. He or she must be registered for that offering.

2. That offering must have status confirmed.

Specification FEb is a rewrite of the subset operator in FEa into quantifiers that follow from the definition of the subset operator. Set A is a subset of B if and only if every element of A is an element of B.

$$(A \subseteq B) \Leftrightarrow (\forall a \in A: \exists b \in B: b=a)$$

The rewrite rule that we have applied is slightly more sophisticated; it is of the following structure:

$$\{ a \mid a \in A \land P(a) \} \subseteq \{ b \mid b \in B \land Q(b) \}$$
$$\Leftrightarrow$$
$$(\forall a1 \in \{ a2 \mid a2 \in A \land P(a2) \}: (\exists b \in B: b=a1 \land Q(b)))$$

SQL does not support all set operators: *union*, *intersection*, and *difference* are available; *symmetric difference* is not, nor is the *subset of* operator. Fortunately, you can rewrite the subset operator using other available set operators:

$$(A \subseteq B) \Leftrightarrow ((A - B) = \varnothing)$$

Set A is a subset of B if and only if the difference A minus B represents the empty set. To check for an empty set in SQL, you would have to apply one more rewrite rule:

$$((A - B) = \varnothing) \Leftrightarrow (\#(A - B) = 0)$$

Instead of checking that A minus B represents the empty set, you now check that the cardinality of A minus B equals zero. The preceding rewrite rules were applied to FEa to end up with SQL expression SEI.

Alternative SEII represents the SQL version for the formal version where the subset operator was rewritten into quantifiers (FEb). Note that (again) the universal quantifier had to be further rewritten into an existential quantifier.

Listing 9-10 gives courses (CODE and DESCR) for which all offerings (and there must be at least one) in 2006 were given by only one trainer, and for which none of these offerings was attended by another trainer.

Listing 9-10. *Query EXQ10(dbs)*

```
FEa:  { c↓{CODE,DESCR}
      | c∈dbs(CRS) ∧ /* there is one trainer for all offerings of this course */
                    (∃e∈dbs(EMP):
                        (∀o∈dbs(OFFR): (o(COURSE)=c(CODE) ∧ o(STATUS)='CONF' ∧
                                        to_year(o(STARTS))=2006) ⇒
                                       o(TRAINER)=e(EMPNO) )
                    ∧ /* course was offered in 2006 */
                    (∃o∈dbs(OFFR): o(COURSE)=c(CODE) ∧ o(STATUS)='CONF' ∧
                                   to_year(o(STARTS))=2006)
                    ∧ /* none of the offerings was attended by another trainer */
                    ¬(∃r∈dbs(REG)⊗
                        (dbs(EMP)⋈{(STUD;EMPNO),(JOB;JOB)})⊗dbs(OFFR):
                            r(COURSE)=c(CODE) ∧ r(STATUS)='CONF' ∧
                            to_year(r(STARTS))=2006 ∧ r(JOB)='TRAINER')
      }
FEb:  { c↓{CODE,DESCR}
      | c∈dbs(CRS) ∧ /* there is one trainer for all offerings of this course */
                    1 = #{ o(TRAINER) | o∈dbs(OFFR) ∧ o(COURSE)=c(CODE) ∧
                                        o(STATUS)='CONF' ∧ to_year(o(STARTS))=2006 }
                    ∧ /* none of the offerings was attended by another trainer */
                    (∀r∈dbs(REG)⊗
                        (dbs(EMP)⋈{(STUD;EMPNO),(JOB;JOB)})⊗dbs(OFFR):
                            (r(COURSE)=c(CODE) ∧ r(STATUS)='CONF' ∧
                            to_year(r(STARTS))=2006) ⇒ r(JOB)≠'TRAINER')
      }
SEI:  select c.CODE
             ,c.DESCR
      from CRS c
      where exists(select e.*
                   from EMP e
                   where not exists(select o2.*
                                    from OFFR o2
                                    where o2.COURSE = c.CODE
                                      and o2.STATUS = 'CONF'
                                      and to_char(o2.STARTS,'YYYY') = '2006'
                                      and o2.TRAINER <> e.EMPNO))
```

```
          and exists(select o1.*
                        from OFFR o1
                       where o1.COURSE = c.CODE
                         and o1.STATUS = 'CONF'
                         and to_char(o1.STARTS,'YYYY') = '2006')
          and not exists(select r.*
                          from REG r
                              ,EMP e
                              ,OFFR o3
                         where r.STUD = e.EMPNO
                           and r.COURSE = o3.COURSE
                           and r.STARTS = o3.STARTS
                           and r.COURSE = c.CODE
                           and o3.STATUS = 'CONF'
                           and to_char(o3.STARTS,'YYYY') = '2006'
                           and e.JOB = 'TRAINER')
SEII: select c.CODE, c.DESCR
      from COURSE c
      where 1 = (select count(distinct o1.TRAINER)
                   from OFFR o1
                  where o1.COURSE = c.CODE
                    and o1.STATUS = 'CONF'
                    and to_char(o1.STARTS,'YYYY') = 2006)
        and not exists(select r.*
                        from REG r
                            ,EMP e
                            ,OFFR o2
                       where r.STUD = e.EMPNO
                         and r.COURSE = o2.COURSE
                         and r.STARTS = o2.STARTS
                         and r.COURSE = c.CODE
                         and o2.STATUS = 'CONF'
                         and to_char(o2.STARTS,'YYYY') = '2006'
                         and e.JOB = 'TRAINER')
```

Note the additional conjunct (the one with comment /* course was offered in 2006 */) inside the specification of FEa to ensure that the universal quantification inside the first conjunct does not involve the empty set.

Specification FEb takes care of this by stating that the cardinality of all distinct trainers, who have given an offering in 2006 for the course, is at least one. By stating that this cardinality should be exactly one, you specify that the course was given by no more than one trainer.

You can translate both formal specifications into SQL; FEa requires a rewrite of the universal quantifier.

Listing 9-11 finds all departments that violate the employee table constraint stating that departments that employ the president or a manager should also employ at least one administrator.

Listing 9-11. *Query EXQ11(dbs)*

```
FEa: { d | d∈dbs(DEPT) ∧
           (∃e1∈dbs(EMP): e1(DEPTNO)=d(DEPTNO) ∧
                           e1(JOB)∈{'PRESIDENT','MANAGER'}) ∧
           ¬(∃e2∈E: e2(DEPTNO)=d ∧ e2(JOB) = 'ADMIN' ) }
FEb: { d | d∈dbs(DEPT) ∧
           (∃e1∈dbs(EMP): e1(DEPTNO)=d(DEPTNO) ∧
                           e1(JOB)∈{'PRESIDENT','MANAGER'}) ∧
           (∀e2∈dbs(EMP): e2(JOB)='ADMIN' ⇒ e2(DEPTNO)≠d(DEPTNO)) }
SEI: select d.*
     from DEPT d
     where exists(select e1.*
                  from EMP e1
                  where e1.DEPTNO = d.DEPTNO
                    and e1.JOB in ('PRESIDENT','MANAGER'))
       and not exists(select e2.*
                      from EMP e2
                      where e2.DEPTNO = d.DEPTNO
                        and e1.JOB = 'ADMIN')
```

Listing 7-26 introduced the formal specification for this table constraint. Using this specification, you can derive the formal expression for query EXQ11. Because you want to find departments that violate this constraint, all you have to do is negate the constraint specification; just prefix the specification with ¬.

Here it is (note that in this specification, free variable E represents an employee table):

```
¬(∀d∈{ e1(DEPTNO) | e1∈E }:
    (∃e2∈E: e2(DEPTNO)=d ∧ e2(JOB)∈{'PRESIDENT','MANAGER'} )
    ⇒
    (∃e3∈E: e3(DEPTNO)=d ∧ e3(JOB)='ADMIN' ) )
```

If you then rewrite this specification by bringing the negation into the quantification, you end up with the following specification (verify this for yourself):

```
(∃d∈{ e1(DEPTNO) | e1∈E }:
    (∃e2∈E: e2(DEPTNO)=d ∧ e2(JOB)∈{'PRESIDENT','MANAGER'} ) ∧
    ¬(∃e3∈E: e3(DEPTNO)=d ∧ e3(JOB)='ADMIN' ) )
```

Formal expression FEa now follows straightforwardly from the preceding rewritten constraint specification. FEb is a rewrite of FEa; a universal quantifier replaces the negated existential quantifier.

You can easily derive the SQL text (SEI) from specification FEa.

A Remark on Negations

You might have noticed that because SQL lacks universal quantification and implication, certain SQL expressions end up having more negations than their formally specified counterpart did. SEII of EXQ9 is a fine example of this; it contains a nested negated existential quantifier.

It is difficult to understand the meaning of such a query. The formal counterpart that employs the universal quantifier is easier to understand.

In general we (humans) have difficulty understanding expressions that contain negations; the more negations, the more difficult it gets for us. Whenever you encounter negations in formal specifications, you should investigate the opportunity of rewriting such a specification into an expression holding fewer negations. You can use the rewrite rules introduced in Part 1 of this book to achieve this.

■**Note** By rewriting formal specifications such that they hold fewer negations, you not only help yourself; you also enable clearer informal specifications that your customer (the user) will definitely appreciate.

Because they are so important, we list rewrite rules that involve negations once again here. Table 9-1 contains various alternatives for the De Morgan, implication, and quantifier rewrite rules.

Table 9-1. *Rewrite Rules with Negations*

Expression		Is Equivalent To
$\neg\neg A$	$\Leftrightarrow$	A
$\neg A \Rightarrow \neg B$	$\Leftrightarrow$	$B \Rightarrow A$
$\neg A \Rightarrow B$	$\Leftrightarrow$	$\neg B \Rightarrow A$
$A \Rightarrow \neg B$	$\Leftrightarrow$	$B \Rightarrow \neg A$
$A \Rightarrow \neg B$	$\Leftrightarrow$	$(A \wedge B) \Rightarrow \text{FALSE}$
$\neg A \wedge \neg B$	$\Leftrightarrow$	$\neg(A \vee B)$
$A \wedge \neg B$	$\Leftrightarrow$	$\neg(\neg A \vee B)$
$\neg A \wedge B$	$\Leftrightarrow$	$\neg(A \vee \neg B)$
$\neg A \vee \neg B$	$\Leftrightarrow$	$\neg(A \wedge B)$
$A \vee \neg B$	$\Leftrightarrow$	$\neg(\neg A \wedge B)$
$\neg A \vee B$	$\Leftrightarrow$	$\neg(A \wedge \neg B)$
$\neg(\exists x \in X: \neg P(x))$	$\Leftrightarrow$	$(\forall x \in X: P(x))$
$(\exists x \in X: \neg P(x))$	$\Leftrightarrow$	$\neg(\forall x \in X: P(x))$
$\neg(\exists x \in X: P(x))$	$\Leftrightarrow$	$(\forall x \in X: \neg P(x))$
$(\exists x \in X: P(x))$	$\Leftrightarrow$	$\neg(\forall x \in X: \neg P(x))$

Sometimes you can get rid of a negation by using knowledge about the constraints of a database design. For instance, if you need to query all offerings that are not canceled, you can equivalently query all offerings that are either scheduled or confirmed. If o represents an offering tuple, then the following rewrite rule will apply:

$$o(\text{STATUS}) \neq \text{'CANC'} \Leftrightarrow o(\text{STATUS}) \in \{\text{'SCHD'}, \text{'CONF'}\}$$

Here you use knowledge about the attribute value set of attribute STATUS.

If—in the course of rewriting expressions—you end up querying employees who don't have a salary of less than 5000, it might be better to query the employees who have a salary equal to or more than 5000 instead. The following rewrite rule applies (e represents an employee tuple):

$$\neg(e(\text{MSAL}) < 5000) \Leftrightarrow e(\text{MSAL}) \geq 5000$$

Our brains dislike negations. Try to avoid negations by rewriting expressions into expressions containing fewer negations. This is not only true for query specifications, but also for constraint specifications (in previous chapters), and data manipulation specifications (in the next chapter).

Chapter Summary

This section provides a summary of this chapter, formatted as a bulleted list. You can use it to check your understanding of the various concepts introduced in this chapter before continuing with the exercises in the next section.

- Queries constitute a crucial application of a database; they enable you to extract information from a database that is relevant for you.

- You can formally represent a query as a function over a database universe. For every database state that you supply as the argument, the function returns the query result.

- Because you supply a database state, the function can reference every table available in the database state to determine the query result.

- To specify a query, you can use all formal concepts introduced in Part 1 of this book. You usually specify the result set of a query as a set of tuples (a table) using the hybrid method. The given set from which you start such a specification is typically one of the tables, or a join of some of the tables available in the database state; you can also use any of the set operators introduced in this book. The predicates inside the query specification are typically compound predicates (they use the various logical connectives), and often employ the universal and existential quantifiers.

- In practice (certainly when you use SQL), the result of a query will always be a table. However, our formal model does not require this.

- When you use SQL as your query language, you should be aware of various limitations. Following are the most notable ones:

  - SQL is not set oriented; you sometimes have to use the distinct keyword.

  - SQL lacks the implication operator; you must rewrite these into disjunctions.

  - Oracle's version of SQL lacks universal quantification; you must rewrite this into existential quantification.

  - SQL lacks the subset operator; you must rewrite this using the other available set operators (union, intersect, and minus).

- Our brains dislike negations. Whenever you specify a query, try to minimize the number of negations in such a specification. Most of the time, you can use the rewrite rules introduced in Part 1 of this book to achieve this. Sometimes you can use simple arithmetic rewrite rules. On occasion, you can achieve this by using constraint knowledge of the database design that you query.

Exercises

Develop both formal and SQL expressions for these queries.

Note In the following exercises, there may be queries that cannot be answered with the given database. In these cases, you should give arguments why the answer cannot be given.

---

1. Give the number and name of employees who belong to department 10.

2. Give the number and name of employees who do not belong to department 10, 11, 12, or 15.

3. Give the number and name of employees who belong to departments 10 and 11.

4. Give the number and name of employees who belong to a department that is a subdepartment of department 10.

5. Ascertain that the constraint of there being at most one president is not violated.

6. Give the number and name of administrators older than 35 who have a monthly salary of more than 2000.

7. Give the number and name of managers who earn the maximum of their grade.

8. Give the number and name of the trainers who actually worked as such in at least one course in 2004.

9. Give the number and name of the trainers who did not work as such in any course in 2004.

10. Give the number, name, and salary of every manager who earns less than any of his employees.

11. Find a query with answer "yes" if COURSE is uniquely identifying in OFFR and "no" if otherwise. Does the answer "yes" imply that COURSE is a key of OFFR?

12. Give of every manager: his or her number, name, and salary of every one of his or her subordinate employees.

13. Give for every employee whose manager is managed by another employee (supermanager): number and name of the employee and of his or her super-manager.

14. Give of every manager and of every one of his or her direct subordinates who is a manager: number, name, and date hired.

15. Give of every manager and of every one of his or her subordinates who is a manager: number, name, and date when they got the manager's job.

16. Give the number and name of employees who left in 2006 and came back in that same year.

17. Give the number and name of employees who left in 2006 and did not come back.

18. Give the number of persons that left and the number that entered department 10 in 2006.

19. Give the number of persons in department 10 at the end of 2006.

20. List the following for the course "Designing Databases" that started on March 4, 2006: for every registered student, username, name, job, and evaluation.

21. Give for every one of the courses (with CODE) DB1, DB2, DB3, the duration, and for every offering (with a begin date) in 2006: begin date, status, and number of registered students.

22. Give per department (DEPTNO and DNAME) the number of administrators, trainers, sales representatives, and managers.

23. Give all data of salary grades where every employee (that is, employee who is assigned to this grade) is earning more than the salary grade's upper limit minus 500 dollars.

24. Give all (managed) employees who are assigned to a higher salary grade than their boss's salary grade.

25. Give the courses for which every canceled offering in 2006 had at least one student registered for that offering.

26. Give the employees (EMPNO and ENAME) who attended (at least) one offering for all design courses (course category equals 'DSG') in 2006.

27. List all employees who have received a raise of more than 20 percent in the year 2006.

CHAPTER 10

Data Manipulation

Through executing *transactions*, you can manipulate the data in a database. In this chapter we'll demonstrate how you can specify a transaction in a formal way. We won't formally introduce any new concepts; we've already presented all the ingredients for specifying transactions.

The section "Formally Specifying Transactions" gradually develops how you can specify a transaction. You'll learn that you can specify a transaction as a *function over the database universe* at hand. For every database state, this function returns another database state that reflects the intended changes of the transaction. In this section, we'll also give two examples to familiarize you with this formal concept of a transaction.

The section "Example Transactions Over DB_UEX" provides example transactions for the database universe that was introduced in Chapter 7. For the second time in this book, you'll see the use of SQL. Every example transaction will be accompanied by one or more equivalent SQL data manipulation language (DML) statements; that is, INSERT, UPDATE, and DELETE statements. You'll learn that expressing certain transactions in SQL requires executing more than one DML statement.

Note We assume you have a working knowledge of SQL DML statements. It is not the goal of this book to teach SQL.

In preparation for the next chapter (11) where you'll be introduced to the challenges of implementing data integrity constraints using an SQL DBMS, we'll also (somewhat) discuss which data integrity constraints a given transaction might violate. It is up to the DBMS to validate these *involved* data integrity constraints for the given transaction. The DBMS should reject the intended changes of the transaction if the resulting database state violates any of the involved constraints.

As usual, you'll find a "Chapter Summary" at the end, followed by an "Exercises" section.

Formally Specifying Transactions

Next to data retrieval, transaction execution is the second most important application of a database. By executing transactions, you can maintain the database and ensure that its state remains a valid representation of the (changing) real world. In this section, we'll demonstrate how you can formally specify transactions.

Let's start with a simple example using the database design that was introduced in Chapter 7. Take a look at tuple tcrs1. It represents a new course than needs to be inserted into the database:

```
tcrs1 := { (CODE;'AM4DP')
         , (DESC;'Applied Mathematics for Database Professionals')
         , (CAT;'DSG')
         , (DUR;5) }
```

For your convenience, we repeat the definitions of characterization chr_CRS, tuple universe tup_CRS, and table universe tab_CRS in Listing 10-1. All involved attribute, tuple, and table constraints with regards to the CRS table structure are in this listing.

Listing 10-1. *Definitions of chr_CRS, tup_CRS, and tab_CRS*

```
chr_CRS :=
{ ( CODE;  CRSCODE-TYP                       )
, ( DESCR; varchar(40)                       )
, ( CAT;   { s | s∈varchar(3) ∧
                 s∈{'DSG','GEN','BLD'} }     )
, ( DUR;   { n | n∈number(2,0) ∧ 1 ≤ n ≤ 15 } )
}

tup_CRS :=
{ c | c∈Π(chr_CRS) ∧ c(CAT) = 'BLD' ⇒ t(DUR) ≤ 5
}

tab_CRS :=
{ C | C∈℘(tup_CRS) ∧ (∀c1,c2∈C: c1(CODE) = c2(CODE) ⇒ c1 = c2)
}
```

■**Note** tcrs1 does not violate any attribute or tuple constraints for the CRS table structure; or put differently, tcrs1 is an element of tuple universe tup_CRS.

Here is a first attempt to formally specify the transaction of inserting tcrs1 into the CRS table structure. We could specify this transaction as a function, say Tx1a, over DB_UEX. For a given database state in DB_UEX, say dbs, function Tx1a returns a database state that reflects the insertion of tcrs1 into the CRS table structure.

```
Tx1a(dbs) := { (EMP;  dbs(EMP) )
             , (SREP; dbs(SREP))
             , (MEMP; dbs(MEMP))
             , (TERM; dbs(TERM))
             , (DEPT; dbs(DEPT))
             , (GRD;  dbs(GRD) )
```

```
        , (CRS;   dbs(CRS) ∪ {tcrs1} )
        , (OFFR; dbs(OFFR))
        , (REG;   dbs(REG) )
        , (HIST; dbs(HIST)) }
```

As you can see, function Tx1a yields another database state that holds the same ten table structures as dbs. This resulting database state differs from dbs only for the CRS table structure; tuple tcrs1 has been added. For all other table structures, the resulting database state holds the corresponding tables that dbs holds.

Let's apply Tx1a to the "empty database state" (that is, the database state in which all table structures hold the empty table). Here is the empty database state, which we'll name db_empty. We introduced you to this database state in Exercise 12 in Chapter 7.

```
db_empty := { (EMP;   ∅)
            , (SREP;  ∅)
            , (MEMP;  ∅)
            , (TERM;  ∅)
            , (DEPT;  ∅)
            , (GRD;   ∅)
            , (CRS;   ∅)
            , (OFFR;  ∅)
            , (REG;   ∅)
            , (HIST;  ∅) }
```

In Exercise 12 in Chapter 7, you established that db_empty is an element of DB_UEX. Therefore, you can apply function Tx1a to it. Applying function Tx1a to db_empty, denoted by Tx1a(db_empty), results in the following database state:

```
Tx1a(db_empty) = { (EMP;   ∅)
                 , (SREP;  ∅)
                 , (MEMP;  ∅)
                 , (TERM;  ∅)
                 , (DEPT;  ∅)
                 , (GRD;   ∅)
                 , (CRS;   {tcrs1} )
                 , (OFFR;  ∅)
                 , (REG;   ∅)
                 , (HIST;  ∅) }
```

Note that the application of Tx1a to db_empty results in a database state that is (again) an element of DB_UEX; the resulting database state conforms to all static constraints that were specified as part of the definition of DB_UEX. However, this isn't true in general. Let's take a look at applying Tx1a to the following database state (dbs1):

```
dbs1 :=
  { (EMP;   ∅)
  , (SREP;  ∅)
  , (MEMP;  ∅)
  , (TERM;  ∅)
  , (DEPT;  ∅)
```

```
, (GRD;  ∅)
, (CRS; { { (CODE;'AM4DP'), (DESC;'AM4DP workshop')
          , (CAT;'DSG'),    (DUR;1) } })
, (OFFR; ∅)
, (REG;  ∅)
, (HIST; ∅) }
```

Applying transaction Tx1a to database state dbs1 results in a database state that holds the following CRS table:

```
{ { (CODE;'AM4DP'), (DESC;'AM4DP workshop'), (CAT;'DSG'), (DUR;1) }
, { (CODE;'AM4DP'), (DESC;'Applied Mathematics for Database Professionals'),
                                   (CAT;'DSG'), (DUR;5) } }
```

This table clearly violates the table constraint that is specified as part of the definition of tab_CRS, and is therefore not an admissible table for the CRS table structure. Consequently, in this case, Tx1a(dbs1) is *not* an element of DB_UEX. Clearly the current definition of this transaction is flawed, for we don't want a transaction to have the database end up in a state that violates any of the data integrity constraints.

A more proper definition of the transaction that inserts tcrs1 to the database would be this one, named Tx1b. Note that in this definition we are reusing function Tx1a, which was specified earlier in this section.

```
Tx1b(dbs) := dbs      , if Tx1a(dbs)∉DB_UEX
          := Tx1a(dbs), otherwise
```

Transaction Tx1b describes an insertion *attempt*. If the insertion of tcrs1 results in a database state that violates any of the data integrity constraints—that is, the resulting database state is not an element of DB_UEX—then the insertion is refused (also referred to as *rolled back*), and the database state remains the same. Otherwise, the insertion of tcrs1 is allowed (the transaction *executes successfully*, or *commits*):

In this particular example, given a database state dbs, the insertion attempt successfully executes only if the CRS table in dbs does not already contain a tuple where the code attribute value equals 'AM4DP'. However, if that tuple is in fact tcrs1, the insertion attempt succeeds, but in this case does not add a tuple at all. Adding a tuple (through set union) to a table that already contains this tuple does not introduce a new element (tuple) to the table.

Thus far, we are only focusing on attribute, tuple, and table constraints in this discussion. When checking whether Tx1a(dbs) is an element of DB_UEX, you should also consider the database constraints that involve the CRS table structure.

■Note You can determine the involved database constraints for a transaction that inserts a tuple in CRS by simply scanning for the string 'CRS' in the formal specifications of the database constraints.

Here are the involved database constraints (using the short names introduced in Listing 7-39): PSSR6, PTIJ9, PTIJ10, PTIJ12, PTIJ14, PTIJ15, and PODC3. In this particular example, inserting a new CRS tuple into a valid database state—a database state in DB_UEX—will never violate one of these database constraints (you might want to verify this for yourself). Therefore, we need not consider these involved database constraints in the discussion of this example.

■ **Note** The definition of Tx1b does cover all static constraints: attribute, tuple, table, and database.

Last—this should not surprise you—the *state transition* constraints should be involved in the formal definition of a transaction.

Take a look at tuple toffr1. It represents an offering for the AM4DP course that needs to be inserted into the database.

```
toffr1 := { (COURSE;  'AM4DP')
          , (STARTS;  '01-FEB-2007')
          , (STATUS;  'CONF')
          , (MAXCAP;  20)
          , (TRAINER; 1126)
          , (LOC;     'UTRECHT') }
```

This tuple conforms to all attribute and tuple constraints that are specified for the OFFR table structure (see the definitions of chr_OFFR and tup_OFFR in Chapter 7).

Let's assume you'd like to attempt to insert the offr1 tuple into the database whose begin state currently conforms to all static constraints specified in the definition of DB_UEX. We'll further assume that the begin database state for this transaction conforms to the following additional characteristics. In parentheses, we list involved constraints that cause us to list the characteristic.

- CRS holds a tuple that represents the AM4DP course (PSSR6).

- No offerings are in OFFR yet; this is the first one to be inserted (tab_OFFR constraints PTIJ13, PTIJ14, PTIJ15).

- EMP holds a tuple that represents a trainer with employee number 1126, who was hired before February 1, 2006. This trainer is still working for us; that is, he or she has not been terminated (PSSR8, PTIJ11, PTIJ12, PODC7).

- DEPT holds a tuple that represents a department located in Utrecht. The aforementioned trainer is working in this department (PSSR7, PODC3).

Three other static constraints involve OFFR: PTIJ10, PODC4, and PODC5. However, these three cannot be violated by a transaction that inserts a new CRS tuple. They all involve the REG table structure too. The second characteristic in the preceding bulleted list, together with the fact that the begin state must be a valid one (that is, contained in DB_UEX), imply that there are no tuples in REG. This in turn means that the database state conforms (and remains conformed after the insertion of offr1) to PTIJ10, PODC4, and PODC5.

Given the preceding characteristics, the transaction of inserting tuple toffr1 would successfully execute. However, note that toffr1 represents a *confirmed* offering. The definition of our state transition universe (ST_UEX from Chapter 8) contains the specification of a state transition constraint stating that new offerings must start with status *scheduled* (constraint STC2, in Listing 8-8). Clearly this transaction violates constraint STC2.

A correct definition of the transaction that attempts to insert offr1, say Tx2, would be as follows.

For a database state dbs in DB_UEX, let

```
Tx2a(dbs) := { (EMP;  dbs(EMP) )
             , (SREP; dbs(SREP))
             , (MEMP; dbs(MEMP))
             , (TERM; dbs(TERM))
             , (DEPT; dbs(DEPT))
             , (GRD;  dbs(GRD) )
             , (CRS;  dbs(CRS) )
             , (OFFR; dbs(OFFR) ∪ {toffr1} )
             , (REG;  dbs(REG) )
             , (HIST; dbs(HIST)) }
```

and let

```
Tx2b(dbs) := dbs       , if Tx2a(dbs)∉DB_UEX
          := Tx2a(dbs), otherwise
```

then,

```
Tx2(dbs) := Tx2b(dbs), if (dbs,Tx2b(dbs))∈ST_UEX
         := dbs       , otherwise
```

The definition of Tx2a describes the insertion of toffr1. Tx2b ensures that this conforms to all static constraints. The definition of Tx2 ensures that the transaction conforms to all state transition constraints too. It does so by adding the condition that the ordered pair consisting of the begin state and the end state for the transaction is an element of the state transition universe.

Often a transaction modifies only a few of the table structures involved in a database design; many table structures remain unchanged. An alternative (and somewhat shorter) way of specifying Tx2a, that more explicitly shows this fact, is as follows:

```
Tx2a(dbs) := dbs↓{EMP,SREP,MEMP,TERM,DEPT,GRD,CRS,REG,HIST}
            ∪
           { (OFFR; dbs(OFFR) ∪ {toffr1}) }
```

Here we use function limitation (↓) to add all unchanged table structures to the end state, and through union (∪) we add the table structure(s) that the transaction modifies.

The next section will present some more example transactions over DB_UEX to familiarize you further with formally specifying transactions.

Example Transactions Over DB_UEX

This section will provide example transactions. For every transaction, we'll present you with the following:

- An informal description for the transaction

- One or more formal expressions to specify the transaction

- One or more SQL specifications that implement the transaction in an SQL DBMS

Along the way, you'll see that SQL has limitations that cause you to execute more than one DML statement to implement a given transaction.

Listings 10-1 through 10-7 introduce the example transactions. All transactions will be named ETXi (example *transaction* i), where i represents a sequence number. In the formal specifications given for each transaction, dbs will represent the begin state for the transaction (an element of DB_UEX). The various alternative formal expressions will be named FEc (*formal expression* c), where c represents a character (a, b, c, and so on).

In the SQL specifications, we'll use the table structure names introduced by database characterization DB_CHREX (see Listing 7-38) as the table names available for INSERT, UPDATE, and DELETE statements. Alternative SQL specifications will be named SEr (SQL *expression* r), where r represents a Roman numeral (I, II, III, and so on).

In the following formal expressions, we'll specify a transaction as a function similar to the way Tx1a and Tx2a (always resulting in a modified database state) were specified in the previous section. However, we intend—as discussed in the previous section—that all static and dynamic constraints should remain satisfied; that is, that the transaction rolls back whenever either the resulting database state is not an element of DB_UEX, or the ordered pair representing the transition from the begin state to the end state is not an element of ST_UEX.

In the previous section, you saw two examples of a transaction that inserts a single tuple. Take a look at the example in Listing 10-2. It specifies a transaction that inserts (potentially) multiple tuples. Listing 10-2 registers all administrators that have been hired in the past quarter (91 days) for the offering of course AM4DP that starts on March 1, 2007.

Listing 10-2. *Transaction ETX1(dbs)*

```
FEa: dbs↓{EMP,SREP,MEMP,TERM,DEPT,GRD,CRS,OFFR,HIST}
       ∪
     { (REG; dbs(REG)
             ∪
           { { (COURSE;'AM4DP'       )
             ,(STARTS;'01-mar-2007')
             ,(STUD;  e(EMPNO)      )
             ,(EVAL;  -1            ) }
             | e∈dbs(EMP) ∧ e(JOB)='ADMIN' ∧ e(HIRED) ≥ sysdate-91
                                           ∧ e(HIRED) ≤ sysdate } ) }

SEI: insert into REG(STUD,EVAL,COURSE,STARTS)
     select e.EMPNO, -1, 'AM4DP', '01-mar-2007'
     from EMP e
     where e.JOB = 'ADMIN'
       and e.HIRED between sysdate - 91 and sysdate
```

This transaction only changes the REG table structure; the tuples that result from a query on the EMP table are added to it. In these tuples, attributes COURSE, STARTS, and EVAL are set to values 'AM4DP', '01-mar-2007', and -1, respectively. Attribute STUD ranges over all employee numbers of administrators that were hired in the past 91 days.

In the formal specification, the order of the attribute-value pairs enumerated inside the query part of this specification does not matter. However, in the SQL expression, the order of the value expressions listed in the second line (the one starting with keyword SELECT) must match the order of the attributes listed in the first line (following keyword INSERT).

Note In SQL, embedded queries such as the one displayed in SEI are often referred to as *subqueries*.

Finally, you should recognize that because the subquery in SEI selects EMPNO (the uniquely identifying attribute in the EMP table structure), there is no need to include the distinct keyword right after the select keyword.

Another common transaction is the deletion of tuples from the database. Listing 10-3 gives an example that deletes registrations. Listing 10-3 deletes all registrations of student 3124 for scheduled or confirmed offerings that start in the future.

Listing 10-3. *Transaction ETX2(dbs)*

```
FEa: dbs↓{EMP,SREP,MEMP,TERM,DEPT,GRD,CRS,OFFR,HIST}
        ∪
     { (REG; { r | r∈dbs(REG) ∧
                  ¬ ( r(STUD) = 3124 ∧
                      r(STARTS) > sysdate ∧
                      ⤶{ o(STATUS) | o∈dbs(OFFR) ∧
                                     o↓{COURSE,STARTS} = r↓{COURSE,STARTS} }
                  ∈{'SCHD','CONF'} )
              } ) }
FEb: dbs↓{EMP,SREP,MEMP,TERM,DEPT,GRD,CRS,OFFR,HIST}
        ∪
     { (REG; { r↓{STUD,COURSE,STARTS,EVAL} | r∈dbs(REG)⊗dbs(OFFR) ∧
                                             ( r(STUD) ≠ 3124 ∨
                                               r(STARTS) ≤ sysdate ∨
                                               r(STATUS) = 'CANC' )
              } ) }
FEc: dbs↓{EMP,SREP,MEMP,TERM,DEPT,GRD,CRS,OFFR,HIST}
        ∪
     { (REG; dbs(REG) -
             { r | r∈dbs(REG) ∧ r(STUD) = 3124 ∧ r(STARTS) > sysdate ∧
                   ⤶{ o(STATUS) | o∈dbs(OFFR) ∧
                                  o↓{COURSE,STARTS} = r↓{COURSE,STARTS} }
                   ∈{'SCHD','CONF'}
             } ) }
SEI: delete from REG r
```

```
where r.STUD = 3124
  and r.STARTS > sysdate
  and (select o.STATUS
         from OFFR o
        where o.COURSE = r.COURSE
          and o.STARTS = r.STARTS) in ('SCHD','CONF') )
```

Specification FEa reinitializes the REG table structure with the result from a query that is based on dbs(REG). The query retrieves all registrations that should *remain* in the database state; that is, all tuples that do not represent a registration of student 3124, for an offering in the future that has status confirmed or scheduled.

FEb does something similar, only now the query is based on a join between REG and OFFR. Note that in this specification, compared to FEa, we have rewritten the negation according to De Morgan. The query now retrieves all registrations that are either not for student 3124, or that are for an offering that starts in the past (including today), or that have status canceled.

The way FEc specifies this transaction might be the most intuitive. It specifies a table that contains all the registrations that need to be deleted, and then subtracts that—using the difference operator (–)—from dbs(REG). This specification is much like the way you specify this transaction using SQL (see SEI).

As you'll understand by now, in our formalism a transaction is specified by defining, for every possible begin state, what the end state for the transaction will be. This involves specifying a table for every table structure. In contrast, with SQL you only specify the *change in data* that the transaction achieves; you needn't specify data that remains unchanged.

Right now you're probably thinking that formally specifying transactions is rather tedious. However, you should realize that the SQL expression for the preceding transaction ETX2 is actually a shorthand notation. It specifies that the SQL table variable REG is (re)assigned its begin state value minus the result set of a query that is essentially specified by the WHERE clause of the DELETE statement.

■**Note** Using the mathematical methodology presented in this book, you can also develop formal shorthand expressions. Bert De Brock in his book *Foundations of Semantic Databases* (Prentice Hall, 1995) develops these for common types of transactions (such as deleting tuples from a table structure). However, because this involves introducing a few more somewhat complex mathematical concepts, we won't develop formal shorthand in this book. We refer the interested reader to Chapter 7 of De Brock's book.

There is an important point to be made with regards to the ways ETX2 is specified in Listing 10-2. They all involve the OFFR table structure to determine if the offering has status scheduled or confirmed. In fact, this involvement is not required. Given constraint PODC6 (canceled offerings cannot have registrations), in conjunction with the attribute-value set of the STATUS attribute in OFFR (only three values are allowed: scheduled, confirmed, and canceled), you can *deduce* that if there is a registration for an offering, then that offering will either have status scheduled or confirmed. There is no need for you to specify this in the transaction.

Here are equivalent formal and SQL specifications for transaction ETX2:

FEa: dbs↓{EMP,SREP,MEMP,TERM,DEPT,GRD,CRS,OFFR,HIST}
    ∪
    { (REG; { r | r∈dbs(REG) ∧ ¬ (r(STUD) = 3124 ∧ r(STARTS) > sysdate) }) }
SEII: delete from REG r
    where r.STUD = 3124
      and r.STARTS > sysdate

You can consider these specifications to be more efficient; a DBMS will likely require fewer resources to execute the transaction if specified in this less complex way.

Rewriting formal specifications—be they transactions, queries, or even constraints—using knowledge of already established data integrity constraints, into less complex specifications, is referred to as *semantic optimization*.

■**Note** A true relational DBMS should be capable of performing this semantic optimization automatically for us. Unfortunately, DBMSes that perform such sophisticated semantic optimizations are still unavailable. This is primarily because current DBMSes still have poor support for declaratively specified data integrity constraints. This poor declarative support is also the reason why this book has Chapter 11.

Another common transaction is updating tuples in a database. Listing 10-4 gives an example that updates the maximum capacity of certain offerings. It doubles the maximum capacity of all future offerings planned in Amsterdam.

Listing 10-4. *Transaction ETX3(dbs)*

FEa: dbs↓{SREP,MEMP,TERM,EMP,DEPT,GRD,CRS,REG,HIST}
    ∪
    { (OFFR; { o | o∈dbs(OFFR) ∧ ¬ (o(STARTS) > sysdate ∧ o(LOC) = 'AMSTERDAM') }
        ∪
        { o↓{COURSE,STARTS,STATUS,TRAINER,LOC}
          ∪ { (MAXCAP; 2 * o(MAXCAP)) }
           | o∈dbs(OFFR) ∧ o(STARTS) > sysdate ∧ o(LOC) = 'AMSTERDAM' }
) }
SEI: update OFFR o
    set o.MAXCAP = 2 * o.MAXCAP
    where o.STARTS > sysdate
      and o.LOC = 'AMSTERDAM'

Specification FEa clearly demonstrates that updating a subset of tuples can be seen as first deleting these tuples and then reinserting them with updated attribute values. The first operand of the union operator, at the fourth line of the definition of FEa, represents the OFFR table from which future offerings in Amsterdam have been deleted. The second operand of this union operator represents the reinsertion of these offerings with a doubled maximum capacity.

Again, as shown by expression SEI, SQL offers a convenient shorthand to specify an update transaction.

We continue with another example update transaction. Transaction ETX4 in Listing 10-5 updates the salary of certain employees. Note that state transition constraint STC5 (see Listing 8-8) requires that updates of salary must be logged in the HIST table structure; more precisely, the MSAL values *of the begin state* need to be logged. Listing 10-5 increases the salary of all trainers working in a department at location Denver by 10 percent.

Listing 10-5. *Transaction ETX4(dbs)*

```
FEa:  dbs↓{SREP,MEMP,TERM,DEPT,GRD,CRS,OFFR,REG}
          ∪
      { (HIST; dbs(HIST)
                  ∪
              { { (EMPNO; e(EMPNO)  )
                 ,(UNTIL; sysdate   )
                 ,(DEPTNO;e(DEPTNO) )
                 ,(MSAL;  e(MSAL)   ) }
                | e∈dbs(EMP)⊗dbs(DEPT) ∧ e(JOB) = 'TRAINER' ∧ e(LOC) = 'DENVER' }
      ) }
          ∪
      { (EMP; { e | e∈dbs(EMP) ∧ ¬ (e(JOB) = 'TRAINER' ∧
                              ↵{ d(LOC) | d∈dbs(DEPT) ∧
                                            d(DEPTNO) = e(DEPTNO) }
                          = 'DENVER') }
                  ∪
              { e↓{EMPNO,ENAME,BORN,JOB,HIRED,SGRADE,USERNAME,DEPTNO}
                ∪ { (MSAL; 1.1 * e(MSAL)) }
                | e∈dbs(EMP) ∧ e(JOB) = 'TRAINER' ∧
                              ↵{ d(LOC) | d∈dbs(DEPT) ∧ d(DEPTNO) = e(DEPTNO) }
                          = 'DENVER' }
      ) }
SEI:  insert into HIST(EMPNO,UNTIL,DEPTNO,MSAL)
      (select e.EMPNO, sysdate, e.DEPTNO, e.MSAL
       from EMP e
       where e.job ='TRAINER'
         and 'DENVER' = (select d.LOC
                         from DEPT d
                         where d.DEPTNO = e.DEPTNO));
      update EMP e
      set e.MSAL = 1.1 * e.MSAL
      where e.job ='TRAINER'
         and 'DENVER' = (select d.LOC
                         from DEPT d
                         where d.DEPTNO = e.DEPTNO)
SEII: update EMP e
      set e.MSAL = 1.1 * e.MSAL
      where e.job ='TRAINER'
```

```
     and 'DENVER' = (select d.LOC
                       from DEPT d
                       where d.DEPTNO = e.DEPTNO);
   insert into HIST(EMPNO,UNTIL,DEPTNO,MSAL)
   (select e.EMPNO, sysdate, e.DEPTNO, e.MSAL / 1.1
    from EMP e
    where e.job ='TRAINER'
      and 'DENVER' = (select d.LOC
                        from DEPT d
                        where d.DEPTNO = e.DEPTNO))
```

Specification FEa for transaction ETX4 assigns new values to both the HIST and EMP table structures, at the same time. It inserts into HIST the results of a query based on a join between EMP and DEPT, thereby logging, as required by constraint STC5, the current MSAL and DEPTNO values of the tuples that are about to be updated (loosely speaking). It also updates EMP in the requested way. The specifications of these tables (the "new" HIST table and the "new" EMP table) both refer to dbs, the begin state of the transaction.

In SQL, you cannot add rows to one table, and change rows of another table, using one statement. You are required to specify (separately) an INSERT statement and an UPDATE statement, *and choose an order* in which these two statements are to be serially executed. We have indicated the serial execution in SEI and SEII by separating the two DML statements with a semicolon.

Expressions SEI and SEII differ in the chosen order of the two statements. An SQL DBMS will provide an intermediate database state that already reflects the modifications made by the first DML statement to the second DML statement. This statement (and subqueries embedded within it) will "see" this intermediate database state.

■**Note** This is often the default behavior of an SQL DBMS. We'll have more to say on these intermediate database states in Chapter 11.

This *side effect* doesn't occur in our formalism; FEa references the begin state only. This side effect is why, in SEII, the subquery retrieving the tuples that need to be logged (inserted) into the HIST table structure needs to perform a *division* by 1.1; it sees the modifications (increased salaries) resulting from the UPDATE statement that executed first.

Let's take a look at another update transaction. Listing 10-6 specifies the transaction of canceling a scheduled offering. Note that static constraint PODC6 ("Canceled offerings cannot have registrations;" see Listing 7-43) requires that all registrations for the offering (if any) must be deleted. Listing 10-6 cancels the offering for course J2EE that starts on February 14, 2007.

Listing 10-6. *Transaction ETX5(dbs)*

```
FEa:   dbs↓{SREP,MEMP,TERM,DEPT,GRD,CRS,EMP,HIST}
         ∪
       { (REG; { r | r∈dbs(REG) ∧ (r(COURSE) ≠ 'J2EE' ∨ r(STARTS) ≠ '14-feb-2007') }
       ) }
```

∪
{ (OFFR; { o | o∈dbs(OFFR) ∧ ¬ (o(COURSE) = 'J2EE' ∧
                                           o(STARTS) = '14-feb-2007') }

                    ∪
              { o↓{COURSE,STARTS,MAXCAP,TRAINER,LOC}
                 ∪ { (STATUS; 'CANC') }
                 | o∈dbs(OFFR) ∧ o(COURSE) = 'J2EE' ∧ o(STARTS) = '14-feb-2007' }
) }

SEI: delete from REG r
         where r.COURSE = 'J2EE'
           and r.STARTS = '14-feb-2007';
         update OFFR o
         set o.STATUS = 'CANC'
         where o.COURSE = 'J2EE'
           and o.STARTS = '14-feb-2007'
SEII: update OFFR o
         set o.STATUS = 'CANC'
         where o.COURSE = 'J2EE'
           and o.STARTS = '14-feb-2007';
         delete from REG r
         where r.COURSE = 'J2EE'
           and r.STARTS = '14-feb-2007'

Formal expression FEa should be straightforward by now; it specifies the deletion of zero or more registrations and an update of a single offering. SQL expressions SEI and SEII again only differ in the order of execution of the required two DML statements to implement this transaction in an SQL DBMS.

In contrast with ETX4, one of the alternative orders of execution has a prominent disadvantage. SEII creates an intermediate database state that potentially violates a static constraint. However, the second DML statement will always correct the violation.

Suppose the offering of the J2EE course on Valentine's Day already had at least one registration. Then, the first DML statement—setting the status of the offering to canceled—will create a database state that violates constraint PODC6. The second DML statement—the deletion of corresponding registrations—will repair this; it modifies the intermediate database state into one that conforms to PODC6 (it "fixes the violation").

This state of affairs in alternative SEII is very risky. If the intermediate database state (that violates a constraint) is queried by other application code, executing within the *same* transaction, then results of these queries might be incorrect. Or, maybe even worse, subqueries inside the second DML statement can produce false results.

Note We assume here that application code executing within *other* transactions can never see these intermediate database states. This is indeed the case in Oracle's SQL DBMS (we'll come back to this in Chapter 11 when we discuss the transaction isolation mode offered by Oracle).

For instance, say that you want to query the number of scheduled or confirmed offerings that have at least one registration. Let's call this query EXQ11. Here is a formal specification for EXQ11:

$$EXQ11(dbs) = \#\{\ o\ |\ o \in dbs(OFFR) \land o(STATUS) \in \{\text{'SCHD'},\text{'CONF'}\} \land$$
$$(\exists r \in dbs(REG): r{\downarrow}\{COURSE,STARTS\} = o{\downarrow}\{COURSE,STARTS\})\ \}$$

In SQL this query might look like this:

```
select count(*)
from OFFR o
where o.STATUS in ('SCHD','CONF')
  and exists (select r.*
              from REG r
              where r.COURSE = o.COURSE
                and r.STARTS = o.STARTS)
```

The application developer might have been very smart and semantically optimized the query into the following:

$$EXQ11(dbs) = \#\{\ r{\downarrow}\{COURSE,STARTS\}\ |\ r \in dbs(REG)\ \}$$

This translates to the following query in SQL:

```
select count(*)
from (select distinct r.COURSE, r.STARTS
      from REG r)
```

Here the developer has used constraint PODC6, which implies that if there is a registration for some offering, then this offering cannot have status canceled. So, by counting distinct (offering) foreign key values in REG, you are effectively counting offerings that have at least one registration and have status scheduled or confirmed.

If this semantically rewritten query would execute in the middle of SEII's version of transaction ETX5, then obviously the result would be one too many; it also counts the canceled offering whose registrations are about to be—but haven't been yet—deleted.

We'll have more to say about this phenomenon in Chapter 11.

Let's give two more examples of transactions. Listing 10-7 defines an update transaction that involves subqueries to determine new attribute values. Listing 10-7 updates the commission of sales reps. For every sales rep, increase the commission by 2 percent of the average monthly salaries of all sales reps (including the one being updated) that work in the same department as the one being updated.

Listing 10-7. *Transaction ETX6(dbs)*

```
FEa:   dbs↓{MEMP,TERM,DEPT,GRD,REG,OFFR,CRS,EMP,HIST}
         ∪
       { (SREP; { s↓{EMPNO,TARGET}
                   ∪ { (COMM; 1.02 *
                             (AVG e1∈{ e | e∈dbs(EMP) ∧
                                           e(DEPTNO)∈{ e2(DEPTNO) | e2∈dbs(EMP) ∧
                                               e2(EMPNO) = s(EMPNO) } ∧
```

```
                                                e(JOB) = 'SALESREP' }
                               : e1(MSAL))
                    ) }
                 | s∈dbs(SREP) }
        ) }
SEI:  update SREP s
      set COMM = (select 1.02 * avg(e1.MSAL)
                    from EMP e1
                    where e1.DEPTNO = (select e2.DEPTNO
                                        from EMP e2
                                        where e2.EMPNO = s.EMPNO)
                      and e1.JOB = 'SALESREP')
```

Note that, in contrast with prior update transaction examples, this is an unrestricted update; all rows of SREP are modified.

For your convenience, here is the structure of the AVG operator as we have formally defined it in Chapter 5:

```
(AVG x∈S: f(x))
```

For every element x that can be chosen from set S, the average operator evaluates expression f(x) and computes the average of all such evaluations. In expression FEa, this operator is used as follows:

```
(AVG e1∈{ all salesreps working in same department as salesrep s(EMPNO) }
  : e1(MSAL))
```

As you can see in expression SEI, SQL allows you to specify subqueries within the set clause of an UPDATE statement. However, note that in these cases, the subquery should always retrieve exactly one row with just one column.

Listing 10-8 defines a DELETE transaction; salary grades that are currently not "used" are deleted from GRD. The listing deletes salary grades that have no employee assigned to them.

Listing 10-8. *Transaction ETX7(dbs)*

```
FEa:  dbs↓{SREP,MEMP,TERM,DEPT,REG,OFFR,CRS,EMP,HIST}
      ∪
      { (GRD; { g | g∈dbs(GRD) ∧ ¬(∃e∈dbs(EMP): e(SGRADE) = g(GRADE) } ) }
SEI:  delete from GRD g
      where not exists (select e.*
                         from EMP e
                         where e.SGRADE = g.GRADE)
```

Despite the "not exists" restriction, transaction ETX7 is still likely to fail, given the last table constraint specified in the definition of table universe tab_GRD (see Listing 7-31). In fact, it would only successfully execute when either the lowest (and zero or more of its direct successors), or the highest (and zero or more of its direct predecessors) salary grades are the only ones that are deleted. In all other cases, the table constraint would be violated and thus the transaction rolled back.

There is an exercise at the end of this chapter for you to specify an UPDATE statement that fixes such a violation.

Chapter Summary

This section provides a summary of this chapter, formatted as a bulleted list. You can use it to check your understanding of the various concepts introduced in this chapter before continuing with the exercises in the next section.

- You can formally specify a transaction as a function over a database universe. For every database state, this function returns another database state that reflects the modifications intended by the transaction.

- You can specify this function using the set theory and logic introduced in Part 1 in conjunction with the various table operators introduced in Part 2.

- Transactions start out in a valid database state and they should always end up in a valid database state; they must leave the database in a state that conforms to all constraints.

- Every transaction is in fact a transaction *attempt*. The DBMS should ensure that a transaction is rolled back when the resulting database state does not conform to all static constraints, or when the state transition is not covered by the state transition universe.

- In SQL a transaction is implemented as one or more data manipulation language (DML) statements that execute serially, one after the other, in an order determined by you.

- You cannot choose the order of these DML statements arbitrarily. Subsequent DML statements query a modified (intermediate) database state; the modifications of prior DML statements executed in the transaction are made visible to them by the SQL DBMS.

- Sometimes the intermediate database state is in violation of one or more data integrity constraints. Such a situation is undesirable, because queries executed against such a database state might deliver wrong results.

- Semantically optimized (sub) queries run a particularly high risk of producing false results in these circumstances.

Exercises

1. List all involved data integrity constraints for transaction ETX1. Also discuss the properties that the begin state should have for transaction ETX1 to execute successfully.

2. Transaction ETX2 might violate constraint PODC4; if the removal of a registration for student 3124 brings the number of registrations for a *confirmed* offering below six, then this constraint is violated. Amend the specification (both formal and SQL) for ETX2, such that as many as possible registrations for student 3124 are deleted, without violating constraint PODC4.

3. Determine the static data integrity constraints that might get violated by the SQL UPDATE statement of transaction ETX4.

4. Suppose transaction ETX7 creates a database state that indeed violates the discussed table constraint. Choose a strategy to fix this by updating the remaining salary grades. Formally specify your strategy and supply an SQL UPDATE statement for it.

5. Specify, both formally and with SQL, the following transaction: increase the monthly salary of all administrators working in department 40 by 5 percent. If the update requires the modification of the salary grade, then modify the salary grade too.

6. Specify, both formally and with SQL, the following transaction: remove all data of employees who have been terminated more than five years ago. What issues with regards to constraints will this transaction encounter?

The Implementation

La pratica deve basarsi su una valida teoria.
(Practice should always be based upon a sound knowledge of theory.)

Leonardo da Vinci (1452–1519)

CHAPTER 11

Implementing Database Designs in Oracle

Thus far this book's main focus has been on formally specifying a database design. Of course, you want to do more than just specify a database design; you usually would like to *implement* it using some DBMS. In this chapter we turn our attention towards implementing a database design.

Given the background of both authors, this chapter focuses specifically on implementing a database design in Oracle's SQL DBMS. We'll assume you're familiar with the PL/SQL language—Oracle's procedural programming language. We assume concepts such as database triggers, packages, procedures, and functions are known concepts.

Note We refer you to the standard Oracle documentation available on the Internet (http://tahiti. oracle.com) if you are unfamiliar with any of the PL/SQL concepts that you'll encounter in this chapter.

This will be a less formal chapter. We'll use SQL terminology (such as *row* and *column*) when referring to SQL constructs. We'll still use formal terminology when referring to the formal concepts introduced in this book.

The first few sections (through the section "Implementing Data Integrity Code") establish some concepts with regards to implementing business applications on top of a database. You'll also see that three distinctly different strategies exist to implement data integrity constraints.

Sections then follow that deal with implementing table structures, attribute constraints, and tuple constraints (through the section "Implementing Tuple Constraints").

The section "Table Constraint Implementation Issues" is a rather large section. It introduces the challenges that you're faced with when implementing multi-tuple constraints (that is, table or database constraints). A big chunk of this section will explore various constraint validation execution models. These execution models range from rather inefficient ones to more sophisticated (efficient) ones.

The sections "Implementing Table Constraints" and "Implementing Database Constraints" cover the implementation of table and database constraints, respectively, using one of the execution models introduced in the section "Table Constraint Implementation Issues." This is followed by an exploration of the implementation of transition constraints (the section "Implementing Transition Constraints").

The section "Bringing Deferred Checking into the Picture" deals with deferring the validation of constraints—a nasty phenomenon that cannot be avoided given that you implement a database design in an SQL DBMS.

At the end of this chapter we introduce you to the RuleGen framework: a framework that can help you implement data integrity constraints in Oracle's SQL DBMS, and that applies many of the concepts explained throughout this chapter.

This chapter does not have an "Exercises" section.

If you're familiar with a different SQL DBMS, then most of the concepts discussed in this chapter will probably also apply. We can't be sure though, given our background. The discussion that involves serializing transactions is likely Oracle specific. Of course, the actual code examples will have to be done differently given another SQL DBMS.

Introduction

Thus far this book's main focus has been to show you how a database design can be formally specified. To that end, we've introduced you to a bit of set theory and a bit of logic. Set theory and logic are the required mathematical tools that enable you to deal with professionally, talk about, manage, and document a database design. Also, as you have seen, a database design is much more than just table structures; the data integrity constraints are by far the most important part of a database design.

Of course, you want to do more than just *specify* a database design; you usually would like to *implement* it using some DBMS, and build *business applications* on top of it.

Unfortunately there are no true relational DBMSes available to us; we are forced to use an SQL DBMS to implement a database design. Implementing a database design in an SQL DBMS, as you'll see in the course of this chapter, poses quite a few challenges—not so much in the area of implementing the table structures, but mainly in the area of implementing the involved data integrity constraints.

As you'll see in the course of this chapter, SQL provides us with constructs to state data integrity constraints declaratively; however, not all of these are supported by SQL DBMSes available today. Most notably, the CREATE ASSERTION command—which has been in the official standard of SQL since 1992—is not supported in most SQL DBMSes (including Oracle's).

Before we start investigating these constraint implementation challenges, we'll first broaden our scope by investigating the general software architecture of a *business application*, or, as we prefer to call such an application from here on, a *window-on-data application*. Once we've established this architecture, we'll then, within the context of that architecture, discuss the challenges of implementing a database design.

Note This chapter will be quite different from the previous ones. It contains far less mathematics, although, as you will see, mathematics can still be applied when implementing a database design. We think that this chapter adds value to this book, because in our experience, the challenges investigated in this chapter are often overlooked.

Window-on-Data Applications

A window-on-data (WoD) application is—well, just as it says—an application that provides the user with windows on data. In a WoD application, users navigate through various windows of the application (browser pages, nowadays). Every page in the application either

- Enables the user to compose a data retrieval request, execute it, and then have the retrieved data displayed in the window, or

- Offers the user the possibility of composing a transaction using already retrieved—or newly entered—data, and then execute it.

Because these applications are all about querying and manipulating data, you should spend a fair amount of effort on designing and implementing the underlying table structures and involved integrity constraints necessary to support the application. The database design constitutes the underlying foundation of a WoD application; the quality of a WoD application can only be as good as the quality of the underlying database design.

■**Note** Here actually lay a main motivation for us to start writing this book. The current state of our industry is pretty bad when it comes to focusing on database design capabilities within an IT project. Few IT professionals nowadays are educated in the foundations of the relational model of data. Often, database designs are created that inevitably will cause the business application to not perform well, and/or be difficult to maintain. As mentioned earlier, discussing the quality of database designs is not within the scope of this book (it justifies at least another book in itself). We chose to offer you first the necessary tools to enable you to start dealing with database designs in a clear and professional way.

So, in short, a WoD application is all about managing business data. Needless to say, by far the majority of all business applications built on top of a database are WoD applications. This justifies taking a closer look at the general software architecture of this type of application.

In the next section we'll introduce you to a classification scheme for the application code of a WoD application. Later on, when we discuss three implementation strategies for the data integrity constraints of a database design, you'll see that we refer to this code classification scheme.

Classifying Window-on-Data Application Code

In this section, we'll introduce you to a high-level code classification scheme that is at the core of every WoD application. Before we do this, we need to introduce two terms we'll use in defining this classification scheme. These are *data retrieval code* and *data manipulation code*.

Data retrieval code is all code that queries data in the database. In our day-to-day practice these are typically the SQL queries (SELECT expressions) embedded within application code and interacting with the SQL DBMS.

Data manipulation code is all code that changes data in the database. These are the SQL data manipulation language (DML) statements (INSERT, UPDATE, or DELETE) embedded within application code that maintain data in the database.

■Note We'll refer to these three types of DML statements (INSERT, UPDATE, or DELETE) jointly as *update* statements.

Having introduced these two terms, we can now introduce the code classification scheme. All code of a WoD application can be classified into one of the following three code classes:

- Business logic code

- Data integrity code

- User interface code

The following three sections will discuss what we mean by the preceding three code classes.

Business Logic Code (BL Code)

Business logic code can be subdivided into two subclasses: first, code that *composes and executes queries*, and second, code that *composes and executes transactions*.

- *Query composing and executing code*: This is procedural code holding only embedded data retrieval code (that is, query expressions). This code is responsible for composing the actual SQL queries, or conditionally determining which SQL queries should be executed. This code also initiates the execution of these queries and processes the rows returned by the SQL DBMS. We'll refer to this subclass as *read BL code* (*rBL code* for short).

- *Transaction composing and executing code*: This is procedural code holding embedded data manipulation code (that is, SQL DML statements). This code is responsible for composing update statements, or conditionally determining which update statements should be executed. This code also initiates the execution of these statements. Depending upon the return code(s) given by the SQL DBMS, this code might also execute the commit or rollback processing for the transaction. Note that data retrieval code will often be part of (the procedural code of) transaction composition. We'll refer to this class as *write BL code* (*wBL code* for short).

Write BL code attempts to change the current database state. When it executes, the SQL DBMS should ensure that none of the data integrity constraints gets violated; the resulting database state should satisfy all data integrity constraints.

Often, you'll find code embedded within wBL code whose specific purpose is to verify that the transaction that gets executed won't result in a state that violates any of the involved data integrity constraints. We consider this constraint-verifying code not part of the wBL code class, but rather part of the *data integrity code* class discussed in the next section.

Data Integrity Code (DI Code)

Data integrity code is all *declarative* or *procedural* code that deals with verifying the continued validity of data integrity constraints. Whenever wBL code executes transactions, the data manipulation statements that get executed as part of such transactions can potentially violate data integrity constraints. If this is indeed the case, data integrity code will ensure that such a statement fails and that the changes it made are rolled back.

Note We deliberately consider DI code to be in a distinct class by itself and not part of the business logic code class. Most other books and articles dealing with *business logic* often remain fuzzy about whether DI code is considered part of business logic or not.

For the majority of the data integrity constraints—in fact, all but attribute and tuple constraints—DI code will have to execute data retrieval code (queries) to determine if a given data manipulation statement is allowed or not. For multi-tuple constraints, DI code will always need to execute queries (inspecting other involved rows) to verify that the resulting database state still satisfies all data integrity constraints.

For example, consider the "at most one president allowed" table constraint defined in Listing 7-26 (table universe tab_EMP). When a transaction attempts to insert a president, you should run a *constraint validation query* either *before* execution of the insert or *after* execution of the insert, to verify that the insert is allowed given this constraint.

If you decide to validate whether the constraint remains satisfied before the actual execution of the insert, you could execute the following constraint validation query:

```
select 'there is already a president'
from emp
where job='PRESIDENT'
  and rownum=1
```

If this query returns a row, then obviously the insert must not be allowed to proceed; inserting another president will clearly create a database state that violates this constraint.

In the other case—executing a query after the insert—you could run the following query:

```
select count(*)
from emp
where job='PRESIDENT'
```

If this query returns more than 1, then the constraint will be violated and the insert must be rolled back.

Ideally you would want that, given the *declaration* of all constraints, the DBMS automatically deduces and executes these constraint validation queries (alongside some conditional code either to refrain execution of a DML statement or to force a DML statement rollback). A DBMS that provides this service makes the task of the developer who codes business logic a lot easier.

Note If you're familiar with Oracle, you'll know that Oracle's SQL DBMS can perform this service only for a limited number of types of constraints.

You can subdivide the DI code class into five subclasses, one per type of constraint:

1. Code that verifies attribute constraints

2. Code that verifies tuple constraints

3. Code that verifies table constraints

4. Code that verifies database constraints

5. Code that verifies transition constraints

As you'll see shortly, you can state the required DI code for some constraints *declaratively* in an SQL DBMS (which is then responsible for maintaining the constraint). However, you need to develop the code for most of them manually; that is, you are responsible for the implementation. This means that you need to design and write *procedural code* to maintain the constraint yourself.

Note There are two high-level implementation strategies for creating DI code procedurally; either you make use of *database triggers*, or you embed DI code within wBL code. We'll discuss the former one in more detail in the remainder of this chapter.

User Interface Code (UI Code)

UI code is code that determines the look and feel of a business application. It is responsible for the front end of the business application that the user deals with when using the application. UI code either

- Creates user interface for the user—the *look* of the business application—and typically displays retrieved data within the user interface, or

- Responds to user interface events initiated by the user and then modifies the user interface—the *feel* of the business application.

Creating and/or modifying the user interface always requires embedded calls to business logic code. This BL code will return the data to the UI code for display, and/or will change data as part of the transaction requested by the user. Depending upon the results of these embedded BL code calls, UI code will modify the user interface accordingly.

As a summary, Figure 11-1 illustrates the correlation between the different WoD application code classes that we've introduced in this section.

Note In Figure 11-1, the reason why the DI code box is deliberately drawn *outside* the DBMS box is because application developers who develop wBL code need to implement the majority of DI code procedurally (as will become obvious in the course of this chapter).

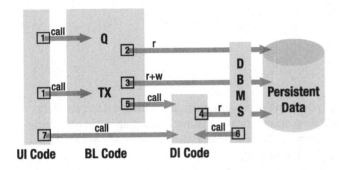

Figure 11-1. *WoD application code classes*

This figure illustrates the following relations between the code classes (note that the numbers in this list refer to the numbers inside Figure 11-1):

1. UI code holds calls to rBL code (queries) or wBL code (transactions).

2. rBL code holds embedded data retrieval code that reads data from the database.

3. wBL code holds embedded data manipulation code that writes to the database. wBL code often also holds embedded queries reading the database.

4. DI code requires the execution data retrieval code.

5. DI code is typically called from wBL code.

6. DI code can also be called by the DBMS via *database triggers* (see the next section), which fire as a result of the execution of DML statements originating from wBL code.

7. Sometimes you'll see that UI code calls DI code directly; this is often done to create a responsive, more user-friendly user interface.

Implementing Data Integrity Code

In this section you'll find a brief exploration of the aforementioned strategies for implementing DI code in Oracle's SQL DBMS. We'll also discuss a few related topics.

Alternative Implementation Strategies

As mentioned in the previous section, when transactions execute, you should run DI code to verify that all data integrity constraints remain satisfied. There are three different strategies to ensure execution of DI code when a WoD application attempts to execute a transaction:

- Declarative

- Triggered procedural

- Embedded procedural

Declarative

In the *declarative* strategy, you simply declare the constraints that are involved in your database design to the DBMS. The DBMS then automatically ensures—hopefully in an efficient manner—that offending DML statements will be rolled back when they try to create a database state that violates any of the declared constraints.

Note that to be able to declare constraints to the DBMS, you first require (some form of) a formal specification of these constraints that states exactly *what* the constraint is. The strength of the declarative strategy is that you just tell the DBMS *what* the constraint is; that is, there is no need for you to write any DI code. In essence, the declaration of the constraint to the DBMS constitutes the DI code.

Once you've declared a constraint, the DBMS then has the challenge of computing *how* best to check the constraint in an efficient manner; it is tasked to generate (hopefully) *efficient* DI code and ensure this code is automatically executed at the appropriate times when transactions are processed.

■**Note** You'll see in the course of this chapter that the word "efficient" in the preceding sentence is imperative.

Oracle's SQL DBMS allows you to specify certain constraints declaratively either as part of the create table command, or separately (after the table has already been created) through the alter table add constraint command.

Starting from the section "Implementing Attribute Constraints" onwards, you'll find a full treatment of constraints that you can specify declaratively. As a preview, Listing 11-1 contains an example of adding a constraint to an already created table. It shows the SQL syntax for declaring the second table constraint in Listing 7-26 (the table universe for EMP) stating that {USERNAME} is a key.

Listing 11-1. *Declaring a Key Using SQL*

```
alter table EMP add constraint EMP_K2 unique (USERNAME);
```

Through the preceding alter table SQL statement, you declare {USERNAME} as a key for the EMP table structure. This command allows you to give the constraint a name (in the preceding case it is named EMP_K2). You'll need to use this name if you want to drop the constraint.

▪Note If you don't supply a name, the DBMS will generate one for you.

We've chosen to use only the `alter table add constraint` statement in our examples throughout this chapter, so that we can gradually build the implementation of the database design. You could have declared every declaratively added constraint instead as part of the `create table` statement. You can find the SQL expressions that declare constraints of the UEX database design as part of the `create table` statement online at http://www.rulegen.com/am4dp.

Triggered Procedural

In the *triggered procedural* strategy, you don't declare the constraint (the *what*) to the DBMS. Instead, you are tasked to write procedural DI code (the *how*) yourself. And, in conjunction, you also tell the DBMS *when* to execute your DI code by creating *triggers* that call your DI code. You can view a trigger as a piece of procedural code that the DBMS will automatically execute when certain events occur. Let's explain this a bit more.

▪Note Triggers can serve many purposes. Executing DI code to enforce data integrity is only one such purpose (and the one we'll be focusing on in this chapter).

Every trigger is associated with a table structure and will automatically be executed (*fired*) by the DBMS whenever a transaction executes a DML statement against that table structure. The trigger code—which executes as part of the same transaction—can then check whether the new database state still satisfies all constraints.

Oracle's SQL DBMS offers the 12 different types of triggers for each table structure, which are defined in the SQL standard:

- Four *insert triggers*: One that fires before an INSERT statement starts executing (referred to as the *before statement insert trigger*), one that fires right before an actual row is inserted (*before row insert trigger*), one that fires after a row has been inserted (*after row insert trigger*), and finally one that fires after completion of an INSERT statement (*after statement insert trigger*).

- Four *update triggers*: Similar to the insert triggers, there are four types of update triggers—before statement, before row, after row, and after statement.

- Four *delete triggers*: The same four types.

The statement triggers (before and after) will only fire once per (triggering) DML statement. The row triggers will fire as many times as there are rows affected by the DML statement. For instance, an UPDATE statement that increases the monthly salary of all employees in the employee table (say there are currently ten) will cause the before and after row update triggers each to fire ten times. The before and after statement update triggers will only fire once each in this case.

Row-level triggers are able to refer to the column values of the rows that are affected by the triggering DML statement. Before and after row insert triggers can inspect all column values of the new rows (the ones that are inserted). Before and after row delete triggers can inspect all columns of the old rows (the ones that are deleted). Before and after row update triggers can inspect both all column values of the old rows and all column values of the new rows.

■**Note** An UPDATE statement replaces one set of rows (the "old" ones) by another (the "new" ones).

If you aren't already familiar with the various types of table triggers available in Oracle, we refer you to the Oracle manuals for more information on this. In the rest of this chapter, we assume you are familiar with them.

There isn't an easy way for statement-level triggers to reference the rows that are affected by the triggering DML statement; they either see the (old) table as it existed before the start of the DML statement (before trigger), or the resulting (new) table as it exists after completion of the DML statement (after trigger). You can enable statement-level triggers to see the affected rows, but it requires some sophisticated coding on your part. Later on in this chapter, you'll discover that this is actually a requirement in order to be able to develop *efficient* DI code in the triggered procedural strategy. We'll then demonstrate how this can be done.

To illustrate the use of a trigger as a means to implement DI code, here is an example. Let's take a look at implementing a trigger for the "at most one president allowed" table constraint of the EMP table structure. Listing 11-2 shows the SQL syntax for implementing such a trigger that is attached to the EMP table structure.

Listing 11-2. *Attaching a Trigger to a Table Using SQL*

```
create trigger EMP_AIUS
after insert or update on EMP
declare pl_num_presidents number;
begin
  --
  select count(*) into pl_num_presidents
  from EMP
  where job='PRESIDENT';
  --
  if pl_num_presidents > 1
  then
    raise_application_error(-20999,'Not allowed to have more than one president.');
  end if;
  --
end;
/
```

The way this trigger is created (in the second line: after insert or update) ensures that the DBMS executes the procedural code of the trigger whenever BL code inserts or updates an employee (the *when* of this constraint). The trigger will fire immediately after execution of such an insert or update. Therefore, the embedded code will see a database state that reflects the changes made by the insert or update.

The body of the trigger (that is, the procedural code between declare and end), shown in Listing 11-2, represents the *how* of this constraint. First a query is executed to retrieve the number of presidents in the EMP table. Then, if this number is more than one, the trigger generates an error by calling raise_application_error. This call raises an SQL exception, which in turn forces the triggering DML statement to fail and the changes it made to be undone. In this case, the DBMS will perform this DML statement rollback for you, contrary to the embedded procedural strategy that's described hereafter.

Note that it would be inefficient to have this trigger also fire for DELETE statements. This particular constraint cannot be violated when a transaction deletes rows from the EMP table structure; if there is at most one president before deleting a row from EMP, then there will still be at most one president after deletion of the row.

In the triggered procedural strategy, you—the DI code developer—need to think about not only when DI code *should be run*, but also when it would be *unnecessary to run* DI code. This is part of ensuring that DI code is efficiently implemented. Of course, in the declarative strategy you needn't think about either of these things.

■**Note** The trigger in Listing 11-2 now fires for every type of INSERT and every type of UPDATE statement executed against the EMP table structure. This is still rather inefficient. For instance, if you insert a new clerk or update the monthly salary of some employee, the trigger really needn't be run. In both of these cases (similar to a DELETE statement, discussed earlier) the triggering DML statement can never violate the constraint.

Apart from being suboptimal in terms of efficiency, we need to address a more serious issue about the trigger in Listing 11-2: it is not complete when it comes to implementing the given constraint. There are still issues, which we will address in more detail in the section "Table Constraint Implementation Issues," in the area of transactions executing concurrently.

Embedded Procedural

Finally, in the *embedded procedural* strategy to implement DI code, you again need to write the DI code (the *how*) yourself. Instead of creating triggers that call your DI code, you now embed the DI code into the wBL code modules that hold the DML statements that might cause constraints to be violated. DI code then executes as part of the execution of wBL code.

This is probably by far the most used procedural strategy for implementing DI code in WoD applications.

■**Note** In this case, "most used" strategy certainly doesn't imply "best" strategy.

Let's take a look at an example. Assume the application supplies a page where the user can enter data for a new employee to be inserted. The user supplies attributes ENAME, BORN, JOB, and DEPTNO. The BL code determines the other employee attributes (EMPNO, SGRADE, MSAL, HIRED, and USERNAME) according to rules that were agreed upon with the users. Listing 11-3 lists the procedure the UI code calls to insert a new employee. It holds BL code first to determine the other employee attributes, and then executes an INSERT statement. Immediately following this INSERT statement, the BL code runs embedded DI code to ensure the "at most one president" constraint remains satisfied.

Listing 11-3. *Embedding DI Code in wBL Code*

```
create procedure p_new_employee
(p_ename  in varchar
,p_born   in date
,p_job    in varchar
,p_deptno in number) as
--
pl_sgrade   number;
pl_msal     number;
pl_hired    date;
pl_username varchar(15);
--
begin
  -- Determine monthly start salary.
  select grade, llimit into pl_sgrade, pl_msal
  from grd
  where grade = case p_job
                  when 'ADMIN'     then 1
                  when 'TRAINER'   then 3
                  when 'SALESREP'  then 5
                  when 'MANAGER'   then 7
                  when 'PRESIDENT' then 9;
  -- Determine date hired.
  pl_hired := trunc(sysdate);
  -- Determine username.
  pl_username := upper(substr(p_ename,1,8));
  -- Now insert the new employee row. Set a transaction savepoint first.
  savepoint sp_pre_insert;
  -- Use EMP_SEQ sequence to generate a key.
  insert into emp(empno,ename,job,born,hired,sgrade,msal,username,deptno)
  values(emp_seq.nextval,p_ename,p_job,p_born,pl_hired,pl_sgrade
       ,pl_msal,pl_username,p_deptno);
  -- Verify 'at most one president' constraint.
  if p_job = 'PRESIDENT'
  then
    declare pl_num_presidents number;
    begin
      --
```

```
      select count(*) into pl_num_presidents
      from EMP
      where job='PRESIDENT';
      --
      if pl_num_presidents > 1
      then
        -- Constraint is violated, need to rollback the insert.
        rollback to sp_pre_insert;
        raise_application_error(-20999,
                          'Not allowed to have more than one president.');
      end if;
    end;
  end if;
end;
```

The embedded DI code following the INSERT statement very much resembles the code in the body of the trigger listed in Listing 11-2. It is a more efficient implementation than the INSERT statement trigger; the DI code is executed only when a president is inserted.

Also note that in this procedural strategy—in contrast to the triggered procedural strategy— it is up to the developer to force a statement rollback explicitly. In the preceding code, this is done by setting a transaction savepoint just prior to executing the INSERT statement, and performing a rollback to that savepoint whenever the constraint is found to be violated.

There is another more serious drawback of the embedded procedural strategy. You now have to replicate DI code for a given constraint into every wBL code module that holds DML statements that might potentially violate the constraint. In this strategy, all necessary DI code for a given constraint is typically scattered across various wBL code modules. Often, when wBL code of a WoD application needs to be changed, you'll forget to change (add or remove) the necessary DI code. Even more so, when an actual constraint of a database design needs to be changed, it is often difficult to locate all wBL code modules that hold embedded DI code for the constraint.

Note This drawback also applies in some extent to the triggered procedural strategy. The example trigger given in Listing 11-2 is actually shorthand for two triggers: an update trigger and an insert trigger. DI code for the constraint can be considered scattered across two triggers. In more complex cases of constraints, you'll need more triggers to implement the DI code; you could need as many as three times the number of table structures involved in the constraint (an insert, an update, and a delete trigger per involved table structure). However, with the triggered procedural strategy, this drawback is not as bad as it can get in a WoD application that was built using the embedded procedural strategy.

The embedded procedural strategy has the same issues in the area of transactions executing concurrently (we'll explain these in the section "Table Constraint Implementation Issues").

Order of Preference

It should not be a surprise that the declarative strategy is highly preferable to the two procedural strategies. Not only will a declaratively stated constraint free you of the burden of developing DI code, it will likely outperform any self-developed procedural implementation. Don't forget that it also frees you of the burden of maintaining this code during the WoD application's life cycle!

■**Note** This last remark assumes that the DBMS vendor has done its research with respect to designing and implementing an efficient *execution model* for DI code. In the section "Table Constraint Implementation Issues," we'll introduce you to various execution models, ranging from inefficient ones to more efficient ones.

However, as you're probably aware, you can state only a limited set of constraint types declaratively in Oracle's SQL DBMS. Note that this is not due to an inherent deficiency in the SQL standard, but rather due to the poor implementation of this language in an SQL DBMS. For implementing constraints that cannot be declared to the DBMS, we prefer to follow the triggered procedural strategy. Following are the main two reasons why we prefer the triggered over the embedded procedural strategy:

- Like declared constraints, the triggered procedural strategy cannot be subverted.

- The triggered procedural strategy is likely to create a more manageable code architecture; DI code isn't replicated in lots of BL code. DI code is fully detached from all BL code, and is therefore better manageable (the BL code itself, by the way, will be better manageable too).

■**Note** The second reason assumes that triggers will only hold DI code. Embedding BL code in triggers is generally considered a bad practice.

The embedded procedural strategy is the worst strategy of all; it can obviously be subverted, simply by using some other application (perhaps a general-purpose one supplied by the DBMS vendor) to update the database.

As you'll see starting from the section "Table Constraint Implementation Issues" and onwards, when we start dealing with table constraints and database constraints (that is, multi-tuple constraints), implementing efficient DI code for these constraints through triggers is far from being a trivial task.

Obviously, the type of effort involved in implementing different constraints within one class (attribute, tuple, table, database, transition) is the same. Also, the complexity involved in implementing DI code for constraints probably increases as the scope of data increases. The remainder of this chapter will offer guidelines for implementing the table structures of a database design and, in increasing scope order, for implementing the DI code for the involved constraints. Here is an overview of the remaining sections of this chapter:

- The section "Implementing Table Structures" deals with implementing the table structures in Oracle's SQL DBMS.

- The section "Implementing Attribute Constraints" discusses how to implement attribute constraints.

- The section "Implementing Tuple Constraints" discusses how to implement tuple constraints.

- The section "Table Constraint Implementation Issues" acts as a preface for the sections that follow it. In this section, we'll introduce you to various issues that come into play when developing triggers to implement DI code for multi-tuple constraints. This section will also elaborate on different execution models.

- The section "Implementing Table Constraints" discusses how you can state some table constraints declaratively, and how to design triggers for checking all other table constraints.

- The section "Implementing Database Constraints" discusses how you can state some database constraints declaratively, and how to design triggers for checking all other database constraints.

- The section "Implementing Transition Constraints" discusses an approach for implementing DI code for transition constraints.

- The section "Bringing Deferred Checking into the Picture" explains the need for deferring the execution of DI code for certain types of constraints.

- The section "The RuleGen Framework" introduces you to RuleGen, a framework that supports implementing DI code using the triggered procedural strategy, and that takes care of many of the issues discussed in this chapter.

Implementing Table Structures

Whenever you implement a database design in an SQL DBMS, you usually start with creating the table structures. Through the `create table` command, you implement the table structures of your database design within the SQL DBMS. In this chapter, we'll implement the UEX database design one on one. Specifically, we'll create an SQL table-per-table structure.

Note It is not the goal of this book to investigate *denormalization* (for improving performance) or other reasons that could give rise to deviation from the formally specified database design. Moreover, it's generally our personal experience that such one-on-one implementation usually provides excellent performance given the optimizer technology available in Oracle's current SQL DBMS.

Creating a table in an SQL DBMS involves the following:

- Choosing a name for the table structure (we've done this formally in the *database characterization*)

- Declaring names for the columns (we've done this formally in the *characterizations*)

- Declaring data types for the columns (also done in the *characterizations*)

As for the last bullet, unfortunately the support is rather immature for creating user-defined types—representing the attribute-value sets—that can be used in a create table statement. For instance, we cannot do the following:

```
-- Create a type to represent the value set for the EMPNO attribute.
-- Note this is not valid Oracle syntax.
create type empno_type under number(4,0) check(member > 999);
/
-- Create a type to represent the enumeration value set for the JOB attribute.
-- Invalid syntax.
create type job_type under varchar(9)
          check(member in ('ADMIN','TRAINER','SALESREP','MANAGER','PRESIDENT'));
/
-- Now use the empno_type and job_type types in the create table statement.
create table EMP
(empno    empno_type not null
,job      job_type    not null
,...);
```

In all practicality, we're forced to use built-in data types provided by the SQL DBMS. In the case of Oracle, the most commonly used built-in data types are varchar, number, and date. These will suffice for our example database design.

In the next section ("Implementing Attribute Constraints"), you'll see that with the use of the SQL alter table add constraint statement, you can still in effect implement the attribute-value sets. The column data types declared in the create table statements act as supersets of the attribute-value sets, and by adding constraints you can narrow down those supersets to exactly the attribute-value sets that were specified in the characterizations for the table structures.

Listings 11-4 through 11-13 show the create table statements for the UEX example database design.

Listing 11-4. *Create Table for GRD Table Structure*

```
create table  grd
( grade     number(2,0)   not null
, llimit    number(7,2)   not null
, ulimit    number(7,2)   not null
, bonus     number(7,2)   not null);
```

■**Note** The not null alongside every column indicates that no NULLs are allowed in that column. In such cases, we say that the column is *mandatory*.

Listing 11-5. *Create Table for EMP Table Structure*

```
create table  emp
( empno       number(4,0)  not null
, ename       varchar(8)   not null
, job         varchar(9)   not null
, born        date         not null
, hired       date         not null
, sgrade      number(2,0)  not null
, msal        number(7,2)  not null
, username    varchar(15)  not null
, deptno      number(2,0)  not null);
```

Listing 11-6. *Create Table for SREP Table Structure*

```
create table  srep
( empno       number(4,0)  not null
, target      number(6,0)  not null
, comm        number(7,2)  not null);
```

Listing 11-7. *Create Table for MEMP Table Structure*

```
create table  memp
( empno       number(4,0)  not null
, mgr         number(4,0)  not null);
```

Listing 11-8. *Create Table for TERM Table Structure*

```
create table  term
( empno       number(4,0)  not null
, left        date         not null
, comments    varchar(60));
```

■**Note** In our example, the user doesn't always want to supply a value for COMMENTS when an employee has been terminated. Oracle doesn't allow an empty string in a mandatory column. To prevent the users from entering some random varchar value in these cases (for instance, a space), this column has been made *optional* (sometimes called *nullable*), meaning that NULLs are allowed to appear in this column.

Listing 11-9. *Create Table for HIST Table Structure*

```
create table  hist
( empno        number(4,0)  not null
, until        date         not null
, deptno       number(2,0)  not null
, msal         number(7,2)  not null);
```

Listing 11-10. *Create Table for DEPT Table Structure*

```
create table  dept
( deptno       number(2,0)  not null
, dname        varchar(12)  not null
, loc          varchar(14)  not null
, mgr          number(4,0)  not null);
```

Listing 11-11. *Create Table for CRS Table Structure*

```
create table  crs
( code         varchar(6)   not null
, descr        varchar(40)  not null
, cat          varchar(3)   not null
, dur          number(2,0)  not null);
```

Listing 11-12. *Create Table for OFFR Table Structure*

```
create table  offr
( course       varchar(6)   not null
, starts       date         not null
, status       varchar(4)   not null
, maxcap       number(2,0)  not null
, trainer      number(4,0)
, loc          varchar(14)  not null);
```

■**Note** For reasons we'll discuss in the section "Implementing Database Constraints," the TRAINER attribute has been defined as nullable; we'll use NULL instead of the special value -1 that was introduced in this attribute's attribute-value set.

Listing 11-13. *Create Table for REG Table Structure*

```
create table  reg
( stud         number(4,0)  not null
, course       varchar(6)   not null
, starts       date         not null
, eval         number(1,0)  not null);
```

In the relational model of data, all attributes in a database design are mandatory. Therefore, you can consider it a disappointment that in the SQL standard by default a column is nullable; SQL requires us to add not null explicitly alongside every column to make it mandatory.

The next section deals with the aforementioned "narrowing down" of the built-in data types that were used in the create table statements.

Implementing Attribute Constraints

We now revisit the matter with regards to the term *attribute constraints* (mentioned in the section "Classification Schema for Constraints" in Chapter 7).

Formally, a characterization just attaches attribute-value sets to attributes. Attaching an attribute-value set to an attribute can be considered an attribute constraint. However, in practice you implement database designs in SQL DBMSes that are notorious for their poor support of user-defined types. User-defined types would have been ideal for implementing attribute-value sets. However, as discussed in the section "Implementing Table Structures," you can't use them to do so. Instead, you must use an appropriate superset (some built-in data type, as shown in the previous section) as the attribute-value set of a given attribute. Luckily you can use declarative SQL check constraints to narrow down these supersets to exactly the attribute-value set that was specified in the characterizations. During implementation, we refer to these declarative check constraints as the attribute constraints of an attribute.

All attribute constraints can—and, given our preference in strategies, *should*—be stated as declarative check constraints. You can declare these constraints using the alter table add constraint statement.

Listing 11-14 shows the declaration of six check constraints that are required to declaratively implement the attribute-value sets for the EMP table structure as defined in the definition of chr_EMP in Listing 7-2. We'll discuss each of these after the listing.

Listing 11-14. *Attribute Constraints for EMP Table Structure*

```
alter table EMP add constraint emp_chk_empno check (empno > 999);
alter table EMP add constraint emp_chk_job
                            check (job in ('PRESIDENT','MANAGER','SALESREP'
                                          ,'TRAINER','ADMIN'  ));
alter table EMP add constraint emp_chk_brn   check (trunc(born) = born);
alter table EMP add constraint emp_chk_hrd   check (trunc(hired) = hired);
alter table EMP add constraint emp_chk_msal  check (msal > 0);
alter table EMP add constraint emp_chk_usrnm check (upper(username) = username);
```

As you can see from this listing, all check constraints are given a name. The name for the first one is emp_chk_empno. It narrows down the declared data type for the empno column, number(4,0), to just numbers consisting of four digits (greater than 999).

Once this constraint is declared and stored in the data dictionary of Oracle's SQL DBMS, the DBMS will run the necessary DI code whenever a new EMPNO value appears in EMP (through an INSERT statement), or an existing EMPNO value in EMP is changed (through an UPDATE statement). The DBMS will use the constraint name in the error message that you receive, informing you whenever an attempt is made to store an EMPNO value in EMP that does not satisfy this constraint.

Constraint emp_chk_job (the second one in the preceding listing) ensures that only the five listed values are allowed as a value for the JOB column.

Constraints emp_chk_brn and emp_chk_hrd ensure that a date value (which in the case of Oracle's SQL DBMS always holds a time component too) is only allowed as a value for the BORN or HIRED columns, if its time component is truncated (that is, set to 0:00 midnight).

Constraint emp_chk_msal ensures that only positive numbers—within the number(7,2) superset—are allowed as values for the MSAL column.

Finally, constraint emp_chk_usrnm ensures that values for the USERNAME column are always in uppercase.

Listings 11-15 through 11-23 supply the attribute constraints for the other table structures of the UEX database design.

Listing 11-15. *Attribute Constraints for GRD Table Structure*

```
alter table GRD add constraint grd_chk_grad check (grade > 0);
alter table GRD add constraint grd_chk_llim check (llimit > 0);
alter table GRD add constraint grd_chk_ulim check (ulimit > 0);
alter table GRD add constraint grd_chk_bon1 check (bonus > 0);
```

Listing 11-16. *Attribute Constraints for SREP Table Structure*

```
alter table SREP add constraint srp_chk_empno check (empno > 999);
alter table SREP add constraint srp_chk_targ  check (target > 9999);
alter table SREP add constraint srp_chk_comm  check (comm > 0);
```

Listing 11-17. *Attribute Constraints for MEMP Table Structure*

```
alter table MEMP add constraint mmp_chk_empno check (empno > 999);
alter table MEMP add constraint mmp_chk_mgr   check (mgr > 999);
```

Listing 11-18. *Attribute Constraints for TERM Table Structure*

```
alter table TERM add constraint trm_chk_empno check (empno > 999);
alter table TERM add constraint trm_chk_lft   check (trunc(left) = left);
```

Listing 11-19. *Attribute Constraints for HIST Table Structure*

```
alter table HIST add constraint hst_chk_eno  check (empno > 999);
alter table HIST add constraint hst_chk_unt  check (trunc(until) = until);
alter table HIST add constraint hst_chk_dno  check (deptno > 0);
alter table HIST add constraint hst_chk_msal check (msal > 0);
```

Listing 11-20. *Attribute Constraints for DEPT Table Structure*

```
alter table DEPT add constraint dep_chk_dno check (deptno > 0);
alter table DEPT add constraint dep_chk_dnm check (upper(dname) = dname);
alter table DEPT add constraint dep_chk_loc check (upper(loc) = loc);
alter table DEPT add constraint dep_chk_mgr check (mgr > 999);
```

Listing 11-21. *Attribute Constraints for CRS Table Structure*

```
alter table CRS add constraint reg_chk_code check (code = upper(code));
alter table CRS add constraint reg_chk_cat  check (cat in ('GEN','BLD','DSG'));
alter table CRS add constraint reg_chk_dur1 check (dur between 1 and 15);
```

Listing 11-22. *Attribute Constraints for OFFR Table Structure*

```
alter table OFFR add constraint ofr_chk_crse check (course = upper(course));
alter table OFFR add constraint ofr_chk_strs check (trunc(starts) = starts);
alter table OFFR add constraint ofr_chk_stat
                            check (status in ('SCHD','CONF','CANC'));
alter table OFFR add constraint ofr_chk_trnr check (trainer > 999)
alter table OFFR add constraint ofr_chk_mxcp check (maxcap between 6 and 99);
```

■**Note** You might be wondering how an SQL DBMS deals with constraint ofr_chk_trnr whenever it encounters NULLs in the TRAINER column. We'll discuss this at the end of this section.

Listing 11-23. *Attribute Constraints for REG Table Structure*

```
alter table REG add constraint reg_chk_stud  check (stud > 999);
alter table REG add constraint reg_chk_crse  check (course = upper(course));
alter table REG add constraint reg_chk_strs  check (trunc(starts) = starts);
alter table REG add constraint reg_chk_eval  check (eval between -1 and 5);
```

If a declarative check constraint evaluates to UNKNOWN, usually arising from the use of NULLs, then the SQL standard considers the constraint satisfied; the check evaluates to TRUE. Beware; you'll observe the opposite behavior in the PL/SQL programming language. Here a Boolean expression evaluating to unknown is handled as FALSE. To illustrate this, take a look at the following trigger definition; it is *not* equivalent to check constraint ofr_chk_trnr:

```
create trigger ofr_chk_trnr
after insert or update on OFFR
for each row
begin
  if not (:new.trainer > 999)
```

```
  then
    raise_application_error(-20999,'Value for trainer must be greater than 999.);
  end if;
end;
```

The declarative check constraint will allow a NULL in the TRAINER column, whereas the preceding trigger won't allow a NULL in the TRAINER column. You can fix this discrepancy by changing the fifth line in the preceding trigger definition into the following:

```
if not (:new.trainer > 999 or :new.trainer IS NULL)
```

The trigger is now equivalent to the declarative check constraint.

We continue by investigating how you can implement tuple constraints (the next level after attribute constraints) in Oracle's SQL DBMS.

Implementing Tuple Constraints

Before we deal with the implementation of tuple constraints, we need to confess something up front. The formal methodology that has been developed in this book is based on 2-valued logic (2VL). The science of 2VL is sound; we've explored propositions and predicates in Chapters 1 and 3 and developed some rewrite rules with it. However, in this chapter we'll make various statements about predicates that are expressed in SQL. As demonstrated by the preceding trigger and attribute constraint ofr_chk_trnr in Listing 11-22, due to the possible presence of NULLs SQL doesn't apply 2VL; instead it applies 3-valued logic (3VL). The most crucial assumption in 3VL is that, besides the two truth values TRUE and FALSE, a third value represents "possible" or UNKNOWN.

■**Note** 3VL is counterintuitive, as opposed to the classical 2VL. We won't provide an in-depth discussion of 3VL here; you can find a brief exploration of 3VL in Appendix D.

We admit up front that we're taking certain liberties in this chapter. By using NOT NULL on almost all columns in the SQL implementation of the example database design, we're in effect avoiding 3VL issues. Without the use of NOT NULL, various statements we're making about logical expressions in this chapter would be open to question.

As you saw in Chapter 1, conjunction, disjunction, and negation are *truth functionally complete*. Therefore, you can rewrite every formally specified tuple constraint into an equivalent specification that uses just the three connectives that are available in SQL.

Once transformed in such a way, all tuple constraints can—and therefore should—be stated declaratively as check constraints. You can use the alter table add constraint statement to declare them to the DBMS. Let's demonstrate this using the tuple constraints of the EMP table structure. For your convenience, we repeat the tuple universe definition tup_EMP here:

```
tup_EMP :=
{ e | e∈Π(chr_EMP) ∧
        /* We hire adult employees only */
        e(BORN) + 18 ≤ e(HIRED) ∧
        /* Presidents earn more than 120K */
        e(JOB) = 'PRESIDENT' ⇒ 12*e(MSAL) > 120000 ∧
        /* Administrators earn less than 5K */
        e(JOB) = 'ADMIN' ⇒ e(MSAL) < 5000 }
```

The preceding three tuple constraints can be stated as follows (see Listing 11-24).

Note The preceding three constraints are formally expressed in 2VL, but the three constraints expressed in SQL in Listing 11-24 are in 3VL. In this case, the constraints expressed in 3VL are equivalent to the formally expressed constraints only because we have carefully declared all involved columns to be mandatory (NOT NULL).

Listing 11-24. *Tuple Constraints for EMP Table Structure*

```
alter table EMP add constraint emp_chk_adlt
                    check ((born + interval '18' year) <= hired);
alter table EMP add constraint emp_chk_dsal
                    check ((job <> 'PRESIDENT') or (msal > 10000));
alter table EMP add constraint emp_chk_asal
                    check ((job <> 'ADMIN') or (msal < 5000));
```

The implementation of the first constraint, named emp_chk_adlt, uses date arithmetic (the + interval operator) to add 18 years to a given born date value.

Because SQL only offers three logical connectives (and, or, not), you are forced to transform the second and third tuple constraints—both involving the implication connective—into a disjunction. In case you've forgotten the important rewrite rule that enables you to do so, here it is once more:

$$(P \Rightarrow Q) \Leftrightarrow ((\neg P) \vee Q)$$

Once again, you should be aware that this transformation might not be safe in general, because when you're using SQL you're in the world of 3VL, not the 2VL world from which the rewrite rule is taken. If NULL is permitted in any of the columns involved, you'll need to think about how these constraints work in SQL's 3VL logic.

Given that the tuple constraints are declared in the way shown in Listing 11-24, the DBMS will ensure that rows that violate any of them are rejected.

In Listings 11-25 through 11-28, you can find the implementation of the tuple constraints for table structures GRD, MEMP, CRS, and OFFR. The other remaining table structures in the example database design don't have tuple constraints.

Listing 11-25. *Tuple Constraints for GRD Table Structure*

```
alter table GRD add constraint  grd_chk_bndw  check (llimit <= (ulimit - 500));
alter table GRD add constraint  grd_chk_bon2  check (bonus < llimit);
```

Listing 11-26. *Tuple Constraints for MEMP Table Structure*

```
alter table MEMP add constraint  mmp_chk_cycl  check (empno <> mgr);
```

Listing 11-27. *Tuple Constraints for CRS Table Structure*

```
alter table CRS add constraint  reg_chk_dur2  check ((cat <> 'BLD') or (dur <= 5));
```

Listing 11-28. *Tuple Constraints for OFFR Table Structure*

```
alter table OFFR add constraint  ofr_chk_trst
                   check (trainer is not null or status in ('CANC','SCHD'));
```

The accompanying formal specification for the tuple constraint stated in Listing 11-28 was the following:

```
tup_OFFR :=
{ o | o∈ P(chr_OFFR) ∧
      /* Unassigned TRAINER allowed only for certain STATUS values */
      o(TRAINER) = -1 ⇒ o(STATUS)∈ {'CANC','SCHD'}
}
```

After a rewrite of the implication into a disjunction, this changes into the following:

```
tup_OFFR :=
{ o | o∈ P(chr_OFFR) ∧
      /* Unassigned TRAINER allowed only for certain STATUS values */
      o(TRAINER) ≠ -1 ∨ o(STATUS)∈ {'CANC','SCHD'}
}
```

Because we have decided to represent the -1 with a NULL in the implementation of the OFFR table structure (again for reasons that will be explained later on), the first disjunct changes to trainer is not null in the preceding check constraint.

We'll end this section on implementing tuple constraints with an observation that is also valid for the constraint classes that follow hereafter.

It is good practice to write all tuple constraints in conjunctive normal form (CNF; see the section "Normal Forms" in Chapter 3). This might require you to apply various rewrite rules first. By rewriting a constraint into CNF, you'll end up with as many conjuncts as possible, where each conjunct represents a separately implementable constraint. For tuple constraints, you would create one declarative check constraint per conjunct. This in turn has the advantage that the DBMS reports violations of tuple constraints in *as detailed a way as possible*.

Let's explain this.

> ■**Note** We again assume that SQL's 3VL behaves in a 2VL fashion because all columns that are involved in constraints are mandatory.

Suppose you create one check constraint for a tuple constraint that is—when rewritten in CNF—of the form A ∧ B. When that check constraint gets violated, all you know (in 2VL) is that A ∧ B is not TRUE. This, using the laws of De Morgan, translates as either A is not TRUE or B is not TRUE. Wouldn't it be nicer if you knew exactly which one of the two was FALSE? If you would have created two separate check constraints (one for A and one for B), the DBMS could report which one of the two was causing the violation (or maybe they both are). In other words, by rewriting a constraint specification into CNF and implementing each conjunct separately, you'll get more detailed error messages.

As mentioned earlier, this observation also applies to the constraint classes that follow (table, database, and transition).

Table Constraint Implementation Issues

Up until now, everything has been straightforward concerning the implementation of data integrity constraints. However, when you increase the scope from tuple constraints to table constraints, and thus start dealing with constraints that span multiple tuples, implementing efficient DI code rapidly becomes much more complex.

The main reason for this complexity is the poor support for declaring these constraints to the DBMS. You can state only two types of table constraints declaratively: uniquely identifying attributes (keys) and subset requirements referencing back to the same table, in which case a subset requirement is a table constraint (foreign key to the same table).

Implementing all other types of table constraints requires you to develop procedural DI code. In practice, this means that you'll often have to resort to the triggered procedural strategy.

> ■**Note** We think there's a reason why DBMS vendors offer us such poor declarative support. We'll reveal this reason in the course of this section.

We'll introduce you to the complexity involved in implementing table constraints by illustrating different DI code *execution models*. In the first (rather large) subsection that follows, we'll illustrate six different execution models, ranging from very inefficient to more efficient. As you'll see, implementing more efficient execution models for DI code is also more complex.

To explain every execution model clearly, we'll be using two example table constraints and show how these constraints are implemented in every execution model. The constraints we'll use are the last one specified in table universe tab_EMP in Listing 7-26 and the last one specified in table universe tab_DEPT in Listing 7-30. For your convenience, we repeat the formal specifications of these two constraints here (note that in these specifications E represents an employee table and D represents a department table).

```
/* A department that employs the president or a manager */
/* should also employ at least one administrator        */
( ∀d∈ E⇓{DEPTNO}:
  ( ∃e2∈ E: e2(DEPTNO) = d(DEPTNO) ∧ e2(JOB) ∈ {'PRESIDENT','MANAGER'} )
    ⇒
  ( ∃e3∈ E: e3(DEPTNO) = d(DEPTNO) ∧ e3(JOB) = 'ADMIN' )
)
/* You cannot manage more than two departments */
( ∀m∈ D⇓{MGR}: #{ d | d∈D ∧ d(MGR) = m(MGR) } ≤ 2 )
```

Next to implementing an efficient execution model, another—rather serious—issue comes into play when implementing DI code for table constraints. This concerns *transaction serialization*. Given that Oracle's SQL DBMS can execute transactions concurrently, you must ensure that the queries inside DI code for a given constraint are executed in a serializable way: Oracle's SQL DBMS does not guarantee serializability. We'll explain this issue to you in detail in the section "DI Code Serialization."

DI Code Execution Models

This section will discuss various execution models for implementing DI code for table constraints following the triggered procedural strategy. However, before doing so we'll first provide you with a few preliminary observations with regards to the timing of DI code execution in relation to the DML statement execution.

Some Observations

With an SQL DBMS, you update the database by executing INSERT, UPDATE, or DELETE statements. Each of these statements operates on just one target table structure in just one manner—it's either an INSERT, or an UPDATE, or a DELETE. Typically, transactions need to change more than one table, or possibly just one table in more than one manner. Therefore, your transactions in general consist of multiple DML statements that are serially executed one after the other.

You implicitly start a transaction when the first DML statement is executed. A transaction is explicitly ended by either executing a COMMIT statement (requesting the DBMS to persistently store the changes made by this transaction), or by executing a rollback statement (requesting the DBMS to abort and undo the changes made by the current transaction). After ending a transaction, you can start a new one again by executing another (first) DML statement. All changes made by a transaction—that has not yet committed—are only visible to that transaction; other transactions cannot see these changes. Once a transaction commits, the changes it made become visible to other transactions.

■**Note** Here we're assuming that the DBMS is running in the read-committed isolation mode—the mode most often used within Oracle's installed base.

Of course, all constraints must be satisfied at the end of a transaction (when it commits). That is to say, you don't want a transaction to commit successfully while the database state, produced by the serial execution of its DML statements so far, violates one of the constraints. But what about the database states that exist in between the execution of two DML statements inside the same transaction? Should these database states always satisfy all constraints too, or might they be in violation of some constraints, as long as the last database state (the one that the transaction commits) satisfies all constraints?

For the time being, we disallow that these intermediate database states violate any database constraint.

■**Note** However, we'll revisit this question in the section "Bringing Deferred Checking into the Picture," where you'll see that to implement certain transactions using Oracle's SQL DBMS, we must allow certain constraints to be temporarily violated in one of the intermediate database states.

A DML statement that attempts to create a database state that violates a constraint will fail; in the following execution models we'll ensure that the changes of such a DML statement will be rolled back immediately, while preserving the database state changes made by prior DML statements that executed successfully inside the transaction.

In Table 11-1 you can find an example transaction that executes four DML statements; the table shows the database state transitions that occur within this transaction.

Table 11-1. *Database State Transitions Inside a Transaction*

Time	Start DB State	DML	End DB State	Comment
0	dbs0	DML0;	dbs1	Transaction starts. dbs1 is a valid state.
1	dbs1	DML1;	dbs2	dbs2 violates a constraint; DML1 is rolled back.
2	dbs1	DML2;	dbs3	dbs3 is a valid state.
3	dbs3	DML3;	dbs4	dbs4 violates a constraint; DML3 is rolled back.
4	dbs3	commit;	dbs3	dbs3 is committed and made visible to other transactions.

Our execution model will be based on triggers. As mentioned before, triggers are associated with a table structure and will automatically be executed ("fired") by the DBMS if a DML statement changes the content of that table. The code inside the trigger body can then check whether the new database state satisfies all constraints. If the state does not satisfy all constraints, then this code will force the triggering DML statement to fail; the DBMS then ensures that its changes are rolled back.

You should be aware of a limitation that row triggers have (the ones that fire for each affected row). These triggers are only allowed to query the state of *other* table structures; that is, they are not allowed to query the table structure on which the triggering DML statement is currently operating. If you try this, you'll hit the infamous *mutating table* error (ORA-04091: table ... is mutating, trigger/function may not see it).

The very valid reason why Oracle's SQL DBMS disallows you to do this is to prevent *nondeterministic behavior*. That's because if your row triggers would be allowed to query a table structure that a DML statement is currently modifying, then these queries would perform a dirty read within the transaction. These queries see intermediate table states that only exist while the triggering DML statement is being executed row by row. Depending upon the order in which the SQL optimizer happens to process the rows, the outcome of these queries can be different. This would cause nondeterministic behavior, which is why Oracle's DBMS won't allow you to query the "mutating" table.

Given the essence of a table constraint—that is, it involves multiple rows in a table—the DI code for a table constraint will always require you to execute queries against the table that has been modified; however, the mutating table error prevents you from doing so. Therefore, row triggers are not suitable to be used as containers of DI code for table constraints.

Before statement triggers see the start database state in which a DML statement starts execution. After statement triggers see the end database state created by the execution of a DML statement. Because DI code needs to validate the end state of a DML statement, you are left with no more than three after statement triggers per table structure (insert, update, and delete) on which to base an execution model.

Given these observations, we can now go ahead and illustrate six different execution models for DI code. In discussing the execution models, we'll sometimes broaden the scope to also include database constraints.

Execution Model 1: Always

In the first execution model (EM1), whenever a DML statement is executed, then the corresponding after statement trigger will hold code that sequentially executes the DI code for every constraint. In this model, every intermediate database state (including the last one) is validated to satisfy all constraints.

This execution model only serves as a starting point; you would never want to make use of this model, because it's highly inefficient. For instance, if a DML statement changes the EMP table structure, then this execution model would then also run the DI code to check constraints that do not involve the EMP table structure. Obviously, this is completely unnecessary because these other table structures remain unchanged; constraints that don't involve the table structure upon which the triggering DML statement operates need not be validated.

Let's quickly forget this model, and move on to a more efficient one.

Execution Model 2: On-Involved-Table

This execution model (EM2) very much resembles EM1. The only difference is that you now make use of the knowledge of what the involved table structures are for each constraint. You only run DI code for a given constraint, if the table structure that is being changed by a DML statement is involved in the constraint (hence the "On-Involved-Table" in the section title).

Let's take a closer look at how the example table constraint of the EMP table structure is implemented in this execution model. Remember, this was the constraint: "A department that employs the president or a manager should also employ at least one administrator." You can formally derive the constraint validation query that you need to execute for verifying whether a new database state still satisfies this constraint. The way to do this is by translating the formal specification into an SQL WHERE-clause expression and then executing a query that evaluates the truth value of this expression. You can use the DUAL table to evaluate the expression. Let's demonstrate this. Here is the formal specification of this table constraint:

(∀d∈ E⇓{DEPTNO}:
  (∃e2∈ E: e2(DEPTNO) = d(DEPTNO) ∧ e2(JOB) ∈ {'PRESIDENT','MANAGER'})
  ⇒
  (∃e3∈ E: e3(DEPTNO) = d(DEPTNO) ∧ e3(JOB) = 'ADMIN')
)

Before you can translate the formal specification into an SQL expression, you'll need to get rid of the universal quantifier and implication. Following is the rewritten version of the specification.

Tip Try to rewrite this specification yourself; start by adding a double negation in front of the preceding specification.

¬ (∃d∈ E⇓{DEPTNO}:
  (∃e2∈ E: e2(DEPTNO) = d(DEPTNO) ∧ e2(JOB) ∈ {'PRESIDENT','MANAGER'})
  ∧
  ¬ (∃e3∈ E: e3(DEPTNO) = d(DEPTNO) ∧ e3(JOB) = 'ADMIN')
)

This now easily translates to SQL (we're naming this constraint EMP_TAB03).

Note The DUAL table in Oracle is a single-column, single-row system table. It is most often used to have the SQL engine evaluate either a SELECT-clause expression or a WHERE-clause expression. The following code displays the latter usage.

```
select 'Constraint EMP_TAB03 is satisfied'
from DUAL
where not exists(select d.DEPTNO
                from EMP d
                where exists(select e2.*
                            from EMP e2
                            where e2.DEPTNO = d.DEPTNO
                              and e2.JOB in ('PRESIDENT','MANAGER'))
                  and not exists(select e3.*
                            from EMP e3
                            where e3.DEPTNO = d.DEPTNO
                              and e3.JOB = 'ADMIN'))
```

In EM2, you would create three after statement triggers for this constraint on only the EMP table structure (the one involved in this constraint). These triggers hold the preceding query to verify that the new database state still satisfies this constraint. Listing 11-29 shows these three triggers combined into one create trigger statement.

Listing 11-29. *EM2 DI Code for Constraint EMP_TAB03*

```
create trigger EMP_AIUDS_TAB03
after insert or update or delete on EMP
declare pl_dummy varchar(40);
begin
  --
  select 'Constraint EMP_TAB03 is satisfied' into pl_dummy
  from DUAL
  where not exists(select d.DEPTNO
                     from EMP d
                   where exists(select e2.*
                                  from EMP e2
                                where e2.DEPTNO = d.DEPTNO
                                  and e2.JOB in ('PRESIDENT','MANAGER'))
                     and not exists(select e3.*
                                      from EMP e3
                                    where e3.DEPTNO = d.DEPTNO
                                      and e3.JOB = 'ADMIN'));
  --
exception when no_data_found then
  --
  raise_application_error(-20999,'Constraint EMP_TAB03 is violated.');
  --
end;
```

■ Note A DBMS could, by parsing the declared formal specification of a constraint, *compute* what the involved tables are. Also, the DBMS could *compute* the validation query that needs to be run to validate whether a constraint is still satisfied (all this requires is the application of rewrite rules to end up with a specification that can be translated into an SQL expression). Therefore, the DBMS could generate the preceding trigger. In other words, this execution model could be fully supported by a DBMS vendor *in a declarative way*!

Listing 11-30 shows the three triggers representing the DI code for constraint DEPT_TAB01 using this execution model.

Listing 11-30. *EM2 DI Code for Constraint DEPT_TAB01*

```
create trigger DEPT_AIUDS_TAB01
after insert or update or delete on DEPT
declare pl_dummy varchar(40);
begin
  --
  select 'Constraint DEPT_TAB01 is satisfied' into pl_dummy
  from DUAL
```

```
where not exists(select m.DEPTNO
                 from DEPT m
                 where 2 < (select count(*)
                            from DEPT d
                            where d.MGR = m.MGR));
  --
exception when no_data_found then
  --
  raise_application_error(-20999,'Constraint DEPT_TAB01 is violated.');
  --
end;
/
```

This execution model is still inefficient. For instance, when you update the name of an employee, then this execution model will validate constraint EMP_TAB03. Obviously, because the ENAME column is not involved at all in this constraint, DML statements that update ENAME should never give rise to the need to check constraint EMP_TAB03. A similar inefficiency applies to constraint DEPT_TAB01; for instance, EM2 will validate this constraint when you update the location of a department (whereas attribute LOC is not involved in constraint DEPT_TAB01). The next execution model addresses this inefficiency.

Execution Model 3: On-Involved-Column(s)

This execution model (EM3) is the same as EM2 in the cases where the DML statement is an INSERT or a DELETE. However, when updates occur you now also make use of the knowledge of what the involved attributes are (per table structure) for each constraint. For a given constraint, there's only a need for this constraint to be validated if involved attributes get modified by the UPDATE statement. INSERT and DELETE statements always involve all attributes, and therefore give rise to a need for constraints that involve the table structure to be validated whenever they occur (irrespective of the attributes involved in the constraint).

Let's again demonstrate this using the example table constraint EMP_TAB03. In this case, the insert and delete triggers remain the same as in EM2. You only change the update trigger to be more efficient. Simply by scanning the formal specification of constraint EMP_TAB03, you can discover the attributes that are involved; for this constraint these are DEPTNO and JOB. Whenever UPDATE statements occur, you now only execute the DI code that was developed in EM2 when the UPDATE statement changes either the DEPTNO or the JOB (or both) attributes.

■Note You'll probably easily understand that an update of JOB can violate this constraint. For instance, in a given department, when you promote an administrator to become a trainer, it might well be the case that you just "removed" the single administrator who was required to be in that department, because that department also employs the president or a manager. Also, for instance, when you promote a trainer to become a manager, this might be the first manager in the department. This now would require that the department also employ an administrator. Similar scenarios apply to updates of DEPTNO; if you switch a manager who is currently working in department 10 to start working in department 20, then this manager might be the first manager in department 20, therefore . . . , and so on.

The SQL standard allows you to specify these columns in update triggers. The update trigger will then only fire if one of the involved columns has been changed. Here is how you would code the after statement update trigger in Oracle (see Listing 11-31).

Listing 11-31. *EM3's More Efficient Update Trigger for Constraint EMP_TAB03*

```
create trigger EMP_AUS_TAB03
after update of DEPTNO,JOB on EMP
declare pl_dummy varchar(40);
begin
  --
  select 'Constraint EMP_TAB03 is satisfied' into pl_dummy
  from DUAL
  where not exists(select d.DEPTNO
                   from EMP d
                   where exists(select e2.*
                                from EMP e2
                                where e2.DEPTNO = d.DEPTNO
                                  and e2.JOB in ('PRESIDENT','MANAGER'))
                     and not exists(select e3.*
                                    from EMP e3
                                    where e3.DEPTNO = d.DEPTNO
                                      and e3.JOB = 'ADMIN'));
  --
exception when no_data_found then
  --
  raise_application_error(-20999,'Constraint EMP_TAB03 is violated.');
  --
end;
/
```

The second line in Listing 11-31 specifies the involved columns.

Note As was the case with EM2, a DBMS vendor can also easily support this execution model declaratively. The extra work the DBMS needs to do for EM3, compared to EM2, is to parse all constraints. It does this not only to determine the table structure(s) that are involved for EM2, but also to determine per table structure what the involved attribute(s) are. The DBMS can then implement the more sophisticated update trigger automatically.

Listing 11-32 displays the optimized DI code for constraint DEPT_TAB01 in the case of UPDATE statement execution (note that only the MGR attribute is involved in this constraint).

Listing 11-32. *DI Code for DEPT_TAB01 in Case of Updates*

```
create trigger DEPT_AUS_TAB01
after update of MGR on DEPT
declare pl_dummy varchar(40);
begin
  --
  select 'Constraint DEPT_TAB01 is satisfied' into pl_dummy
  from DUAL
  where not exists(select m.DEPTNO
                   from DEPT m
                   where 2 < (select count(*)
                              from DEPT d
                              where d.MGR = m.MGR));
  --
exception when no_data_found then
  --
  raise_application_error(-20999,'Constraint DEPT_TAB01 is violated.');
  --
end;
/
```

There is a way to further improve on the efficiency of this execution model. For a given constraint, you can sometimes deduce that an INSERT statement (into one of the involved table structures) or a DELETE statement (on one of the involved table structures) can never violate the constraint. In the case of table constraint EMP_TAB03, neither can be deduced. You could be inserting a president, in which case the constraint should be validated. Or, you could be deleting an administrator, in which case the constraint should be validated too. However, in the case of table constraint DEPT_TAB01, you can deduce that deleting a department can never violate this constraint.

The next execution model addresses this further optimization with regards to INSERT or DELETE statements.

Execution Model 4: On-Involved-Column(s) Plus Polarity-of-Involved-Tables

This execution model (EM4) is the same as EM3 when the triggering DML statement is an UPDATE statement. However, when inserts or deletes occur, you now also make use of the knowledge of what the *polarity* of an involved table structure is per constraint.

The polarity of a table structure for a given constraint is defined to be *positive* if inserts into that table structure can violate the constraint and deletes cannot. The polarity of a table structure for a given constraint is *negative* if deletes from that table structure can violate the constraint and inserts cannot. The polarity of a table structure is defined to be *neutral* if both an insert and a delete give rise to a need for the constraint to be validated. The polarity of a table structure for a given constraint is undefined if the table structure is not involved in the constraint.

If the polarity of a table structure for a given constraint is neutral, then EM4 is equivalent to EM3; there is no opportunity for you to further optimize (in comparison to EM3) the insert or delete trigger. However, if it is positive or negative, then you can further optimize the DELETE or INSERT statement trigger, respectively; in fact, you can drop them.

Let's demonstrate this by examining the DI code for constraint DEPT_TAB01. As mentioned earlier, only inserting a department can potentially violate this constraint; if all department managers currently manage no more than two departments, then deleting a department can never violate this constraint. We say that the DEPT table structure has a positive polarity with regards to the DEPT_TAB01 constraint. In this case you can optimize the delete trigger not to run any DI code at all for DEPT_TAB01; you simply needn't create the DEPT DELETE statement trigger that would have been created in EM3 for constraint DEPT_TAB01.

Note Scientific research has shown that a DBMS can also fairly easily compute the polarity of an involved table structure for a given (formally specified) constraint. This again implies that a DBMS vendor should be capable of supplying us with full declarative multi-tuple constraint support using execution model EM4.

Still, execution model EM4 sometimes runs DI code when there is no need to. For instance, considering constraint EMP_TAB03, when you insert a *sales rep*, or delete a *trainer*, EM4 will run the DI code for constraint EMP_TAB03. But obviously, because neither sales reps nor trainers play any role in this constraint, then inserts and/or deletes of them should never give rise to the need to check constraint EMP_TAB03. The next execution model addresses this inefficiency.

Execution Model 5: On-Transition-Effect-Property

This execution model (EM5) assumes the availability of a *transition effect* of a given DML statement that has just been executed. The transition effect describes the actual rows that have been affected by the DML statement, including—in the case of an UPDATE statement— how these rows have been modified.

As you'll see shortly, the transition effect provides a convenient means for an after statement trigger to see which rows precisely have been affected by the triggering DML statement. By inspecting the transition effect in the after statement trigger, you are able to address the inefficiency mentioned earlier for EM4.

You can implement the transition effect as a view that only holds rows directly after the processing of a DML statement. After statement triggers that fire can access the view to determine exactly which rows have been inserted, deleted, or updated.

In this execution model, we assume the availability of three transition effect (TE) views for each table structure:

- The *insert TE view* named v_[table name]_ite: This view will show the row(s) that a triggering INSERT statement has just inserted. It is empty (holds no rows) if the triggering statement is not an INSERT.

- The *update TE view* named v_[table_name]_ute: This view will show the row(s) that a triggering UPDATE statement has just updated; this view shows both old and new values of modified columns. It is empty if the triggering statement is not an UPDATE.

- The *delete TE view* named v_[table_name]_dte: This view will show the row(s) that a triggering DELETE statement has just deleted. It is empty if the triggering statement is not a DELETE.

Currently, Oracle's SQL DBMS does not provide you with a transition effect (there is at least one other DBMS vendor that does supply it). However, you can develop a row and a statement trigger for each table structure that do the necessary bookkeeping to provide these three TE views.

Take a look at Listing 11-33. It shows the necessary DI code required to maintain the transition effect of the EMP table structure. The row triggers use the session temporary table EMP_TE to store the transition effect. On top of this table, the three TE views are defined.

Listing 11-33. *DI Code for Maintaining Transition Effect of EMP Table Structure*

```
create global temporary table EMP_TE
(DML       char(1)  not null check(DML in ('I','U','D'))
,ROW_ID    rowid
,EMPNO     number(4,0)
,JOB       varchar(9)
,HIRED     date
,SGRADE    number(2,0)
,MSAL      number(7,2)
,DEPTNO    number(2,0)
,check(DML<>'I' or ROW_ID is not null)
,check(DML<>'U' or ROW_ID is not null)
,check(DML<>'D' or ROW_ID is null)
) on commit delete rows
/
create trigger EMP_BIUDS_TE
before insert or update or delete on EMP
begin
  -- Reset transition effect before every DML statement execution.
  delete from EMP_TE;
  --
end;
/
create trigger EMP_AIUDR_TE
after insert or update or delete on EMP
for each row
begin
  -- Conditionally maintain the transition effect.
  if INSERTING
  then
    -- Only store 'pointer' to affected row.
    insert into EMP_TE(DML,ROW_ID) values('I',:new.rowid);
  elsif UPDATING
  then
    -- Store snapshot of old version of row, plus pointer to new version.
```

```
          insert into EMP_TE(DML,ROW_ID,EMPNO,JOB,HIRED,SGRADE,MSAL,DEPTNO)
          values ('U',:new.rowid,:old.empno,:old.job,:old.hired
                              ,:old.sgrade,:old.msal,:old.deptno);
       elsif DELETING
       then
          -- Store snapshot of old version of row.
          insert into EMP_TE(DML,ROW_ID,EMPNO,JOB,HIRED,SGRADE,MSAL,DEPTNO)
          values ('D',null,:old.empno,:old.job,:old.hired
                          ,:old.sgrade,:old.msal,:old.deptno);
       end if;
       --
end;
/
create view V_EMP_ITE as
select e.*
from EMP_TE te
     ,EMP e
where DML='I'
   and te.ROW_ID = e.ROWID
/
create view V_EMP_UTE as
select e.EMPNO    as N_EMPNO  ,e.JOB    as N_JOB   ,e.HIRED    as N_HIRED
      ,e.SGRADE   as N_SGRADE ,e.MSAL   as N_MSAL  ,e.DEPTNO   as N_DEPTNO
      ,te.EMPNO   as O_EMPNO  ,te.JOB   as O_JOB   ,te.HIRED   as O_HIRED
      ,te.SGRADE  as O_SGRADE ,te.MSAL  as O_MSAL  ,te.DEPTNO  as O_DEPTNO
from EMP_TE te
     ,EMP e
where DML='U'
   and te.ROW_ID = e.ROWID
/
create view V_EMP_DTE as
select EMPNO,JOB, HIRED,SGRADE,MSAL,DEPTNO
from EMP_TE
where DML='D'
/
```

Note In the transition effect, you need to maintain only the columns that are involved in any of the (multi-row) constraints that involve the EMP table structure. This is why the preceding code does not maintain columns ENAME, BORN, and USERNAME: these three columns aren't involved in any of the constraints of DB_UEX.

Given the preceding code, you can now create more efficient after INSERT and DELETE statement triggers for constraint EMP_TAB03. Remember that in EM4 the DI code for this constraint would needlessly run if a sales rep was inserted or a trainer deleted.

Using the transition effect, you can now precisely code when the constraints need to be validated on execution of INSERT statements or DELETE statements:

- *For inserts*: Only when the statement inserts a president or a manager should you need to check whether there is an administrator (in the same department).

- *For deletes*: Only when the statement deletes an administrator should you need to check whether there (still) is another administrator, in case the department employs a manager or president.

In all other cases of INSERT or DELETE statements, it is not required to validate constraint EMP_TAB03.

In Listing 11-34 you can find the modified insert and delete triggers. These now first query the transition effect to verify if one of the preceding properties is TRUE, and if so, only then execute the query that validates constraint EMP_TAB03.

Listing 11-34. *EM5's More Efficient Insert and Delete Triggers for Constraint EMP_TAB03*

```
create trigger EMP_AIS_TAB03
after insert on EMP
declare pl_dummy varchar(40);
begin
    -- If this returns no rows, then EMP_TAB03 cannot be violated.
    select 'EMP_TAB03 must be validated' into pl_dummy
    from DUAL
    where exists (select 'A president or manager has just been inserted'
                from v_emp_ite
                where JOB in ('PRESIDENT','MANAGER'));
    --
    begin
        --
        select 'Constraint EMP_TAB03 is satisfied' into pl_dummy
        from DUAL
        where not exists(select d.DEPTNO
                        from EMP d
                        where exists(select e2.*
                                    from EMP e2
                                    where e2.DEPTNO = d.DEPTNO
                                        and e2.JOB in ('PRESIDENT','MANAGER'))
                            and not exists(select e3.*
                                        from EMP e3
                                        where e3.DEPTNO = d.DEPTNO
                                            and e3.JOB = 'ADMIN'));
    --
exception when no_data_found then
    --
    raise_application_error(-20999,'Constraint EMP_TAB03 is violated.');
    --
    end;
```

```
exception when no_data_found then
    -- No need to validate EMP_TAB03.
    null;
    --
end;
/
create trigger EMP_ADS_TAB03
after delete on EMP
declare pl_dummy varchar(40);
begin
  -- If this returns no rows, then EMP_TAB03 cannot be violated.
  select 'EMP_TAB03 must be validated' into pl_dummy
  from DUAL
  where exists (select 'An administrator has just been deleted'
                from v_emp_dte
                where JOB='ADMIN');
    --
  begin
    --
    select 'Constraint EMP_TAB03 is satisfied' into pl_dummy
    from DUAL
    where not exists(select d.DEPTNO
                     from EMP d
                     where exists(select e2.*
                                  from EMP e2
                                  where e2.DEPTNO = d.DEPTNO
                                    and e2.JOB in ('PRESIDENT','MANAGER'))
                        and not exists(select e3.*
                                       from EMP e3
                                       where e3.DEPTNO = d.DEPTNO
                                         and e3.JOB = 'ADMIN'));
    --
  exception when no_data_found then
    --
    raise_application_error(-20999,'Constraint EMP_TAB03 is violated.');
    --
  end;
exception when no_data_found then
    -- No need to validate EMP_TAB03.
    null;
    --
end;
/
```

You might have noticed that with the availability of the transition effect, you can now also write a more efficient update trigger. For instance, updating a trainer to become a sales rep does not require executing DI code for EMP_TAB03.

Written as a query on DUAL, here is the property to look for, which would require EMP_TAB03 to be validated in case of the execution of an UPDATE statement:

```
select 'EMP_TAB03 is in need of validation'
from DUAL
where exists(select  'Some department just won a president/manager or
                      just lost an administrator'
             from v_emp_ute
             where (n_job in ('PRESIDENT','MANAGER') and
                    o_job not in ('PRESIDENT','MANAGER')
                or (o_job='ADMIN' and n_job<>'ADMIN')
                or (o_deptno<>n_deptno and
                   (o_job='ADMIN' or n_job in ('PRESIDENT','MANAGER')))))
```

You can use the preceding query to create a more efficient update trigger in the same way as was shown for the insert and delete triggers in Listing 11-34.

We refer to these queries on the transition effect views hereafter as *transition effect queries* (TE queries).

■**Note** We don't know whether the DBMS can compute the TE queries (looking for the constraint-specific property) used in this execution model. Investigating the scientific research done in this area does not provide us with a clear answer to this question. Therefore, we cannot decisively say whether a DBMS should in principle be capable of supplying us with full declarative multi-tuple constraint support using execution model EM5.

Listing 11-35 supplies the triggers for implementing the second example table constraint using execution model EM5. It assumes the code for maintaining the transition effect views for the DEPT table structure has already been set up in a similar way as the transition effect for EMP was set up in Listing 11-33. Note that constraint DEPT_TAB01 does not require a delete trigger.

Listing 11-35. *EM5 Implemention of DI Code for Constraint DEPT_TAB01*

```
create trigger DEPT_AIS_TAB01
after insert on DEPT
declare pl_dummy varchar(40);
begin
  -- If this returns no rows, then DEPT_TAB01 cannot be violated.
  select 'DEPT_TAB01 must be validated' into pl_dummy
  from DUAL
  where exists (select 'A row has just been inserted'
                from v_dept_ite);
  --
  begin
    --
```

```
      select 'Constraint DEPT_TAB01 is satisfied' into pl_dummy
      from DUAL
      where not exists(select m.DEPTNO
                       from DEPT m
                       where 2 < (select count(*)
                                  from DEPT d
                                  where d.MGR = m.MGR));
      --
    exception when no_data_found then
      --
      raise_application_error(-20999,'Constraint DEPT_TAB01 is violated.');
      --
    end;
exception when no_data_found then
    -- No need to validate DEPT_TAB01.
    null;
    --
end;
/
create trigger DEPT_AUS_TAB01
after update on DEPT
declare pl_dummy varchar(40);
begin
  -- If this returns no rows, then DEPT_TAB01 cannot be violated.
  select 'DEPT_TAB01 must be validated' into pl_dummy
  from DUAL
  where exists (select 'A department manager has just been updated'
                from v_dept_ute
                where o_mgr<>n_mgr);
  --
  begin
    --
    select 'Constraint DEPT_TAB01 is satisfied' into pl_dummy
    from DUAL
    where not exists(select m.DEPTNO
                     from DEPT m
                     where 2 < (select count(*)
                                from DEPT d
                                where d.MGR = m.MGR));
    --
  exception when no_data_found then
    --
    raise_application_error(-20999,'Constraint DEPT_TAB01 is violated.');
    --
  end;
exception when no_data_found then
    -- No need to validate DEPT_TAB01.
```

```
      null;
      --
end;
/
```

Note that in the case of constraint DEPT_TAB01, execution models EM4 and EM5 are equivalent.

The question might arise whether testing for a certain property in the transition effect defeats its purpose. That's because if performing this test is as costly as is running the actual constraint validation code, then what is your gain? In answer to this question, we can make the following observations:

- The number of rows in the transition effect is usually much smaller than the number of rows in the table structures that are involved in the constraint.

- The transition effect is always in cache, which cannot be said about all rows in the involved table structures.

- The TE query itself will normally be much simpler than the query that is conditionally run to validate the constraint.

The examples shown have demonstrated this last observation. Together with the first two observations, this should then answer the question; a TE query does not defeat its purpose (efficiency of DI code).

Furthermore, there is a second—more important—purpose for *guarding* constraint validation with TE queries. Preventing unnecessary execution of queries that validate the constraint will strongly benefit the concurrency of transactions. We'll deal with this aspect in the next subsection, "DI Code Serialization."

There is one more way to further optimize the efficiency of execution model EM5. This involves executing a more efficient query to validate the constraint. Up until now you've derived these queries directly from the formal specifications of the constraints, and as such they validate the *full* constraint predicate.

In the case of EMP_TAB03, the query validates whether *every* department satisfies the predicate that is quantified (if there is a president/manager, then there is an administrator). In the case of DEPT_TAB01, the query validates whether *every* department manager is not managing more than two departments. Often, given a triggering DML statement, it suffices to execute a query that validates a *weaker* predicate.

For instance, if an INSERT statement inserts a manager for department 10 into the EMP table structure, then theoretically you would only have to validate whether the quantified predicate is still satisfied *for department 10 only*. Likewise, if an UPDATE statement changes the manager for some department, then you would only have to validate whether this new department manager isn't managing more than two departments.

The last execution model addresses this opportunity for further increasing the efficiency of DI code.

Execution Model 6: On-Transition-Effect-Property Plus Optimized-Query

This execution model (EM6) resembles EM5 in that it also requires a transition effect for each table structure; you now use this transition effect in a slightly more sophisticated manner, so that you can determine the weaker predicate.

Instead of just looking for a property in the transition effect to guard execution of a constraint validation query, you now also use the transition effect to supply values that can be used to optimize the validation query. For instance, in the case of EMP_TAB03, you can use the transition effect to determine for which department(s) the weaker predicate must be checked; this should always result in executing a more efficient validation query. In the case of DEPT_TAB01, you can use the transition effect to find out for what MGR value(s) the weaker predicate must be checked.

Listing 11-36 shows you how to do this. It shows the EM6 version of the insert, update, and delete triggers for constraint EMP_TAB03.

Listing 11-36. *EM6 Implemention of DI Code for Constraint EMP_TAB03*

```
create trigger EMP_AIS_TAB03
after insert on EMP
declare pl_dummy varchar(40);
begin
  --
  for r in (select distinct deptno
            from v_emp_ite
            where JOB in ('PRESIDENT','MANAGER'));
  loop
  begin
    -- Note: this now uses r.deptno value from preceeding TE query.
    select 'Constraint EMP_TAB03 is satisfied' into pl_dummy
    from DUAL
    where not exists(select e2.*
                     from EMP e2
                     where e2.DEPTNO = r.DEPTNO
                       and e2.JOB in ('PRESIDENT','MANAGER'))
       or exists(select e3.*
                 from EMP e3
                 where e3.DEPTNO = r.DEPTNO
                   and e3.JOB = 'ADMIN'));
    --
  exception when no_data_found then
    --
    raise_application_error(-20999,
     'Constraint EMP_TAB03 is violated for department '||to_char(r.deptno)||'.');
    --
  end;
  end loop;
end;
/
create trigger EMP_ADS_TAB03
after delete on EMP
declare pl_dummy varchar(40);
begin
  --
```

```
    for r in (select distinct deptno
              from v_emp_dte
              where JOB='ADMIN');
  loop
  begin
    --
    select 'Constraint EMP_TAB03 is satisfied' into pl_dummy
    from DUAL
    where not exists(select e2.*
                     from EMP e2
                     where e2.DEPTNO = r.DEPTNO
                       and e2.JOB in ('PRESIDENT','MANAGER'))
        or exists(select e3.*
                  from EMP e3
                  where e3.DEPTNO = r.DEPTNO
                    and e3.JOB = 'ADMIN'));
    --
  exception when no_data_found then
    --
    raise_application_error(-20999,
     'Constraint EMP_TAB03 is violated for department '||to_char(r.deptno)||'.');
    --
  end;
  end loop;
end;
/
create trigger EMP_AUS_TAB03
after update on EMP
declare pl_dummy varchar(40);
begin
  --
  for r in (select n_deptno as deptno
            from v_emp_ute
            where (o_job not in ('PRESIDENT','MANAGER') or updated_deptno='TRUE')
              and n_job in ('PRESIDENT','MANAGER')
            union
            select o_deptno as deptno
            from v_emp_ute
            where (n_job<>'ADMIN' or updated_deptno='TRUE')
              and old_job ='ADMIN')
  loop
  begin
    --
    select 'Constraint EMP_TAB03 is satisfied' into pl_dummy
    from DUAL
    where not exists(select e2.*
                     from EMP e2
```

```
                        where e2.DEPTNO = r.DEPTNO
                          and e2.JOB in ('PRESIDENT','MANAGER'))
          or exists(select e3.*
                    from EMP e3
                    where e3.DEPTNO = r.DEPTNO
                      and e3.JOB = 'ADMIN'));
      --
   exception when no_data_found then
      --
      raise_application_error(-20999,
        'Constraint EMP_TAB03 is violated for department '||to_char(r.deptno)||'.');
      --
   end;
   end loop;
end;
/
```

■**Note** The `distinct` keyword inside the preceding TE queries possibly prevents multiple executions of the same constraint validation query in case the UPDATE statement affected more than one row.

Because the example constraints happen to be universal quantifications, finding the weaker predicate in the cases of EMP_TAB03 and DEPT_TAB01 is trivial. However, this is not always the case; the weaker predicate can also be rather complex to discover. This all depends on the specification of the constraint. Again, we don't know if it is possible at all whether, instead of having to discover it yourself, you can have the DBMS automatically compute the weaker predicate (including the TE query) given a declared formal specification of a constraint.

DI Code Serialization

You should be aware of another major issue when implementing DI code yourself. This issue applies irrespective of whether you follow the triggered procedural strategy or the embedded procedural strategy.

In Oracle's SQL DBMS, transactions execute concurrently. At any point in time there can be many *open* transactions; that is, transactions that have started but that have not yet committed. As mentioned earlier in this chapter, an open transaction cannot see the changes made by other concurrent open transactions. This has serious ramifications in the area of correctness of the DI code. As we'll demonstrate in a moment, the root cause of the issue lies in the fact that the constraint validation query, which executes as part of the DI code, assumes that all data it reads—or failed to read due to the absence of the data—is not currently being changed (or created) by other transactions. The DI code for a given constraint can only correctly implement the constraint if concurrently running transactions, which execute the validation query (embedded in the DI code) of this constraint, are *serialized*.

■**Note** We'll actually demonstrate some of the classical concurrency problems that arise in a DBMS that does not support *serializability* of concurrently executing transactions. If you are unfamiliar with the concept of serializability, then check out some of the references that we've added in Appendix C.

Let's demonstrate this serializability issue by describing a scenario of two concurrently executing transactions that both potentially violate the EMP_TAB03 constraint. For the sake of simplicity, assume that the EMP table structure currently contains a single row representing an administrator working for department 20. Transaction TX1 inserts a manager working for department 20 in the EMP table structure. Transaction TX2 deletes the administrator working for department 20 from the EMP table structure. Now take a look at Table 11-2. It describes a possible scenario of these two transactions executing concurrently.

Table 11-2. *TX1 and TX2 Executing Concurrently*

Time	TX1	TX2	DI Code
t=0	INSERT		Finds the administrator; therefore allows this insert.
t=1		DELETE	Doesn't find a manager; therefore allows the delete.
t=2	COMMIT		
t=3		COMMIT	

At time t=0, transaction TX1 starts. It inserts the manager, which causes the execution of DI code for constraint EMP_TAB03. The constraint validation query that executes as part of this DI code finds the administrator in department 20, which causes the DI code to allow this insert. At time t=1, transaction TX2 starts. It deletes the only row in the EMP table structure representing the administrator. Deleting an administrator also causes the same DI code for constraint EMP_TAB03 to be executed. The constraint validation query that executes as part of this DI code does not find a manager (or president) working in department 20, which causes the DI code to also allow this delete.

■**Note** At t=1, queries executing within transaction TX2 do not see the uncommitted changes made by transaction TX1.

At t=2, transaction TX1 commits. At t=3, transaction TX2 commits. The database now violates constraint EMP_TAB03; the EMP table structure holds a manager working for department 20, but there is no administrator in that department.

Let's also look at an example within the context of constraint DEPT_TAB01. Assume the DEPT table structure currently holds one department managed by employee 1042. Transaction TX3 inserts a new department that is also managed by employee 1042. Transaction TX4 also inserts a department again managed by employee 1042. Take a look at Table 11-3. It describes a possible scenario of these two transactions executing concurrently.

Table 11-3. *TX3 and TX4 Executing Concurrently*

Time	TX3	TX4	DI Code
t=0	INSERT		Sees 1042 now manages two departments; therefore allows this insert.
t=1		INSERT	Sees 1042 now manages two departments; therefore allows this insert.
t=2	COMMIT		
t=3		COMMIT	

Again, the DI code that executes at t=1 in TX4 does not see the uncommitted department inserted by transaction TX3 at t=0. Both inserts execute successfully. After t=3, the database violates constraint DEPT_TAB01; employee 1042 is managing three departments.

For every multi-tuple constraint, you can devise a scenario of concurrently executing transactions such that upon commit of these transactions the database is in violation of the constraint. Note that this is irrespective of the execution model that is used to implement the DI code.

Now, the question is, can you resolve this issue? The answer is yes. However, it requires that you develop and embed sometimes rather sophisticated serialization code in the DI code to ensure that there can never be *two transactions executing at the same time that involve the same constraint* (that is, that run the validation query of the same constraint).

■**Note** The following section assumes that you are familiar with Oracle's dbms_lock package and the concept of an autonomous transaction. If you're not, then we advise you first to study the Oracle documentation on this package and autonomous transactions.

The trick is that you use the dbms_lock supplied package of Oracle's SQL DBMS. By using this package you can acquire *application locks*, through which you can effectively serialize concurrently executing transactions that involve the same constraint.

Listing 11-37 shows the code of procedure p_request_lock that's built on top of the dbms_lock package, and through which you can request an application lock. This procedure needs to call a dbms_lock module that performs an implicit commit. Because you'll be calling p_request_lock from DI code, which in turn is executed from within a trigger (a context in which you're not allowed to commit), you need to hide this implicit commit from the current transaction. You can do this by use of an *autonomous transaction*. Auxiliary function f_allocate_unique (also in Listing 11-37) implements this autonomous transaction.

Listing 11-37. *Application Lock Services*

```
create function f_allocate_unique
(p_lockname in varchar) return varchar as
--
pragma autonomous_transaction;
--
```

```
pl_lockhandle   varchar(128);
--
begin
  -- This does implicit commit.
  dbms_lock.allocate_unique(upper(p_lockname)
                           ,pl_lockhandle
                           ,60*10); -- Set expiration to 10 minutes.
  --
  return pl_lockhandle;
  --
end;
/
create procedure p_request_lock(p_lockname in varchar) as
--
pl_lockhandle varchar(128);
pl_return number;
--
begin
  --
  -- Go get a unique lockhandle for this lockname.
  --
  pl_lockhandle := f_allocate_unique(p_lockname);
  --
  -- Request the named application lock in exclusive mode.
  -- Allow for a blocking situation that lasts no longer than 60 seconds.
  --
  pl_return :=
  dbms_lock.request(lockhandle        => pl_lockhandle
                   ,lockmode          => dbms_lock.x_mode
                   ,timeout           => 60
                   ,release_on_commit => true);
  --
  if pl_return not in (0,4)
  then
    raise_application_error(-20998,
         'Unable to acquire constraint serialization lock '||p_lockname||'.');
  end if;
  --
end;
/
```

You can now—in this case fairly easily—ensure that two transactions, which both need to run the DI code for constraint DEPT_TAB01, are correctly serialized to prevent the concurrency problem that was demonstrated in Table 11-3. Take a look at Listing 11-38, which shows the DI code for constraint DEPT_TAB01 using execution model EM6, including the necessary calls to p_lock_request to ensure correct serialization.

Listing 11-38. *EM6 Implemention of DI Code for DEPT_TAB01 Including Serialization*

```
create trigger DEPT_AIS_TAB01
after insert on DEPT
declare pl_dummy varchar(40);
begin
  --
  for r in (select distinct mgr as mgr
            from v_dept_ite)
  loop
  begin
    -- Acquire serialization lock.
    p_request_lock('DEPT_TAB01');
    --
    select 'Constraint DEPT_TAB01 is satisfied' into pl_dummy
    from DUAL
    where 2 >= (select count(*)
                from DEPT d
                where d.MGR = r.MGR);
    --
  exception when no_data_found then
    --
    raise_application_error(-20999,'Constraint DEPT_TAB01 is violated '||
                             'for department manager '||to_char(r.MGR)||'.');
    --
  end;
  end loop;
  --
end;
/
create trigger DEPT_AUS_TAB01
after update on DEPT
declare pl_dummy varchar(40);
begin
  --
  for r in (select distinct n_mgr as mgr
            from v_dept_ute)
  loop
  begin
    -- Acquire serialization lock.
    p_request_lock('DEPT_TAB01');
    --
    select 'Constraint DEPT_TAB01 is satisfied' into pl_dummy
    from DUAL
    where 2 >= (select count(*)
                from DEPT d
                where d.MGR = r.MGR);
    --
```

```
exception when no_data_found then
  --
  raise_application_error(-20999,'Constraint DEPT_TAB01 is violated '||
                          'for department manager '||to_char(r.MGR)||'.');
  --
end;
end loop;
  --
end;
/
```

The scenario that was described in Table 11-3 now executes as follows (see Table 11-4).

Table 11-4. *Serialization of TX3 and TX4*

Time	TX3	TX4	DI Code
t=0	INSERT		Sees 1042 now manages two departments; therefore allows this insert.
t=1		INSERT	Blocks on the serialization lock (execution of DI code is suspended).
t=2	COMMIT		(Within 60 seconds.)
t=3			TX4 is released from block, DI code resumes execution.
t=4			DI code sees 1042 now manages three departments and the insert fails.

On t=1, transaction TX4 will start waiting for transaction TX3 to release the application lock. Right after t=2, this waiting ends and execution of DI code is resumed. It now executes the constraint validation query, and finds that the insert in TX4 is not allowed because it would make employee 1042 the department manager of three departments.

You've now fixed the serialization issue: two transactions that both require executing the DEPT_TAB01 validation query can never execute simultaneously. However, the locking scheme that is implemented might be a bit too coarse. For instance, if TX4 were to insert a department that is managed by someone else (that is, not employee 1042), then TX4 will,also block, whereas it really needn't in this case for the DI code to enforce the constraint correctly.

Given the use of EM6 in Listing 11-38, you can implement a more granular locking scheme for this constraint, by changing the calls to p_request_lock to the following:

```
p_request_lock('DEPT_TAB01'||to_char(r.mgr));
```

Instead of always requesting an application lock whose name is constant ('DEPT_TAB01'), you now request an application lock whose name is dependent upon the *case* that is in need to be checked. Now two transactions inserting a department managed by different employees are allowed to execute simultaneously.

■**Note** Only EM6 allows you to implement this more granular locking scheme.

We'll end this section with a few concluding remarks related to serializability, further clarifying why vendors offer such poor support for the declarative strategy to implement constraints.

Recall the various execution models to which you've been introduced. Not only will less efficient execution models more often execute nonoptimized constraint validation queries than is necessary, but they'll also acquire serialization locks more often than is necessary. For instance, if you were to add serialization lock calls into DI code built using EM1, then effectively you'd only allow one transaction at a time; there cannot be any concurrent execution of transactions in this execution model. In EM2, this is relaxed to only one transaction at a time per table structure. Going further through all the remaining execution models, the level of concurrency increases each time.

Next to the remarks made earlier about the DBMS maybe not being able to compute neither the TE queries nor the optimized constraint validation queries, similar remarks apply to the DBMS being able to compute what the most optimal serialization lock calls should be. A lazy strategy that ensures correctness of DI code execution is always to acquire an exclusive application lock for each constraint (as shown in Listing 11-38). However, it is likely that you won't accept the unnecessary degraded concurrency of your DBMS that comes along with it.

Having extensively investigated the issues around implementing efficient DI code for table constraints using the triggered procedural strategy in this section, the next section will only offer you a summary of guidelines for implementing DI code for table constraints.

Implementing Table Constraints

As demonstrated by the previous section, it is here at the table constraint level where things rapidly become more complex. You can state only two types of table constraints declaratively: uniquely identifying attributes (keys), and subset requirements referencing back to the same table (in which case a subset requirement is a table constraint).

Here's an example that demonstrates the use of SQL primary key constraints and unique key constraints (see Listing 11-39).

Listing 11-39. *Declarative Implementation of the Keys of the DEPT Table Structure*

```
alter table DEPT add constraint DEPT_key1 primary key(deptno);
after table DEPT add constraint DEPT_key2 unique(dname,loc);
```

The example database design doesn't involve a subset requirement at the table level. In the next section you'll see how you can state database-level subset requirements declaratively.

Given the section "Table Constraint Implementation Issues," you might perhaps realize now why the DBMS vendor doesn't offer you the possibility of including queries inside declarative constraints; it's likely that a DBMS cannot offer a better execution model than EM4, and it's also likely that you won't accept the imposed serialization of transactions that comes along with EM4.

For instance, the following SQL statement, which attempts to implement DEPT_TAB01 declaratively, is not allowed:

```
-- Invalid "alter table add constraint" syntax for Oracle.
alter table DEPT add constraint dept_tab01 check
                    (not exists(select m.DEPTNO
                                from DEPT m
                                where 2 < (select count(*)
                                           from DEPT d
                                           where d.MGR = m.MGR)))
```

You must implement procedural DI code yourself for all other types of table constraints. Developing and implementing efficient DI code is not an easy task. As shown when the various execution models were investigated, it requires the following high-level stepping stones for each constraint:

1. Translate the formal specification into a constraint validation query.

2. Develop code to maintain transition effects.

3. Devise TE queries that ensure the constraint validation query is only run when necessary.

4. Discover a means to optimize the constraint validation query by having the TE query provide values that can be used in the validation query.

5. Devise and add a serialization strategy to the DI code.

However, you'll experience that by implementing table constraints regularly and becoming proficient in doing so, implementing table constraints procedurally is in general quite doable.

Implementing Database Constraints

As you probably know, declarative support for implementing database constraints is only available for subset requirements; in SQL a subset requirement is expressed by declaring a *foreign key*. Let's take a look at implementing subset requirement PSSR1 from our example database design:

```
PSSR1(EMP,DEPT) :=
      /* Employee works for a known department */
      { e(DEPTNO) | e∈EMP } ⊆ { d(DEPTNO) | d∈DEPT }
```

In SQL, this subset requirement is stated as follows:

```
alter table emp add constraint emp_fk_dept
                    foreign key(deptno) references dept(deptno);
```

SQL requires that the set of attributes that are referenced constitute a key. In the preceding example, this is the case; DEPTNO is uniquely identifying in DEPT. However, in the following case—requirement PSSR7—LOC does not constitute a key in DEPT. Therefore, you cannot implement PSSR7 by declaring a foreign key.

```
PSSR7(OFFR,DEPT) :=
    /* Courses take place in locations where we have a department */
    { o(LOC) | o∈OFFR } ⊆ { d(LOC) | d∈DEPT }
```

If you try the following `alter table` command, the SQL DBMS will give you an error:

```
-- Invalid because dept(loc) is not a key.
alter table offr add constraint offr_fk_dept
                        foreign key(loc) references dept(loc);
```

There are other scenarios where a foreign key cannot be used to implement a subset requirement declaratively. Some of the subset requirements in the example database design reference a *subset* of the tuples in the referenced table structure; this is quite common. Here is an example:

```
PSSR2(DEPT,EMP) :=
    /* Dept mgr is a known employee, excluding admins and president */
    { d(MGR)   | d∈DEPT } ⊆
    { e(EMPNO) | e∈EMP ∧ e(JOB) ∉ {'ADMIN','PRESIDENT'} }
```

You can declare a foreign key from DEPT to EMP as follows:

```
alter table offr add constraint offr_fk_dept
                        foreign key(loc) references dept(loc);
```

This foreign key will enforce that only known employees are referenced; it will still allow administrators or the president to manage a department. There is no declarative possibility to specify that a subset of the employees is only allowed to be referenced; you'll need to write additional procedural code for this.

A similar restriction applies to the cases where only a *subset* of the rows needs to reference the key values in rows of another table. This is the case in subset requirement PSSR8:

```
PSSR8(OFFR,EMP) :=
    /* Trainer of course offering is a known trainer */
    { o(TRAINER) | o∈OFFR ∧ o(TRAINER) ≠ -1 } ⊆
    { e(EMPNO)   | e∈EMP ∧ e(JOB) = 'TRAINER' }
```

It is not possible to declare to the DBMS that only the subset of OFFR rows where TRAINER≠-1 each references a known trainer.

There is a trick that you can apply in this case, though. By choosing to use a NULL instead of value -1 as a means to represent that no trainer has been assigned yet, you enable yourself to declare a foreign key, at least, to enforce that trainer assignments reference a known employee. Again, you still need to develop additional procedural code to implement the restriction at the other end (only employees where JOB='TRAINER' are allowed to be referenced).

Now let's spend a little time investigating this; before you build additional procedural code, it would be wise first to think about what the *remaining predicate* to be implemented would be here (given that the foreign key already does some work to implement PSSR8). To be more precise, can you rewrite PSSR8 into a conjunction where one conjunct covers exactly what the foreign key already implements declaratively, and the other conjunct covers what remains to be implemented procedurally? Here it is.

$(\forall o \in OFFR: o(TRAINER) \neq -1 \Rightarrow (\exists e \in EMP: e(empno) = o(trainer))) \wedge$
$(\forall t \in (OFFR \Diamond\Diamond \{(trainer; empno)\}) \otimes EMP: t(job) = 'TRAINER')$

The preceding first conjunct states that for every offering the assigned trainer should be a known employee; this represents what the foreign key implements. The second conjunct states that for all tuples in the join of OFFR (which requires attribute renaming) and EMP, the JOB attribute should hold value 'TRAINER'; this represents what remains to be implemented procedurally. By the way, do you recognize the predicate pattern of the second conjunct? It is in fact a *tuple-in-join* predicate.

Note You'll probably intuitively comprehend that the second predicate is exactly what remains to be implemented procedurally for PSSR8. It is worth mentioning that you could actually *formally prove* that the preceding conjunction is logically equivalent with the PSSR8 predicate. It requires the development of more rewrite rules with regards to quantifiers, and a few concepts with regards to how formal proofs are to be set up (both of which we haven't done in this book).

Procedurally implementing database constraints is done in a similar way as table constraints; it just requires developing more triggers because multiple table structures are involved now. Take a look at Listing 11-40. It lists all necessary triggers using EM6 (including serialization logic) for implementing the remaining tuple-in-join predicate listed earlier to complete the PSSR8 implementation. In this case, you require an after statement update trigger on the EMP table structure, and an after INSERT statement trigger together with an after statement update trigger on the OFFR table structure.

Listing 11-40 does not list the necessary global temporary table, pre-statement trigger, after row triggers, and view definitions to maintain the transition effect views; you need to set these up for both the OFFR and EMP table structures in a similar way, as shown in Listing 11-33.

Listing 11-40. *EM6 Implemention of DI Code for Remaining PSSR8 Predicate*

```
create trigger EMP_AUS_PSSR8
after update on EMP
declare pl_dummy varchar(40);
begin
  -- Changing a trainers job, requires validation of PSSR8.
  for r in (select n_empno as empno
              from v_emp_ute e
              where (e.O_empno=e.n_empno and e.n_job<>'TRAINER' and e.o_job='TRAINER')
                or (e.O_empno<>e.n_empno and e.n_job<>'TRAINER'))
  loop
  begin
    -- Acquire serialization lock.
    p_request_lock('PSSR8'||to_char(r.empno));
    --
    select 'Constraint PSSR8 is satisfied' into pl_dummy
    from DUAL
```

```
          where not exists(select 'This employee is assigned as a trainer to an offering'
                            from OFFR o
                            where o.TRAINER =  r.empno);
          --
      exception when no_data_found then
          --
          raise_application_error(-20999,'Constraint PSSR8 is violated '||
                                'for employee '||to_char(r.empno)||'.');
          --
      end;
      end loop;
      --
  end;
  /
  create trigger OFFR_AIS_PSSR8
  after insert on OFFR
  declare pl_dummy varchar(40);
  begin
    -- Inserting an offering, requires validation of PSSR8.
    for r in (select distinct trainer
                from v_offr_ite i)
    loop
    begin
      -- Acquire serialization lock.
      p_request_lock('PSSR8'||to_char(r.trainer));
      --
      select 'Constraint PSSR8 is satisfied' into pl_dummy
      from DUAL
      where not exists(select 'This employee is not a trainer'
                        from EMP e
                        where e.EMPNO =  r.trainer
                          and e.JOB   <> 'TRAINER');
      --
    exception when no_data_found then
        --
        raise_application_error(-20999,'Constraint PSSR8 is violated '||
                              'for trainer '||to_char(r.trainer)||'.');
        --
    end;
    end loop;
    --
  end;
  /
  create trigger OFFR_AUS_PSSR8
  after update on OFFR
  declare pl_dummy varchar(40);
  begin
```

```
-- Updating the trainer of an offering, requires validation of PSSR8.
for r in (select distinct n_trainer as trainer
           from v_offr_ute u
           where o_trainer<>n_trainer)
loop
begin
  -- Acquire serialization lock.
  p_request_lock('PSSR8'||to_char(r.trainer));
  --
  select 'Constraint PSSR8 is satisfied' into pl_dummy
  from DUAL
  where not exists(select 'This employee is not a trainer'
                    from EMP e
                    where e.EMPNO =  r.trainer
                      and e.JOB   <> 'TRAINER');
  --
exception when no_data_found then
  --
  raise_application_error(-20999,'Constraint PSSR8 is violated '||
                          'for trainer '||to_char(r.trainer)||'.');
  --
end;
end loop;
--
end;
/
```

We'll end this section with an observation about the poor declarative support for multi-tuple constraints offered by DBMS vendors.

Because we believe that it is not possible for a DBMS vendor to program an algorithm that accepts an arbitrarily complex predicate and then computes efficient TE queries, a minimal validation query, and optimal serialization code to implement execution model EM6, we should not expect full support for multi-tuple constraints—in a practical, usable and acceptable way—from these vendors in the future. The best we can hope for is that database researchers first come up with more common classes of constraints and develop convenient shorthands for these. The DBMS vendors, in their turn, should then provide us with new declarative constructs, consistent with these shorthands, to state these common classes of constraints easily to the DBMS. Given such a common class declaration, the DBMS vendor should be able to program an algorithm that provides us with an EM6-like execution model under the covers to implement the constraint.

■Note We've hinted at a few common classes of constraints in this book for which DBMS vendors should offer us full declarative support: specialization, generalization, and tuple-in-join constraints. Also, in the area of subset requirement constraints—where we currently only have the SQL foreign key construct available to us—more declarative variations should be offered.

This concludes the investigation of developing DI code for database constraints. The next section takes a look at implementing transition constraints.

Implementing Transition Constraints

Please go back to Listing 8-8 and take a moment to recall the transition constraints of our example database universe.

Do you notice that the way the state transition constraints are specified is not different from the way you would specify a database constraint? They are predicates that involve two or more parameters of type table. Of course, in the case of transition constraints, these parameters always represent old and new snapshots of involved table structures. But in essence, a transition constraint is a predicate involving multiple table structures. This means that the complexity involved in implementing DI code for transition constraints is in principle not different from the complexity involved in database constraints.

A transition constraint deals with a transaction's begin state and end state. As explained before, transactions are implemented in SQL by the consecutive execution of DML statements. Such implementation not only creates intermediate database states, but—in the context of this section—also creates *intermediate state transitions*. Formally you would only need to validate the transition from the begin state to the end state of the transaction. DI code for transition constraints should only execute after the last DML statement of the transaction has created the end state; that is, its execution should be deferred to the end of the transaction.

In the section "Bringing Deferred Checking into the Picture," you'll find a brief exploration of deferring execution of DI code. For now we'll demonstrate how you can develop DI code for transition constraints (in the triggered procedural strategy), such that all intermediate state transitions satisfy them too.

■**Note** As you probably know, there is no support whatsoever in current SQL DBMSes to implement transition constraints declaratively.

If you start thinking about implementing transition constraints, you'll immediately hit this question: "In an after statement trigger, how do I query the old snapshot of an involved table structure?" The answer happens to be simple. In Oracle's SQL DBMS you can use *flashback queries* to do exactly that: query an old snapshot of a table structure.

To be able to use a flashback query on a table structure, you'll somehow need to administer what the *system change number* was when the transaction started. You can do this using a packaged variable, or a session temporary table. Note that only the table structures whose old snapshot is involved in any of the state transition constraints will ever need to be queried using a flashback query. So it is safe to administer the system change number only when a DML statement changes one of these table structures; you can use pre-statement triggers for this that determine the current system change number via `dbms_flashback.get_system_change_number` and store that in the packaged variable or session table. In the following example, we'll assume these triggers are already in place.

We'll now present you with an exploration of implementing the DI code for state transition constraint STC5.

```
STC5(HISTB,EMPB,HISTE,EMPE) :=
        /* New history records must accurately reflect employee updates */
        ( ∀h∈(HISTE⇓{EMPNO,UNTIL} − HISTB⇓{EMPNO,UNTIL})⊗HISTE:
            h(UNTIL) = sysdate ∧
            ( ∃e1∈ EMPB, e2∈ EMPE:
              e1↓{EMPNO,MSAL,DEPTNO} = h↓{EMPNO,MSAL,DEPTNO} ∧
              e2(EMPNO) = h(EMPNO) ∧
              ( e2(MSAL) ≠ e1(MSAL) ∨ e2(DEPTNO) ≠ e1(DEPTNO) ) ) )
```

For maintaining this constraint, you only need to develop an after INSERT statement trigger on the HIST table structure. Listing 11-41 lists this trigger. Note how the formal specification is again translated fairly easily into a constraint validation query. The following code assumes the availability of a transition effect view and also assumes the availability of function f_get_start_scn to retrieve the previously stored system change number.

Listing 11-41. *EM6 Implemention of DI Code for STC5 (Without Serialization)*

```
create or replace trigger HIST_AIS_STC5
after insert on HIST
declare pl_dummy varchar(40);
begin
  -- Inserting a history record, requires validation of STC5.
  for r in (select empno,until
              from v_hist_ite i)
  loop
  begin
    --
    select 'Constraint STC5 is satisfied' into pl_dummy
    from DUAL
    where exists (select 'The history record is OK'
                  from HIST h
                  where h.EMPNO = r.empno
                    and h.UNTIL = r.until
                    and h.UNTIL = sysdate
                    and exists(select 'A corresponding update on EMP'
                               from EMP as of scn f_get_tx_start_scn e1
                                   ,EMP e2
                               where e1.EMPNO   = h.EMPNO
                                 and e1.MSAL    = h.MSAL
                                 and e1.DEPTNO  = h.DEPTNO
                                 and e2.EMPNO   = h.EMPNO
                                 and (e2.MSAL<>e1.MSAL or e2.DEPTNO<>e1.DEPTNO)));
  exception when no_data_found then
    --
    raise_application_error(-20999,'Constraint STC5 is violated '||
                            'for history record '||to_char(r.empno)||'/'||
```

```
                                                    to_char(r.until)||'.');
      --
   end;
   end loop;
   --
end;
```

Devising a serialization strategy for DI code of transition constraints is not trivial. For instance, consider the following scenario (in Table 11-5) of two concurrently executing transactions: TX5 and TX6.

Table 11-5. *Serialization of TX5 and TX6*

Time	TX5	TX6	Comment
t=0	DML1;		TX5 starts; DML1 does not involve the EMP table structure.
t=1		UPDATE	TX6 starts; it updates the salary of employee 1042.
t=2		INSERT	TX6 inserts corresponding history record; STC5 DI code fires.
t=3		COMMIT	TX6 ends.
t=4	INSERT		TX5 inserts similar history record for 1042, STC5 DI code fires.

Given Oracle's read-committed isolation level, when the DI code for constraint STC5 fires at t=4, it sees the change in salary for employee 1042 established by transaction TX6. The old snapshot from t=0 did not have this change. The new snapshot (that is, the current one at t=4) does have this change because TX6 has already committed at t=4. STC5's DI code could there-fore approve the history record insert performed by TX5 (given, of course, that it correctly reflects the salary update). Adding serialization lock calls won't help in this case; any locks acquired by the DI code running in TX6 will already have been released at t=4.

Obviously, the reason why the current setup of STC5's DI code doesn't work correctly is because it wrongly deduces that the change it sees with respect to the EMP table structure is due to prior DML statements in the *same* transaction.

We've given you this example to show that implementing DI code for (at least some) state transition constraints is by far not trivial and definitely requires further investigation.

■**Note** At the time of the writing of this book we have not yet fully investigated the issues with respect to correctly serializing state transition DI code. In this case, a possible fix could be to have the constraint vali-dation query (the flashback query) run in Oracle's `serializable` isolation level. Queries that run in this mode won't see changes made by other transactions that were committed after the current transaction began; you only see the changes that the current transaction made. Unfortunately you cannot change the isolation mode of a single query; you would have to resort to running the whole transaction in Oracle's `serializable` mode.

In the next section you'll find an exploration of another issue that we have ignored up to now.

Bringing Deferred Checking into the Picture

So far we've been assuming that during the serial execution of DML statements in a transaction, every intermediate database state should satisfy all constraints; all required DI code is run immediately at statement level using after DML-triggers. However, you'll sometimes require that the execution of DI code be deferred to the end of the transaction.

Why Deferred Checking?

There is a class of data integrity constraints that will always need to be temporarily violated during the transaction, and rechecked in a deferred way at the end of the transaction. An example of this is a specialization constraint. Take a look at constraint PSPEC1 from our example database design:

```
PSPEC1(EMP,SREP) :=
    /* Sales reps have a target and a commission */
    { e(EMPNO) | e∈EMP ∧ e(JOB) = 'SALESREP' } =
    { s(EMPNO) | s∈SREP }
```

Because with SQL, you cannot insert both the EMP row and the SREP row at the same time, a transaction that inserts a new sales representative will have to issue two inserts. Also, irrespective of the order of the inserts, the intermediate database state will violate constraint PSPEC1.

This example gives us a first reason why, in our SQL world, you have to deal with temporary constraint violations.

DML Statements Operate on a Single Table Structure

Given our set of data integrity constraints, certain valid database state transitions might well require a DML statement on more than one table structure. Because constraints in the *database constraint* class have a data scope of multiple table structures, there is a good possibility that a database constraint violation will be caused by a first DML statement on one of the involved table structures and that a second DML statement will correct this violation on one of the other involved table structures.

Note the use of the word "possibility." Some transactions will always need to violate a certain database constraint temporarily, regardless of the order in which the DML statements within that transaction are executed (the preceding PSPEC1 is an example of this). However, many database constraints never need deferred checking. The data constrained by them can be kept to satisfy the constraint at all times by issuing the different DML statements *in a specific order* implied by the constraint. For instance, this is the case with a subset requirement. It can always be satisfied by intermediate database states as long as DML statements are executed in the right order; you'll first need to insert a new row to the superset and then to the subset.

In the next section we'll discuss a second shortcoming of the SQL language, which gives rise to deferred checking.

DML Statements Operate in a Single Manner

A DML statement is an INSERT, an UPDATE, or a DELETE statement. However, a valid state transition of one table structure might require more than one type of DML statement to achieve, and thus could possibly give rise to the need to allow temporary violations for table constraints too.

For example, take the following (not very realistic) table constraint: "The number of sales reps plus twice the number of clerks must equal either 100 or zero." Let's look at the transaction of introducing a clerk. Assume that the current EMP table holds 100 sales reps (rendering our table constraint TRUE). As soon as we introduce the new clerk, either by updating the JOB of a sales rep or by inserting a new clerk, we'll always introduce a violation and need a second different type of DML statement to restore the truth of the table constraint.

This shortcoming of the SQL language implies that DI code for certain *table constraints* can be subject to deferred execution too. We'll call table and database constraints that require temporary violations inside transactions, *deferrable* constraints.

Outline of Execution Model for Deferred Checking

If a DML statement, say DML1, introduces a violation within a transaction, then there must be a subsequent DML statement within the same transaction, say DML2, that corrects the violation introduced by DML1 prior to the end of the transaction. On execution of DML1, you would either

- Not want to execute the involved DI code at all, but instead *schedule* it to be executed at the end of the transaction, or

- Have the involved DI code execute in such a way that only if it detects a violation is it scheduled to be *re-executed* at the end of the transaction.

In both cases, if on re-execution of the DI code the constraint is still found to be violated, then the transaction should obviously be prohibited from committing.

So, how do you schedule DI code to be executed at the end of a transaction? Well, you don't; there is no way to achieve this in Oracle's DBMS. A concept enabling you to do this would have been the concept of a *commit trigger*. A commit trigger would fire just prior, as part of the system commit procedure, and it could check the end state that is about to be committed by the transaction. By embedding DI code into this trigger, you could recheck whether subsequent DML statements have resolved all temporary violations of constraints. Only if this is the case does the trigger allow the commit procedure to succeed. Unfortunately, the DBMS doesn't offer the concept of a commit trigger.

However, there is another way that allows you to re-execute DI code of a temporarily violated constraint. In the remainder of this section, we'll provide you with an outline of how you could modify execution model EM6 to also cater for deferred checking.

Take a look at Table 11-6. It describes a transaction that executes four DML statements. Statement DML1 involves constraint C1, which has been identified as a deferrable constraint.

Table 11-6. *Re-Executing DI Code of Deferred Constraint C1*

TX	Comment
`DML1;`	Involves constraint `C1`; DI code fires and finds that `DML1` violates it. DI code allows this.
`DML2;`	DI code of other constraints executes. `C1` DI code is re-executed; finds `C1` is still in violation.
`DML3;`	DI code of other constraints executes. `C1` is rechecked; DI code now finds `C1` is satisfied.
`DML4;`	DI code of other constraints executes. `C1` is no longer rechecked.
`COMMIT;`	

Statement `DML1` introduces a violation of constraint `C1`. Because `C1` has been identified as deferrable, its DI code will not raise an error to force a rollback of `DML1`. Instead, it stores information about the fact that `C1` is currently violated somewhere inside the context of this transaction.

When `DML2` is executed, various other (non-deferrable) constraints might be involved, and the DI code for those constraints is executed accordingly. In our modified execution model, this is now followed by a check of the transaction's context to find out if certain constraints are currently violated. If such a constraint is found, then the modified execution model will now also re-execute the DI code of this constraint. If on recheck the constraint is found to still be in violation, then the context remains unchanged. If on recheck the constraint is found to be satisfied, then the context will be modified to reflect that constraint `C1` is no longer in violation.

In the preceding scenario, statement `DML3` repairs the violation of constraint `C1`. When `DML4` is executed, the execution model now no longer re-executes the DI code for `C1`.

The preceding scenario shows you that you can use the triggers that fire for subsequent DML statements to recheck a deferrable constraint that a preceding DML statement violated.

You have one challenge left now. Can you prevent a commit from successfully executing when the transaction context still holds information stating that one or more deferrable constraints are in violation? The answer is yes, you can.

If the DI code for a given deferrable constraint finds that this constraint is violated, it can store this information in a session temporary table. And if the DI code finds that the constraint is satisfied again, then it deletes the associated record from the session temporary table. You can set up this session temporary table in a way that whenever this table holds a record, a transaction cannot successfully commit. Take a look at Listing 11-42, which defines this session temporary table.

Listing 11-42. *Table for Storing Temporary Violations*

```
create global temporary table current_violations
(constraint_name   varchar(30) not null
,constraint all_satisfied_at_commit check(0=1) initially deferred
,constraint curvio_pk primary key(constraint_name))
on commit preserve rows;
```

Do you see the trick that's used? The way this session temporary table (on commit preserve rows) and the all_satisfied_at_commit constraint (initially deferred) are set up allows DI code to insert records in the current_violations table. However, at the same time it disables transactions from committing successfully when there are still records in this table, thereby preventing transactions from committing when a deferrable constraint is in violation.

As you'll probably agree, bringing deferred execution into the picture complicates the execution model substantially:

- DI code for deferrable constraints must now appropriately insert and delete from the current_violations table.

- You must extend all DI code with procedural code that rechecks all constraints that are currently registered in the current_violations table. To be able to perform the recheck without having to replicate DI code for deferrable constraints, you'll need to move current DI code from the trigger bodies into stored procedures; this enables you to call this code from other triggers too.

- You might want a more efficient execution model than the one outlined so far. Currently a deferrable constraint (one that is in violation) is rechecked on every subsequent DML statement. For a given subsequent DML statement, you can deduce whether rechecking a constraint is even sensible or not. For instance, if a subsequent DML statement operates on a table that is not involved in the deferrable constraint, then this DML statement can never restore a violation of the deferrable constraint. To prevent unnecessary rechecks, you'll only want to run the recheck if the subsequent DML statement is such that it could potentially restore a violation.

Note In fact, you can determine this by using the transition effect to guard such re-execution of DI code for a deferrable constraint. Instead of querying the transition effect to verify if a DML statement can violate a constraint, you now do the inverse: query the transition effect to verify if a DML statement can restore a constraint.

This concludes the outline of an execution model for deferred checking. We wrap up this section with one important observation with regards to deferrable constraints.

There is a serious problem with allowing constraints to be temporarily violated inside transactions. You run the risk of getting incorrect results from queries executing in these transactions. For instance, assume that constraint PSPEC1 is currently violated due to the fact that in the current transaction an insert of a new sales reps into the EMP table structure has not yet been followed by a corresponding insert into the SREP table structure. Now suppose you want to determine the number of sales reps. When you write data retrieval statements, you normally assume that all constraints are satisfied. Under these circumstances, there are two ways to find the number of sales reps:

```
select count(*)
from EMP
where JOB='SALESREP';

select count(*)
from SREP;
```

Note that when PSPEC1 is violated in the way just described, then the first SELECT expression will return the correct result, and the second SELECT expression will return an incorrect result. Actually, in the given intermediate database state you might argue whether the number of sales reps is at all defined, because two supposedly equivalent query expressions return different results. Getting incorrect results is a serious problem when you allow constraints to be temporarily violated.

Note The real solution for preventing this problem is to add the concept of a *multiple assignment* to the SQL language. We refer you to papers written by Chris Date and Hugh Darwen on this subject (see Appendix C).

Having explored various matters concerning the implementation of DI code in a triggered procedural approach, we conclude this chapter with a short introduction to a framework that can assist you in implementing DI code.

The RuleGen Framework

Having seen the various examples of DI code in this chapter, you can imagine that as the number of constraints that you have implemented grows, maintaining them can become quite a challenge. Our example database design only has about 50 multi-tuple constraints. Real-world database designs typically have hundreds—if not over a thousand—multi-tuple constraints, most of which cannot be stated declaratively to the DBMS.

For every constraint that you implement, you are repeating a lot of code over and over again; the parts that differ for each constraint are the *TE queries*, the *validation query*, and the *serialization code*. Wouldn't it be great if you could just register these three for a given constraint and have some piece of software generate all the required row and statement triggers for you?

Over the past few years one of the authors—Toon Koppelaars—has developed a framework, called RuleGen, that does just this. RuleGen implements execution model EM6, including the outlined enhancements necessary to cater for deferrable constraints.

You register a constraint within RuleGen by populating a few tables of its repository. This involves information about the constraint, its involved tables and involved columns, the TE queries, the validation query, and the serialization code. Given this information, RuleGen will fully generate the necessary row and statement triggers for each involved table. Row triggers will maintain the transition effect that the statement triggers use. Statement triggers will validate the necessary constraints.

By the time this book is available, we expect to have made available more information about the RuleGen framework. If you are interested in this framework, you can find up-to-date information, documentation, and papers at http://www.rulegen.com/am4dp. We'll also maintain a download on this site of all DI code for the constraints involved in the example database universe described in this book.

Chapter Summary

This section provides a summary of this chapter, formatted as a bulleted list.

- You usually implement a database design in order to build a business application on top of it. These applications normally are *window-on-data* (WoD) applications. Users query and transact data by using these applications.

- All code of a WoD application can be classified into three classes: *user interface* code (UI code), *business logic* code (BL code), and *data integrity* code (DI code). UI code creates the user interface that the user sees, and it responds to events initiated by the user in the user interface. DI code is responsible for the continued validity of all data integrity constraints as users change data in the database. BL code is responsible for composing and executing queries and transactions.

- This chapter's main focus has been how to implement DI code in an efficient manner.

- You can implement DI code using one of the following three strategies: *declarative*, *triggered procedural*, or *embedded procedural*.

- You can state all attribute and tuple constraints declaratively. You can state only a few table and database constraints declaratively.

- The majority of (multi-row) data integrity constraints must be implemented procedurally. In this chapter, the triggered procedural strategy is preferred over the embedded procedural strategy.

- We introduced you to six execution models for implementing DI code for multi-tuple constraints. These range from rather inefficient (every constraint is fully checked for every DML statement), to rather efficient (a constraint is conditionally checked in a minimal way).

- Given Oracle's standard read-committed isolation level, you must programmatically serialize DI code. Failure to do so can result in constraint violations when transactions execute concurrently. Serializing DI code of transition constraints is particularly difficult.

- Certain constraints cannot be validated at the statement level; they require a deferred execution model of the DI code. Extending the execution models to cater for deferred execution of DI code is not easy. You've seen an outline of how this could be done, which involved setting up a central table where temporary violations are logged.

- If you have many data integrity constraints that require a triggered procedural implementation, then the RuleGen framework can help you manage all DI code for these constraints.

Summary and Conclusions

You've reached the last chapter of this book. In this chapter we'll provide a brief summary first and then give some conclusions.

Summary

In Part 1 of this book, we presented two important mathematical disciplines: logic and set theory. These two disciplines are the most relevant ones in the application of mathematics to the field of databases.

Chapter 1 offered an introduction to logic. We presented the concepts of a *proposition* and a *predicate*, and showed how you can use *logical connectives* (conjunction, disjunction, implication, equivalence, and negation) to describe compound propositions and predicates. The chapter ended by establishing the very important concept of a *rewrite rule*. You've seen many applications of rewrite rules throughout this book; they enable you to transform predicates into other equivalent predicates.

Chapter 2 offered an introduction to set theory. We presented several ways to specify *sets*, discussed the concept of a *subset*, and explored the common set operators *union*, *intersection*, and *difference*. The chapter ended with a treatment of *powersets* and *ordered pairs*. As you saw in Part 2 of this book, set theory provides an excellent language to reliably describe complex database designs, data retrieval, and data manipulation.

Chapter 3 continued the treatment of logic that was started in the first chapter. It introduced you to the key concepts of *universal* and *existential quantification* and identified important rewrite rules concerning these two quantifiers. One of these rewrite rules demonstrated that you can transform the existential quantifier into a universal quantifier, and vice versa—a rewrite rule that has been applied many times in this book.

Chapter 4 continued the set theory basics laid down in Chapter 2, and introduced some more concepts in this area. You saw how you can use a *function* to represent a *tuple*. We've also shown how you can use a special kind of function, a *set function*, to *characterize* something of the real world that needs to be represented in the database.

Chapters 5 and 6 demonstrated how you can apply set theory and logic to describe important concepts in the field of databases. We used these mathematical disciplines to formally describe the following:

- *Tables* and *database states*

- Common table operators such as *projection, extension, restriction*, and *join*—to name a few

- *Tuple, table*, and *database predicates*—the building blocks for specifying constraints

At the end of Chapter 6 we also explored common types of data integrity predicates: *unique identification, subset requirements, specialization, generalization*, and *tuple-in-join* predicates.

Chapter 7 brought everything together and demonstrated the main topic of this book: how you can apply all introduced mathematical concepts to create a solid database design specification (a *database universe*). The layered approach in which this was done gives us a good and clear insight into the relevant data integrity constraints. It established several classes of constraints: *attribute, tuple, table*, and *database* constraints. Chapter 8 explored another class of constraints: *state transition constraints*. As you've seen, you can also specify this class of constraints in a formal way. Clear insight in all involved constraints is a prerequisite to performing a reliable and robust implementation of the design using an SQL DBMS.

Chapters 9 and 10 discussed the application of the mathematics in the areas of specifying *data retrieval* (queries) and *data manipulation* (transactions).

Finally, in Chapter 11 we explored the challenges of implementing a database design—specifically all its data integrity constraints—in a well-known SQL DBMS (Oracle). As you've seen, for some classes of constraints, the implementation is trivial (they can be declared to the DBMS), but for other classes of constraints the implementation turns out to be a complex task. Implementing an efficient execution model, serializing transactions, and sometimes deferring the execution of checking the constraints are some of the aspects that make this task a serious challenge.

Note Many subjects haven't been covered in this book. For instance, you can further explore the mathematics to come up with other useful rewrite rules. Also, a treatment on how to provide formal proofs isn't included; being able to prove that a given transformation of a predicate is correct is sometimes very convenient. Also, in this book we chose to offer you only the necessary formal tools so that you can start dealing with database designs in a clear and professional way. We have specifically not covered subjects such as the following: what is a good database design, what are the criteria by which you can measure this, what about data redundancy, and the various normal forms in database design. Covering these topics justifies at least another book in itself.

Conclusions

The unique aspect of this book is captured by its title: applied mathematics for database professionals. We've described two disciplines of mathematics that can act as high-quality toolsets for a database professional. We've described how to apply these toolsets in the area of data integrity constraints.

Data integrity constraints add semantic value to the data captured by a database design by describing how the table structures represent the real world that we work in. For this reason, data integrity constraint specifications are an integral part of a database design specification. The formal methodology described in this book enables us to specify a database design precisely, and in particular to specify all involved data integrity constraints precisely.

Here is quote that reiterates the importance of data integrity constraints:

> *It should be clear that integrity constraints are crucially important, since they control the correctness of the data. In many ways, in fact, integrity constraints are the most important part of the system.*

C. J. Date, What Not How (Addison-Wesley, 2000)

Why are *formal* constraint specifications so important?

Well, if we use plain English, or some awkward derivative, to express data integrity constraints we'll inevitably hit the problem of how the English sentence maps, unambiguously, into the database design. Different software developers will implement such specifications diversely, because they all try to convert the sentence—everybody in his or her own way—to something that will map into the database design, and then code it.

Every informal language is bound to be ambiguous. This is unsolvable. An informal or natural language effort to capture data integrity constraints will always fail in exposing, unambiguously, how such a constraint maps into the database design, because there exists no mapping from the informal natural language to the formal world of a database design. This data integrity constraint problem is inevitable unless we adopt a formal methodology. With a formal language, we can unambiguously describe how a constraint maps into a database design.

Within the IT profession we should recognize that database design is a task for properly educated database professionals. Their education must involve enough set theory and logic, including how these disciplines can be applied in the field of designing databases. This book aims to provide this formal education.

How can you start applying this knowledge in your job as a database professional? Here's a little roadmap that you can adopt.

1. Whenever you design your next database, start by specifying the involved data integrity constraints in a formal way. Specify them as data integrity predicates and adopt the classification scheme introduced in Chapters 7 and 8.

2. Apply this formalism to queries too, especially the more complex ones. Use rewrite rules in the formal world to come up with expressions that can easily be transformed to SQL.

3. Finally, you can move on to specifying transactions formally too. This should avoid all ambiguities when software is developed to implement the business logic of a WoD application.

You'll get the biggest gains from step 1. It ensures that there is a documented single truth of the meaning (semantics) of the database design, which in turn makes certain that all software developers will understand and therefore use the database design in the same way.

Once you formally specify the database design, a good implementation of the database design becomes possible. We've discussed various strategies for implementing the important part of every database design: the data integrity constraints.

Implementing data constraints declaratively is easy. Implementing data constraints procedurally is by far not a trivial task (as discussed in Chapter 11). It's time consuming and will produce more lines of complex procedural code than you might have expected (part of which can be generated, though). The current status of DBMS technology, such as Oracle's SQL DBMS, enables us to implement database designs in a robust way; that is, including the DI code for all data integrity constraints in a triggered procedural way.

Still, few database professionals actually do this. Why? Probably because designing DI code that is fully detached from BL code (the triggered procedural strategy) is indeed truly complex given the current state of DBMSes available to us. However, this neglects the big picture. Failing to fully detach DI code from BL code implies not being able to efficiently maintain and manage the DI code and thus the constraints.

We should not underestimate the gains we receive once all DI code is implemented separately. Data integrity constraints have then finally become manageable. There is an interesting opportunity for DBMS vendors to evolve their products into data integrity constraint engines. It is up to the scientific world to come up with more meaningful subclasses of constraints first. The DBMS vendors, in their turn, should then provide us with new declarative constructs at the DBMS level to implement these easily.

Once more declarative constructs are available, there is not only a huge potential of much more rapid construction of WoD applications, but also the potential of achieving considerable savings in the cost of maintaining such an application.

PART 4

Appendixes

APPENDIX A

Formal Definition of Example Database

In this appendix, we deliver the formal specification of the example database design used throughout this book.

The section "Bird's Eye Overview" provides a bird's-eye overview of the example database; it shows a picture of the ten tables with their relationships, and it provides brief informal descriptions of those tables and relationships.

We then present you with a definition of the *database skeleton* DB_S. In the section "Database Skeleton DB_S" you can find the involved attributes for each table, including a brief description for each attribute.

The biggest section of this appendix is the section "Table Universe Definitions," providing the ten *table universe* definitions. For each table, you'll find the table universe specification that formally defines all attribute, tuple, and table constraints that are applicable for that table, alongside the external predicate (describing the meaning of the table to the user).

The appendix ends with the definition of the *static* database constraints through a specification of the *database universe* DB_UEX in the section "Database Universe DB_UEX," followed by the *dynamic* constraints through a specification of the *state transition universe* TX_UEX in the section "State Transition Universe TX_UEX." The following table summarizes the structure of this appendix and shows how the specification of the example database design is built up, starting from a skeleton all the way up to a database and state transition universe.

Table A-1. *Appendix Structure*

Section	Specifies	Description
"Database Skeleton DB_S"	DB_S	Lists the table and column names
"Table Universe Definitions"	tab_XXX	Provides the characterization, tuple universe, and table universe for each of the ten tables
"Database Characterization DBCH"	DBCH	Maps each table to its table universe
"Database Universe DB_UEX"	DB_UEX	Lists all static database constraints
"State Transition Universe TX_UEX"	TX_UEX	Lists all dynamic database constraints

Bird's Eye Overview

Figure A-1 shows a diagram of the ten tables (represented by rounded-corner boxes) that make up our sample database design, and their mutual relationships (represented by arrows).

Each of these arrows indicates a *subset requirement* that is applicable between a pair of tables. These subset requirements indicate that some projection of the table at the beginning of the arrow should always be a subset of some projection of the table to which the arrow is pointing. The majority of these arrows represent what is often called *many-to-one relationships*, and will eventually end up as *foreign key constraints* during the implementation phase. However, this is not always the case, as you have seen in Chapter 11.

We'll give the exact meaning of each arrow in the database universe specification DB_UEX in the fifth section of this appendix.

Our database holds employees (EMP) and departments (DEPT) of a company. Some of the arrows indicate the following:

- An employee is working for a department.

- A department is managed by an employee.

- An employee is assigned to a salary grade (GRD).

Employee history (HIST) records are maintained for all salary and/or "works-for-department" changes; every history record describes a period during which one employee was assigned to one department with a specific salary.

We hold additional information for all sales representatives in a separate table (SREP). We hold additional information for employees who no longer work for the company (that is, they have been terminated or they resigned) in a table TERM. We hold additional information for all managed employees (MEMP); that is, employees who have a manager assigned to them.

The database further holds information about courses (CRS), offerings (OFFR) of those courses, and registrations (REG) for those course offerings. Some more arrows show the following:

- An offering must be taught by a trainer who works for the company.

- An offering is of an existing course.

- A registration records one employee as an attendee for one course offering.

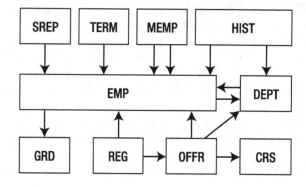

Figure A-1. *Picture of example database*

Database Skeleton DB_S

In this section, you'll find a specification of the skeleton DB_S for the sample database.

A *database skeleton* defines our vocabulary; for each table we introduce a table alias, and for each table we introduce the names of the involved attributes for that table. We won't give the external predicates for the tables here; you can find these in the definition of the table universes in the next section of this appendix.

A database skeleton is a set-valued function; for each table this function yields the set of attributes (heading) of that table. Our database skeleton DB_S for the sample database is defined in Listing A-1.

Listing A-1. *Database Skeleton Definition*

```
DB_S = { (EMP;                        -- Employees
                { EMPNO           /* Employee number          */
                , ENAME           /* Employee name            */
                , JOB             /* Employee job             */
                , BORN            /* Date of birth            */
                , HIRED           /* Date hired               */
                , SGRADE          /* Salary grade             */
                , MSAL            /* Monthly salary           */
                , USERNAME        /* Username                 */
                , DEPTNO    } )   /* Department number        */
       , (SREP;                        -- Sales Representatives
                { EMPNO           /* Employee number          */
                , TARGET          /* Sales target             */
                , COMM      } )   /* Commission               */
       , (MEMP;                        -- Managed Employees
                { EMPNO           /* Employee number          */
                , MGR       } )   /* Manager: employee number */
       , (TERM;                        -- Terminated Employees
                { EMPNO           /* Employee number          */
                , LEFT            /* Date of leave            */
                , COMMENTS } )    /* Termination comments     */
       , (DEPT;                        -- Departments
                { DEPTNO          /* Department number        */
                , DNAME           /* Department name          */
                , LOC             /* Location                 */
                , MGR       } )   /* Manager: employee number */
       , (GRD;                         -- Salary Grades
                { GRADE           /* Grade code               */
                , LLIMIT          /* Lower salary limit       */
                , ULIMIT          /* Upper salary limit       */
                , BONUS     } )   /* Yearly bonus             */
       , (CRS;                         -- Courses
                { CODE            /* Course code              */
                , DESCR           /* Course description       */
                , CAT             /* Course category          */
```

```
                , DUR       } )    /* Duration of course in days   */
      , (OFFR;                     -- Course Offerings
                { COURSE         /* Code of course               */
                , STARTS         /* Begin date of this offering  */
                , STATUS         /* Scheduled, confirmed, ...    */
                , MAXCAP         /* Max participants capacity    */
                , TRAINER        /* Trainer: employee number     */
                , LOC       } )  /* Location                     */
      , (REG;                        -- Course Registrations
                { STUD           /* Student: employee number     */
                , COURSE         /* Course code                  */
                , STARTS         /* Begin date course offering   */
                , EVAL      } )  /* Evaluation                   */
      , (HIST;                       -- Employee History Records
                { EMPNO          /* Employee number              */
                , UNTIL          /* History record end date      */
                , DEPTNO         /* Department number            */
                , MSAL      } ) } /* Monthly salary              */
```

Table Universe Definitions

This section provides formal definitions of the ten table universes of our sample database. For each table, you'll find four subsections:

- The *external predicate* for the table, describing the meaning of the attributes of the table to the database users.

- The *characterization*, attaching *attribute-value sets* to each attribute.

  The naming convention is chr_<table alias>.

- The *tuple universe*, defining the tuple constraints (if any) for the table.

  The naming convention is tup_<table alias>.

- The *table universe*, defining the table constraints for the table.

  The naming convention is tab_<table alias>.

Note The tuple universe specifications build on the characterization specifications; the table universe specifications, in turn, build on the tuple universe specifications.

Chapter 7 explained the following:

- An *attribute-value set* acts as the data type for the corresponding attribute.

- A *tuple universe* acts as the data type for a *tuple variable* of the table at hand.

- A *table universe* acts as the data type for a corresponding *table variable*.

You'll notice that the attribute-value sets are always defined by first drawing values from the base data types that are available in current SQL database management systems (that is, NUMBER, VARCHAR, and DATE) and then narrowing down these sets by specifying attribute constraints. In doing so, the attribute constraint expression to implement with the SQL CHECK clause is made explicit.

Where deemed necessary, you'll find embedded comments (/* ... */) explaining the formal definition.

All tuple, table, database, and dynamic constraints are sequentially numbered for easy reference.

Some Convenient Sets

In our database definition, four sets occur frequently: employee numbers, department numbers, salary-related amounts, and course codes. Therefore, we define them here so we can refer to them by name. You could consider them user-defined data types:

```
EMPNO_TYP   = { n | n∈number(4,0) ∧ n > 999      }
DEPTNO_TYP  = { n | n∈number(2,0) ∧ n > 0        }
SALARY_TYP  = { n | n∈number(7,2) ∧ n > 0        }
CRSCODE_TYP = { s | s∈varchar(6)  ∧ s = upper(s) }
```

Table Universe for EMP

> **External Predicate:** *The employee with employee number EMPNO has name ENAME, job JOB, was born at BORN, is hired at HIRED, has a monthly salary of MSAL dollars within the SGRADE salary grade, is assigned to account USERNAME, and works for the department with department number DEPTNO.*

The following three listings (A-2, A-3, and A-4) show the attribute-value sets, the tuple universe, and the table universe for EMP, respectively.

Listing A-2. *Characterization chr_EMP*

```
chr_EMP :=
{ ( EMPNO;  EMPNO_TYP                            )
, ( ENAME;  varchar(9)                           )
, ( JOB;    { s | s∈varchar(8) ∧
                  s∈{'PRESIDENT','MANAGER'
                    ,'SALESREP','TRAINER','ADMIN'} )
, ( BORN;   date                                 )
```

```
, ( HIRED;   date                                    )
, ( SGRADE; { n | n∈number(2,0) ∧ n > 0 }            )
, ( MSAL;    SALARY_TYP                               )
, ( USERNAME; { s | s∈varchar(15) ∧
                    upper(USERNAME) = USERNAME }      )
, ( DEPTNO; DEPTNO_TYP                                )
}
```

Listing A-3. *Tuple Universe tup_EMP*

```
tup_EMP :=
{ e | e∈Π(chr_EMP) ∧
      /* We hire adult employees only                           r1 */
      e(BORN) + 18 ≤ e(HIRED)
      ∧
      /* A president earns more than 10K monthly                r2 */
      e(JOB) = 'PRESIDENT' ⇒ e(MSAL) > 10000
      ∀̈
      /* Administrators earn less than 5K monthly               r3 */
      e(JOB) = 'ADMIN' ⇒ e(MSAL) < 5000
}
```

Listing A-4. *Table Universe tab_EMP*

```
tab_EMP :=
{ E | E∈℘(tup_EMP) ∧
      /* EMPNO uniquely identifies an employee tuple            r4 */
      ( ∀e1,e2∈E: e1(EMPNO) = e2(EMPNO) ⇒ e1 = e2 )
      ∧
      /* USERNAME uniquely identifies an employee tuple         r4 */
      ( ∀e1,e2∈E: e1(USERNAME) = e2(USERNAME) ⇒ e1 = e2 )
      ∧
      /* At most one president allowed                          r5 */
      #{ e | e∈E ∧ e(JOB) = 'PRESIDENT' } ≤ 1
      ∧
      /* A department that employs the president or a manager   r6 */
      /* should also employ at least one administrator           */
      ( ∀d∈{ e1(DEPTNO) | e1∈E }:
        ( ∃e2∈E: e2(DEPTNO) = d ∧ e2(JOB) ∈ {'PRESIDENT','MANAGER'} )
          ⇒
        ( ∃e2∈E: e2(DEPTNO) = d ∧ e2(JOB) = 'ADMIN' )
      )
}
```

Table Universe for SREP

External Predicate: *The sales representative with employee number* EMPNO *has an annual sales target of* TARGET *dollars and a yearly commission of* COMM *dollars.*

The following three listings (A-5, A-6, and A-7) show the attribute-value sets, the tuple universe, and the table universe for SREP, respectively.

Listing A-5. *Characterization chr_SREP*

```
chr_SREP :=
{ ( EMPNO;  EMPNO_TYP                        )
, ( TARGET; { n | n∈number(5,0) ∧ n > 9999 } )
, ( COMM;   SALARY_TYP                       )
}
```

Listing A-6. *Tuple Universe tup_SREP*

```
tup_SREP :=
{ s | s∈Π(chr_SREP) }
```

Listing A-7. *Table Universe tab_SREP*

```
tab_SREP :=
{ S | S∈℘(tup_SREP) ∧
     /* EMPNO uniquely identifies a tuple                      r7 */
     ( ∀s1,s2∈S: s1(EMPNO) = s2(EMPNO) ⇒ s1 = s2 )
}
```

Table Universe for MEMP

External Predicate: *The employee with employee number* EMPNO *is managed by the employee with employee number* MGR.

The following three listings (A-8, A-9, and A-10) show the attribute-value sets, the tuple universe, and the table universe for MEMP, respectively.

Listing A-8. *Characterization chr_MEMP*

```
chr_MEMP :=
{ ( EMPNO;  EMPNO_TYP          )
, ( MGR;    EMPNO_TYP          )
}
```

Listing A-9. *Tuple Universe tup_MEMP*

```
tup_MEMP :=
{ m | m∈Π(chr_MEMP) ∧
        /* You cannot manage yourself                                    r8 */
        m(EMPNO) ≠ m(MGR)
}
```

Listing A-10. *Table Universe tab_MEMP*

```
tab_MEMP :=
{ M | M∈℘(tup_MEMP) ∧
        /* EMPNO uniquely identifies a tuple                             r9 */
        ( ∀m1,m2∈S: m1(EMPNO) = m2(EMPNO) ⟹ m1 = m2 )
}
```

Table Universe for TERM

External Predicate: *The employee with number* EMPNO *has resigned or was fired at date* LEFT *due to reason* COMMENTS.

The following three listings (A-11, A-12, and A-13) show the attribute-value sets, the tuple universe, and the table universe for TERM, respectively.

Listing A-11. *Characterization chr_TERM*

```
chr_TERM :=
{ ( EMPNO;    EMPNO_TYP  )
, ( LEFT;     date       )
, ( COMMENTS; varchar(60) )
}
```

Listing A-12. *Tuple Universe tup_TERM*

```
tup_TERM :=
{ t | t∈Π(chr_TERM) }
```

Listing A-13. *Table Universe tab_TERM*

```
tab_TERM :=
{ T | T∈℘(tup_TERM) ∧
        /* EMPNO uniquely identifies a tuple                            r10 */
        ( ∀t1,t2∈T: t1(EMPNO) = t2(EMPNO) ⟹ t1 = t2 )
}
```

Table Universe for DEPT

External Predicate: *The department with department number DEPTNO has name DNAME, is located at LOC, and is managed by the employee with employee number MGR.*

The following three listings (A-14, A-15, and A-16) show the attribute-value sets, the tuple universe, and the table universe for DEPT, respectively.

Listing A-14. *Characterization chr_DEPT*

```
chr_DEPT :=
{ ( DEPTNO; DEPTNO_TYP                                       )
, ( DNAME;  { s | s∈varchar(12) ∧ upper(DNAME) = DNAME } )
, ( LOC;    { s | s∈varchar(14) ∧ upper(LOC) = LOC }     )
, ( MGR;    EMPNO_TYP                                        )
}
```

Listing A-15. *Tuple Universe tup_DEPT*

```
tup_DEPT :=
{ d | d∈Π(chr_DEPT) }
```

Listing A-16. *Table Universe tab_DEPT*

```
tab_DEPT :=
{ D | D∈ ℘(tab_DEPT) ∧
      /* Department number uniquely identifies a tuple            r11 */
      ( ∀d1,d2∈D: d1(DEPTNO) = d2(DEPTNO) ⇒ d1 = d2 )
      ∧
      /* Department name and location uniquely identify a tuple   r12 */
      ( ∀d1,d2∈D:
        d1↓{DNAME,LOC} = d2↓{DNAME,LOC} ⇒ d1 = d2 )
      ∧
      /* You cannot manage more than two departments              r13 */
      ( ∀m∈{ d(MGR) | d∈D }: #{ d | d∈D ∧ d(MGR) = m } ≤ 2 )
}
```

Table Universe for GRD

External Predicate: *The salary grade with ID GRADE has a lower monthly salary limit of LLIMIT dollars, an upper monthly salary limit of ULIMIT dollars, and a maximum net monthly bonus of BONUS dollars.*

The following three listings (A-17, A-18, and A-19) show the attribute-value sets, the tuple universe, and the table universe for GRD, respectively.

Listing A-17. *Characterization chr_GRD*

```
chr_GRD :=
{ ( GRADE;  { n | n∈number(2,0) ∧ n > 0 } )
, ( LLIMIT; SALARY_TYP                    )
, ( ULIMIT; SALARY_TYP                    )
, ( BONUS;  SALARY_TYP                    )
}
```

Listing A-18. *Tuple Universe tup_GRD*

```
tup_GRD :=
{ g | g∈Π(chr_GRD) ∧
        /* Salary grades have a bandwidth of at least 500 dollars      r14 */
        g(LLIMIT) ≤ g(ULIMIT) - 500
        ∧
        /* Bonus must be less than lower limit                         r15 */
        g(BONUS) < g(LLIMIT)
}
```

Listing A-19. *Table Universe tab_GRD*

```
tab_GRD :=
{ G | G∈℘(tup_GRD) ∧
        /* Salary grade code uniquely identifies a tuple              r16 */
        ( ∀g1,g2∈G: g1(GRADE) = g2(GRADE) ⇒ g1 = g2 )
        ∧
        /* Salary grade lower limit uniquely identifies a tuple       r17 */
        ( ∀g1,g2∈G: g1(LLIMIT) = g2(LLIMIT) ⇒ g1 = g2 )
        ∧
        /* Salary grade upper limit uniquely identifies a tuple       r18 */
        ( ∀g1,g2∈G: g1(ULIMIT) = g2(ULIMIT) ⇒ g1 = g2 )
        /* A salary grade overlaps with at most one (lower) grade     r20 */
        ( ∀g1∈G:
          ( ∃g2∈G:  g2(LLIMIT) < g1(LLIMIT) )
            ⇒
          #{ g3 | g3∈G ∧ g3(LLIMIT) < g1(LLIMIT) ∧
                        g3(ULIMIT) ≥ g1(LLIMIT) ∧
                        g3(ULIMIT) < g1(ULIMIT) } = 1
        )
}
```

Table Universe for CRS

External Predicate: The course with code CODE has description DESCR, falls in course category CAT, and has duration of DUR days.

The following three listings (A-20, A-21, and A-22) show the attribute-value sets, the tuple universe, and the table universe for CRS, respectively.

Listing A-20. *Characterization chr_CRS*

```
chr_CRS :=
{ ( CODE;  CRSCODE_TYP                           )
, ( DESCR; varchar(40)                           )
           /* Course category values: Design, Generate, Build        */
, ( CAT;   { s | s∈varchar(3) ∧
                 s∈{'DSG','GEN','BLD'} }          )
           /* Course duration must be between 1 and 15 days          */
, ( DUR;   { n | n∈number(2,0) ∧ 1 ≤ n ≤ 15 } )
}
```

Listing A-21. *Tuple Universe tup_CRS*

```
tup_CRS :=
{ c | c∈Π(chr_CRS) ∧
      /* Build courses never take more than 5 days              r21 */
      c(CAT) = 'BLD' ⇒ t(DUR) ≤ 5
}
```

Listing A-22. *Table Universe tab_CRS*

```
tab_CRS :=
{ C | C∈℘(tup_CRS) ∧
      /* Course code uniquely identifies a tuple                r22 */
      ( ∀c1,c2∈C: c1(CODE) = c2(CODE) ⇒ c1 = c2 )
}
```

Table Universe for OFFR

External Predicate: The course offering for the course with code COURSE that starts at STARTS, has status STATUS, has a maximum capacity of MAXCAP attendees, is taught by the employee with employee number TRAINER, and is offered at location LOC.

The following three listings (A-23, A-24, and A-25) show the attribute-value sets, the tuple universe, and the table universe for OFFR, respectively.

Listing A-23. *Characterization chr_OFFR*

```
chr_OFFR :=
{ ( COURSE;   CRSCODE_TYP                    )
, ( STARTS;   date                           )
, ( STATUS;   { s | s∈varchar(4) ∧
              /* Three STATUS values allowed:                    */
                    s∈{'SCHD','CONF','CANC'} } )
              /* Maximum course offering capacity; minimum = 6   */
, ( MAXCAP;   { n | n∈number(2,0) ∧ n ≥ 6 }  )
              /* TRAINER = -1 means "no trainer assigned" (see r23)  */
, ( TRAINER; EMPNO_TYP ∪ { -1 }              )
, ( LOC;      varchar(14)                    )
}
```

Listing A-24. *Tuple Universe tup_OFFR*

```
tup_OFFR :=
{ o | o∈Π(chr_OFFR) ∧
              /* Unassigned TRAINER allowed only for certain STATUS values    r23 */
      o(TRAINER) = -1 ⇒ o(STATUS)∈{'CANC','SCHD'}
}
```

Listing A-25. *Table Universe tab_OFFR*

```
tab_OFFR :=
{ O | O∈ ℘(tup_OFFR) ∧
      /* Course code and begin date uniquely identify a tuple          r24 */
      ( ∀o1,o2∈O:
        o1↓{COURSE,STARTS} = o2↓{COURSE,STARTS} ⇒ o1 = o2 )
      ∧
      /* Begin date and (known) trainer uniquely identify a tuple       r25 */
      ( ∀o1,o2∈{ o | o∈O ∧ o(TRAINER) ≠ -1 }:
        o1↓{STARTS,TRAINER} = o2↓{STARTS,TRAINER} ⇒ o1 = o2 )
}
```

Table Universe for REG

> *External Predicate:* The employee whose employee number is STUD has registered for the course offering of course COURSE that starts at STARTS, and has rated the course with an evaluation score of EVAL.

The following three listings (A-26, A-27, and A-28) show the attribute-value sets, the tuple universe, and the table universe for REG, respectively.

Listing A-26. *Characterization chr_REG*

```
chr_REG :=
{ ( STUD;    EMPNO_TYP          )
, ( COURSE; CRSCODE_TYP         )
, ( STARTS; date                )
  /* -1: too early to evaluate; 0: not (yet) evaluated;      */
  /* 1-5: regular evaluation values (from 1=bad to 5=excellent)  */
, ( EVAL;    { n | n∈number(1,0)
                  ∧ -1 ≤ n ≤ 5  } )
}
```

Listing A-27. *Tuple Universe tup_REG*

```
tup_REG :=
{ r | r∈Π(chr_REG) }
```

Listing A-28. *Table Universe tab_REG*

```
tab_REG :=
{ R | R∈℘(tup_REG) ∧
          /* Attendee and begin date(!) uniquely identify a tuple    r26 */
          ( ∀r1,r2∈R:
            r1↓{STUD,STARTS} = r2↓{STUD,STARTS} ⇒ r1 = r2 )
          ∧
          /* Offering is evaluated,                             */
          /* or it is too early to evaluate the offering       r27 */
          ( ∀r1,r2∈R:
            ( r1↓{COURSE,STARTS} = r2↓{COURSE,STARTS} )
            ⇒
            ( ( r1(EVAL) = -1 ∧ r2(EVAL) = -1 ) ∨
              ( r1(EVAL) ≠ -1 ∧ r2(EVAL) ≠ -1 )
            ) )
}
```

Table Universe for HIST

> **External Predicate:** *At date* UNTIL, *for employee whose employee number is* EMPNO, *either the department or the monthly salary (or both) have changed. Prior to date* UNTIL, *the department for that employee was* DEPTNO *and the monthly salary was* MSAL.

The following three listings (A-29, A-30, and A-31) show the attribute-value sets, the tuple universe, and the table universe for HIST, respectively.

Listing A-29. *Characterization chr_HIST*

```
chr_HIST :=
{( EMPNO;  EMPNO_TYP  )
,( UNTIL;  date       )
,( DEPTNO; DEPTNO_TYP )
,( MSAL;   SALARY_TYP )
}
```

Listing A-30. *Tuple Universe tup_HIST*

```
tup_HIST :=
{ h | h∈Π(chr_HIST) }
```

Listing A-31. *Table Universe tab_HIST*

```
tab_HIST :=
{ H | H∈ ℘(tup_HIST) ∧
      /* Employee number and end date uniquely identify a tuple       r28 */
      ( ∀h1,h2∈H: h1↓{EMPNO,UNTIL} = h2↓{EMPNO,UNTIL} ⇒ h1 = h2 )
      ∧
      /* Either department number or monthly salary (or both)         r29 */
      /* must have changed between two consecutive history records      */
      ( ∀h1,h2∈H:
        ( h1(EMPNO) = h2(EMPNO) ∧
          h1(UNTIL) < h2(UNTIL) ∧
          ¬ ( ∃h3∈T: h3(EMPNO) = h1(EMPNO) ∧
                     h3(UNTIL) > h1(UNTIL) ∧
                     h3(UNTIL) < h2(UNTIL) )
        ) ⇒
        ( h1(MSAL) ≠ h2(MSAL) ∨ h1(DEPTNO)  ≠ h2(DEPTNO) )
      )
}
```

Database Characterization DBCH

The database characterization DBCH attaches the ten table universes (as defined in the previous section of this appendix) to their corresponding table aliases; see Listing A-32. As such, the database characterization "revisits" the database skeleton and provides many more details.

Listing A-32. *Database Characterization DBCH*

```
DBCH :=
{ ( EMP;  tab_EMP  )
, ( SREP; tab_SREP )
```

```
, ( MEMP; tab_MEMP )
, ( TERM; tab_TERM )
, ( DEPT; tab_DEPT )
, ( GRD;  tab_GRD  )
, ( CRS;  tab_CRS  )
, ( OFFR; tab_OFFR )
, ( REG;  tab_REG  )
, ( HIST; tab_HIST )
}
```

Database Universe DB_UEX

As you can see in Listing A-33, the database universe DB_UEX is built on top of the database characterization DBCH. The specification of DB_UEX contains all static database constraints.

Listing A-33. *Database Universe DB_UEX*

```
DB_UEX :=
{ v | v∈Π(DBCH) ∧
   /* ================================================================== */
   /* Start of Subset Requirements                                       */
   /* ================================================================== */
   /* Employee works for a known department                      r30 */
   { e(DEPTNO) | e∈v(EMP) } ⊆ { d(DEPTNO) | d∈v(DEPT) }
   ∧
   /* Dept mgr is a known employee, excluding admins and president  r31 */
   { d(MGR)   | d∈v(DEPT) } ⊆
   { e(EMPNO) | e∈v(EMP) ∧ e(JOB) ∉ {'ADMIN','PRESIDENT'} }
   ∧
   /* Employees can report to the president or a manager only      r32 */
   { m(MGR)   | m∈v(MEMP) } ⊆
   { e(EMPNO) | e∈v(EMP) ∧ e(JOB) ∈ {'PRESIDENT','MANAGER' } }
   ∧
   /* A termination is for a known employee; not everyone has left  r33 */
   { t(EMPNO) | t∈v(TERM) } ⊂ { e(EMPNO) | e∈v(EMP) }
   ∧
   /* Employee has a known salary grade                           r34 */
   { e(SGRADE) | e∈v(EMP) } ⊆ { g(GRADE) | g∈v(GRD) }
   ∧
   /* Course offering is for a known course                       r35 */
   { o(COURSE) | o∈v(OFFR) } ⊆ { c(CODE) | c∈v(CRS) }
   ∧
   /* Courses take place in locations where we have a department   r36 */
   { o(LOC) | o∈v(OFFR) } ⊆ { d(LOC) | d∈v(DEPT) }
   ∧
   /* Trainer of course offering is a known trainer               r37 */
```

```
{ o(TRAINER) | o∈v(OFFR) ∧ o(TRAINER) ≠ -1 } ⊆
{ e(EMPNO) | e∈v(EMP) ∧ e(JOB) = 'TRAINER' }
∧
```

/* Course registration is for a known employee   r38 */
```
{ r(STUD) | r∈v(REG) } ⊆ { e(EMPNO) | e∈v(EMP) }
∧
```

/* Course registration is for a known course offering   r39 */
```
{ r↓{COURSE,STARTS} | r∈v(REG) } ⊆
{ o↓{COURSE,STARTS} | o∈v(OFFR) }
∧
```

/* History record is for a known employee   r40 */
```
{ h(EMPNO) | h∈v(HIST) } ⊆ { e(EMPNO)} | e∈v(EMP) }
∧
```

/* History record is for a known department   r41 */
```
{ h(DEPTNO) | h∈v(HIST) } ⊆ { d(DEPTNO)} | d∈v(DEPT) }
∧
```

```
/* =================================================================== */
/* End of Subset Requirements; Start of Specialization Rules           */
/* =================================================================== */
```
/* Sales reps have a target and a commission   r42 */
```
{ e(EMPNO) | e∈v(EMP) ∧ e(JOB) = 'SALESREP' } =
{ s(EMPNO) | s∈v(SREP) }
∧
```

/* Everybody, excluding the president, is a managed employee r43 */
```
{ e(EMPNO) | e∈v(EMP) ∧ e(JOB) ≠ 'PRESIDENT' } =
{ m(EMPNO) | m∈v(MEMP) }
∧
```

```
/* =================================================================== */
/* End of Specializations; Start of Tuple-in-Join Rules                */
/* =================================================================== */
```
/* Monthly salary must fall within assigned salary grade   r44 */
```
( ∀e∈v(EMP), g∈v(GRD):
    e(SGRADE) = g(GRADE) ⇒ g(LLIMIT) ≤ e(MSAL) ≤ g(ULIMIT)
) ∧
```
/* Leave date must fall after hire date   r45 */
```
( ∀e∈v(EMP), t∈v(TERM):
    e(EMPNO) = t(EMPNO) ⇒ e(HIRED) < t(LEFT)
) ∧
```
/* Sales reps cannot earn more than the employee they report to r46 */
```
( ∀s∈v(SREP), es,em∈v(EMP), m∈v(MEMP):
  ( s(EMPNO)=es(EMPNO) ∧ es(EMPNO)=m(EMPNO) ∧ m(MGR) = em(EMPNO) )
    ⇒
  ( es(MSAL) + s(COMM)/12 < em(MSAL)      )
) ∧
```
/* Non-sales reps cannot earn more than the employee they report to r47 */
```
( ∀e,em∈v(EMP), m∈v(MEMP):
  (e(EMPNO)=m(EMPNO) ∧ m(MGR) = em(EMPNO) ∧ e(JOB) ≠ 'SALESREP')
```

$\Rightarrow$
(e(MSAL) < em(MSAL)   )
) $\wedge$
/* No history records allowed before hire date   r48 */
($\forall e \in v(EMP)$, h$\in$v(HIST):
    e(EMPNO) = h(EMPNO) $\Rightarrow$ e(HIRED) < h(UNTIL)
) $\wedge$
/* No history records allowed after leave date   r49 */
($\forall t \in v(TERM)$, h$\in$v(HIST):
    t(EMPNO) = h(EMPNO) $\Rightarrow$ t(LEFT) > h(UNTIL)
) $\wedge$
/* You cannot register for offerings in 1st four weeks on the job   r50 */
($\forall e \in v(EMP)$, r$\in$v(REG):
    e(EMPNO) = r(STUD) $\Rightarrow$ e(HIRED) + 28 $\leq$ r(STARTS)
) $\wedge$
/* You cannot register for offerings given at or after leave date   r51 */
($\forall t \in v(TERM)$, r$\in$v(REG), c$\in$v(CRS):
  (t(EMPNO) = r(STUD) $\wedge$ r(COURSE) = c(CODE))
    $\Rightarrow$
  (t(LEFT) $\geq$ r(STARTS) + c(DUR)   )
) $\wedge$
/* You cannot register for overlapping course offerings   r52 */
($\forall e \in v(EMP)$, r1,r2$\in$v(REG), o1,o2$\in$v(OFFR), c1,c2$\in$v(CRS):
  (e(EMPNO) = r1(STUD) $\wedge$
    r1$\downarrow$\{COURSE,STARTS\} = o1$\downarrow$\{COURSE,STARTS\} $\wedge$
    o1(COURSE)   = c1(COURSE) $\wedge$
    e(EMPNO)   = r2(STUD) $\wedge$
    r2$\downarrow$\{COURSE,STARTS\} = o2$\downarrow$\{COURSE,STARTS\} $\wedge$
    o2(COURSE) = c2(COURSE)
) $\Rightarrow$
  (o1$\downarrow$\{COURSE,STARTS\} = o2$\downarrow$\{COURSE,STARTS\} $\vee$
    o1(STARTS) $\geq$ o2(STARTS) + c2(DUR) $\vee$
    o2(STARTS) $\geq$ o1(STARTS) + c1(DUR)
)) $\wedge$
/* Trainer cannot teach courses before hire date   r53 */
($\forall e \in v(EMP)$, o$\in$v(OFFR):
    e(EMPNO) = o(TRAINER) $\Rightarrow$ e(HIRED) $\leq$ o(STARTS)
) $\wedge$
/* Trainer cannot teach courses at or after leave date   r54 */
($\forall t \in v(TERM)$, o$\in$v(OFFR), c$\in$v(CRS):
  (t(EMPNO) = o(TRAINER) $\wedge$ o(COURSE) = c(CODE))
    $\Rightarrow$
  (t(LEFT) $\geq$ o(STARTS) + c(DUR)   )
) $\wedge$
/* Trainer cannot register for offerings taught by him/herself   r55 */
($\forall r \in v(REG)$, o$\in$v(OFFR):
    r$\downarrow$\{COURSE,STARTS\} = o$\downarrow$\{COURSE,STARTS\} $\Rightarrow$

```
            r(STUD) ≠ o(TRAINER)
  ) ∧
/* Trainer cannot teach different courses simultaneously        r56 */
( ∀o1,o2∈v(OFFR), c1,c2∈v(CRS):
  ( o1(TRAINER) = o2(TRAINER) ∧
    o1(COURSE)  = c1(CODE)    ∧
    o2(COURSE)  = c2(CODE)
  ) ⇒
  ( o1↓{COURSE,STARTS} = o2↓{COURSE,STARTS} ∨
    o1(STARTS) ≥ o2(STARTS) + c2(DUR)        ∨
    o2(STARTS) ≥ o1(STARTS) + c1(DUR)
) ) ∧

/* Employee cannot register for course offerings that overlap    r57 */
/* with another course offering where he/she is the trainer        */
( ∀e∈v(EMP), r∈v(REG), o1,o2∈v(OFFR), c1,c2∈v(CRS):
  ( e(EMPNO)    = r(STUD)                       ∧
    r↓{COURSE,STARTS} = o1↓{COURSE,STARTS} ∧
    o1(COURSE) = c1(CODE)                       ∧
    e(EMPNO)    = o2(TRAINER)                   ∧
    o2(COURSE) = c2(CODE)
  ) ⇒
  ( o1↓{COURSE,STARTS} = o2↓{COURSE,STARTS} ∨
    o1(STARTS) ≥ o2(STARTS) + c2(DUR)        ∨
    o2(STARTS) ≥ o1(STARTS) + c1(DUR)
) ) ∧
/* ==================================================================== */
/* End of Tuple-in-Join Rules; Start of Other Database Rules           */
/* ==================================================================== */
/* Department manager must work for a department he/she manages   r58 */
( ∀d1∈v(DEPT): { e(DEPTNO)| e∈v(EMP) ∧ e(EMPNO)=d1(MGR)} ⊆
                { d2(DEPTNO)| d2∈v(DEPT) ∧ d2(mgr)=d1(mgr) } )
/* Active employee cannot be managed by terminated employee       r59 */
{ t1(EMPNO) | t1∈v(TERM) } ∩
{ m(MGR) | m∈v(MEMP) ∧
          ¬ ( ∃t2∈v(TERM): t2(EMPNO) = m(EMPNO) ) } = ∅
∧
/* Department cannot be managed by a terminated employee          r60 */
{ t(EMPNO) | t∈v(TERM) } ∩ { d(MGR) | d∈v(DEPT) } = ∅
∧
/* At least half of the course offerings (measured by duration)   r61 */
/* taught by a trainer must be 'at home base'                       */
( ∀e1∈{ o1(TRAINER) | o1∈v(OFFR) ∧ o1(STATUS) ≠ 'CANC' }:
  ( ∑t∈{ o2∪c2| d2∈v(DEPT) ∧ e2∈v(EMP) ∧ o2∈v(OFFR) ∧ c2∈v(CRS) ∧
                e2(EMPNO)  = e1          ∧
                e2(EMPNO)  = o2(TRAINER) ∧
                e2(DEPTNO) = d2(DEPTNO)  ∧
                o2(COURSE) = c2(CODE)    ∧
```

```
                    o2(STATUS) ≠ 'CANC'        ∧
                    c2(LOC)    = d2(LOC)
            } : t(DUR)
    ) ≥
    ( Σt∈{ o3∪c3| d3∈v(DEPT) ∧ e3∈v(EMP) ∧ o3∈v(OFFR) ∧ c3∈v(CRS) ∧
                    e3(EMPNO)  = e1           ∧
                    e3(EMPNO)  = o3(TRAINER) ∧
                    e3(DEPTNO) = d3(DEPTNO)  ∧
                    o3(COURSE) = c3(CODE)    ∧
                    o3(STATUS) ≠ 'CANC'       ∧
                    c3(LOC)    ≠ d3(LOC)
            } : t(DUR)
) ) ∧
```

/* Offerings with 6+ registrations must have status confirmed   r62 */
```
( ∀o∈v(OFFR):
  #{ r | r∈v(REG) ∧
        r↓{COURSE,STARTS} = o↓{COURSE,STARTS} } ≥ 6
  ⇒
  o(STATUS) = 'CONF'
) ∧
```

/* Number of registrations cannot exceed maximum capacity of offering r63 */
```
( ∀o∈v(OFFR):
  #{ r | r∈v(REG) ∧
        r↓{COURSE,STARTS} = o↓{COURSE,STARTS} } ≤ o(MAXCAP)
) ∧
```

/* Canceled offerings cannot have registrations   r64 */
```
( ∀o∈v(OFFR): o(STATUS) = 'CANC'
                    ⇒
              ¬( ∃r∈v(REG): r↓{COURSE,STARTS} = o↓{COURSE,STARTS} )
) ∧
```

/* You are allowed to teach a certain course only if: r65 */
/* 1. You have been employed for at least one year, or   */
/* 2. You have attended that course first and the trainer of that   */
/*   course offering attends your first teach as participant   */
```
( ∀o1∈v(OFFR):
  /* If this is the 1st time this trainer gives this course ...        */
  ( ¬∃o2∈v(OFFR):
        o1↓{COURSE,TRAINER} = o2↓{COURSE,TRAINER} ∧
        o2(STARTS) < o1(STARTS)
  ) ⇒
  ( /* then there should be an attendee in the classroom ...          */
    ( ∃r1∈v(REG):
        r1↓{COURSE,STARTS} = o1↓{COURSE,STARTS} ∧
        /* who has given this course at an earlier date ...           */
        ( ∃o3∈v(OFFR):
          o3(TRAINER) = r1(STUD)  ∧
          o3(COURSE) = o1(COURSE) ∧
```

```
            o3(STARTS) < o1(STARTS) ∧
    /* and *that* course was attended by the current trainer      */
            ( ∃r2∈v(REG):
                o3↓{COURSE,STARTS} = r2↓{COURSE,STARTS} ∧
                r2(STUD) = o1(TRAINER)
        ) ) ) ∨
    /* or, this trainer has been employed for at least one year     */
        ( ↵{ e(HIRED) | e∈v(EMP) ∧ e(EMPNO) = o1(TRAINER) } <
            o1(STARTS)  - 365
        )
      )
    )
    /* ================================================================= */
    /* End of Other Database Rules                                       */
    /* ================================================================= */
}
```

State Transition Universe TX_UEX

The *state transition universe* TX_UEX is defined by first generating the Cartesian product of the database universe DB_UEX (as defined in the section "Database Universe DB_UEX" of this appendix) with itself. You can view the result of this Cartesian product as the set of all possible transactions. In this state transition universe TX_UEX, every transaction is depicted as an ordered pair (b;e), where b stands for the database state in which the transaction began and e stands for the database state in which the transaction ends. As you can see in Listing A-34, the definition of TX_UEX restricts this set to hold only *valid* transactions, through specifying the *dynamic* (also called *state transition* or *transaction*) constraints.

■**Note** In this section we use sysdate to denote the moving point "now."

Listing A-34. *Transaction Universe TX_UEX*

```
TX_UEX :=
{ (b;e) | b∈DB_UEX ∧ e∈DB_UEX ∧
    /* Monthly salary can only increase                              r66 */
    ( ∀e1∈b(EMP), e2∈e(EMP):
        e1(EMPNO) = e2(EMPNO) ⇒ e1(MSAL) ≤ e2(MSAL)
    ) ∧
    /* New offerings must start with status SCHED                    r67 */
    ( ∀o1∈e(OFFR)⇓{COURSE,STARTS} - b(OFFR)⇓{COURSE,STARTS}:
        ↵{ o2(STATUS) | o2∈e(OFFR) ∧ o2↓{COURSE,STARTS} = o1↓{COURSE,STARTS} }
        = 'SCH'
```

```
) ∧
/* Valid offering status transitions are:                            r68 */
/* SCHED -> CONF, SCHED -> CANC, CONF -> CANC                             */
( ∀o1∈b(OFFR), o2∈e(OFFR):
  o1↓{COURSE,STARTS} = o2↓{COURSE,STARTS}
    ⇒
  ( o1(STATUS) = o2(STATUS) ∨
    ( o1(STATUS) = 'SCH'  ∧ o2(STATUS) = 'CONF' ) ∨
    ( o1(STATUS) = 'SCH'  ∧ o2(STATUS) = 'CANC' ) ∨
    ( o1(STATUS) = 'CONF' ∧ o2(STATUS) = 'CANC' )
) ) ∧
/* No updates allowed to history records                              r69 */
( ∀h1∈b(HIST), h2∈e(HIST):
  h1↓{EMPNO,UNTIL} = h2↓{EMPNO,UNTIL}
    ⇒
  ( h1(DEPTNO) = h2(DEPTNO) ∧ h1(MSAL) = h2(MSAL) )
) ∧
/* New history records must accurately reflect employee updates       r70 */
( ∀h1∈e(HIST)⇓{EMPNO,UNTIL} − b(HIST)⇓{EMPNO,UNTIL}:
  ( ∃h2∈e(HIST):
    h2↓{EMPNO,UNTIL} = h1↓{EMPNO,UNTIL} ∧
    h2(UNTIL) = sysdate ∧
    ( ∃e1∈b(EMP), e2∈e(EMP):
      e1↓{EMPNO,MSAL,DEPTNO} = h2↓{EMPNO,MSAL,DEPTNO} ∧
      e2(EMPNO) = h2(EMPNO) ∧
      ( e2(MSAL) ≠ e1(MSAL) ∨ e2(DEPTNO) ≠ e1(DEPTNO) )
) ) ) ∧
/* New registration tuples must start with EVAL = -1                  r71 */
( ∀r1∈e(REG)⇓{STUD,STARTS} − b(REG)⇓{STUD,STARTS}:
  ( ∃r2∈e(REG):
    r2↓{STUD,STARTS} = r1↓{STUD,STARTS} ∧ r2(EVAL) = -1
) ) ∧
/* Transitions for evaluation must be valid                           r72 */
/* and cannot occur before start date of offering                         */
( ∀r1∈b(REG), r2∈e(REG):
  r1↓{STUD,STARTS} = r2↓{STUD,STARTS} ∧ r1(EVAL) ≠ r2(EVAL)
    ⇒
  ( ( r1(EVAL) = -1 ∧ r2(EVAL) = 0 ∧ r2(STARTS) ≥ sysdate ) ∨
    ( r1(EVAL) = 0 ∧ r2(EVAL) ∈ {1,2,3,4,5} )
) )
}
```

APPENDIX B

Symbols

Table B-1. *Mathematical Symbols Related to Sets and Functions*

Symbol	Description	Examples
:=	Is defined as	P1 := x > y
$\in, \notin$	Is (not) an element of	$x \in A, y \notin A$
=, ≠	Is (not) equal to	
≥, ≤, <, >	Other comparison operators	
⊆	Is a subset of	A ⊆ B
⊇	Is a superset of	A ⊇ B
⊂	Is a proper subset of	A ⊂ B
⊃	Is a proper superset of	A ⊃ B
∪	Union	A ∪ B
∩	Intersect	A ∩ B
−	Difference	A − B
÷	Symmetric difference	A ÷ B
×	Cartesian product	A × B
⊗	Natural join	A ⊗ B
∅	The empty set	
(;)	Ordered pair	(EMPNO; 102)
◊	Function composition	f◊g
◊◊	Attribute renaming	T◊◊g
dom	Domain of a function	dom(F)
rng	Range of a function	rng(F)
π_1	First coordinate of a pair	π_1(a;b)
π_2	Second coordinate of a pair	π_2(a;b)
N	The set of natural numbers	
Z	The set of all integers	
↓	Limitation of a tuple	t↓{...}
⇓	Projection of a table	T⇓{...}

Continued

Table B-1. *Continued*

Symbol	Description	Examples
$\wp$	Powerset of a set	$\wp A$, $\wp\{\ldots\}$
Π	Product of a set function	$\Pi(F)$
#	Cardinality of a set	#A, #$\{\ldots\}$
SUM	Sum (of f over A)	$\text{SUM}x \in A$: f(x)
AVG	Average (of f over A)	$\text{AVG}x \in A$: f(x)
MAX	Maximum (of f over A)	$\text{MAX}x \in A$: f(x)
MIN	Minimum (of f over A)	$\text{MIN}x \in A$: f(x)
⌐	Choose operator	⌐S, ⌐$\{a\}$

Table B-2. *Mathematical Symbols Related to Logic*

Symbol	Description	Examples
t, T	TRUE	
f, F	FALSE	
$\exists$	Existential quantifier	$\exists x \in S$: y < 42
$\forall$	Universal quantifier	$\forall y \in S$: y ≥ 27
$\wedge$, $\vee$, $\neg$	And, or, not	P $\wedge$ (Q $\vee \neg$R)
$\Rightarrow$	Implication	P $\Rightarrow$ Q
$\Leftrightarrow$	Equivalence	P $\Leftrightarrow$ Q

APPENDIX C

Bibliography

This appendix provides a reference for further background reading.

Original Writings That Introduce the Methodology Demonstrated in This Book

Brock, Bert de. *Foundations of Semantic Databases*. Upper Saddle River, NJ: Prentice Hall, 1995.

Brock, Bert de. *De Grondslagen van Semantische Databases* (in Dutch). Schoonhoven, The Netherlands: Academic Service, 1989.

Recommended Reading in the Area of the Underlying Mathematical Theories

Hodges, Wilfred. *Logic*. Harmondsworth, England: Pelican Books, 1977.

Gray, Peter M. D. *Logic, Algebra and Databases*. Chichester, England: Ellis Horwood Limited, 1984.

Stanat, Donald F. and David F. McAllister. *Discrete Mathematics in Computer Science*. Englewood Cliffs, NJ: Prentice Hall, 1977.

Seminal Writings That Introduce the General Theory of Data Management

Codd, E. F. "Derivability, Redundancy and Consistency of Relations Stored in Large Data Banks." San Jose, CA: IBM Research Report RJ599, 1969.

Codd, E. F. *The Relational Model For Database Management, Version 2*. Reading, MA: Addison-Wesley, 1990.

Recommended Reading on Relational Database Management

Date, C. J. *Database In Depth: Relational Theory for Practitioners*. Sebastopol, CA: O'Reilly, 2005.

Date, C. J. *The Relational Database Dictionary*. Sebastopol, CA: O'Reilly, 2006.

Date, C. J. and Hugh Darwen. *Databases, Types, and the Relational Model: The Third Manifesto*. Reading, MA: Addison-Wesley, 2006.

Date, C. J. *What Not How: The Business Rules Approach to Application Development.* Reading, MA: Addison-Wesley, 2000.

Date, C. J. with Hugh Darwen. "Multiple Assignment." Database Foundation Paper #3 at `http://www.dbdebunk.com`, 2004.

Research Papers on Implementing Data Integrity Constraints and Related Subjects

Widom, Jennifer and Sheldon J. Finkelstein. "Set-Oriented Production Rules in Relational Database Systems." In *ACM SIGMOD International Conference on Management of Data Proceedings* 259–70, May 1990.

Ceri, Stefano and Jennifer Widom. "Deriving Production Rules for Constraint Maintenance." In *VLDB Conference Proceedings* 566–77, 1990.

Simon, Eric, Jerry Kiernan, and Christophe de Maindreville. "Implementing High Level Active Rules on Top of a Relational DBMS." In *VLDB Conference Proceedings* 315–26, 1992.

Behrend, Andreas, Rainer Manthey, and Birgit Pieper. "An Amateur's Introduction to Integrity Constraints and Integrity Checking in SQL." In *BTW Conference Proceedings*, 2001.

Grefen, Paul W.P.J. "Combining Theory and Practice in Integrity Control: A Declarative Approach to the Specification of a Transaction Modification Subsystem." In *VLDB Conference Proceedings* 581–91, 1993.

Simon, Eric and Angelika Kotz-Dittrich. "Promises and Realities of Active Database Systems." In *VLDB Conference Proceedings* 642–53, 1995.

Ceri, Stefano, Roberta J. Cochrane, and Jennifer Widom. "Practical Applications of Triggers and Constraints: Successes and Lingering Issues." In *VLDB Conference Proceedings* 254–62, 2000.

Eswaran, K. P., J. N. Gray, R. A. Lorie, and I. L. Traiger. "The Notions of Consistency and Predicate Locks in a Database System." In *Communications of the ACM*, 1976.

Jacobs, Ken. "Concurrency Control, Transaction Isolation and Serializability in SQL92 and Oracle7." Technical report, Oracle White Paper Part No A33745, 1995.

Previous Related Writings of the Authors

Haan, Lex de. *Mastering Oracle SQL and SQL*Plus.* Berkeley, CA: Apress, 2004.

Haan, Lex de. *Leerboek ORACLE SQL* (in Dutch). Schoonhoven, The Netherlands: Academic Service, 1993.

Koppelaars, A. V. "Business Rules, Classification and Implementation." In *IOUW Conference Proceedings*, 1994.

Koppelaars, A. V. "Business Rules, Guidelines for Deferred Checking." In *EOUG Conference Proceedings*, 1995.

Koppelaars, A.V. "Business Rules, Specification and Classification." *IOUG SELECT Newsmagazine*, January 1995.

Koppelaars, A.V. "The Specification and Implementation of Business Rules." In *ASPAC IOUW Conference Proceedings*, 1995.

Koppelaars, A. V. "Business Rules: All You Need to Know When Implementing Them." In *EOUG Conference Proceedings*, 1996.

Nulls and Three (or More) Valued Logic

*N*ote *from the author: Much of the text in this appendix was originally part of Chapter 3—the last chapter that Lex had been able to spend time on at the end of 2005. Being called "Mr. NULL," as some of you might know, he produced quite a bit of text on the topic of NULLs and 3-valued logic (3VL) as part of Chapter 3. By the time Chapter 3 review comments were in and I (Toon) started working on them, I decided that it would be better, for Chapter 3, to move all text with regards to NULLs and 3VL out of Chapter 3 and into this appendix.*

During his career, my coauthor dedicated quite a bit of time to investigating the phenomenon of a NULL "value" in SQL DBMSes and to researching the 3 (or more) valued logic that arises from it. I just used NULLs (cautiously) in my job as a database professional. Because it was difficult to integrate my perspective on this subject into Lex's text, I chose to split this appendix into two sections.

In the first section ("To Be Applicable or Not"), I'll give you my thoughts on NULLs in SQL DBMSes from a database design point of view.

The second section, "Three (or More) Valued Logic," consists of a "cut and paste" of Lex's text on 3VL from the original version of Chapter 3. I did incorporate the review comments (from Jonathan Gennick and Chris Date), which Lex never had the time to study, into his text.

To Be Applicable or Not

As you saw in Chapter 11, the example database design introduced in this book hardly contains any *nullable* attributes; all attributes in all table structures, with the exception of TRAINER in OFFR, and COMMENTS in TERM, are mandatory (NOT NULL, in SQL terminology). You'll probably find a lot more nullable attributes in the database designs that you deal with in your daily job, right?

Most likely the main reason why an attribute is left optional is the *inapplicability* of the value that could have been stored in it for certain rows. Let me explain this. Optional attributes are usually introduced in database designs for one of the following three reasons:

- The data values that could have been stored are *inapplicable*.

- The data values are *not yet applicable*.

- The values are *nice to know* (if known), but not mandatory.

The next three sections will briefly discuss these reasons.

Inapplicable

Inapplicable data values arise from the failure to design specializations. This is the main reason of the manifestation of optional attributes in the implementation of a database design. By not introducing separate table structures to hold the attributes that are only applicable for a certain subset of the tuples in a given table structure, you'll end up with optional attributes.

In the example database design in Chapter 7, we specifically introduced SREP and MEMP to prevent the following optional attributes in EMP:

- TARGET and COMM: Only applicable for (the subset of) sales representatives

- MGR: Only applicable for managed employees; that is, everybody but the president

Frequently, you'll find that neither SREP nor MEMP are introduced, and that attributes TARGET, COMM, and MGR are nullable attributes in the EMP table structure. With a bit of luck, all the following four CHECK constraints accompany them:

```
CHECK( JOB<>'SALESREP' or (TARGET is not null and COMM is not null) )
CHECK( JOB='SALESREP' or (TARGET is null and COMM is null) )
CHECK( JOB='PRESIDENT' or MGR is not null )
CHECK( JOB<>'PRESIDENT' or MGR is null )
```

The first two constraints represent the following two implications, specifying when the TARGET and COMM attributes should hold a value and when not:

$$(\text{JOB} = \text{'SALESREP'}) \Rightarrow (\text{TARGET is not null and COMM is not null})$$
$$(\text{JOB} <> \text{'SALESREP'}) \Rightarrow (\text{TARGET is null and COMM is null})$$

Note that the implications have been rewritten into disjunctions.

The last two CHECK constraints represent the implications specifying when the MGR attribute should hold a value and when not:

$$(\text{JOB} <> \text{'PRESIDENT'}) \Rightarrow (\text{MGR is not null})$$
$$(\text{JOB} = \text{'PRESIDENT'}) \Rightarrow (\text{MGR is null})$$

Note Often you'll find that the second and fourth CHECK constraints are erroneously left unspecified.

The preceding four CHECK constraints would implement the applicability requirements of these specialization attributes, given that they are part of the EMP table structure. They are the counterparts of database constraints PSPEC1 and PSPEC2 found in the example database design.

Not Yet Applicable

Not yet applicable data values also arise from failing to design specializations. As we mentioned in Chapter 7, the example database design holds two rather tricky hacks. The attribute-value sets of the TRAINER attribute in the OFFR table structure, and the EVAL attribute in the REG table structure, hold a special -1 value. In both cases, this value is used to signify that the attribute value is not yet applicable.

Apparently there are two sorts of offerings: offerings with a trainer assigned to them and offerings without one assigned to them. The following tuple constraint, taken from the example database universe specification, describes when a trainer needn't be assigned yet (here o represents an offering tuple):

```
/* Unassigned TRAINER allowed only for canceled and scheduled offerings */
o(TRAINER) = -1 ⇒ o(STATUS)∈{'CANC','SCHD'}
```

Note that this tuple constraint specifies that confirmed offerings must have an assigned trainer, and canceled or scheduled offerings may have an assigned trainer.

We can make a similar remark about registrations: some registrations include an evaluation score for the course offering, and some of them don't yet. In this case, no constraint describes exactly when registrations hold an evaluation and when not. The table constraint specified in the table universe tab_REG does state that whenever one registration of an offering holds an evaluation, then all registrations of that offering should hold an evaluation. Here's the specification of that constraint (R represents a registration table):

```
/* Offering is evaluated by all attendees, or it is too early to */
/* evaluate the offering */
( ∀r1,r2∈R:
   ( r1↓{COURSE,STARTS} = r2↓{COURSE,STARTS} )
     ⇒
   ( ( r1(EVAL) = -1 ∧ r2(EVAL) = -1 ) ∨
     ( r1(EVAL) ≠ -1 ∧ r2(EVAL) ≠ -1 )
   )
) )
```

In the actual implementation of these kinds of designs, you'll often see that the special -1 value from the formal specification has been transformed to a NULL in an SQL DBMS.

However, in a properly designed database, we should have created a specialization for both the offering table design and the registration table design such that each holds the attribute that is not always applicable in the current database design (TRAINER for offering and EVAL for registration). The attribute-value sets of these two attributes then do not hold the special -1 value, and in the implementation these specialization attributes will have become mandatory attributes. In case of the offering specialization, you should then also specify an appropriate database constraint replacing the tuple constraint that currently describes when a trainer must be assigned.

Nice to Know

The third reason why optional attributes are introduced in database designs is a subtle variation of the preceding reason. When optional attributes are introduced due to the second reason, you'll typically find one or more data integrity constraints at the tuple, table, or database level that precisely describe when the attribute value is indeed applicable. In the absence of any such constraint, we regard the value of an optional attribute as "nice to know."

In the implementation of the example database design, the COMMENTS attribute of the TERM table structure is an example of this category. The users apparently just allow a missing value for this attribute.

Implementation Guidelines

If an optional attribute is of the category "nice to know" (and thus not involved in any constraints), then chances are that this attribute is also not involved in any business logic. It's probably an attribute that is predominantly used in reports, just to be printed on paper, or displayed on screen. As such, the NULLs stored in the column seldom give rise to the various issues surrounding the use of NULLs described in the next section. It is more convenient just to deal with the optional attribute, instead of creating a separate specialization table that holds the attribute as a mandatory attribute, and which would require the use of outer joins to always try to retrieve the value.

Note If you're unfamiliar with the concept of an outer join, we refer you to the Oracle documentation.

It is our opinion that inapplicable data values—the ones introduced due to the first reason—should be avoided at all times. Our main argument for this (besides the avoidance of the issues described in the next section) is that introducing specializations for these attributes benefits the clarity of the overall database design. This is particularly the case when there is not just a single attribute, but a whole group of attributes that would be transferred to one or more specialization tables.

The cases of not yet applicable data values (the second reason) often give rise to heated debates as to how these should be dealt with. From a true relational point of view, you again would have to avoid them by creating specializations accompanied with the relevant constraints describing when tuples should be present in the specializations. If you decide not to, then you should not fail both to specify and implement the accompanying constraints that describe when the values are indeed applicable and when not.

Three (or More) Valued Logic

In this section, Lex briefly explores 3VL. He introduces you to the three-valued truth tables for the three connectives AND, OR, and NOT. He further investigates some problems around the implication connective in 3VL, and various other issues that arise in 3VL.

Unknown

The most crucial assumption in 3VL is that (besides the two values TRUE and FALSE) there is a third value to represent "possible" or (still) UNKNOWN. To avoid misunderstandings, let's start with the following statement: there is nothing wrong with 3-valued (or multi-valued) logic. Many mathematicians have explored this area in the past; one of them worth mentioning is Jan Łukasiewicz (1878–1956).

Note Łukasiewicz also introduced the *Polish notation*, which allows expressions to be written unambiguously without the use of brackets. This is the basis of the *Reverse Polish Notation* (RPN), which many pocket calculators and expression compilers use.

In 3VL, predicates can change their truth values in time, but only from UNKNOWN to TRUE or from UNKNOWN to FALSE. This is rather slippery, because it means that in 3VL the value UNKNOWN seems to be somewhat special. This description is too vague anyway; we need formal rules, definitions, and truth tables. We'll look at those details in a minute.

3VL is counterintuitive, as opposed to the classical 2-valued logic (2VL). The main reason is that you lose the *tertium non datur* (the principle of the excluded middle). That is, if P is unknown, then ¬P is unknown as well, which in turn means that P ∨ ¬P is unknown. Consider the following famous Aristotelian example. "Tomorrow a sea battle will take place" is neither TRUE nor FALSE—it is unknown—yet the sentence "Either tomorrow there will be a sea battle, or tomorrow there won't be a sea battle" is certainly true (in reality). However, it is unknown in 3VL, hence the counterintuitive nature.

Another problem arises from the fact that if two predicates are "possible" (that is, their truth value could possibly be TRUE), then their conjunction is also "possible." However, this is obviously wrong if one of them is a negation of the second. Ludwik Stefan Borkowski (1914–1993) proposed to "fix" this problem by introducing a 4-valued logic (4VL); this indeed makes the preceding problem disappear, but the solution is unsatisfactory and ad hoc.

Furthermore, 3VL does *not* solve the problem of handling missing information; it does not allow you to represent the reason why information is missing. At the end of this section, you'll see that Ted Codd proposed a 4VL in 1990, to distinguish between applicable and inapplicable values. However, a 4VL doesn't tell you what to do if you don't know whether a certain attribute value is applicable or not; for example, if commission is applicable for sales reps only, but you don't know the job of a certain employee, what should you do with the commission attribute of that employee? One NULL implies 3VL, two NULLs (applicable and inapplicable) imply 4VL, n NULLs imply (n+2)-valued logic. Using the technique of full induction, you can prove that you'll end up with an infinite number of (meanings of) NULLs, and a corresponding infinite number of truth values. To repeat part of this paragraph's opening sentence: 3VL does *not* solve the problem of handling missing information.

Even worse, 3VL is not only counterintuitive in itself; it is ill-implemented in the SQL standard. Probably one of the biggest blunders in the SQL standard in this respect is that in an attribute of the BOOLEAN data type, a NULL represents the logical value UNKNOWN. Wasn't a NULL supposed to represent the fact that you don't know the value? There are more examples of such mistakes in the SQL standard.

You'll have to revisit all tautologies (and therefore all rewrite rules) from 2VL to check whether they're still valid in 3VL; you'll find out that several tautologies don't hold anymore.

Actually, you could even argue that we should use different names and symbols for the connectives in 3VL; after all, they are different from the "corresponding" connectives in 2VL.

Truth Tables of Three-Valued Logic

Tables D-1 through D-3 show the three standard truth tables for the negation, conjunction, and disjunction connectives in 3VL.

Table D-1. *Three-Valued Truth Table for NOT (Negation)*

P	¬P
T	F
U	U
F	T

¬P is still FALSE if P is TRUE, and vice versa. However, the negation is not the complement operator anymore, because the negation of UNKNOWN is UNKNOWN.

Table D-2. *Three-Valued Truth Table for AND (Conjunction)*

P	Q	P ∧Q
T	T	T
T	U	U
T	F	F
F	T	F
F	U	F
F	F	F
U	T	U
U	U	U
U	F	F

As you can see, P ∧ Q is only TRUE if both P and Q are TRUE. The result is FALSE if at least one of the operands is FALSE, and the three remaining combinations result in UNKNOWN.

Table D-3. *Three-Valued Truth Table for OR (Disjunction)*

P	Q	P ∨Q
T	T	T
T	U	T
T	F	T
F	T	T
F	U	U
F	F	F
U	T	T
U	U	U
U	F	U

P ∨ Q is only FALSE if both P and Q are FALSE. The result is TRUE if at least one of the operands is TRUE, and there are again three combinations with result UNKNOWN.

Missing Operators

You almost never see a truth table for the implication and the equivalence in 3VL. The most likely reason for the absence of the implication is that it is tough to come up with a good definition. It turns out that in 3VL, the implication connective is not definable in terms of conjunction and negation, or disjunction and negation. Remember the following implication rewrite rule from 2VL:

$$(P \Rightarrow Q) \Leftrightarrow (\neg P \vee Q)$$

If you'd define the implication in 3VL according to this rewrite rule, you'd end up in the situation that $P \Rightarrow P$ would evaluate to UNKNOWN if P is UNKNOWN; obviously, in any logic you would like this to be TRUE. The last row in Table D-4 shows the problem.

Table D-4. *An Attempt to Define Three-Valued Implication and Equivalence Connectives*

P	Q	P ⇒Q	P ⇔ Q
T	T	T	T
T	F	F	F
T	U	U	U
F	T	T	F
F	F	T	T
F	U	T	U
U	T	T	U
U	F	U	U
U	U	U?	U?

Also, if $P \Rightarrow Q$ and $Q \Rightarrow P$, you want P to be equivalent with Q. These problems are all related to the fact that the negation is not the complement operator anymore. Actually, Jan Łukasiewicz proposed a truth table for the implication where the two U? values in the last row are both a T instead—so he "fixed" the problem by sacrificing a tautology (the implication rewrite rule).

Three-Valued Logic, Tautologies, and Rewrite Rules

If you want to use any of the rewrite rules we identified in 2VL, you'll have to check them first against the truth tables of 3VL; as you'll find out, several tautologies and rewrite rules from 2VL are not necessarily also valid in 3VL. Listing D-1 shows two examples of such tautologies.

Listing D-1. *Examples of 2VL Tautologies That Are Not Valid in 3VL*

```
P ∨ ¬P
P ⇔ P
```

Handling Three-Valued Logic

Consider the following two rather obvious statements (in an SQL context):

- A row shows up in a table (or in the result of a query) or it doesn't.

- A constraint gets violated or it doesn't.

There are no other possibilities; therefore, these are two-valued issues. However, in 3VL, predicates have three possible outcomes: TRUE, FALSE, or UNKNOWN. Unfortunately, there is no intuitive interpretation for this third possible outcome. To give you an idea of the inconsistencies, look at Table D-5 where you see the difference between evaluating the predicate, say P, of a WHERE clause of an SQL query compared with checking the predicate of an SQL CHECK constraint.

Table D-5. *Predicate Evaluation in SQL: Queries vs. Constraints*

P(row)	WHERE P(row)	CHECK(P(row))
T	Row accepted	Row satisfies constraint
F	Row rejected	Row violates constraint
U	Row rejected	Row satisfies constraint

As you can see, FALSE and UNKNOWN lead to the same result for WHERE clauses in queries, whereas TRUE and UNKNOWN lead to the same effect in constraints. The third line in the preceding table shows the discrepancy; a row will violate the predicate (and therefore not be retrieved) when the predicate is part of a WHERE clause. However, that row will satisfy the predicate when evaluated by a CHECK constraint that is defined on a table that receives this row.

If you want to get control over 3VL in ISO-standard SQL, it is a good idea to think in terms of the three SQL functions introduced in Table D-6. They allow you to create a 2VL layer on top of 3VL, thus providing more explicit control over the three Boolean values TRUE, FALSE, and UNKNOWN.

Table D-6. *The IS {TRUE|FALSE|UNKNOWN} Operators in SQL*

P	IS TRUE (P)	IS FALSE (P)	IS UNKNOWN (P)
T	T	F	F
F	F	T	F
U	F	F	T

Note that UNKNOWN does not appear in the last three columns of Table D-6. Therefore, these three operators enable you to map three-valued expressions to 2VL.

Listing D-2 shows some rewrite rules based on the operators defined in Table D-6.

Listing D-2. *Some Rewrite Rules in 4VL Using the IS Operators*

```
IS TRUE ( P ) ⇔ ( P ∧ ¬ ( IS UNKNOWN (P) ) )
IS FALSE ( P ) ⇔ (¬P ∧ ¬ ( IS UNKNOWN (P) ) )
IS TRUE  ( ¬P ) ⇔ ( IS FALSE (P) )
```

IS FALSE (¬P) ⇔ (IS TRUE (P))
IS TRUE (P ∧ Q) ⇔ (IS TRUE (P) ∧ IS TRUE (Q))
IS TRUE (P ∨ Q) ⇔ (IS TRUE (P) ∨ IS TRUE (Q))
IS FALSE (P ∧ Q) ⇔ (IS FALSE (P) ∨ IS FALSE (Q))
IS FALSE (P ∨ Q) ⇔ (IS FALSE (P) ∧ IS FALSE (Q))
IS TRUE (∃x∈S: P) ⇔ (∃x∈S: (IS TRUE (P)))
IS FALSE (∃x∈S: P) ⇔ (∀x∈S: (IS FALSE (P)))
IS FALSE (∀x∈S: P) ⇔ (∃x∈S: (IS FALSE (P)))
IS UNKNOWN (∃x∈S: P) ⇔ (¬∃x∈S: (IS TRUE (P)) ∧ ∃y∈S: (IS UNKNOWN (P)))
IS UNKNOWN (∀x∈S: P) ⇔ (¬∃x∈S: (IS FALSE (P)) ∧ ∃y∈S: (IS UNKNOWN (P)))

You can prove all these tautologies by using three-valued truth tables, or by using a combination of 3VL rewrite rules you proved before.

Four-Valued Logic

In E. F. Codd's *The Relational Model for Database Management: Version 2* (Addison-Wesley, 1990), he proposes a revision of the first version of the relational model, RM/V1. Earlier, in 1979, he presented a paper in Tasmania with the title "Extending the Database Relational Model to Capture More Meaning," naming the extended version RM/T (T for Tasmania). The features of RM/T were supposed to be gradually incorporated into the sequence of versions RM/V2, RM/V3, and so on.

The most debatable sections of the RM/V2 book are Chapter 8 ("Missing Information") and Section 12.4 ("Manipulation of Missing Information"). In these sections, Codd proposes a 4VL in an attempt to make a distinction between the two most common reasons why information is missing: applicable and inapplicable, represented with the two discernible values A and I, respectively. The truth tables he provides appear in Table D-7.

Table D-7. *Four-Valued Truth Tables for NOT, OR, and AND*

P	¬P			
T	F			
A	A			
I	I			
F	T			
∨	**T**	**A**	**I**	**F**
T	T	T	T	T
A	T	A	A	A
I	T	A	I	F
F	T	A	F	F
∧	**T**	**A**	**I**	**F**
T	T	A	I	F
A	A	A	I	F
I	I	I	I	F
F	F	F	F	F

Note that the last two truth tables use a slightly different format from all other truth tables you saw so far in this book. They are formatted as a matrix where the four rows represent the four possible truth values for P, and the four columns represent the four possible values for Q, respectively. This can be done because the disjunction and conjunction connectives are commutative; in the regular truth table format, those two truth tables would have needed sixteen rows each.

Note that introducing the two discernible values A and I also implies that you have to revisit the outcome of arithmetic operators and string concatenation; Ted Codd proposed the behavior shown in Listing D-3, where x denotes a regular numeric attribute value and s denotes a regular character string value.

Listing D-3. *Arithmetic Operators and Concatenation Revisited in 4VL*

```
a + a = a        a || a = a
i + i = i        i || i = i
x + a = a        s || a = a
a + i = i        a || i = i
x + i = i        s || i = i
```

As stated before, the whole idea of introducing two discernible values (a and i) to replace the NULL (and the corresponding 4VL) must be considered as one of Ted Codd's few mistakes, in hindsight. But it is always easy to criticize afterwards; the importance of Ted Codd's original paper cannot be overestimated.

Answers to Selected Exercises

Chapter 1 Answers

Exercise 1

a. This is a FALSE proposition.

b. Predicate. It is equivalent to the predicate x > 0.

c. This is a FALSE proposition.

d. This is a TRUE proposition.

e. This is a FALSE proposition.

Exercise 2

If you compare the truth tables for A ∧ B and A | B, you'll notice a pattern:

A	B	A∧B	A∣B
T	T	T	F
T	F	F	T
F	T	F	T
F	F	F	T

Whenever expression A ∧ B is TRUE, expression A | B is FALSE, and vice versa. In other words, the first expression is the negation of the second expression. This should bring you straight to the solution for expressing the AND in terms of the NAND:

$$(A \wedge B) \Leftrightarrow \neg \ (A \mid B)$$

If you compare the truth tables for A ∨ B and A | B, you'll again notice a pattern:

A	B	A∨B	A|B
T	T	T	F
T	F	T	T
F	T	T	T
F	F	F	T

The truth values for A ∨ B read downwards in the truth table, and equal the truth values for A | B, if read upwards in the truth table. So, if you were first to generate the four combinations of values for A and B the other way around and then computed the truth values for the NAND on those, you should find the solution. Generating "the other way around" is the same as negating the original input values of A and B. Extending the preceding truth table with the negations of A and B will give you the following truth table:

A	B	A∨B	A|B	¬A	¬B	(¬A)	(¬B)
T	T	T	F	F	F	T
T	F	T	T	F	T	T
F	T	T	T	T	F	T
F	F	F	T	T	T	F

The third column now equals the last column, so you can conclude the following:

(A ∨ B) ⇔ ((¬A) | (¬B))

Exercise 3

Truth Table for (P ∧ P) ⇔ P

P	P	P∧P
T	T	T
F	F	F

Truth Table for (¬¬ P) ⇔ P

P	¬P	¬¬P
T	F	T
F	T	F

Truth Table for $(P \lor Q) \Leftrightarrow (Q \lor P)$

P	Q	P ∨ Q	Q ∨ P
T	T	T	T
T	F	T	T
F	T	T	T
F	F	F	F

Truth Table for $((P \land Q) \land R) \Leftrightarrow (P \land (Q \land R))$

P	Q	R	P ∧ Q	(P ∧ Q) ∧ R	Q ∧ R	P ∧ (Q ∧ R)
T	T	T	T	T	T	T
T	T	F	T	F	F	F
T	F	T	F	F	F	F
T	F	F	F	F	F	F
F	T	T	F	F	T	F
F	T	F	F	F	F	F
F	F	T	F	F	F	F
F	F	F	F	F	F	F

Truth Table for $((P \land Q) \lor R) \Leftrightarrow ((P \lor R) \land (Q \lor R))$

P	Q	R	P ∧ Q	(P ∧ Q) ∨ R	P ∨ R	Q ∨ R	(P ∨ R) ∧ (Q ∨ R)
T	T	T	T	T	T	T	T
T	T	F	T	T	T	T	T
T	F	T	F	T	T	T	T
T	F	F	F	F	T	F	F
F	T	T	F	T	T	T	T
F	T	F	F	F	F	T	F
F	F	T	F	T	T	T	T
F	F	F	F	F	F	F	F

Truth Table for $\neg(P \lor Q) \Leftrightarrow (\neg P \land \neg Q)$

P	Q	P ∨ Q	¬(P ∨ Q)	¬P	¬Q	¬P ∧ ¬Q
T	T	T	F	F	F	F
T	F	T	F	F	T	F
F	T	T	F	T	F	F
F	F	F	T	T	T	T

The following table proves the second De Morgan law $\neg(P \wedge Q) \Leftrightarrow (\neg P \vee \neg Q)$ by using available rewrite rules.

Derivation		Comments
$\neg(P \wedge Q)$	$\Leftrightarrow$	Double negation (twice)
$\neg(\neg\neg P \wedge \neg\neg Q)$	$\Leftrightarrow$	First law of De Morgan (right to left)
$\neg\neg(\neg P \vee \neg Q)$	$\Leftrightarrow$	Double negation
$(\neg P \vee \neg Q)$		

Exercise 4

b. Using available rewrite rules.

Derivation		Comments
$P \Rightarrow Q$	$\Leftrightarrow$	Rewrite implication into disjunction
$\neg P \vee Q$	$\Leftrightarrow$	Commutativity
$Q \vee \neg P$	$\Leftrightarrow$	Double negation
$\neg\neg Q \vee \neg P$	$\Leftrightarrow$	Rewrite disjunction into implication
$\neg Q \Rightarrow \neg P$		

d. $\neg(P \Rightarrow Q) \Leftrightarrow (P \wedge \neg Q)$, using available rewrite rules.

Derivation		Comments
$\neg(P \Rightarrow Q)$	$\Leftrightarrow$	Rewrite implication into disjunction
$\neg(\neg P \vee Q)$	$\Leftrightarrow$	De Morgan
$\neg\neg P \wedge \neg Q$	$\Leftrightarrow$	Double negation
$P \wedge \neg Q$		

f. $((P \Rightarrow Q) \wedge (P \Rightarrow \neg Q)) \Leftrightarrow \neg P$, using truth table.

P	Q	$P \Rightarrow Q$	$\neg Q$	$P \Rightarrow \neg Q$	$(P \Rightarrow Q) \wedge (P \Rightarrow \neg Q)$	$\neg P$
T	T	T	F	F	F	F
T	F	F	T	T	F	F
F	T	T	F	T	T	T
F	F	T	T	T	T	T

Exercise 5

You can use truth tables or existing rewrite rules. Alternatively, you can bring up a valuation for the involved variables for which the predicate evaluates to FALSE (that is, you give a counter example).

a. P ⟹ (P ∧ Q)

Counter Example: P = TRUE and Q = FALSE

Derivation	
TRUE ⟹ (TRUE ∧ FALSE)	⟺
TRUE ⟹ FALSE	⟺
FALSE	

Therefore P ⟹ (P ∧ Q) is *not* a tautology.

b. P ⟹ (P ∨ Q)

Using Existing Rewrite Rules

Derivation		Comments
P ⟹ (P ∨ Q)	⟺	Rewrite the implication into a disjunction
¬P ∨ (P ∨ Q)	⟺	Associativity
(¬P ∨ P) ∨ Q	⟺	Special case
TRUE ∨ Q	⟺	Special case
TRUE		

Therefore P ⟹ (P ∨ Q) is a tautology.

f. (P ⟹ Q) ⟹ (P ∧ Q) is not a tautology.

Counter Example: P = FALSE and Q = TRUE

Derivation	
(FALSE ⟹ TRUE) ⟹ (FALSE ∧ TRUE)	⟺
(TRUE) ⟹ (FALSE)	⟺
FALSE	

Note that the value of Q did not really matter: P = FALSE and Q = FALSE is a second counter example.

Chapter 2 Answers

Exercise 1

a. TRUE; 3 is an element of set A.

b. Meaningless; the left operand should be a set.

c. TRUE; the empty set is a subset of every set.

d. FALSE; there are only five elements in A, none of which is the empty set.

e. TRUE.

f. FALSE; again there are only five elements in A, none of which is the set $\{3,4\}$.

Exercise 2

a. $\{3, 5, 7, 9\}$

b. $\varnothing$

c. $\{0\}$

Exercise 3

a. $\{\ z \in \mathbf{N} \mid sqrt(z) \in \mathbf{N}\ \}$

b. $\{\ z \in \mathbf{N} \mid mod(z,2) = 0\ \}$

c. $\{\ p \in \mathbf{N} \times \mathbf{N} \mid \pi_1(p) + \pi_2(p) < 11\ \}$

Exercise 4

a. $\{3,4,5,7,9\}$

c. $\{1,8\}$

f. Depends on the operator precedence. If $A - (B \cap C)$ is meant, then $\{1,2,8\}$. If $(A - B) \cap C$ is meant, then $\{2\}$.

Exercise 6

a. TRUE.

b. TRUE.

f. TRUE.

g. FALSE.

n. There are ten distinct subsets of S that have two elements. You can construct these subsets as follows. Pick a first element from S. You have five possible choices for this. Then pick a second element from S, excluding the first-picked element. You have four possible choices for this. This gives a total of five times four, which equals twenty choices of two elements from S. However, because the order of the choices does not matter, we have to divide twenty by two, resulting in ten possible subsets of S with only two elements.

Exercise 7

Expression	=	≠	⊂	⊄	∈	∉
∅ ... ∅	T			T		T
∅ ... {∅}		T	T		T	
{∅} ... {∅}	T			T		T
{∅} ... {{∅}}		T		T	T	
1 ... S		T			T	
{1} ... S		T	T			T
{1,2} ... S		T	T		T	
{1,2,3} ... S		T	T			T
{1,2,{1,2}} ... S		T	T			T
{1,{1}} ... S		T		T		T
∅ ... S		T	T			T
{∅} ... S		T		T		T
#S ... S		T				T

Chapter 3 Answers

Exercise 2

a. TRUE; all elements in set A are greater than 1.

b. TRUE; 5 is an element that exists in B for which, when chosen for variable x, $\mod(x,5) = 0$.

c. FALSE; if you choose element 2 in A for x and choose 1 in B for y, then $x + y = 3$, which is not greater than or equal to 4. Because there exists such a combination for x and y, the given predicate does not hold for all values x and y, and is therefore FALSE. The predicate would be TRUE if you redefine set B to {3,5,7,9}.

d. TRUE; for each element that you can choose from A, there is always an element in y that can be picked such that $x + y = 11$. For $x = 2, 4, 6, 8$, pick $y = 9, 7, 5, 3$, respectively.

e. FALSE; there is no value in set B such that if you add that value to every available value in set A, the result of every such addition would always be 11. The predicate would be TRUE if you redefined set A such that it only holds *one* element, which effectively downgrades the inner universal quantification to an existential quantification. For $A = \{2\}$ you can choose $y = 9$. For $A = \{4\}$ you can choose $y = 7$. For $A = \{6\}$ you can choose $y = 5$. For $A = \{8\}$ you can choose $y = 3$. Another option would be to redefine set A to the empty set. The inner universal quantification will then be TRUE, irrespective of the expression $(x + y = 11)$. As long as B has at least one element, the full predicate will then always be TRUE.

f. TRUE; choose 2 in A for both x and y. You might think that it is not allowed to choose the same value twice, but it is in this case. Variables x and y are bound independently to set A. The binding of y to (the inner) A is not influenced by the value you choose for x that is bound to the outer A.

Exercise 3

a. $\forall x \in A: \text{div}(x,2) = 0$

b. $\forall x \in B: x < 9$

c. $\exists x \in A: \exists y \in A: \exists z \in A: x \neq y \wedge y \neq z \wedge z \neq x \wedge x + y + z = 18$

Exercise 4

a. $\forall x \in A: x \geq 5$

b. $\exists x \in B: \text{mod}(y,2) = 0$

Exercise 7

To prove this equivalence you start with either the left or right side of the equivalence and apply a series of rewrite rules such that you end up with the other side. Let's start with the left side:

$$\neg(\ \exists x \in S: \forall y \in T: P(x,y)\ )$$

Note that you can view this expression as follows: $\neg(\exists x \in S:\ R(x)\ )$, where $R(x) = (\ \forall y \in T: P(x,y)\ )$. Now you can apply the third rewrite rule of Listing 2-15, which has the following result:

$$(\ \forall x \in S:\ \neg R(x)\ )$$

Substituting the expression for R(x) back into this gives the following result:

(∀x∈S: ¬(∀y∈T: P(x,y)))

Now you can apply the fourth rewrite rule of Listing 2-15 to the inner (negated) universal quantification, which has the following result:

(∀x∈S: ∃y∈T: ¬P(x,y))

This ends the proof of the given equivalence.

Chapter 4 Answers

Exercise 3

a. Function.

b. Function.

c. Function.

d. Function.

e. Specified in the enumerative method, the set is { (a;f), (b;e), (b;f) }. This is not a function.

f. This is not a function. The first pair holds a second coordinate that is not in A. The second pair holds a first coordinate that is not in B.

Exercise 6

a. The expression evaluates to { (X;1), (Y;3), (Z;2), (R;1) }. This is a function.

b. The expression evaluates to { (X;1) }. This is a function.

c. The expression evaluates to { (X;1), (Y;3), (X;2) }. This is not a function; the first coordinate X appears twice.

Exercise 7

a. { { (a;1), (b;1) }, { (a;1), (b;2) } }

b. ∅

Exercise 8

a. { (ean;9786012), (price;24.99) }

c. { (descr;'A very nice book') }

Exercise 11

a. The left side evaluates to { {(empno;104)}, {(empno;106)}, {(empno;102)} }: a set of three functions. The right side evaluates to { {(empno;103)}, {(empno;104)}, {(empno;105)}, {(empno;106)} }; this is a set of four functions. The proposition is FALSE.

b. This expression evaluates to { {(deptno;10)}, {(deptno;20)} } ⊂ { {(deptno;10)}, {(deptno;20)} , {(deptno;30)} }. This proposition is TRUE; the set of two functions at the left is indeed a proper subset of the set of three functions at the right.

Chapter 5 Answers

Exercise 1

a. This is not a table; not all tuples have the same domain.

b. This is a table; in fact it is the empty table.

c. This is a table over {partno}.

d. This is a table over {suppno,sname,location}.

e. This is a table over {partno,pname,price}.

Exercise 2

a. { p | p∈∏(chr_PART) ∧ p(name)='hammer' ⇒ p(price)>250 }

b. { p | p∈∏(chr_PART) ∧ p(price)<400 ⇒ p(name)≠'drill' }, or
{ p | p∈∏(chr_PART) ∧ p(name)='drill' ⇒ p(price)≥400 }

c. { p | p∈∏(chr_PART) ∧ p(partno) ∈ {10,15,20} ⇒ p(instock)≤42 }

Exercise 3

E1 holds five tuples: the four tuples from table P and tuple {(partno;201)}. Because they do not all share the same domain, E1 is not a table.

E2 holds five tuples that all share the domain {partno,pname,price}; it is therefore a table.

Exercise 4

E6, the join of S and SP, is a table over {partno,suppno,available,reserved,sname,location}. It holds the six tuples from SP that have been extended with the supplier name and location.

E8 represents the Cartesian join of S and P. It is a table over {partno,pname,price,suppno, sname,location}, and holds eight tuples.

Exercise 5

P1 states that for all pairs of parts that can be chosen from table P, the two parts have different part numbers. This is a FALSE proposition because the formal specification allows a pair to hold the same part twice.

P2 states that for all pairs of *different* parts (chosen from table P), the two parts have different part numbers. This is a TRUE proposition.

Chapter 6 Answers

Exercise 1

a. This proposition states that all even-numbered parts (in table PAR1) have a price of less than or equal to 15. This is a TRUE proposition.

b. If you rewrite this proposition into a universal quantification, you'll see that it states that all parts are priced 5 and are currently in stock. Obviously this is a FALSE proposition.

c. If you rewrite the implication into a disjunction, you'll see that this proposition states that there are six parts in PAR1 for which we either have 10 or less items in stock, or that cost 10 or less. This is a TRUE proposition; all six parts in PAR1 satisfy the implication.

Exercise 4

This involves specifying three subset requirements and one additional constraint to state that every tuple in EMP1 has a corresponding tuple in one of the specializations.

$$
\begin{aligned}
&\text{TRN1}\!\Downarrow\!\{\text{empno}\} \subseteq \text{EMP1}\!\Downarrow\!\{\text{empno}\} \;\wedge \\
&\text{MAN1}\!\Downarrow\!\{\text{empno}\} \subseteq \text{EMP1}\!\Downarrow\!\{\text{empno}\} \;\wedge \\
&\text{CLK1}\!\Downarrow\!\{\text{empno}\} \subseteq \text{EMP1}\!\Downarrow\!\{\text{empno}\} \;\wedge \\
&(\forall\; e \in \text{EMP1}: \; e(\text{job})=\text{'TRAINER'} \Rightarrow (\exists\; t \in \text{TRN1}: \; t(\text{empno})=e(\text{empno})) \;\wedge \\
&\qquad\qquad\qquad e(\text{job})=\text{'MANAGER'} \Rightarrow (\exists\; m \in \text{MAN1}: \; m(\text{empno})=e(\text{empno})) \;\wedge \\
&\qquad\qquad\qquad e(\text{job})=\text{'CLERK'}\;\; \Rightarrow (\exists\; c \in \text{CLK1}: \; c(\text{empno})=e(\text{empno})))
\end{aligned}
$$

Exercise 5

This involves specifying three subset requirements and a few additional constraints stating that all tuples in EMP1 are covered by exactly one tuple in one of the specializations.

TRN1⇓{empno} ⊆ EMP1⇓{empno} ∧
MAN1⇓{empno} ⊆ EMP1⇓{empno} ∧
CLK1⇓{empno} ⊆ EMP1⇓{empno} ∧
TRN1⇓{empno} ∩ MAN1⇓{empno} = ∅ ∧
TRN1⇓{empno} ∩ CLK1⇓{empno} = ∅ ∧
MAN1⇓{empno} ∩ CLK1⇓{empno} = ∅ ∧
#EMP1 = #TRN1 + #MGR1 + #CLK1

Exercise 7

This is a tuple-in-join predicate. We join EMP1 with CLK1 on the empno attribute, and then join back to EMP1 on the manager attribute (which requires attribute renaming).

(∀ e∈ (EMP1⊗CLK1)⊗(EMP1◊◊{(manager;empno),(m_deptno;deptno)}):
    e(deptno)=e(m_deptno))

This is a FALSE proposition; the managers of clerks 105 and 107 work in a different department.

Chapter 7 Answers

Exercise 2

Predicate o(STATUS)='CONF' ⇒ o(TRAINER)≠-1 is equivalent to predicate o(TRAINER)=-1 ⇒ o(STATUS)∈{'CANC','SCHD'}. This is a manifestation of the following rewrite rule:

(A ⇒ B) ⇔ (¬B ⇒¬A)

Your response should therefore be that adding that tuple constraint does not add anything.

Exercise 3

```
tab_MEMP :=
  { M | M∈ ℘(tup_MEMP) ∧
        /* EMPNO uniquely identifies a tuple */
        ( ∀m1,m2∈M: m1(EMPNO) = m2(EMPNO) ⇒ m1 = m2 ) ∧
        ( ∀m∈M: |{ e| e∈M ∧e(MGR)=m(MGR) }| ≤ 10 )
  }
```

When designing this constraint, you might want to check with the users whether the TERM table structure should play a role in this constraint.

Exercise 6

Of the thirteen elements that are in tab_RESULT (see Listing 7-25), only the following two can be combined with the given LIMIT table:

```
{ ∅
, { { (POPULATION;'DP'),      (COURSE;'set theory'), (AVG_SCORE;'C') }
  , { (POPULATION;'DP'),      (COURSE;'logic'),      (AVG_SCORE;'B') }
  , { (POPULATION;'NON-DP'), (COURSE;'set theory'), (AVG_SCORE;'E') }
  , { (POPULATION;'NON-DP'), (COURSE;'logic'),      (AVG_SCORE;'D') } }
}
```

All other result tables either have an average score of A for database pros, or an average score of F for non-database pros; these are prohibited by the database constraint given in DB_U2.

Exercise 7

You can express this by stating that for every department manager, the department number of the department that employs the manager must be an element of the set of department numbers of departments managed by this manager.

```
PTIJ5(EMP,DEPT) :=
    ( ∀d1∈DEPT⇓{MGR}: ⌐{ e(DEPTNO)| e∈EMP ∧ e(EMPNO)=d1(MGR)} ∈
                       { d2(DEPTNO)| d2∈DEPT ∧ d2(mgr)=d1(mgr) } )
```

Note that this is now no longer a tuple-in-join predicate.

Exercise 9

Constraints PTIJ3 and PTIJ4 prevent these cycles.

Exercise 11

The given constraint is abstractly of the following form:

$$(\forall o \in OFFR: (P(o) \Rightarrow (Q(o,REG) \land R(o,OFFR))))$$

Here P, Q, and R are predicates with free variables o, o plus REG, and o plus OFFR, respectively. You can rewrite this predicate form into this:

$$(\forall o \in OFFR: (P(o) \Rightarrow Q(o,REG)) \land (P(o) \Rightarrow R(o,OFFR)))$$

You can rewrite this, in turn, into the following conjunction:

$$(\forall o \in OFFR: P(o) \Rightarrow Q(o,REG)) \land (\forall o \in OFFR: P(o) \Rightarrow R(o,OFFR))$$

Note that the second conjunct now only involves the OFFR table structure and therefore is a table predicate.

Chapter 8 Answers

Exercise 3

```
STC(EMPB,EMPE) :=
  (∀e1∈EMPB, e2∈EMPE: (e1(EMPNO) = e2(EMPNO) ∧ e1(MSAL) > e2(MSAL))
                   ⇒ e1(SGRADE) < e2(SGRADE))
```

Exercise 4

```
STC2(OFFRB,OFFRE) :=
  /* New offerings must start with status SCHED */
  ( ∀o∈(OFFRE⇓{COURSE,STARTS}-OFFRB⇓{COURSE,STARTS})⊗OFFRE: o(STATUS)='SCHD' )
```

Exercise 5

We assume that addition has been defined on the date data type. By adding 31 days we formally specify the "one month."

```
STC(EMPB,EMPE) :=
  ( ∀e∈(EMPE⇓{EMPNO}−EMPB⇓{EMPNO})⊗EMPE: e(HIRED)<=sysdate+31 )
```

Exercise 6

If you rewrite the conclusion of STC7's quantified implication into conjunctive normal form, you'll end up with six conjuncts. In the same way as exercise 11 in Chapter 7, you can then rewrite the implication into a conjunction of six implications. From that, you can rewrite the universal quantification into a conjunction of six quantifications.

You can rewrite STC3 into a conjunction as follows:

```
( ∀o1∈OFFRB, o2∈OFFRE:
    (o1↓{COURSE,STARTS} = o2↓{COURSE,STARTS} ∧ o1(STATUS) ≠ o2(STATUS))
    ⇒ (o1(STATUS)='SCHD' ⇒ (o2(STATUS)='CONF' ∨ o2(STATUS)='CANC') )
∧
( ∀o1∈OFFRB, o2∈OFFRE:
    (o1↓{COURSE,STARTS} = o2↓{COURSE,STARTS} ∧ o1(STATUS) ≠ o2(STATUS))
    ⇒ (o1(STATUS)='CONF' ⇒ o2(STATUS)='CANC') )
```

Exercise 9

In the following specification, CRSE represents the CRS table in the end state. You'll need to join to CRS to determine the last day of the offering.

```
STC7(REGB,REGE) :=
  ( ∀r1∈REGB, r2∈REGE⊗(CRSE◊◊{(COURSE;CODE),(DUR;DUR)}):
    (r1↓{STUD,STARTS} = r2↓{STUD,STARTS} ∧ r1(EVAL) ≠ r2(EVAL))
    ⇒
    ( ( r1(EVAL) = -1 ∧ r2(EVAL) = 0 ∧ r2(STARTS) ≤ sysdate ∧
                                       r2(STARTS)+r2(DUR) ≥ sysdate )∨
      ( r1(EVAL) = 0 ∧ r2(EVAL) ∈ {1,2,3,4,5} ) ) ) )
```

Chapter 9 Answers

Exercise 1

```
{ t↓{empno,name} | t∈dbs(EMP) ∧ t(deptno)=10 }
```

```
select e.EMPNO, e.NAME
from EMP e
where e.deptno=10
```

Exercise 3

Note that an employee belongs to exactly one department. You can try to retrieve an answer for this question but it will always be the empty set (table).

```
{ t↓{empno,name} | t∈dbs(EMP) ∧ t(deptno)=10 ∧ t(deptno)=20}
```

```
select e.EMPNO, e.NAME
from EMP e
where e.DEPTNO=10 and e.DEPTNO=20
```

Exercise 5

```
{ (message;'Constraint is violated') | x∈{1} ∧
                          #{ e | e∈dbs(EMP) ∧ e(job)='PRESIDENT' } > 1 }
∪
{ (message;'Constraint is satisfied') | x∈{1} ∧
                          #{ e | e∈dbs(EMP) ∧ e(job)='PRESIDENT' } ≤ 1 }
```

```
select 'Constraint is violated'
from DUAL
where 1 < (select count(*)
           from EMP e
           where e.job='PRESIDENT')
```

```
union
select 'Constraint is satisfied'
from DUAL
where 1 >= (select count(*)
            from EMP e
            where e.job='PRESIDENT')
```

Exercise 7

There are a few ways to interpret "managers." A manager is either an employee whose job equals MANAGER, or an employee who is managing other employees, or an employee who is managing a department, or any combination of these. We'll give queries for the first two interpretations.

$\{$ e↓$\{$empno,name$\}$ | e∈dbs(EMP)⊗(dbs(GRD)◊◊$\{$(sgrade;grade),(ulimit;ulimit)$\}$) ∧
                    e(job)='MANAGER' ∧ e(msal)=e(ulimit) $\}$

$\{$ e↓$\{$empno,name$\}$ | e∈dbs(EMP) ∧ e(empno) ∈ $\{$ m(mgr) | m∈dbs(MEMP) $\}$ ∧
                    e(msal)=⌐$\{$ g(ulimit) | g∈dbs(GRD) ∧ g(grade)=e(sgrade) $\}$

```
select e.EMPNO, e.NAME
from EMP e
where e.JOB='MANAGER'
  and e.MSAL = (select g.ULIMIT
               from GRD g
               where g.GRADE = e.SGRADE)
select e.EMPNO, e.NAME
from EMP e
where e.EMPNO in (select m.MGR
                  from MEMP m)
  and e.MSAL = (select g.ULIMIT
               from GRD g
               where g.GRADE = e.SGRADE)
```

Exercise 10

The way this question has been expressed suggests the meaning of "manager" as an employee who is managing other employees (MEMP table structure). In this case the answer to the question is easy: ∅. No such manager exists, because there are two tuple-in-join constraints that state that managers always earn more than the employees they manage.

You could also interpret "his employees" as the employees who work in the department(s) that the "manager" manages. We'll provide the query for this case:

$\{$ em↓$\{$empno,name,msal$\}$ | em∈dbs(EMP)⊗(dbs(DEPT)◊◊$\{$(empno;mgr),(mdeptno;deptno)$\}$)
                    ∧((∃e∈dbs(EMP): e(job)≠'SALESREP' ∧
                                    e(deptno)=em(mdeptno) ∧
                                    e(msal)>em(msal)) ∨
                    (∃e∈dbs(EMP)⊗dbs(SREP):

```
                                    e(job)≠'SALESREP' ∧
                                    e(deptno)=em(mdeptno) ∧
                                    e(msal)+e(comm)/12>em(msal))) }
```

```
select distinct /* Must use distinct! */
       em.EMPNO, em.NAME, em.MSAL
from EMP em
    ,DEPT d
where d.MGR = em.EMPNO
  and (exists (select 'One of "his employees" earns more (non salesrep case)'
               from EMP e
               where e.job <> 'SALESREP'
                 and e.DEPTNO = d.DEPTNO
                 and e.MSAL > em.MSAL)
       or
       exists (select 'One of "his employees" earns more (salesrep case)'
               from EMP e
                   ,SREP s
               where e.EMPNO = s.EMPNO
                 and e.DEPTNO = d.DEPTNO
                 and e.MSAL + s.COMM/12 > em.MSAL))
```

Exercise 13

```
{ {(empno;e(empno)),(name;e(name)),(smempno;sm(empno)),(smname;sm(name))}
   | e∈dbs(EMP) ∧ m1∈dbs(MEMP) ∧ m2∈dbs(MEMP) ∧ sm∈dbs(EMP)∧
     e(empno)=m1(empno) ∧ m1(mgr)=m2(empno) ∧ m2(mgr)=sm(empno) }
```

```
select e.EMPNO, e.NAME, sm.EMPNO as SMEMPNO, sm.NAME as SMNAME
from EMP e
    ,MEMP m1
    ,MEMP m2
    ,EMP sm
where e.EMPNO = m1.EMPNO
  and m1.MGR = m2.EMPNO
  and m2.MGR = sm.EMPNO
```

Exercise 21

```
{ c↓{code,dur} ∪
   {(2006_offerings; { o↓{starts,status} ∪
                      {(students; #{ r| r in dbs(REG) ∧
                                     r↓{course,starts}=o↓{course,starts} })}
                      | o∈dbs(OFFR) ∧ o(course)=c(code) ∧ year(o(starts))=2006 }
   )}
```

```
        | c∈dbs(CRS) ∧ c(code) ∈ {'DB1','DB2','DB3'} }

   select c.CODE, c.DUR, o.STARTS, o.STATUS
         ,(select count(*)
            from REG e
           where e.COURSE = o.COURSE
             and e.STARTS = o.STARTS) as students
   from CRS c
       ,OFFR o
   where c.CODE in ('DB1','DB2','DB3')
     and c.CODE = o.COURSE
     and to_char(o.STARTS,'YYYY') = '2006'
```

Note that the SQL expression repeats CRS information.

Chapter 10 Answers

Exercise 1

First, the two table constraints are involved:

```
/* Attendee and begin date uniquely identify a tuple */
( ∀r1,r2∈R:
   r1↓{STARTS,STUD} = r2↓{STARTS,STUD} ⇒ r1 = r2 )

/* Offering is evaluated by all attendees, or it is too early to */
/* evaluate the offering */
( ∀r1,r2∈R:
   ( r1↓{COURSE,STARTS} = r2↓{COURSE,STARTS} )
     ⇒
   ( ( r1(EVAL) = -1 ∧ r2(EVAL) = -1 ) ∨
     ( r1(EVAL) ≠ -1 ∧ r2(EVAL) π -1 )
 ) )
```

The first constraint can be violated if one of the administrators has already been registered for the offering.

The second constraint cannot be violated by transaction ETX1 irrespective of the begin state (assuming March 1 is still in the future; that is, other registrations already present still reflect EVAL=-1).

PTIJ8 (you cannot register for offerings in the first four weeks on the job) is involved and cannot be violated by ETX1 given the e.HIRED between sysdate - 91 and sysdate predicate in the WHERE clause.

PTIJ9 (you cannot register for offerings given at or after leave date) is involved. For ETX1 the begin state should reflect that all administrators who have been hired in the past three months are still working for the company.

PTIJ10 (you cannot register for overlapping courses) is involved. For ETX1 the begin state should reflect that none of these administrators are already registered for another offering that overlaps with the March 1 AM4DP offering.

PTIJ13 (trainer cannot register for offerings taught by him/herself) is involved. This one cannot be violated because administrators cannot act as the trainer for an offering.

PTIJ15 (you cannot register for offering that overlaps with another one where you are the trainer) is involved. For the same reason mentioned with PTIJ13, this one cannot be violated either.

PODC4 (offerings with more than six registrations must have status confirmed) is involved. Depending upon the current number of registrations, the current status for the offering, and the number of administrators that get registered for the AM4DP offering, this constraint might well get violated by ETX1.

PODC5 (number of registrations cannot exceed maximum capacity of offering) is involved. This one too will get violated by ETX1, depending on the current number of registrations and the number added by ETX1.

PODC6 (canceled offerings cannot have registrations) is involved; it will get violated if the current status of the offering equals 'canceled'.

Exercise 3

The following integrity constraints are involved in the UPDATE statement of transaction ETX4: PTIJ1, PTIJ3, PTIJ4, PTIJ6, and PTIJ7. All of these except PTIJ3 run the risk of being violated by the statement.

Index

forums.apress.com

FOR PROFESSIONALS BY PROFESSIONALS™

JOIN THE APRESS FORUMS AND BE PART OF OUR COMMUNITY. You'll find discussions that cover topics of interest to IT professionals, programmers, and enthusiasts just like you. If you post a query to one of our forums, you can expect that some of the best minds in the business—especially Apress authors, who all write with *The Expert's Voice*™—will chime in to help you. Why not aim to become one of our most valuable participants (MVPs) and win cool stuff? Here's a sampling of what you'll find:

DATABASES

Data drives everything.

Share information, exchange ideas, and discuss any database programming or administration issues.

INTERNET TECHNOLOGIES AND NETWORKING

Try living without plumbing (and eventually IPv6).

Talk about networking topics including protocols, design, administration, wireless, wired, storage, backup, certifications, trends, and new technologies.

JAVA

We've come a long way from the old Oak tree.

Hang out and discuss Java in whatever flavor you choose: J2SE, J2EE, J2ME, Jakarta, and so on.

MAC OS X

All about the Zen of OS X.

OS X is both the present and the future for Mac apps. Make suggestions, offer up ideas, or boast about your new hardware.

OPEN SOURCE

Source code is good; understanding (open) source is better.

Discuss open source technologies and related topics such as PHP, MySQL, Linux, Perl, Apache, Python, and more.

PROGRAMMING/BUSINESS

Unfortunately, it is.

Talk about the Apress line of books that cover software methodology, best practices, and how programmers interact with the "suits."

WEB DEVELOPMENT/DESIGN

Ugly doesn't cut it anymore, and CGI is absurd.

Help is in sight for your site. Find design solutions for your projects and get ideas for building an interactive Web site.

SECURITY

Lots of bad guys out there—the good guys need help.

Discuss computer and network security issues here. Just don't let anyone else know the answers!

TECHNOLOGY IN ACTION

Cool things. Fun things.

It's after hours. It's time to play. Whether you're into LEGO® MINDSTORMS™ or turning an old PC into a DVR, this is where technology turns into fun.

WINDOWS

No defenestration here.

Ask questions about all aspects of Windows programming, get help on Microsoft technologies covered in Apress books, or provide feedback on any Apress Windows book.

HOW TO PARTICIPATE:

Go to the Apress Forums site at **http://forums.apress.com/**.
Click the New User link.

You Need the Companion eBook

Your purchase of this book entitles you to buy the companion PDF-version eBook for only $10. Take the weightless companion with you anywhere.

We believe this Apress title will prove so indispensable that you'll want to carry it with you everywhere, which is why we are offering the companion eBook (in PDF format) for $10 to customers who purchase this book now. Convenient and fully searchable, the PDF version of any content-rich, page-heavy Apress book makes a valuable addition to your programming library. You can easily find and copy code—or perform examples by quickly toggling between instructions and the application. Even simultaneously tackling a donut, diet soda, and complex code becomes simplified with hands-free eBooks!

Once you purchase your book, getting the $10 companion eBook is simple:

❶ Visit **www.apress.com/promo/tendollars/**.

❷ Complete a basic registration form to receive a randomly generated question about this title.

❸ Answer the question correctly in 60 seconds, and you will receive a promotional code to redeem for the $10.00 eBook.

2855 Telegraph Avenue • Suite 600 • Berkeley, CA 94705

eBookshop

THE EXPERT'S VOICE™

Offer valid through 12/07.